PENGUIN BOOKS

PRIVATE LIVES, PUBLIC SPIRIT: BRITAIN 1870–1914

Jose Harris is a Fellow of St Catherine's College and Reader in Modern History at the University of Oxford. She is a graduate of Cambridge and used to teach at the London School of Economics. Her previous works include *Unemployment and Politics* and *William Beveridge: A Biography*.

THE PENGUIN SOCIAL HISTORY OF BRITAIN

General Editor: J. H. Plumb

Other titles in this series:

Maurice Keen: *English Society in the Later Middle Ages 1348–1500*
Joyce Youings: *Sixteenth-Century England*
Roy Porter: *English Society in the Eighteenth Century*
John Stevenson: *British Society 1914–1945*
Arthur Marwick: *British Society Since 1945*

JOSE HARRIS

PRIVATE LIVES, PUBLIC SPIRIT: BRITAIN 1870–1914

PENGUIN BOOKS

PENGUIN BOOKS

Published by the Penguin Group
Penguin Books Ltd, 27 Wrights Lane, London W8 5TZ, England
Penguin Putnam Inc., 375 Hudson Street, New York, New York 10014, USA
Penguin Books Australia Ltd, Ringwood, Victoria, Australia
Penguin Books Canada Ltd, 10 Alcorn Avenue, Toronto, Ontario, Canada M4V 3B2
Penguin Books (NZ) Ltd, Private Bag 102902, NSMC, Auckland, New Zealand

Penguin Books Ltd, Registered Offices: Harmondsworth, Middlesex, England

First published by Oxford University Press 1993
Published in Penguin Books 1994
10 9 8 7 6 5 4

Copyright © Jose Harris, 1993
All rights reserved

The moral right of the author has been asserted

Printed in England by Clays Ltd, St Ives plc

FOR
ALICE MAYO
AND
FREDA
BROWN

Preface

The writing of this book coincided with something of a revolution in historical fashion. When I first set out a decade ago, many historians were still moved by a vision of social history as 'total history'—of a discipline that aspired to track down, explain, and encapsulate the objective, interlocking, patterned reality of the past. Ten years later perceptions of the past have become much more nuanced, idiosyncratic, private, and relativist. Texts, artefacts, and language have replaced institutions, movements, and social forces as the substance of what social history is supposed to be about. To borrow a potent phrase used by Sir John Clapham about the years 1866–73, there has been since the early 1980s a 'gigantic hinge' in historical perception. My own view is that the 'objective' history of society is neither so wholly explicable as was often believed in the not-very-distant past, nor so utterly ungraspable as many appear to believe in the immediate present. Nevertheless, like all historical writing this book echoes the passing fashions of the age. My hope is that the creaking of the gigantic hinge may not be too crudely obvious.

I should like to acknowledge the help and support of colleagues, students, family, and friends. Andrew Miles and Youssef Cassis kindly lent me their (then unpublished) work in progress. My research students Mark Bevir, Sandra den Otter, and James Webster fortuitously worked upon themes which stimulated and nourished my own thoughts on this period. Fellow historians whose ideas I have borrowed or stolen are too numerous to mention, but I owe a particular debt of gratitude over many years to Pat Thane and Colin Matthew, both of whom shared with me the teaching of undergraduate courses germane to this book. Long-ago conversations with Asa Briggs, Barbara Caine, Bob and Sandra Holton, Theda Skocpol, Jay Winter, and Alan MacBriar (doubtless long forgotten by them) influenced my thinking on certain key issues. My colleague Peter Dickson kindly weeded out some overgrowths of florid prose, and made many helpful comments. Audrey Hiscock and Susan Seville typed the earlier chapters and taught me to do the later ones myself, and generally gave assistance far beyond the call of secretarial duty. Rosy Addison gave invaluable practical and moral support at a crucial moment. Sir John Plumb, the general editor of the Penguin Social History, was unfailingly patient with my slow production. I am further indebted to Colin Matthew, John Prest and Keith Thomas for identifying and correcting a number of errors, both factual and typographical, that crept into the edition published in 1993 by Oxford University Press. My husband, Jim Harris, read the text from the standpoint of the general reader, and cheered me up immensely by seeming to enjoy it. My son, Hugh, survived my immersion in Victorian literature on child care and forgave me for much neglect; but only his mounting indignation at my prolonged failure to finish this book eventually brought it to an end.

The book is dedicated to my grandmother and mother, who were born respectively at the beginning and end of the period covered. Both were keen amateur historians of their own society, and both supplied some unique personal insights. They would have found many of my ideas puzzling; but I have tried to include nothing that they would have found too grossly at odds with their sense of the subjective reality of those now vanished times.

Contents

I

Themes and Interpretations:
An Overview of British Society 1870–1914

I. CONTINUITY AND CHANGE

Historians of the twentieth century have been sharply divided about whether the First World War was a gigantic crossroads, or merely a transient episode, in the domestic history of British society. No one doubts the importance of the war as a cluster of epic events—military, organizational, geopolitical, apocalyptic, and merely human; but whereas some see those events as profoundly changing the structure of social, political, and economic power in Britain, others argue that such shifts had already been occurring over many decades and that the war merely accelerated a less dramatic but more fundamental process of evolutionary change. The tension between these two perceptions of the war—as a time bomb of total change and as a more humble pressure-cooker of gradualist evolution—haunts the social history of the previous half-century. Were the social structure and social character of Britain in the late Victorian and Edwardian period a natural and logical prelude to the society that developed later in the twentieth century? Or was it a fundamentally different kind of society, one that was wrenched into an alternate mould by the dramatic and traumatic impact of 1914–19?

It is a truism to say that in all societies there are elements of both change and continuity, and Britain in the late nineteenth and early twentieth centuries was no exception; but because of the epic and overwhelming character of the First World War it is peculiarly difficult to identify the character of the earlier society except through the distorting prism of hindsight. Many features of pre-war society—changes in the structure of family life, the emergence of the labour movement, the challenge of feminism, the investigation of poverty, the rise of aesthetic modernism, and the growth of moral and religious uncertainty—seem to anticipate concerns of the later twentieth century; and it is perhaps too easy to assume that they are part of a historical continuum. On the other hand, other aspects of Edwardian life—the fashionable predominance of a leisure aristocracy, the sheer intensity of the poverty of the poor, the omnipresence of infant death, the restricted scope of central government, and the ingenuous confidence in the future of the British Empire (and indeed of European civilization in general)—seem so utterly remote from a later age that it is tempting to see them as part of a wholly vanished society, swept away by a sudden, extraneous, and unpredictable cataclysm, as utterly and irrevocably as Pompeii and Herculaneum.

Such contrasts extend not only to social institutions and structures but to the spheres of thought and artistic consciousness. Thus Virginia Woolf recalled the pre-war years as an age of primal innocence, when lovers sang like singing-birds; while Thomas Hardy, long before the war, conjured up a vision of modern society as a puppet-drama of determinism and disenchantment. The social basis of these conflicting perceptions will be one of the major themes explored in this book, though there is no suggestion here that social change moved in a coherent, unilinear way, or that changing social consciousness was crudely reducible to material and institutional forces. Indeed, anyone who looks closely at the social history of late Victorian and Edwardian Britain cannot but be struck by the immensely varied, contradictory, and fissiparous quality of many of the movements, values, and institutions there encountered. Preconceived 'Victorian' and 'Edwardian' archetypes rapidly dissolve in the face of a riotous pluralism of human experience embracing government, religion, work, family, moral attitudes, popular culture, and sexual relationships. One reason why accounts of social life in this period vary so widely is the immense diversity of objective reality itself, which has misled historians into widely conflicting generalizations about such questions as whether the late Victorians were sexually repressed, whether the working classes swore and beat their children, whether social welfare policies were dominated by eugenics and social Darwinism, and whether religious belief was in terminal decline. The Edwardian decade in particular was full of articulate and embattled pressure groups, urging military conscription, physical jerks, 'national efficiency' and 'duty and discipline' upon what they perceived as the slothful and indifferent mass of their fellow citizens. Yet the existence of such groups does not prove, as many historians appear to assume, that Edwardian society was hyper-authoritarian, any more than it proves that it was libertarian and lax. All it shows is that social norms and expectations were widely varying, and that groups and individuals differed profoundly from each other. In what follows I have doubtless at many points lapsed into generalizations of this kind; indeed, the writing of the history of a national society seems inconceivable without them. But I have tried as far as possible to convey a counterbalancing impression of idiosyncrasy, nuance and diversity. If the overall effect is ramshackle and amorphous, then so be it. Great Britain between 1870 and 1914 was in many respects precisely that: a ramshackle and amorphous society, characterized by a myriad contradictory trends and opinions, and capable of evolving contingently in many different ways. It was not (despite the fashionable jargon of the Edwardian era) a coherent 'organism', still less a 'corporation', a 'system', or a 'machine'.

Britain in this period was also, in a sense that presents peculiar difficulties for the would-be 'social' historian, a society without determinate boundaries. It is a problem endemic to all writing on social history that its subject-matter has no precisely defined context. It lacks the pre-ordained geographical and institutional core of political history and the unifying methodological focus of economic history. And one looks in vain among the great theoreticians of the social sciences for any precise and authoritative definition of what 'society' actually is. Most authors of social history books adopt a pragmatic solution to this problem, by treating 'society' as though it were simply coterminous with the sum of social relationships within a given nation-state; and that is largely the approach adopted here. Yet to allow 'society' to be defined by political geography is an unsatisfactory solution, even for a relatively centralized and self-contained nation-state (like, say, twentieth-century Sweden). It is far *more* problematic for late nineteenth- and early twentieth-century Britain, where internal social arrangements were highly localized and fragmented; which embraced four different national cultures and not just one; which was affected by transnational forces common to all European societies; and which traded with and governed much of the world. To deal satisfactorily with all these layers of organization and social interaction is beyond the scope of a single volume; but I have tried where possible to shift my analysis from the macroscopic to the microscopic, from the core to the periphery, and back again—to give some sense of a 'society' that stretched from the village street to the African veldt, from the parish to the globe.*

Within this context of great diversity and complexity—and of widely differing perceptions of historical change—what clues can be discovered that give shape and meaning and coherence to the social history of Britain between 1870 and 1914? Were there any overarching themes, trends, movements and principles that help us to make sense of changing social structure and social relationships? Contemporaries themselves tried to interpret the unfolding history of British society in a variety of ways, including the advance of 'progress', the historic mission of the Anglo-Saxon race, the rise of the 'common man', the competitive struggle between nations, the shift from *laissez-faire* to monopoly capitalism and the movement from 'individualism' to 'collectivism'. Both in the 1870s and the 1900s there were some who saw Britain as decadent and doomed, others who saw her as the pioneer and pattern of the future of the human race. Such theories in themselves tell us much about the social thought and consciousness of the period, but they do not necessarily reveal to us the most salient features of contemporary social structure. What, if any, were the crucial, overarching themes in the history of social institutions, values, organization, and change?

II. THE IMPACT OF EMPIRE

The very fact of British economic and political power in the wider world was in itself a major determinant of the character of domestic society throughout the period, perhaps more markedly so in the 1900s than in the mid-Victorian era. Between 1870 and 1914 Britain extended and consolidated her sovereign power and informal influence in many parts of Africa and Asia. She fought continuous colonial wars and won most of them. Her Royal Navy policed the seven seas, keeping routes open for global free trade (including the trade of her commercial rivals). During the 1880s Britain lost her position as the undisputed leader of the world's industrial powers, but down to 1914 she was still by far the largest trading

* Take as an example of this problem *The Masonic Year Book for 1914, published under the Authority of the Grand Lodge of England.* This informative little book lists the office-holders, addresses, and diary of events of every masonic lodge and chapter throughout England, Wales, Scotland, Ireland, the Empire, Germany, Scandinavia, Argentina, China, Japan, and the United States. Clearly there was a close network of social relationships at work here, but it was a network that was simultaneously both more intimately parochial and more international than any nation-state.

and carrying nation. And after the eclipse of Paris in the Franco-Prussian war, London became and remained the major discount centre, clearing-house, and capital market of the world.

This global activity as a great imperial and trading power reacted upon society at home in a myriad different ways. The absolute commitment of British governments to international free trade (a commitment challenged but not toppled in the 1900s) meant that, more markedly than anywhere else in Europe, British society was vulnerable to the perpetual changes and collapses wrought by the pressure of world markets. There were many countervailing pressures of locality and custom, but in the last resort patterns of employment, settlement, taste, consumption, and value were all subordinate to the pursuit of 'comparative advantage'. The results of this could be seen most starkly in the 1880s when, alone among European countries, Britain chose not to protect home producers against American wheat, with a consequent collapse of archaic rural communities, an explosion of migration to great cities, a rapid rise in living standards for those in secure employment, and an invisible revolution in the structure of class power. But it could be seen also more diffusely in a certain latent instability throughout the industrial world, in an assumption that change was a norm of life in a way that had not been true in past ages. Similarly, the rapid advance of the financial sector meant that by the turn of the century British society was having to adapt to new forms of economic life and thought, long before it had fully absorbed the social consequences of industrial change and agricultural decline. The result was increasingly a society in which rootlessness was endemic and in which people felt themselves to be living in many different layers of historic time. As a resident in a Surrey village observed in 1912, city commuters and week-enders who formed the fashionable advance guard of the metropolitan England of George V were living cheek by jowl with cottagers who were scraping a living from residual common land, and whose way of life and mental horizons had changed very little since the reign of George III.

Other distinctive social consequences flowed from the fact of Empire. The Empire brought little profit to the British people at large (if anything, the global balance sheet was in the reverse direction); but it provided select individuals with innumerable outlets for employment, enterprise, adventure, status, and prestige. It absorbed indigent peers, ambitious members of the educated middle classes, political idealists, economic migrants, freebooters, social misfits, and the merely violent and aggressive; and it thus acted both as a brake on domestic social innovation and as a powerful safety-valve for domestic discontents. Moreover, the very existence of

Empire lent a certain distinctive flavour to domestic social attitudes and political thought. Far more powerfully than any explicit racial ideology, the mere fact of imperial dominion lent credence to widely disseminated assumptions about the superiority of British institutions and the British race (assumptions that were widespread long before social Darwinism came on the scene to give them an air of scientific authenticity). Travel within the Empire gave an international and cosmopolitan veneer to many sectors of British society; but it was cosmopolitanism of a peculiar kind, in that both linguistically and culturally it was so strongly Anglocentric. (The 'colonial experience man with his brown shiny boots', enshrined in Australasian folk song, knew far less of the continent and culture of Europe than his predecessor on the grand tour a generation before.) At an intellectual and scientific level the Empire opened up knowledge about plants, animals, religions, climates, geology, geography, and the sheer diversity and complexity of the human race—whose impact on both British and wider European consciousness has scarcely begun to be mapped by modern historians. Images of the sea and of Britain's oceanic dominion were deeply woven into national self-consciousness: into history, poetry, music, and the idioms of everyday life. And the Empire also reacted strongly upon certain key features of British domestic politics. Its role in high strategy lies outside the scope of this volume; but, at a more day-to-day level, imperial visions injected a powerful strain of hierarchy, militarism, 'frontier mentality', administrative rationality, and masculine civic virtue into British political culture, at a time when domestic political forces were running in quite the opposite direction, towards egalitarianism, 'progressivism', consumerism, popular democracy, feminism and women's rights.

III. THE EMERGENCE OF CLASS

A second major theme of the period was the evolution of 'class' as an increasingly powerful and comprehensive category in social structure and organization. Britain had of course been laterally divided by functional class-division since the onset of industrialization, if not before; and many earlier periods, most notably the Chartist epoch of the 1840s, had experienced acute class segregation and tension. But many historians of differing ideological persuasions have identified the last quarter of the nineteenth century as the period in which the tentacles of class became all-embracing, in which all other social and cultural attributes became reducible to class categories, and in which the finely shaded hierarchical gradations of pre-industrial society increasingly resolved themselves into two major and mutually exclusive class-formations: a property-owning 'ruling class' that embraced aristocrats, capitalists, and professionals, and a largely property-less 'working class', whose culture and institutions gradually subsumed all other subordinate groups. The dominance of class categories has been graphically demonstrated by many different kinds of historical study: by Eric Hobsbawm's account of a distinctive, national, homogeneous working-class culture rooted in the common experience of advanced mass production; by F. M. L. Thompson's portrayal of a new upper class whose leisure pursuits and cultural pastimes were rural and 'aristocratic', but whose business interests were firmly in the City; and by Peter Clarke's portrayal of the 'electoral sociology' of the period as one in which political loyalties rooted in religion and locality increasingly gave way to more material issues of redistribution and social welfare.

Such accounts accurately reflect many of the dominant themes of the period; and, by any standards, late Victorian and Edwardian Britain was a society ridden to its deepest roots by both objective and subjective indices of social class. Quite apart from the stratifying impact of property distribution and large-scale machine-production, between 1870 and 1914 the organization of work, schools, housing, welfare, culture, and recreation all conspired to compartmentalize British society on class lines; and such divisions were intensified by the erosion of older, supra-class social relationships and by the increasingly national scale and rational character of institutional growth. Class arrangements were viewed by many contemporaries as perfectly natural and non-pathological: there was nothing self-consciously discriminatory about provision for 'the housing of the working classes' or in exempting the children of higher-rate-payers from compulsory attendance at school. Even principled believers in equality before the law continually lapsed into systematic class bias (as in the bankruptcy reforms of the 1860s, which abolished imprisonment for business debtors but retained imprisonment for 'contempt of court' in respect of 'small debtors' too poor to pay their debts). The state itself was continually poised between a liberal ideal of neutrality and even-handedness, and the day-to-day reality that state institutions at all levels, from Whitehall to the parish, were manned by administrative personnel from above the ranks of the manual working class.

Yet it may be questioned whether the growth of class stratification was quite so recent, unilinear, comprehensive, and materially based as many accounts imply. Britain in the earlier Victorian period contained many residues of an older form of social division that was not so much functional as tribal: different groups of people cohabited in the same territory as their ancestors had done for centuries, linked to each other by little more than the fact of a common tongue. Though largely obliterated by migration and industrial change, traces of this kind of division survived down to 1914, and partly account for the immense variety of cultural habits among people and communities of identical class standing. Religious affiliation at the start of the period was perhaps *more* class-related than Clarke and others have allowed: indeed, to be a member of a Nonconformist church in the 1860s and 1870s was in itself, for many people, a species of class-affiliation, albeit not of a purely material kind. In other words, denominational loyalty in mid-Victorian Britain was not so much an alternative to class loyalty as class in another guise. And, conversely, at the end of the period religion was still in certain settings an *independent* variable in politics, and one that was as likely to negate as to reinforce class identity (as could clearly be seen in pan-class Protestant reactions to Irish Home Rule). At all times, ethnic and gender divisions were tangentially related to class divisions, but certainly not wholly reducible to them (as was demonstrated by Irish opposition to Liberal tax and education reforms, and by the way in which many trade union leaders treated women in the labour force not as fellow-members of the same class but as subordinate representatives of a rival and inferior sex).

Furthermore, one may doubt the objective validity of a predominantly two-class model. The rise of the organized labour movement in the 1880s and 1890s polarized political analysis into a dualistic mould; and political rhetoric tended to shape as well as to reflect social facts. But throughout the period and in all sectors of society there were micro-divisions and conflicts within class groups, as well as macro-divisions and conflicts between the two giant formations of capital and labour. Snobbery, class rivalry, and social differentiation cropped up at least as often between groups that were close to each other in status as between those that were far apart. Whole worlds of meaning were conveyed by microscopic household practices, such as whether one washed in the morning or the evening, in the bathroom, in the bedroom, or at the kitchen sink; and upper, middle, and working classes were all vertically divided into a 'serious portion' and a 'gay and rowdy portion', between what Matthew Arnold called 'the heirs of the Puritans' and the devotees of 'beer, gin and fun'. Moreover, although the extent of social mobility in Britain during this period is far from clear, such information as is available suggests that the most open and frequently traversed class frontier was that between the upper-working class and the lower-middle class (a frontier whose limits were greatly enlarged by the growth of teaching, clerical, and other tertiary occupations). By contrast, movement from the ranks of the very poor into the upper-working class was virtually nil, a fact which corroborates the impression of many people at the time, that the top and bottom layers of the lower classes lived virtually on different planets. (A Labour Party report of 1910 sharply differentiated between the genuine working class and 'those who are allowed . . . to wander about parading their sores and propagating their kind'; whilst a spokesman for the TUC described the 'unemployable' as a 'menace to the state'.) At the other end of the social scale, much contemporary evidence supports the view that a new, metropolitan upper class was emerging, forged out of the mutual investment interests and marriage ties of the aristocracy and the City; but many property-owners were left out of this new class-formation, including the vast bulk of the provincial, professional, and industrial bourgeoisie. As Harold Perkin has shown, an occupational category like 'solicitor' might span an enormous arena of social status, from landed gentry to lower-middle class. And, tempting as it is to view Edwardian politics through the lens of hindsight, it must not be forgotten that the major class, party, and constitutional battles of the pre-war era were those fought not between capital and labour but between protectionists and free traders, between Unionists and Home Rulers, between the landed aristocracy and the reformist middle class.

Moreover, for all its immense importance, class was never all-inclusive. In spite of the intensification of class division and class-consciousness in many spheres, there were throughout the period individuals, institutions and groups who confounded or transcended conventional class expectations. Though Oxford and Cambridge remained haunts of upper-class privilege, this was far less true of other universities: at Glasgow, for example, one-third of the students in 1911 were from working-class homes.* The universities extension movement, the new polytechnics set up by the London School Board and, after 1902, the county council grammar schools began a slow process, not of dismantling the class system, but of loosening its bonds for selected individuals. Rising real incomes, new openings for white-collar employment, and the mass production of consumer goods,

---

* Even Oxford had its monuments to social change. Dr Joseph Wright (1855–1930), research assistant to Max Muller, was the son of a Lancashire labourer and had worked in the mills from the age of 7. At 15 Wright could neither read nor write, but proceeded to acquire an education through night school, London external matriculation, and the universities of Freiburg and Heidelberg. He became Professor of Comparative Philology at Oxford in 1901. His career was highly atypical: but it deserves to be set against the more familiar, but fictional, example of Thomas Hardy's *Jude the Obscure*.

particularly clothing, led to a slow but perceptible convergence in the outward appearance and manners of different social groups: in the 1900s working people, especially young women, looked much more like their middle-class equivalents than they had done a generation before, and foreign observers noted that, in marked contrast with sartorial habits on the Continent, the 'Sunday-best' clothes of many workers in Britain were identical with the everyday clothes of the middle class.* There was also some foreshadowing of a phenomenon noted much more strongly thirty years later by Mass Observation, that the British on holiday 'moved up a class': they exchanged their everyday habits for the clothes, food, spending patterns, resorts, and recreations of the class above them. From the 1870s onwards perceptions of what constituted a 'gentleman', a 'lady', and an 'esquire' were rapidly democratized (to such an extent that such terms were increasingly abandoned by their ancient possessors, the beneficiaries of independent incomes derived from land). Moreover, in the 1880s blithe assumptions among the majority about the inexorable normality of class began to be challenged by the bad conscience of a minority (that famous 'class-consciousness of sin' so poignantly described by Beatrice Webb's autobiography).

Finally, by the 1900s all strands of political thought in Britain were being invaded by notions of 'organic' corporate identity and common citizenship, which implicitly or explicitly condemned the class model of society; and it had become an outstanding feature even of British socialist thought that it sought not to wage but to transcend the class war, by promotion of a classless moral commonwealth. Within the labour movement there was much resentment against the class biases of the law, but much affirmation also of an opposite (and very traditional) view: that the British state and British justice were somehow different in kind from the corrupt tyrannies of the Continent. This popular expectation of state neutrality can be perceived even in the midst of the Taff Vale crisis, which—more than any other episode of the period—fuelled working-class suspicions that law and government were merely part of a bosses' state. Trade union comment on the Taff Vale decision does not support the view

---

* Edwardian photographs of mass meetings of the unemployed and of queues outside labour exchanges throw some doubt upon the suggestion of Professor Hobsbawm that the national identity and separateness of the new working class was symbolized by the ubiquity of the cloth cap among working men. In fact most of the unemployed wore Charlie Chaplin-style bowler hats, an article of male apparel that was also worn by all but the most fashionable of the middle and upper classes; and throughout the organized labour movement the kind of cap worn by Keir Hardie was far less common than the 'democratic bowler'.

that Edwardian trade unionists saw the law as automatically stacked against them; on the contrary it suggests that the decision was seen as startlingly out of line with the evenhandedness that organized labour had come to expect from British judges. As the presidential address to the 1901 conference of the Trades Union Congress remarked: 'Following so closely upon the decision of the Law Lords in cases arising under the Workmen's Compensation Act—the provisions of which have been interpreted in a broad-minded and, generally speaking, satisfactory manner, so far as the interests of the workman are concerned—the recent decision is as astounding as it was unexpected.'

IV. INDIVIDUALISM AND COLLECTIVISM

Another much-discussed thematic core of the period is the transition from 'individualism' to 'collectivism', classically propounded by A. V. Dicey in his *Lectures on Law and Opinion* in 1906 and reaffirmed with much greater vehemence and detail in his second edition of 1914. Dicey highlighted the cultural revolution in the relationship between British government and society which he perceived as having taken place since 1870. Private, local, and community provision of services had been continually encroached upon by the expansion of central government; freedom of contract and the rule of law had been increasingly displaced by administrative authorities wielding discretionary powers; pressure groups and organized classes were increasingly looking to legislation to satisfy their sectarian interests; and a broad popular political philosophy, in which individuals made their own plans of life and looked to the state only for law and order, had progressively given way to a holistic organic philosophy, in which state and society were seen as logically prior to individual citizens, and as responsible for their welfare. Such a transformation Dicey saw as underlying the 'new Liberal' social legislation of the late 1900s and embodied *par excellence* in the Old Age Pensions Act of 1908, which replaced the norm of private rational planning for old age by the norm of collective provision as a citizen-entitlement.

Dicey's account was quickly taken up and echoed by Fabian historians like the Webbs, who welcomed what Dicey deplored; and—as with the rhetoric of class polarization—it became a contributory part of the process it was trying to explain. Like the theme of class stratification, the dichotomy between individualism and collectivism continues to haunt social analysis of the period; and certainly there was much structural and institutional change that supports the collectivization thesis. Government employment increased fourfold between 1870 and 1914; central and local public expenditure increased tenfold (even though prices were falling till the late 1890s and then only gently rising); and there was a continuous stream of new specialist administrative departments (the Local Government Board in 1870, the Labour Department of the Board of Trade in 1893, the Board of Agriculture in 1894, and the Board of Education in 1899). There was, moreover, something in the claim that the constitutional principle of keeping the state aloof from pressure groups and asserting the autonomy of Parliament, so strongly affirmed by Sir Robert Peel's generation, was being progressively eroded by the populist, charismatic politics of Gladstone, Chamberlain, and Lloyd George.

Recent historians, however, have been almost unanimous in finding Dicey's analysis crude and unsatisfactory. At the most basic level it glossed over the fact that there had been a great deal of administrative interventionism in early and mid-Victorian Britain (public health, Poor Law, factory acts, and so on), and it grossly exaggerated the degree of advancing state-encirclement in the Edwardian era. It ignored the fact that, outside the narrow spheres of contract law and utilitarian philosophy, the older society was full of organic customary relationships (often themselves by no means free of corruption) embodied in local communities, churches, guilds, co-operatives, organized and unorganized philanthropy, and what the mid-Victorians called 'industrial feudalism'. These relationships constituted the 'social collectivism' approvingly identified by the Charity Organisation Society theorist Helen Bosanquet (who, no less than Dicey himself, was fiercely hostile to the mechanical collectivism of the administrative state). Similarly, Dicey's account ignored the rapid penetration of market relationships in the later nineteenth century into many spheres previously occupied by that older-style organicism: the displacement of friendly societies by industrial assurance companies, the eclipse of subscriptions by fees in hospitals, medicine, and private education, and the advance of commercialized leisure and spectator sports were a few cases in point. It was partly the dwindling capacity of that older collectivism to bear the brunt of these new market forces (exhibited in the decimation of endowed charities by agricultural depression, the limits imposed on 'self-help' by irregular employment, and the futility of face-to-face philanthropy in one-class urban ghettos) that brought about new styles of social intervention by an often reluctant centralized state. In other words, far from being the antipodes of each other, the growth of the state and the growth of the market were inextricably intertwined.

Moreover, just as there was more than one form of collectivism, so there was more than one form of individualism. As was pointed out by many contemporary social theorists, from T. H. Green and the Webbs through to Max Weber and Emil Durkheim, the advance of collectivism might in certain circumstances be the predicate of certain types of individualism rather than their antithesis. When, in 1911, old-age pensions were extended for the first time to paupers, the immediate response was a mass emigration of old men and women from the workhouse into the anonymity of the outside world—an affirmation of individualism within the bosom of collectivism wholly overlooked by Dicey. On a wider level, the release of the individual psyche by the removal of social impediments to 'self-realization' was a major rationale of political thought in the post-Gladstonian era. Throughout the period there were many aspects of modern urban and industrial life pressing individuals into an apparently more uniform and communal mould; but the very same pressures also generated the opposite process—the proliferation of an infinite variety of tastes, styles, functions, habits, and beliefs, and an accentuated emphasis on private life and personal relationships. The evolution of a highly privatized psychological individualism was perhaps most conspicuous in the upper reaches of society, among such cliques as the Souls, the Apostles, and the nascent Bloomsbury Group; but less extreme versions were widely apparent in more humdrum spheres—in attitudes to religion, leisure, marriage, and home and family life. The feminist movement laid great emphasis upon the 'self-sovereignty' of a woman's 'own person', be she wife, worker, suffragist, or common prostitute. 'The grey expanse of life today', wrote H. G. Wells at the dawn of the new century, 'is grey, not in its essence, but because of the minute, confused mingling and mutual cancelling of many-coloured lives.'

V. From 'Ancient Constitution' to 'Great Society'

Class, collectivism and Empire were closely bound up with a fourth major theme of the period: the evolution of a new kind of national polity, and the interaction of that polity with social and cultural life. The period 1870 to 1914 was preceded and followed by two major Reform Acts, both of which radically transformed the size and the nature of the popular franchise; and it may appear that, apart from the lesser reform act of 1884, the period was one of marking time in the constitutional arena, an era of relative tranquillity between two more dramatic and grandiose episodes in the long-term transition from aristocratic to democratic power. This impression is to a certain extent correct: the late Victorian and Edwardian era was not so much an age of substantive constitutional change (though there was some of that) but of the working out of earlier changes, and the anticipation of future ones, within the arena of society, culture, popular attitudes, and mass organization.

The 1867 Reform Act and the contest that surrounded it had been more than just an exercise in extending the number of votes: it had been a public statement about the nature of British society, about property, hierarchy, culture, gender, citizenship, and national identity. The clear aim of both Conservative and Liberal franchise reformers of the 1860s had been not to create a new kind of public polity, but to consider which members of British society could be grafted on to the old one. In spite of the earlier admission of Catholics and Jews to voting rights, the conception of the political nation in the 1860s was still closely bound up with historic Protestantism; and party identity still echoed a cluster of political and religious myths that dated back to the English Civil War. The language of the 1867 reform debates was heavily laden with references to the ancient constitution, the sterling independence of the Anglo-Saxon freeman, and the republic of civic virtue. The admission to the constitution of urban male householders who paid their own rates was very deliberately designed to maintain that ancient tradition of a limited polity of independent freemen, and to exclude those deemed incapable of political and economic independence (women, lunatics, agricultural labourers, and the 'residuum' of the casual poor). The idea of 'class representation' within the electorate—which was later to become anathema to orthodox constitutional theorists—was treated in 1867 as curiously uncontentious, as meaning little more than the bringing in of another 'estate of the realm'. Almost immediately, however, the 1867 Reform Act proved to be a Trojan Horse for constitutional, political, and, ultimately, social transformation. Legal decisions of the late 1860s and 1870s increasingly interpreted the term 'household' to include tenancy of multi-occupied dwellings; and the revival of 'compounding' in 1873 (whereby tenants of non-resident landlords were deemed to be ratepayers) almost accidentally extended the franchise to include many inhabitants of slum tenements. The 1884 Reform Act brought in agricultural labourers and more than doubled the Irish vote, thereby creating for the first time a substantial Roman Catholic bloc within the national electorate.

The result of these constitutional growths was not mere institutional change (though there was much of that in the emergence of caucuses and mass parties and the growing professionalization of politics); more fundamentally, it was the evolution of a new kind of mass political culture, rooted in a wholly different social basis from the limited polity of the past.

Within this new culture, mass organization and class, group and ethnic interests began to press upon and transform the traditional concerns of high politics. Protestantism gave way to pluralism and ultimately to the 'secularization'* of political life; and the mere fact of citizenship increasingly challenged property, moral character, education, and economic independence as the basis of civil rights.

The transition from one culture to another was never complete within this period: manhood suffrage and the removal of the franchise disqualification for paupers came only in 1918, complete womanhood suffrage only in 1929. Throughout the period something like 40 per cent of the male householders notionally entitled to vote were absent from the electoral registers (through migration, receipt of poor relief, gerrymandering, or mere negligence). Women of all kinds were excluded from the parliamentary franchise; and the fact that ratepaying women could vote in local government elections and actually stand for office in School Board and Poor Law elections was less an acknowledgement of democracy under the new regime than of property rights (and of women's traditional 'caring' roles) under the old one. An enlarged franchise did not necessarily mean that the 'will of the people' was more effectively mobilized than in the past: it may, on the contrary, have had the opposite effect, in the form of more apathy, more machine-politics, more manipulation of the phenomena (newly discovered in the 1900s) of 'political irrationality' and 'crowd psychology'. Much acknowledgement of the new social forces was fairly token, such as the appointment in the 1870s of seventy working-class magistrates and the inclusion of titular working-men and titular middle-class women on public inquiries and Royal Commissions. There were always powerful forces buttressing and reinvigorating the older-style polity: inherited tradition, the greater experience and resources of the older political classes, the entrenchment of the rights of ancient communities by the 1884 redistribution of parliamentary seats, and the newer influence of the politics of Empire (which in the 1890s and 1900s drew heavily upon the older philosophies of civic virtue and 'masculine radicalism'). The Edwardian national efficiency movement recast many of these older ideas in a modernist and progressive mould, epitomized by the hero of H. G. Wells's political morality tale *The New Machiavelli* (1911).

Nevertheless, the strength of the new, more democratic polity and its widely ramifying influence should not be discounted. Throughout the

---

* The limited and ambiguous character of this process is discussed more fully in Chapter 6.

period politicians and social observers spoke and behaved as though they believed that the British political system was much more broadly democratic than it actually was, a fact that acted as an invisible but powerful constraint upon public policy in many spheres. The popular language of politics changed very rapidly: the traditional appeal to the 'ancient constitution', still so potent in the 1860s, had almost vanished from the theatre of public debate by the 1880s, to be replaced by an ahistorical frame of reference that was much more populist, pragmatic, and present-minded in tone. When Dicey, at the end of the period, bemoaned the fact that the British had lost the sense of national identity that had been so strong in the mid-Victorian era, he was referring not to the decline of 'nationalism' (the Edwardians were if anything more 'nationalist' than the mid-Victorians), but to a loss of that earlier sense of Britain's epic, principled, constitutional past.

Much of the public life of late Victorian and Edwardian Britain can be seen not just as a struggle between classes and parties, but as a struggle between these two visions of the political nation: between a limited, masculine, property-based polity rooted in a 'protestant' and 'Anglo-Saxon' vision of history (often tinged with classical republicanism); and a comprehensive, pluralist polity based on citizens as individuals, open to all comers (a polity that Graham Wallas at the very end of the period labelled 'the Great Society'). Such a contest clearly had affinities with class and party conflicts, but it was not wholly reducible to them, because members of different classes and parties were found in either camp. Indeed, many groups and individuals in public life were torn simultaneously in both directions: Mr Gladstone, for example, moved enigmatically between one model and the other. The Liberal party throughout the period was *both* a major vehicle for the new mass politics *and* an enclave for many votaries of the older civic ideal (among them some who, like Dicey, Sir Henry Maine, Cecil Rhodes, and Alfred Milner, migrated to Liberal Unionism). Intellectuals on both sides fought their corner with theoretical weapons forged in the arsenals of Greece and Rome. Even the organized labour movement—often seen as the spearhead of the new mass politics—harboured many residues of an older and more exclusive style of politics, in which the skill, independence, and solidarity of the different trade societies were surrogates for the role of 'property' within the wider political community.

The tension between these two visions was a constant undercurrent of the Ulster question, though often overlaid and obscured by the cruder debate about Protestantism and Roman Catholicism. It was deeply enmeshed in the women's question too, since—far more obviously than free market capitalism—it was the ancient tradition of civic virtue that classified male and female gender roles and allocated women to hearth and home. (In Bagehot's words, the *'patria potestas'* was a precondition of civilization, and a nation without patriarchy 'would be conquered like a mob'.) It found echoes in the debate on Jewish immigration, both in Winston Churchill's claim that the Jews were models of ancient traditions of citizenship and in Beatrice Webb's portrayal of the Jewish immigrant as the incarnation of Ricardian rational-economic man—rootless, privatized, and 'deficient in that highest and latest development of human sentiment—social morality'. Above all it was mirrored in the changing social character of British constitutional monarchy—in the shift from the austere, private, 'first-servant-of-the-state' model of monarchy forged by Prince Albert to the much more demotic, spectacular, and stage-managed monarchy that emerged during the last years of Queen Victoria and that was brought to splendid and vulgar fruition in the reign of her son.*

VI. THE NATIONALIZATION OF CULTURE

The shift from a limited to a mass polity did not take place in a vacuum; and more must be said about the underlying structural and cultural changes in this period that, quite apart from the sphere of high politics, were transforming Britain into a more centralized, homogeneous national society. It is tempting to assume that in all 'modern' societies the process of movement from the small to the large and from the local to the national is a simple and unilinear one. It must be stressed, however, that this had not been the uniform experience of Britain in the earlier part of the nineteenth century. It is true that the four nations of the British Isles had constituted a single, unitary sovereign state since the end of the eighteenth century; and both industrialization and classical political economy had set in train large-scale unifying and rationalizing forces. Nevertheless, throughout the early and mid-Victorian periods Britain had remained a society that in numerous ways was fiercely variegated and local. The different cultural, religious and (in the case of Scotland) legal traditions of the four nations; the widely varying occupational and manufacturing specialisms of the new industrial centres; the flourishing municipal culture and civic pride of many provincial cities; and the rise of new, locally based, middle-class élites who challenged the aristocracy for predominance: all combined to produce in

* 'The King's success as a social stage manager', wrote a 'foreign resident' in 1904, 'has been admitted as a European fact.'

the mid-nineteenth century a society that in certain respects was *less* metropolitan than it had been a hundred years before.

Moreover, preservation of local autonomy and custom was seen as a quintessential feature of British national character and culture—in marked contrast to the centralization, rationality, and legalistic uniformity imposed on Continental countries by the legacy of the two Napoleons. Local government was seen as the proper sphere for provision of all 'public goods' except defence and sound currency; and although local authorities had no legal existence other than that conferred on them by Parliament, the local communities that they represented were seen as something more than just convenient administrative subdivisions of a centralized state. This quasi-corporate character of the local community was most clearly seen in the Poor Law, under which individuals had fundamental claims upon the parish of their birth that they did not have upon the nation at large. Utilitarian efforts of the 1830s and 1840s to shift the locus of government away from small communities had proved largely a failure; and, far from dwindling in the face of economic change, the culture and philosophy of localism had enjoyed a tremendous resurgence in the 1840s and 1850s, as part of a nationwide reaction against bureaucratic rationalization. Furthermore, much of the cultural and intellectual life of early Victorian Britain flourished, not in the metropolis, but in the provinces and in Scotland. Numerous literary and philosophical societies, social science and statistical associations, mechanics' institutes, dissenting academies, and individual churches and chapels acted as patrons of high and low culture, seedbeds for scientific observation and experiment, popular media for the dissemination of evolutionary theories and modernist theology, and laboratories of social reform.

This intense and variegated local and provincial culture was still a major strand in British social life between 1870 and 1914. New popular institutions of the period—professional football, county cricket, and the county organization of the post-Crimean Volunteer force—all acted as institutional channels for the continuing cultivation of cross-class local patriotism and civic pride. The establishment of school boards in the 1870s, county councils in 1888 and parish and district councils in 1894 greatly expanded the sphere of popular democracy and largely displaced the aristocracy and gentry from the apex of local communities (though many titled persons reappeared in the 1890s and 1900s as honorific patrons of civic culture). Local democracy was accompanied by the era of 'gas and water' socialism, which encircled urban areas with a network of public utilities. Numerous acts of private legislation enabled local authorities to raise public loans and to engage in ambitious projects: to build town halls, public libraries, hospitals, art galleries, and new civic universities. Such activities ranged from the rampantly philistine to the dazzlingly beautiful, from disinterested public service to gross examples of peculation and class-bias (the high-minded Edwardian 'Guild of Help' movement that flourished in many cities must be set against such unsavoury incidents as the Liverpool police scandals of the early 1890s and the widespread connivance in illegal betting uncovered by the Metropolitan Police Commission in 1908). Throughout the country local communities were vigorous microcosms of many of the wider trends and tensions of late Victorian and Edwardian society: civic virtue vied with civic corruption; community solidarity clashed with class, religious and ethnic tensions; and ambitious women and working-class men struggled to challenge the powerful freemasonry of local, masculine, middle-class business and professional élites.

Yet, all this dynamism and variety notwithstanding, provincial communities in the 1900s were less overwhelmingly dominant in British society and culture than they had been a generation before, and the late Victorian period saw a subterranean shift in the balance of social life away from the locality to the metropolis and the nation. The elements in this shift were complex and only partly visible to contemporaries (not perhaps surprisingly, since many of them only fully worked themselves out many decades later). A factor of fundamental importance was the 'gigantic hinge' dated by Sir John Clapham at around 1870, that decisively shifted the fulcrum of economic life away from the northern provinces to London, away from manufacturing industry to international finance. The collapse of the Paris money market in the Franco-Prussian war and the migration to Britain of many European financiers and bankers made the City of London, always a major financial centre, now the undisputed capital market of the world. Over the next twenty years many country bankers, who for over a century had been unpretentious but crucial engines of local economic growth, moved their firms to London and were swallowed up by much larger, de-localized, joint-stock banks. Between 1870 and 1914 the number of provincial stock exchanges dwindled from ten to two, while the London stock exchange and London's merchant and investment banks increasingly dominated, not domestic industrial finance, but international securities and commodity markets and loans to governments throughout the world. The change in the structure and location of wealth was reinforced by the growth of a new *rentier* class: holders of passive wealth invested in the newly emerging joint-stock enterprises and limited liability companies that had been legalized in the 1850s and 1860s. And it was reinforced also by the agricultural depression of the 1880s, which forced the owners of old estates either to sell up to new wealth-holders or to join them in pursuit of portfolio investments and directorships in the City.

The economic implications of this pivotal shift to finance remain a matter of dispute, but there can be no doubt about its impact on national social structure. Wealth, prestige, fashion, and social status—always greater in London than elsewhere, even in the heyday of the Industrial Revolution—now moved decisively towards the metropolis. Successful provincial businessmen who formerly were content to be local notables now increasingly transferred both their social aspirations and their financial interests to London and the City. Joseph Chamberlain—often regarded as the political flagship of provincial industrial capitalism—is a key example of a Midlands manufacturer who moved his investments to London, his political concerns to the Empire, and his social circle to 'Society' and the aristocratic country house. London 'Society'—that inner circle of those presented at Court, which in the 1850s consisted of a tiny coterie of a few hundred ancient landed families—had by the Edwardian period swollen into an élite of ten thousand, many of them operators in the new financial sectors. Rural landed society—traditionally a nexus of philanthropy, patronage, local government, and inter-class social relationships—had by the 1900s been largely pincered out by democracy and agricultural depression, and was being replaced by what J. N. Figgis called 'delocalised irresponsible wealth', largely detached from rural communities. The change in the balance of social power was mirrored in the creation of new peerages, which from the 1880s onwards included many businessmen who chose no longer to veil their moneyed origins in the purchase of large landed estates (though they continued to purchase small ones as outlets for pleasure and conspicuous consumption). Moreover, the transformation wrought by finance was not confined to business élites: it was seen also in the explosion of stockbrokers, accountants, bank officials, insurance agents, commercial clerks, and copyists who formed a substantial part of the *nouvelles couches sociales* of the late Victorian and Edwardian era. These groups were found in all commercial centres, but above all in the expanding commuter hinterland of suburban Middlesex and Surrey. Their orientation to local and national society—as private citizens in a great nation rather than bigwigs in a small community—was fundamentally different from that of the provincial middle classes of a generation before.

This shift of the centre of gravity from the provinces to the metropolis was paralleled by many other forces making for an increasingly integrated and homogeneous 'national' society. In late nineteenth- and early twentieth-century Britain (by contrast with Imperial Germany, or France under the Third Republic) there were very few proponents of 'centralization' as an administrative principle in its own right, and parish-pump loyalties remained an important part of national self-image and culture. But from the mid-century onwards railways, telegraph, and the postal service had been invisibly transforming individual perceptions of the boundaries of community and national life; while from the 1880s the 'retailing revolution' enormously expanded the horizons of consumers. The increasing scale of economic enterprise and the crystallization of the trade cycle meant that by the third quarter of the nineteenth century new social problems were emerging that were inherently beyond the scope of local administration and finance.

Unemployment in particular was a powerful, though inadvertent, catalyst for the assumption of new responsibilities by an often reluctant central government (significantly, relief of the unemployed was the one major area of social policy whose transfer from local to central authority was recommended by the Royal Commission on the Poor Laws in 1909). The same forces were at work in education: management of schools under the Education Acts of 1870 and 1902 remained firmly in local hands, but visits by inspectors and centralized guidance on school curricula rapidly generated a new national popular culture—a culture that evoked new market responses in the form of mass-circulation newspapers (which in turn began to reinforce the process of mass production of attitudes and cultural unification). Similarly, the growth of public boarding-schools increasingly replaced the old provincial grammar schools and dissenting academies by a new, cosmopolitan, upper-class culture, largely divorced from local roots (and divorced also from the skills and mental outlook of factory management and manufacturing). At the level of higher education one of the major cultural transformations of the period was the migration of intellectual life into the universities, and the absorption of science, history, and political economy into academic departments—in marked contrast to, and at the expense of, the great provincial (and often amateur) flowering of those disciplines a generation before. The new civic universities preserved strong cultural and personal ties with their host cities, but Oxford and Cambridge at the end of the nineteenth century were steadily becoming the academic suburbs of metropolis and Empire.

All these trends were accompanied, particularly towards the end of the nineteenth century, by a gradual renaissance of London as a centre of fashionable and artistic life. New theatres, galleries, and concert halls were opened, London University received its charter, Shakespeare was seriously performed in public for the first time in half a century, and ancient thoroughfares were rebuilt in the neo-classical idiom deemed suitable for the hub of the world's greatest empire. New Continental influences began to invade the metropolis, in the form of opera from Germany, drama from Norway, post-impressionist painting from France, and ballet from Russia. At a time when at least some of the provincial cities were losing their old élites to cosmopolitanism and gentrification, London in the 1890s and 1900s was a much stronger magnet for the educated and ambitious middle classes than it had been a generation before.* Many Edwardian feminists relished the social autonomy, freedom from family ties and opportunities for intellectual employment that were available in London to a much greater extent than in more structured and sheltered provincial communities. And to many overseas visitors London increasingly appeared not as the chief city of England, nor even of the British Empire, but as 'the capital of the human race'.

Finally, mirroring and reinforcing all these other shifts, was a long-drawn-out national revolution in the use of language. Archaic rural dialects had been in decline since the eighteenth century, and by 1870 were far more residual in England than in any other European country. New vernacular styles that evolved during the period—such as cockney rhyming-slang and the 'old codgers' speech of Lancashire and Yorkshire—were no less genuine an expression of popular culture; but unlike the older dialect forms they were at least in part self-consciously fostered by such media as music-halls, almanacs, clubs, recitation, and the popular press. Welsh and Gaelic survived better than the English regional dialects, but were everywhere vulnerable to Anglicizing cultural pressures (and to well-meaning public officials who tried to extend the English language as a form of compulsory social welfare). By the turn of the century 50 per cent of the Welsh still spoke their traditional language, but only 14 per cent of the Irish and 5 per cent of the Scots. Regional accents were also under threat, not so much from extinction, as from social labelling and stigmatization. The 'received standard English' of southeastern England (that is, the English spoken by the upper and middle-classes in London) everywhere established itself as the cultural norm in a descending hierarchy of phonic status: and an American observer in 1881 remarked that the 'ah' sound

---

* An important exception was Dublin, which was much more culturally dynamic in the 1900s than it had been half a century before. But to many Irish nationalists Dublin at this time was less a provincial city than a rival centre of European culture.

in words such as glass, pastor, and father had become the 'surest test of high culture'. Even members of the aristocracy and gentry—whose traditional accents contained strong traces of the now despised regional vowel sounds—cleaned up and 'modernized' their pronunciation (substituting God for Gawd and coffee for corfee). Many teachers under the 1870 education system were passionate missionaries of linguistic conformity, and stern censors of missing aitches and proletarian ain'ts.*

Moreover, the very substance of English was being homogenized in a variety of ways. Gentility, officialdom, and standardization increasingly drove out many old idiosyncratic phrases, while advanced mass production substituted numerous classically based neologisms for the rich customary vocabulary of older industrial and agricultural life. Perhaps most pervasive of all, there came creeping down from the fashionable upper classes a certain vacuous cosmopolitanism of expression that reduced all utterance to exaggerated clichés of praise or blame. 'Nice, jolly, charming, and bore' were the four words left in the English language, remarked a character in Disraeli's *Lothair* in 1870. By 1900 'topping', 'ripping', 'terribly decent', and 'absolutely frightful' were part of the new national dialect of the younger middle classes.† Such modes of speech imperceptibly reinforced the wider role of language as a badge of social status, and they acted as a powerful force for restructuring an older, regional, variegated, and customary society along more uniform, national and horizontal lines.

VII. Sex and Gender

Cutting across and complicating the major themes of Empire, state, social class, and the nationalization of culture was what sounded to many like a more muted melody in a minor key: the issues of sex, gender and the legal and personal relationships between men and women. The question of women's roles and women's rights had come to the fore in public debate in the 1860s, with the (unsuccessful) demand for female enfranchisement and the (partially successful) demand for women's secondary and higher education. The subsequent three decades have often been viewed as a period

---

* Though the missing aitch was itself part of the new, delocalized mode of speech. Virtually unknown outside London before the 1880s, its rapid spread thereafter was a graph of the 'cockneyfication' of the southern working class.

† Lady Bell gave the following as an example of fashionable newspeak in 1907:

And then, do you see, I said 'no'—sort of very loudly, do you see? And really sort of meaning it, don't you know what I mean? And as for him—well, do you see, he was sort of bothered—you see what I mean, don't you?

of quiescence and marking time in women's history, before the emergence in the 1900s of the militant suffragettes. This view is, however, in many ways a misleading one. The last quarter of the nineteenth century was a period of continuous and quite seminal, if partly invisible, change in the perception of women's roles and in the realignment of male–female relationships. Such changes can be detected in many spheres: political, legal, economic, intellectual, personal, and psychological.

During the last third of the nineteenth century a select minority of middle-class women began to play a role in public life in Britain that would have been quite inconceivable only a generation before. The reconstruction of local government between 1870 and 1899 almost inadvertently gave women a toehold in public office for the first time—a toehold which they vigorously exploited in the spheres of education, Poor Law, sanitation, and public health. In the 1880s the campaigns against compulsory vaccination, vivisection, and, above all, against the Contagious Diseases Acts shattered the convention that it was dangerous and improper for a woman to speak in public, even upon such subjects as venereal disease and the vaginal inspection of prostitutes. Both the major political parties set up women's organizations in the 1880s, and by the turn of the century large numbers of Liberal and Conservative women were vigorously campaigning, canvassing, and addressing mass meetings on behalf of male parliamentary candidates for whom they could not vote. The enormous growth of associational culture in late nineteenth-century Britain—under the auspices of churches, charities, pressure groups, and a host of musical, artistic, political, social science, and self-improvement societies—brought thousands of active and organizing women into the quasi-public sphere. Many of them had no self-conscious commitment to specifically 'feminist'* causes, though an increasingly influential and articulate minority was explicitly concerned with advancing women's interests and women's rights.

Parallel changes were evident in many other spheres. Whereas in the mid-Victorian era a husband still retained absolute legal control over his wife's person and property and the right to sole guardianship of their children, from 1870 onwards a series of legislative reforms and judicial decisions gradually conferred upon women and mothers certain autonomous legal rights. Although rising affluence meant that in most areas married women of the working class increasingly withdrew from the labour market,

---

* Though often retrospectively applied to earlier stages of the women's movement, 'feminist' and 'feminism' were neologisms of the 1890s, introduced into the English language from France and North America.

growing awareness of the demographic surplus of females meant that some middle-class women began to seek occupation, status, and economic alternatives to marriage in the forms of education, philanthropy and training for a profession. Education affected women at all levels of society: not simply the small minority who went to the newly founded girls' grammar schools and women's colleges, but the much larger group for whom teaching in elementary schools offered a wholly new kind of occupation and status. In all classes there were women affected by 'that wave of desire for a personal working life' that Clementina Black, the president of the Women's Industrial Council, defined as one of the distinguishing characteristics of the late Victorian age. During these same decades women writers, reformers, and intellectuals began to investigate and challenge many ancient monuments in the landscape of traditional social structure. Women such as Josephine Butler, Ellice Hopkins, and Frances Julia Wedgwood questioned not merely such obvious moral anomalies as the sexual 'double standard' and the rights of husbands to coerce their wives, but more oblique areas of male dominance such as the gendered structure of day-to-day language* and the overwhelmingly masculine characterization of most orthodox accounts of God. Perhaps most fundamentally, the fertility revolution that commenced in the 1870s began tentatively to erode the age-old assumption that a woman was necessarily wholly preoccupied with pregnancy, childbirth, and child care throughout her child-bearing years.

The metamorphosis of women's roles was by no means, however, a simple and continuous process. It was at all times fraught with ambiguity, contingency, and tension—tension that incidentally throws much light upon many other aspects of late Victorian ideology and social structure. As will appear in later chapters, ideas and behaviour relating to women varied widely within and between different social groups; but, even so, numerous autobiographies and memoirs of the period suggest that, above the ranks of the working class, young women who sought a role outside the home—or who sought more freedom within it—almost invariably passed through a period of subterfuge and struggle. The plight, and subsequent flight, of Clara Middleton (George Meredith's 'dainty rogue in porcelain') was not just a story, but a symbol of the age. Women who gained acceptance in

---

* Since 'virtue' was widely equated with female chastity, it should be renamed 'muliertue', wrote Ellice Hopkins in *The Power of Womanhood* in 1899, perhaps the earliest example of the kind of feminist reconstruction of language that came into vogue later in the twentieth century.

public life, as doctors, nurses, academics, social scientists or factory inspectors, did so often only by cloaking themselves to a quite exaggerated degree with modesty, propriety, and other outward trappings of acceptable femininity—and by specializing in corners of their professions deemed peculiarly suitable for women. Even voluntary philanthropy, often portrayed as a conventional outlet for middle-class ladies of the period, was viewed in some powerful quarters as unwomanly and subversive (the novels of the ubiquitous Religious Tract Society, for example, suggest that, for many young women, work on behalf of a Charity Organisation Society might be an act not of social conformity but of radical defiance). Throughout society both 'individualist' and 'collectivist' attitudes to economics and public policy coexisted with large residues of pre-industrial paternalism and patriarchalism in the sphere of private relationships. A growing emphasis upon individual rights that undoubtedly embraced women as well as men was nevertheless tempered by the view that social cohesion, personal morality, reproduction, and family life all required the relative confinement of women to the home—a view shared not just by men but by large numbers of women, who maintained that the sexes occupied generically 'separate spheres'.

Moreover, the shift towards more 'liberal' views was by no means a unilinear one. Changes in the law did not always expand women's rights at the expense of men's. On the contrary, as late as 1899 a jury's decision in the case of *Regina* v. *Clarence* overturned the standard opinion of judges and legal textbooks by asserting a husband's right to rape his wife (even when, as in this case, the husband was suffering from an advanced stage of syphilis). The Vagrancy Act of 1898, which outlawed sexual soliciting, prescribed fines of forty shillings for female offenders, compared with six months' imprisonment with hard labour for soliciting males; but the Act was massively enforced against women, whereas prosecutions of men were virtually unknown. Social acceptance of individual women in public and professional life slowly increased over the period, but this coincided with certain intellectual and institutional pressures that may have had the effect of reinforcing rather than slackening traditional views about sex and gender roles. The work of Darwin, for example, specifically emphasized the role of reproduction in the natural selection process, and suggested that increasing functional differentiation between males and females was a distinguishing feature of the evolution of the higher mammals. The sociology of Herbert Spencer taught that the biological energy absorbed by childbirth precluded the female brain from sharing in 'the latest products of human evolution', namely abstract reasoning and the sentiment of justice (though Spencer, unlike evolutionary theorists, thought that female inferiority was susceptible to cultural change). The new sciences of psychology and gynaecology, even when practised by men who in other spheres were notorious champions of 'progressive' causes, taught for several decades that prolonged education and mental effort were dangerous to women's reproductive processes and a potent source of female ill-health.

Likewise, not all developments in popular culture favoured women. On the contrary, the late Victorian cult of both upper- and lower-class 'clubland' was an almost exclusively, and often aggressively, masculine sphere (women were admitted to only one out of the 512 working-men's clubs that existed in London in 1897). The tremendous centrality of the home in late Victorian society (far more pronounced in most social groups than earlier in the nineteenth century) both enhanced and diminished the status of women, by giving them a forum of moral and economic power but at the same time reinforcing for many their separation from the wider society. Growing fears about Britain's national defence capability and status as a world power tended to intermesh with fears about the changing role of women and the decline in the birth rate. Hostility to women's suffrage, which in the 1860s had emphasized mainly their lack of property rights, by the 1900s concentrated much more upon the notion that a female-dominated electorate would subvert military security. 'Female suffrage would be worse than a German invasion in the way of national calamity', claimed the radical imperialist Leo Maxse in the *National Review* for 1908. And though the need for women's education was widely accepted by the 1900s, rising concern for Empire, family, and general biological improvement meant that gender divisions in programmes of learning were in certain respects *more* pronounced than they had been a generation before. Boys needed instruction in 'courage, self-control, hard work, endurance and protection of the weak', wrote one prominent educationist in 1911; girls, by contrast, needed to be taught 'gentleness, care for the young and helpless, interest in domestic affairs, and admiration for the strong and manly character in men'.

At the same time women themselves varied widely in the practice and perception of their social roles. Almost certainly the majority of late Victorian and Edwardian women saw personal liberation not in terms of entry into the public sphere but of escape from the drudgery of paid employment, protection against excessive childbirth, and possession of a secure and comfortable home. In purely numerical terms, by far the most successful women's organization of the period was the Mothers' Union, founded in 1886, which did not seek to extend women's roles, but campaigned for greater protection, dignity, and status for women within the context of marriage, religion, motherhood, and home. Some feminists denounced 'the rat-poison of housework', but others sought to enhance its social importance and to 'de-feudalize' its social status by the systematic teaching of hygiene, nutrition, child care, and domestic science. A few *fin de siècle* feminists explored lesbianism and free love, but the vast majority of late Victorian and Edwardian campaigners for women's rights opposed sexual experiment or permissiveness, and advocated a strictly monogamous and heterosexual code of behaviour common to both women and men. There was no necessary correlation between a woman's personal position in society and her views about the 'woman question'. Some who were themselves active in the public sphere (such as Mrs Humphry Ward and, for a time, Beatrice Webb) opposed female suffrage and idealized women's domestic function; while many others who were confined to hearth and home favoured legal, economic, and political emancipation. Community of sex and gender might transcend class differences among women, as in the concern of purity reformers with the rights of prostitutes and serving girls, in the efforts of many middle-class feminists to promote women's trade unionism, and in the support of Lancashire mill-girls and London match-girls for the militant suffragettes; but it might also conspicuously fail to do so. Few accounts of the habits of working women, for example, were more censorious and unsympathetic than those of Hilda Martindale, a senior factory inspector and author of many official reports on aspects of working-class life.

Even among those who favoured radical changes in women's status and role, there was much difference of opinion about what those changes should consist of and the best way to attain them—differences that were partly social, partly ideological, partly generational. John Stuart Mill's *The Subjection of Women*, that burst like a time bomb into the sexual arena in 1869, remained throughout the period a bible of the women's movement; but some of its central themes—most notably its portrayal of women as captive victims within marriage and its idealization of women's superior moral sense—seemed to advanced feminists of the 1890s curiously old-fashioned. Frances Power Cobbe, the matriarch of many women's causes in the 1860s and 1870s, wrote with some distaste in her turn-of-the-century autobiography of 'the abrupt-speaking, courtesy-neglecting, slouching, slangy young damsel who may now perhaps carry off the glories of a university degree'. From the 1860s through to the First World War women social reformers were divided between those who thought that the state should offer special protection for women (in the form of factory acts, restrictions on the employment of mothers, and minimum-wage legislation) and those who thought that women should seek only the right to compete freely in the open market with men. The campaign for the repeal of the Contagious Diseases Acts in the 1870s and 1880s sheltered a wide spectrum of reformist thought, embracing those whose main concern was to prevent the licensing of prostitution, those incensed by the double standard applied to men and women, and those more generally alarmed by the threat which the Acts posed to conventional civil liberties. Most conspicuously and dramatically, the women's suffrage movement split apart in 1905 over the issue of the parliamentary vote. On the one hand there was a large bloc of women's organizations, broadly affiliated to Millicent Fawcett's National Union of Women's Suffrage Societies, who saw the vote merely as one item on a long agenda of social, economic and political reforms, which they sought to attain largely by constitutional means. On the other hand, there was the group organized by the Pankhursts and Pethick-Lawrences in the Women's Social and Political Union, who concentrated upon the sole immediate objective of obtaining the vote, and who—partly of their own volition, partly in response to repression by police and courts—increasingly sought to advance their cause by illegal demonstrations and acts of public violence.

Such varying emphases within the women's movement mirrored and interlocked with many other social divisions and trends of the age. The differences of opinion between the followers of Mrs Pankhurst (primarily concerned with the elimination of gender from the existing property franchise) and the followers of Mrs Fawcett (dedicated to promoting the interests of women on a much broader front) to some extent replicated divisions within society at large about the role of class, property, and the state. To many radical middle-class women it seemed that the movement for women's rights was part of a much wider struggle against aristocratic domination and an integral feature of the new mass polity that was emerging during the period on many different fronts. Josephine Butler, for example, believed her challenge to doctors over the Contagious Diseases Acts to be part and parcel of a much wider confrontation with a corrupt, militaristic, masculine aristocracy—though to the historian it may appear that army doctors were no more 'aristocratic' than Mrs Butler herself. Women no less than men were caught up, too, in the moral and ideological transformations of the age. Feminists who had been outraged by the affront to personal liberty posed by the Contagious Diseases Act in the 1860s and 1870s were curiously silent about the Mental Deficiency Act of 1913, which permitted the permanent detention of feeble-minded unmarried mothers dependent on poor relief; indeed, women child-care workers and asylum attendants played a prominent role in the campaign that gave rise to this measure. Even the geography of the women's movement—in particular the migration of the Pankhursts from Lancashire to London, and the wide-ranging network of communications with feminists overseas—reflected the increasingly metropolitan, national, and even international orientation of British social life.

It would be quite wrong, however, to see the emergence of women in this period as merely a secondary aspect of other 'progressive' causes, a fact indicated by the often unexpected way in which attitudes to women's rights and to women's involvement in public life interacted with other social and political themes of the time. Throughout the period many prominent feminists were Conservatives—among them Emily Davies, Frances Power Cobbe, Louisa Creighton, and Lady Constance Lytton. The revolt of some turn-of-the-century feminists against the traditional bonds of marriage—fuelled to some extent by the prevailing panic about venereal disease—travelled far outside the normally optimistic and reformist boundaries of Edwardian progressivism, as may be seen in such writings as Cicely Hamilton's *Marriage as a Trade* (1909) and Christabel Pankhurst's *The Great Scourge and How To End It* (1913). The campaigns for married women's property rights and repeal of the Contagious Diseases Acts were strongly rooted in the middle-class, temperance-promoting, provincial Nonconformity that was one of the mainstays of Gladstonian and post-Gladstonian Liberalism; yet that same stratum of society also contained some of the most implacable opponents of women's claims, not least among them H. H. Asquith, Liberal Prime Minister from 1908 to 1916.

The reactions of men to the women's movement—ranging from the fervent support of a George Butler or a Frederick Pethick-Lawrence to the impassioned hostility of those who 'talked out' women's suffrage bills in the House of Commons between 1907 and 1912—were often deeply rooted in individual psychology and so transcended the usual categories of ideology and social class. Male involvement in organized opposition to women's enfranchisement appears to have been more closely linked to personal temperament, bachelor lifestyles, old-boy networks, and fondness for masculine clubland than to membership of any distinctive social or political group. Some of the most enthusiastic Liberal supporters of popular franchise extension in the 1860s were among the most vehement opponents of women's suffrage a generation later—on the ground that women as a class were inherently lacking in the kind of independence, civic virtue, and 'masculine radicalism' that active citizenship required.

Conversely, Robert Lowe, notorious for his scepticism of the political capacities of working-class males, saw no objection at all to the enfranchisement of middle-class females. The famous Rainbow Circle, which from 1894 until the First World War was the chief dining and debating club of the London progressive intelligentsia, never included a single woman among its members and often listened to lectures that emphasized women's moral and physical incapacity for civic affairs. Most Labour politicians were sympathetic to the women's cause; but the labour movement in general was deeply apprehensive of women's demands, fearing loss of jobs to cut-price female labour and the flooding of the electorate by deferential, Conservative-voting females. Moreover, as many accounts of individual families have shown, there was no necessary connection between public ideology and the private treatment of women. Studies by Pat Jalland, Barbara Caine, and others suggest that there were many households—of all shades of political opinion—in which women enjoyed status, authority, and personal freedom regardless of the economic and legal conventions of the age; and there were other households, such as that of Mr Gladstone himself, in which the subordination of wife and daughters to the interests of the male head went far beyond the bounds that contemporary perceptions of patriarchal entitlement appeared to require.

Such variation in the status of women suggests that a crucial clue to the social structure of the period lay in a large and growing element of contingency and indeterminacy. The most important characteristic of gender roles in the 1900s was not simply that they had changed in a particular way but that, by comparison with the early and mid-Victorian era, the very nature of those roles was increasingly contested and uncertain. This can be discerned not just in the thought and attitudes of campaigners for and against women's issues, but in the thought and attitudes of the vast majority of both sexes who were not actively engaged in either supporting or opposing women's rights. In many areas of social debate in the Edwardian era—on such subjects as health, housing, education, poverty, religion, and crime—one finds numerous almost incidental *obiter dicta* on the subject of the role of women in the wider society. Such commentary frequently took the form either of assuming a traditional role for women or of promoting a new role for them as the publicly protected but domestically confined guardians of a new imperial race. Often, however, the keynote of such writing was a much more confused and indeterminate one. It gave expression to genuine uncertainty and perplexity about current sex and gender roles and about social trends and patterns in the future: about whether declining fertility was a progressive or a recessive force and whether the future of women lay primarily in the family or in the work-force; about the impact of women's work upon health and infant mortality; about the nature of 'modern marriage' and the future status and functions of the family; and about the long-term balance of power between men and women, public and private spheres, the family and the state. As unlikely a source as the Metropolitan Police Commission remarked in 1908 that the answer to all these questions 'depends in the long run, on the settlement of still wider questions connected with the relations of the sexes, as to which public opinion is much divided, and is in a state of flux'.

VIII. 'MODERNITY' AND THE 'LOST DOMAIN'

Imperial expansion, state intervention, class division, encircling cultural uniformity, and latent guerrilla warfare between the sexes seemed to many people at the time to be quintessential features of 'modernity'; and a further key theme of the period was a widely diffused sense of living in a peculiarly 'modern' age. There is of course a sense in which all ages are modern, and historians have been rightly suspicious of attempts to explain history tautologically in terms of a so-called 'modernization' process. Yet the consciousness of living in a new age, a new material context, and a form of society totally different from anything that had ever occurred before was by the turn of the century so widespread as to constitute a genuine and distinctive element in the mental culture of the period. The phrase 'we moderns' was widely used as a self-explanatory expression not just by artists and critics (the self-conscious protagonists of aesthetic modernism) but by economists, lawyers, scientists, anthropologists, and practical men and women of affairs. Yet the meaning of 'modern' was a fluid one, and late Victorian and Edwardian usage differed from that of both earlier and later generations. The term had been used by the earlier Victorians mainly to distinguish 'modern' from 'classical' (or 'mediaeval') times, and this sense was still current later in the century (in, for instance, the establishment of 'modern studies' in many secondary schools, in the founding of the Oxford Modern History School in 1873, and in the publication of the Cambridge Modern History between 1897 and 1911). But over the course of Queen Victoria's reign the subjective time span of modernity grew shorter and shorter, and by the 1870s the term was being widely used to describe 'the way we live now': the age of evolution, plutocracy, gaslight, and feminism, rather than the longer sweep of post-classical European civilization.

This sense of the unique dominance of the present time was immensely reinforced over the next thirty years by a variety of interlocking factors: by the enormous physical growth in the urban environment, by the explosion of scientific knowledge, and by the political and material Europeanization of the globe. Manufacturing processes were transformed in method and scale by the growth of machine tools, mass production, and the rise of a new class of industrial 'managers'. Markets for commodities were increasingly designed not merely to satisfy human wants, but to invent and impose those wants through the new medium of mass advertisement. A demographic revolution began invisibly to transform both the nature of family life and the structure of social and economic dependency. For the first time in British (and perhaps human) history the sheer fact of scarcity receded from the cockpit of social organization, as average per capita income rose from a slender margin of 25 per cent above subsistence in 1870 to a comfortable 150 per cent above subsistence in 1914. And in a myriad mundane but basic ways the regime of nature slackened its hold on human life, as medicine began to cure as well as to kill, as water flowed out of taps and excrement flowed into sewers, as the glare of gas and electricity replaced the age-old illumination of oil-lamp and candle, and as the man-made tempo of great cities increasingly superseded the diurnal, seasonal, and annual rhythms of the natural world.

Such changes may be seen by the historian as merely an acceleration of more gradual processes that had been taking place over the course of many centuries, but they seemed to many people at the time like a quantum leap into a new era of human existence. Past ages of ignorance, scarcity, and irrationality were deemed, not to be wholly done away with, but to be working themselves out 'like a long-division sum'. This sense of living in a new epoch found expression in many contexts and in a variety of ways. There was a marked decline in a popular sense of continuity with past history; and many contemporaries from the 1880s onwards remarked upon the emergence of a new 'race' or 'nation' with no spontaneous memory of past time—a race with an ahistorical mentality that was being forcibly created by mass migration to the cities. Even in villages, folk memory was dying: 'modernized people acquainted with leisure are in every cottage', wrote George Bourne in 1912. Precedent declined in status as a guide to public policy, and its place was usurped by various models of 'social evolution', which became the dominant sociological paradigm of the age. Evolutionary thought led to a certain amount of pessimistic determinism about the human condition; and from the 1880s onwards anxiety about degeneracy and 'physical deterioration' became one of the fashionable idioms of the age. But a more common response was the assumption that evolutionary science, and indeed science generally, was making it more and more possible for social arrangements to be brought under rational, purposive human control. Such assumptions extended to private lives as well as to public policy, and could be seen in the emergence during the 1890s of the 'new woman' (and to a lesser extent of the 'new man'), determined to forge her own role and purposes rather than to accept the prescription of past ages. At the same time social science and social philosophy were transforming the definition and understanding of many social phenomena; and they were also creating a new sense of 'society', not as the narrow concern of the small minority who moved in the public sphere, but as the predicate of individual existence and as the encircling sum of all human affairs.

Such trends formed a distinctive strand in the social thought and action of the late Victorian and Edwardian eras. Indeed, foreign observers remarked that the British were in fact more 'modern' than their own self-awareness led them to believe, but that the chasm between the present and the past was misted over and obscured by the antiquity of their ceremonial institutions. There were many new institutions of the period whose remorselessly modern purposes were clothed by the fig-leaf of invented tradition: the Primrose League, the revival of folk song and May Day, the Edwardian discovery of the 'Dickensian pub', the Dureresque woodcuts of St George and the Dragon adopted as the emblem of the Institute of Social Service (founded in 1906). Such a packaging of the past in the service of modernity seems to point inexorably towards the consumerist mass society of the later twentieth century.

One must be wary, however, both of taking Victorian and Edwardian modernity too much at its own evaluation, and of assuming its necessary connection with history's onward march. It must be remembered that much of what contemporaries perceived as quintessentially modern—such as large, unified, multicultural states and international free trade—proved in fact to be a cul-de-sac for at least the next half-century of European history; and much of what they perceived as quintessentially *anti*-modern—ethnic diversity, Irish nationalism, the cultural self-assertion of 'backward peoples'—were to be key themes of history in later decades of the twentieth century. The same point may be made about many other movements and institutions. The social purity campaign and sexual vigilante groups of the 1880s and 1890s—pilloried by 'modernists' of the 1920s as the quintessence of outmoded Victorian prudery—were a product, not of the older Victorian Britain of sin and Sabbatarianism, but of modern women in a self-consciously modern era, asserting a new 'progressive' principle of self-control for both sexes, against the more archaic tradition of a sexual 'double standard'. Similarly, many features of the Poor Law that later generations found most offensively 'Victorian'—particularly, strict enforcement of the workhouse test and discrimination between 'deserving' and 'undeserving'—were less characteristic of the high Victorian period than of the era of rationalization, modernization, and development of specialist social services within the Poor Law that set in during the period after 1870.

Moreover, there were at all times many different perceptions of what constituted 'the modern'. To some, modernity meant the continuous advance of human and institutional rationality, whereas to others it meant the rise of group hysteria and the era of the crowd. For some it entailed militant scientific positivism of the kind starkly outlined in the presidential address of the physicist John Tyndall to the Belfast meeting of the British Association in 1874: 'We claim, and we shall wrest from theology, the entire domain of cosmological theory. All schemes and systems . . . which infringe upon the domain of science must . . . submit to its control and relinquish all thought of controlling it.' But by the end of the century Tyndall's position seemed crude and untenable even to fellow positivists; and to many late Victorians the way ahead in both scientific and socio-logical understanding appeared to lie in various forms of philosophical idealism, which emphasized the role of 'spirit' and 'consciousness' in the structure of knowledge, without necessarily invoking a supernatural realm. Reaction against positivism also generated, from the 1890s onwards, a powerful current of both Catholic and Protestant theological 'modernism', which asserted that mysticism and prophetic utterance were perfectly compatible with the most advanced forms of material understanding of the modern world. In the spheres of culture and aesthetics there was always a fundamental difference of emphasis between the mainstream of late Victorian and Edwardian modernist thought, with its central emphasis on the social context of human behaviour and the social purpose of art, and a rival undercurrent—exclusively concerned with perception of abstract form—that burst into prominence just before 1914 and came to dominate the modern movement in the 1920s. Some of the cult figures of that earlier modernism—such as H. G. Wells, Arnold Bennett, and John Galsworthy—came to be seen by the generation of Roger Fry, Virginia Woolf, and Wyndham Lewis not merely as old-fashioned but as quin-tessential exponents of the kind of naïve, social-reformist, representational realism that the new wave of modernism was determined to depose.

Differences among intellectuals were mirrored by differing responses to the fact of modernity within society at large (though historians know little enough about how ordinary people reacted to change within the context of their private lives). Throughout the period, and at all levels except the very poorest, British society was characterized by an immensely vigorous associational and reformist culture: by groups of people who constantly came together to improve, reform, rationalize, and revolutionize social institutions and to bring them into harmony with the perceived requirements of the modern world. With a few noteworthy exceptions, the mainstream of writing on economics, sociology, and the analysis and treatment of social problems was optimistic, progressive, and ameliorative in tone, even among those who were highly critical of the structural injustices of capitalism and the effects of free competition. There were many who viewed modernity as a process of liberation, who longed for the wheels of history to turn faster and to grind the residues of the past away. But throughout the period there were also recurrent echoes of the opposite note, even among those who were at the forefront of the modern movement. Thomas Hardy, whose 1870 novel *The Laodicean* was an exuberant celebration of the new society wrought by steam, speed, and technological change, was writing in the 1890s of the 'coming universal wish not to live'. Beatrice Webb, most tireless campaigner in the cause of institutional modernization, constantly confided to her diary her sense of private nausea and ennui at the implications of many of the causes that she was publicly espousing: 'I confess', she wrote in 1902, 'to a certain background of permanent melancholy, the dark consciousness of the meaninglessness of the struggle for life on this miserable little planet.' The cultural wing of Irish nationalism was deeply infused with the desire to escape the repulsive forces of modernity, believed to be characteristic of the Anglo-Saxon world. Sir James Frazer, most pugnacious and confident prophet of the view that scientific naturalism would eventually encompass the whole of human history, passionately mourned the world of myth and mystery—enshrined in the sacrifice of the king in the sacred grove of Nemi—that his own ethnographic studies deliberately set out to destroy. This other face of Edwardian modernity suggests a lurking grief at the memory of a lost domain—a sense that change was inevitable, and in many respects desirable, but that its gains were being purchased at a terrible price. Such varieties and ambiguities are a valuable reminder that 'modernity' was essentially a mental construct rather than an objective, external measuring-rod of the social institutions of the late Victorian and Edwardian age.

IX. PARADOX AND PLURALITY

These themes do not exhaust the central concerns of British society in the forty-four years before the First World War, but they offer a framework for understanding an immensely diverse society at a very contingent and seminal period of history. At least some of these themes were endemic not just in British but in European experience of this period, and were incorporated by contemporary social theorists into a general sociology of the modern world. They were pinpointed and highlighted by such abstract paradigms as Sir Henry Maine's account of the transition from 'status' to 'contract', Ferdinand Tönnies' antinomy of 'Gemeinschaft' and 'Gesellschaft', Bagehot's emphasis on the dissolution of the 'cake of custom' by 'discussion' and 'free choice'. In nearly all branches of political thought there was a shift from viewing society as an aggregation of private individuals to a vision of society as collective, public, evolutionary, and organic. All these theories are both part of the essential subject-matter of the social history of the period and an aid to the imaginative reconstruction of that history. Yet it cannot be emphasized too strongly how often and how unpredictably the course of real historical structures and events defied or deviated from tidy patterns of generalized social theory. For instance, Britain's economic and legal arrangements and dominant political ideas in the late nineteenth century were very far out along the spectrum towards a pure 'Gesellschaft' model of society: and yet 'Gemeinschaft'-type arrangements constantly survived or reasserted themselves in unexpected quarters (in, for example, the tenacious survival of small family businesses, and in the late nineteenth-century emergence of supposedly 'traditional' working-class communities, powerfully bound together by ties of kinship, culture, custom, and class).

Moreover, though Britain was perceived by most contemporary social theorists as the most 'advanced' modern society, there were many respects in which British citizens and social institutions obstinately refused to behave in ways that sociological theory required. Throughout the period Britain's bureaucracy was smaller, her voluntary institutions more extensive, her churches more flourishing, her homicide, suicide, divorce, and illegitimacy rates markedly lower than those of most other European countries—in stark contrast to what Britain's structural modernity might have led one to expect. An analysis through time may emphasize the growth of class division, the rise of collectivism, and the dwindling of firm religious conviction. But a comparative perspective suggests a rather different set of questions, such as why were class relationships so relatively docile, why was British government so unexpectedly limited in scope, and why did religious belief retain such a widely pervasive hold? The same dichotomy prevails in the sphere of public order. The Trafalgar Square riots of the 1880s, the syndicalist strikes of the late 1900s, the endemic threat of Catholic and Protestant violence in Ireland, and the hysterical scenes in the House of Commons over the passing of the 1911 Parliament Act may suggest a society where the legitimacy of state institutions was fragile. However, comparison with the recurrent conspiracies of the French Third Republic, the mass alienation of labour in the German Empire, and the incipient balkanization of south-eastern Europe suggests on the contrary a society where the organs of law and government were quite unusually secure. The constitutional battle of the late 1900s over graduated taxes on income and property should be compared to similar battles during the same period in the German Reichstag or the French Chambre des Députés, where finance ministers tried, but (in marked contrast to their opposite numbers in Britain) singularly failed, to impose centralized direct progressive taxation of any kind. The degree of Irish estrangement before 1914, and the inevitability or otherwise of Ulster rebellion and Irish separation, remain imponderable questions. But, Ireland apart, nothing in the sociological theories of the period (or indeed of subsequent periods) quite prepares one for the extraordinary coexistence of extreme social inequality with respect for and observance of the law, of growing public order with fierce defence of civil liberties, and of endemic structural and economic change with social and institutional cohesion, that characterized British society for most of the period 1870 to 1914.

X. VICTORIANS AND EDWARDIANS

A final word must be said about those well-honed stereotypes, 'Victorian' and its junior partner 'Edwardian'. Throughout this book I have used these terms simply as a convenient shorthand for people who lived in the British Isles during the reigns of Queen Victoria and King Edward the Seventh. I have tried as far as possible to avoid using them as portmanteau terms that indicate a certain preconceived range of moral, religious, political, and economic beliefs and behaviour. Such reified meanings seem to me to have done immense harm to the understanding of nineteenth- and early twentieth-century history, and to be largely unfounded in historical facts. The late nineteenth and early twentieth century represents a unique period in the development of British society, when opinion had been emancipated from an ancient Church–State establishment but in which the homogenizing forces of the new mass media were still in their infancy. The result was a bewildering diversity of beliefs and styles of life.

In the face of this diversity, few universally acknowledged truths about Victorians or Edwardians survive a closer scrutiny. In carrying out research for this book I have come across no real (as opposed to fabulous) Victorians who swathed their piano legs with nether garments, who refused to utter the word 'damn' even when discussing eternal damnation, or who referred to the stomach as 'S'. Victorian and Edwardian upper middle-class women of deep religious conviction—often parodied as pillars of ignorance and prudery—fought tireless campaigns for the civil rights of prostitutes and gave evidence to public inquiries on the nature of sexual diseases. Victorians, notorious for their supposed cult of death and mourning, often shocked Continental visitors by their careless addiction to sociability and pleasure before the dead were in their graves. 'Organized charity', frequently instanced as the characteristic medium for Victorian upper-class dealings with the poor, in fact represented only a tiny part of the spectrum of late nineteenth-century philanthropy, and was constantly at loggerheads with other, more ambitious and disorganized charitable schemes. The Victorian and Edwardian Poor Law harboured many institutions and practices which confirm its reputation for inhumanity, but many others which by the early twentieth century offered high-quality residential and medical services eagerly sought after by the fee-paying middle classes. Victorian and Edwardian attitudes to race were not anachronistically enlightened; but exemplars of social Darwinism and Anglo-Saxon supremacy must be balanced against those who cast their votes for Indians as MPs (there were several Indians in Parliament in the 1890s) or who thought (like Cecil Rhodes) that Anglo-Saxonism was not an ethnic concept but a bundle of constitutional rights.

Similarly, throughout the period, newspapers and other contemporary records teemed with reports of such apparently un-Victorian happenings as rent strikes, pauper strikes, nude bathing in public gardens, lockouts of teachers by elementary schoolchildren, and the beating up of accosting males by organized feminist vigilantes. British diplomacy at the Congress of Berlin was plagued by newspaper leaks from undetected junior Foreign Office officials. Accounts of the mass strikes of 1910-12, which challenged the legitimacy of the British state, reveal that many strikers seized the chance to spend the summer manœuvring on Dartmoor and sleeping under canvas with the Territorial Army. There were unexpected continuities between past and present: even in the heyday of consumer sovereignty, the late Victorian Southern Railway was notorious for its surly waitresses, sawdust sandwiches, and trains that never ran on time. On the other hand, certain cultural landmarks that look superficially familiar prove on closer inspection to be not so. The *Daily Mirror*, for example, founded in 1903, is often cited as a harbinger of the new mass proletarian culture of the later twentieth century; yet the *Mirror* in its early days was an elegant, art-nouveau-style paper catering for moderate middle-class feminists (its first edition denounced 'foolish gossip' about 'the Smart Set', and devoted two articles to the life and work of Professor Theodore Mommsen, the recently deceased historian of ancient Rome).

Such examples and episodes act as a useful antidote to over-simple expectations about past beliefs and values; but they should not in turn be used to construct a new set of false generalizations about the history of social life. They reflect the shifting and multidimensional 'moral kaleidoscope' of British society in the late Victorian and Edwardian age.

2

Demography, Death, and Disease

I. PEOPLE AND CITIES

One of the most striking facts that emerges from the Census of 1871 is that, a hundred years after the onset of the Industrial Revolution, the topography of Great Britain was still in many respects that of a predominantly rural country. Among a population of 31 million throughout the British Isles, nearly two-thirds still lived in rural areas or in towns of less than 10,000 inhabitants. Even in England and Wales, rural and small-town dwellers still acounted for 45 per cent of the populace; and many of those small towns were still much more closely tied to an agricultural rather than a manufacturing economy. Except in a few limited industrial areas the towns were still culturally and socially 'the creature of the country'. Apart from London only five cities housed more than a quarter of a million people; and a map of population distribution would have shown that heavy urbanization was physically confined and concentrated in certain localities: London and Middlesex, Lancashire and Durham, the Midlands counties of Staffordshire and Warwickshire, west-central Scotland, and parts of south Wales. Within the great cities high ground rents and urban congestion were beginning to drive some middle-class residents to the city boundaries (as they had done in London for centuries); but 'suburbia' was still limited as a phenomenon and unknown as a word. An observer writing in 1871 noted that English workmen had a very strong aversion to living far from their place of work, and that there was still a very close connection between workplace and home. Farm labouring was still by far the largest male occupation, and persons employed in agriculture were as numerous as the three 'leading sectors' of the

Industrial Revolution—textiles, transport, and mining—put together. Natural increase in the rural districts meant that they were growing almost as fast as the towns. Moreover, even in heavy industrial areas many urban-dwellers lived within walking distance of green fields. Even in the metropolis, the 1871 Census recorded, there were still large tracts of land where 'the dome of St Paul's and a thin cloud of smoke' were the only signs of urbanity and where 'the larks and nightingales sing in the surrounding glades'. The Census also gave expression to a remarkable sense of unbroken ethnic continuity with past times: the inhabitants of the different localities of the United Kingdom were still perceived as the direct descendants of Saxons, Angles, Danes, and Celts, of those who had risen with Jack Cade and Wat Tyler, and of those who had manned 'the hill fortresses where Caractacus withstood to the last the Roman power'.

The Census of 1871, however, was to be the last decennial survey of population for which this was true. The historic rural mould was irrevocably shattered by the agricultural depression, by the gravitational pull of urban employment, by the development of cheap suburban transport systems— and by a generic leap in the very nature of urban life. Between 1871 and 1881 rural population suffered an absolute decline for the first time since Census records began, whilst urban population increased by over 25 per cent and the population of the most heavily urbanized counties increased by 75 per cent—the fastest decade of urban growth for the whole of the nineteenth century. Within ten years Buckinghamshire, Huntingdonshire, and Oxfordshire lost a quarter of their population. Simultaneously, the sheer physical space occupied by towns massively expanded: by the 1880s Northumberland, Yorkshire, and Derbyshire had joined the heavily urbanized counties, and much of Middlesex and parts of Surrey were being transformed by the extension of the underground railway into metropolitan suburbs. The prolonged building boom of the 1870s and 1880s encircled all towns and cities with the middle- and working-class red or yellow brick suburbs, which remain the most enduring physical monument of the late Victorian age. In the 1890s and 1900s there was a slight slackening of the rate of urban growth, particularly in city centres, but no arrest of the overall process. By 1911, out of a total population of 45 million, 40 per cent lived in towns of over 100,000, in England and Wales more than 50 per cent. Greater London had over seven million inhabitants, fourteen provincial cities had over a quarter of a million, and thirty-nine had over a hundred thousand. Large parts of Cheshire, South Lancashire, Surrey, Essex, Hertfordshire, Leicestershire, Nottinghamshire, and the West Midlands had coagulated into a continuous urban or semi-urban environment. By 1914 only 8 per cent of the British people were employed in agriculture, compared with 27 per cent in Germany and 38 per cent in France. The percentage of the British population living in rural areas and small towns had shrunk to less than a quarter, and for England alone to one-eighth. Perhaps even more significantly, the physical boundaries of town and country were much more blurred than in 1871. The Census of 1911 recorded that many working-class as well as middle-class people, particularly in London, were positively opting to bring up their children in the suburbs. Daily commuting, not just from the suburbs, but from the shires and from the seaside resorts of the south coast, had become common. As rural England declined in productive importance, it was beginning to acquire a new role as the dormitory, nursery, refuge and recreation-ground of urban civilization.

The inner dynamics of this dramatic change in topographical character were complex. The most obvious pressure on the growth of towns was migration in search of work, of the kind that had been occurring since before the start of industrialization, but now greatly intensified by the agricultural decline of the late 1870s and 1880s, and by the global growth of new economic opportunities, not just in Britain but in the Empire and the United States. By the mid-1880s no county in England or Wales, however rural, had less than 10 per cent of migrants in its population, and in London, Middlesex, and Surrey nearly 50 per cent of the population had been born elsewhere. Most migration within England was 'short-journey' migration from countryside to town, and most migrants were young, single working people. Long-distance migration in family groups was largely confined to the Irish: first-generation settlers from Ireland formed 5.86 per cent of the population of England and Wales and 6.18 per cent of Scotland in 1881. A disproportionately high percentage of short-journey migrants were women; and since job opportunities for women were often found in quite different places from those for men, migration frequently produced extreme local distortions in the balance of the sexes. Mining areas, such as Glamorgan, Monmouthshire, and Durham, for example, had a severe shortage of females; whilst areas which employed a large number of domestic servants, such as London, Surrey, and the coastal holiday resorts, had a severe shortage of men. The effects of migration on the growth of towns were compounded by the fact that so many migrants were of child-bearing age—which meant that, even though urban women individually bore fewer children than rural women, the overall reproduction rate in towns was considerably higher than in the countryside. Of children born between 1901 and 1911, no fewer than 80 per cent were born in towns and cities, thus reinforcing the growth of a population whose mental outlook and social experience was almost wholly urban.

The balance between town and countryside—and between males and females—was further affected by patterns of emigration and immigration. The Census of 1871 calculated that of the 1,173 babies being born every day in Britain, 468 would emigrate ('That is still the policy of the British race, and it appears to succeed'). Over six million Britons emigrated between 1871 and 1911, outward movement reaching a peak in the 1870s and again in the 1890s. Most emigrants came from rural areas and nearly three-quarters of them were men, a fact which partly accounts for the growing surplus of women over this period in the national population (and which also helps to explain why so many young women, deprived of the chance of finding husbands in the countryside, sought work in the towns). Over three million foreigners entered Britain, of whom more than two-thirds were birds of passage from Eastern Europe to North America, and many more were merely temporary visitors. About 400,000 people of non-British origin settled as British citizens, of whom a third were Jewish refugees from Germany, Russia, and Poland. Throughout the period there was a large traffic in and out of Britain from and to the different parts of the Empire, but this imperial traffic was made up almost exclusively of persons born in the British Isles. Immigrants from the Asian and African races of the Empire remained at all times negligible in number, although there was no legal barrier to their entry and such people automatically acquired full British citizenship. The Census of 1911 indentified 4,000 persons of Asiatic origin, of whom the vast majority were sailors and students, with a sprinkling of doctors, Members of Parliament, and millionaires. There were also 12,000 persons of African origin and 9,000 West Indians, mainly in Merseyside and South Wales. Immigrants of all kinds settled almost exclusively in large cities: in rural and small-town Britain, foreign faces and accents were as unknown as visitors from the moon.

Movement of population was therefore a crucial feature of growing urbanization; but of no less importance than purely demographic change was the internal structural development of most urban communities. By the 1870s the towns thrown up earlier in the century to house the operatives of the Industrial Revolution were ceasing to be mere appendages of industry, and were becoming important financial, constructional, cultural, and ecological systems in their own right, providing transport, energy, employment, housing, and other social amenities. Even without population growth, urban life and its trappings began to occupy more physical space: hence the continual conversion of rural into urban administrative areas, the carving out of new 'county boroughs', and the growing tendency from the 1890s onwards for towns and cities to decant their population into the neighbouring countryside. Taken together, changing migration patterns and the growth of an autonomous, self-sustaining urban culture had profound implications for the life of the whole of society. At the beginning of the period a majority of town-dwellers were either first-generation immigrants from the countryside or lived in towns which were still closely linked to the rural economy. Many of them had pre-industrial skills, habits, and values which they at least partially transplanted into an urban environment. By 1914 not merely a majority of children, but a majority of urban-dwellers in early and middle life had been born and bred in towns and cities. The Census of 1911 identified a new 'urban type of population', found in its most extreme form in London—a population whose cultural, reproductive, and migratory habits seemed to be totally different from those of city-dwellers of forty years before. This new 'urban type' formed the subject-matter of much late Victorian and Edwardian sociology, and was often identified as a root cause of urban degeneration and racial decay. The significance of such fears and how far they were justified will be discussed in later chapters. In purely numerical terms the 'urban type' by 1914 comprised the vast majority of the British population.

II. Patterns of Fertility

One of the chief statistical characteristics of the 'urban type' was his or her reluctance to bear large numbers of children; and no less striking than the late nineteenth-century migration to towns was the concurrent revolution in habits of fertility. Nothing more clearly demarcates late Victorian from early Victorian Britain than attitudes towards the procreation of children. The early years of Queen Victoria's reign had been haunted by fears that mouths to feed might outrun the means of subsistence: class relationships, social policy, personal morality, and economic thought had all born the imprint of Malthus's warning that 'nature's feast' was limited and that 'arithmetical' increases in production would inexorably be matched by 'geometrical' increases in population size. By the last quarter of the century, however, both scientific and popular thought were running in quite the opposite direction. Although the aggregate population of Britain increased by almost one-half over the period (from 31 million in 1871 to 45 million in 1911), discussion of demographic trends was increasingly concerned not with population explosion but with stagnation and decline. Earlier fears of national famine gave way first of all to confidence that the subsistence problem had solved itself, then to gloomy forebodings of the 'menace of the empty cradle' and national demographic eclipse. Parental irresponsibility, which in the 1840s had been equated with the feckless bearing of large numbers of children, by the 1900s was equated with the bearing of few children or none at all. Virtually no public inquiry of the Edwardian decade failed to express concern about the spectre of population decline; and in 1910 conservatives, socialists and progressive liberals joined together in the National Social Purity Crusade, whose twin aims were discouragement of abortion and birth control and the general 'promotion of public morals'. Social policy, which at the beginning of the period still recalled with horror the 'pauper rabbit warrens' of the Speenhamland era, by 1914 was unofficially encouraging local authorities to make special 'council-house' provision for families with large numbers of children. At the same time, demographic anxiety was increasingly concerned not just with quantity but with quality—with an uneasy awareness that fertility decline was most marked among the rich and well-educated, and that (by 1911) the poorest third of the nation was breeding and rearing two-thirds of the British race.

Paradoxically, the shift of emphasis in demographic thought preceded the onset of decisive changes in national patterns of fertility. A glimpse of the new attitude had been apparent in the Census of 1861, which rejoiced in the fact that rising living standards appeared to be falsifying the predictions of Malthus. By 1871 the Census authorities were deploring the high proportion of unmarried women of child-bearing age and the growing fashion among parents for spacing out the births of their children. Family limitation, the Census darkly hinted, might be appropriate for atheists, papists, and Frenchmen, but not for English artisans and yeomen, whose unique historic mission was to populate the globe. Despite these forewarnings, however, the scarcely perceptible trends of 1871 proved to be the earth-tremors of a seismic change in the shape and structure of the British population. Over the next forty years there was a steady rise in the mean age of marriage, in the proportion of childless marriages, and in the percentage of those who did not marry at all. Census data on marriage rates give some statistical support to those mothers of heroines in Edwardian fiction who complained that 'men have given up marrying nowadays' and that 'marriage has fallen quite out of fashion'.* Among those who did marry, the birth rate began to decline markedly in the late 1870s, and fell

---

* Only half of the male population was married by the age of 30 in the 1900s (compared with over three-quarters in the late 1960s).

dramatically after 1900. Whereas the average marriage contracted in the 1850s produced more than five surviving children and families of ten or more were common, the average marriage contracted in the 1900s produced only three. Illegitimate births also declined, falling in the 1900s to the lowest level on record (just over 3 per cent), even though Edwardian social reformers often thought of illegitimacy as one of the major social problems of the day. The annual rate of reproduction for all live births, legitimate and illegitimate, fell from 34.1 per 1,000 in 1871–2 to 24.5 per 1,000 in 1910–12. Though the decline was most marked among city-dwellers and in higher professional and skilled occupations, scarcely any group or locality in England, Wales, Scotland, or Ireland was untouched by the change. By the 1900s only the wives of miners and quarrymen were producing families as large as those of the mid-Victorian years.

Contemporary observers and social theorists pondered at length about why this decline in fertility occurred, and the question has been no less fascinating to later historians. Commentators in the 1890s sometimes suggested that the strain of urban living and of modern education was eroding human procreative powers; while other, more optimistic, authorities thought that low fertility was a sign of an advanced stage of biological evolution. No firm scientific evidence was ever brought forward to sub-stantiate either of these views, however, and historians have laid much more emphasis on changes in economic structure and aspiration, and on the spread of literacy and biological knowledge. Because the two most marked falls in fertility coincided with the depression of the late 1870s and the downturn of real wages in the 1900s, the limitation of families has often been ascribed to the efforts of parents to maintain living standards in the face of falling incomes. Similarly, historians have pointed to the growing costs of private education among the middle classes, and to the introduction in the 1870s of compulsory state primary education, which withdrew working-class children from the labour market and thus reduced their value as contributors to family income. Children in this period, so it has been argued, ceased to be factors of production and became one amongst many competing objects of consumption, to be weighed in the balance of parental calculation alongside other forms of consumer goods.

Economic motives for family limitation tell us nothing, however, about how such limitation actually came about; and an alternative view has emphasized not so much the economic context as the increasing availability of mechanical methods of contraception and the spread of information about birth-control techniques—particularly after the much-publicized trial of Annie Besant and Charles Bradlaugh for publishing birth-control literature in 1877. The fact that low birth rates in combination with early marriages were often found where female employment was high, as in the Lancashire textile towns, has suggested that birth-control information was probably transmitted by working women through word of mouth. And the fact that both low birth rates and artificial methods of birth control were condemned by the Anglican and Roman Catholic Churches has led some historians to link declining fertility to the advance of 'secularization' and to the dwindling of ecclesiastical and clerical controls.

All of these explanations have some plausibility, but none of them seems wholly adequate to explain the change in child-bearing patterns that occurred so universally between 1870 and 1914. One difficulty with structural explanations of the declining birth rate is that, with some local variation, the decline was a European-wide phenomenon, so it cannot be accounted for in peculiarly British terms. Moreover, explanations which emphasize the economic burden of children have tended to exaggerate the contrast in the child labour market before and after 1870. Full-time child employment before 1870 was much more limited than historians have often supposed, whereas part-time child employment (in conjunction with both part-time and full-time elementary schooling) continued on a large scale down to 1914. Many children continued throughout the period to be what they had always been: namely, useful but not indispensable sources of secondary family income. The economic argument also seems inadequate in explaining the decline in illegitimacy, since most children born out of wedlock were not likely to have been the consequence of prudent, rational, economic calculation.

Information about methods of family limitation is equally patchy and ambiguous. There is much fragmentary evidence to support the view that access to artificial forms of birth control was readily and increasingly available. Advertisements in popular journals and provincial almanacs, for example, suggest that, at least by the 1890s, postal retailing of prophylactics was widespread; and such diverse sources as reports of factory inspectors, social surveys, medical handbooks, and the memoirs of great lovers all made covert reference to rubber sheaths, pessaries, 'coughing after intercourse', withdrawal, and various modes of abortion. The Registrar General in 1908 estimated that 14 per cent of the decline in fertility was due to later marriage, 7 per cent to the falling illegitimacy rate, and 79 per cent to 'deliberate restriction of child-bearing'. On the National Birth Rate Commission at the end of the period both radical doctors and Roman Catholic priests concurred in the view that there was a burgeoning mass demand for 'Malthusian' information ('Young women tell each other; young men tell each other; fathers tell each other', reported one member of the commission, Monsignor Joseph Brown). Against this, however, evidence from more firsthand sources, both literary and oral, suggests that, even in areas of high female employment, knowledge about family limitation among potential parents was in practice very slight. *Letters from Working Women*, collected by the Women's Co-operative Guild just before the First World War, contained some often-cited references to family limitation procedures, including 'taking pills', 'mechanical prevention', and 'trying to destroy life in the early days of pregnancy'. But many of these letters indicated that among a majority of working mothers the practice and even the discussion of birth-control techniques were virtually unknown. Similarly, it is difficult to establish a link between declining family size, birth control and the advance of 'secularization', since at least in urban areas there seems little reason to suppose that people were any more or less susceptible to clerical control than they had been fifty years before. If anything, popular religious influences may have increased at the end of the nineteenth century (see Chapter 6); and it is conceivable that, through the medium of Sunday schools if not of churchgoing, the churches may inadvertently have contributed to population restraint by preaching premarital chastity and prudential postponement of marriage more successfully than at any previous time.

All these qualifications suggest that any simple, uni-causal analysis of fertility decline is doomed to failure; and what little is known about individual practice suggests that decisions about child-bearing were often determined by highly local and idiosyncratic factors. High fertility among miners, for example, was almost certainly linked to high male wages, limited opportunities for female employment, and the early availability of miners' tied cottages, all of which diminished the practical incentives for postponement of births. Attitudes to birth control were partly generational, and young women who entered the labour market in the 1900s appear to have been much more likely to hear about methods of family limitation than their mothers two decades before. Low fertility in predominantly agricultural Ireland (lower throughout the period than in England, Wales, or Scotland) was almost entirely accounted for by the abnormally late postponement of marriage and by unusually high levels of lifelong celibacy, which in turn were a response to the Irish famine of the 1840s (when the Irish *did* eventually marry, often in their late thirties, their fertility was very high). The very fact that a subsistence catastrophe had changed Irish habits so profoundly shows that procreative trends could be modified by experience, even without mechanical intervention. The case of Ireland is a useful reminder that low birth rates were by no means confined to the most 'modern' sectors of society and that high fertility in a pre-industrial context was in no sense an inexorable natural law.

III. PATTERNS OF MORTALITY

Declining fertility was accompanied, though less dramatically and more patchily, by declining mortality. A slight decline in the crude death rate began in the 1860s, but almost certainly this did not reflect improved life expectancy but the high proportion in the population of people in early and middle life. A more significant fall in the age-specific death rate of children and young women (under 25s) occurred in the 1870s. Life expectancy for middle-aged women improved in the 1880s and for middle-aged men in the 1890s. The census of 1911 registered a marked rise in the proportion of the population over 65—a change which may have reflected a slight increase in longevity, but was primarily the long-term legacy of the abnormally high birth rate of two-thirds of a century before. There was only the faintest foreshadowing here of a massive prolongation of the life of old people, which was to become a major theme of demographic transformation later in the twentieth century. At the opposite end of the spectrum, infant mortality (deaths of those under one year) remained high throughout the later decades of the nineteenth century, and soared to a mysterious peak of 163 per 1,000 in 1899, before falling off rapidly after 1902. The life chances of infants were very unevenly distributed, however, between different social groups; and probably no other factor was a more sensitive index of contemporary variations in wealth, environment, child-rearing habits, and access to medical care. Urban infant mortality was 30 per cent higher than rural, illegitimate infant mortality twice as high as legitimate. In the black year of 1899 the rate in London varied from over 200 in the poorer districts of the East End to less than 80 in 'comfortable and airy' Hampstead, Marylebone, and the more salubrious suburbs.

The social basis of death rates for adults followed a different pattern from that for the newly born. Over the whole period from 1871 to 1913 the crude death rate for England and Wales fell from 22.6 per 1,000 to 13.8 per 1,000. No groups and no regions were wholly unaffected by the trend; but as with changes in the birth rate, the death rate varied markedly according to occupation, social class, and the idiosyncrasies of local population structure. Seaside towns, for example, often had high death rates, not because they were unhealthy but because their residents were old. The life tables of private insurance companies showed that throughout the period mortality tended to be lowest among the highest income groups; but this was not invariably so, since there were certain low-paid occupations such as gardening and farm labouring whose mortality was lower than that of certain highly pressured, high-status occupations such as medicine and merchant banking. Moreover, the contrast between rich and poor was largely concentrated in infancy and old age: in middle life the age-specific mortality of the rich was no different from that of the poor living in healthy districts. In many areas the death rate of middle-class women in childbirth was actually higher than among women of the working class; possibly—though this is by no means certain—because the latter were attended by midwives, the former by fashionable doctors practising newfangled but unreliable techniques of obstetric intervention. At all times female life expectancy was superior to that of comparable males. More male babies were born than female babies, but at all ages above infancy females outnumbered males, indicating that women were more resistant than men to hardship and disease.

In nearly every age group, urban mortality was higher than rural mortality (a relationship that was not to be substantially reversed by the impact of superior urban medical services until the 1920s). Between different urban areas, however, the risk of death varied dramatically. Death rates were predictably low in pre-industrial county towns, predictably high in large cities and in heavy manufacturing areas. But even within the latter there were surprising variations between cities and urban areas whose industrial and occupational composition appeared to be very similar. Tyneside was much healthier than Merseyside, for example; while mortality (other than infant) in the Lancashire mill towns was considerably lower than in the Potteries. Birmingham and Nottingham were conspicuously healthier than Manchester and Sheffield. Leicester, whose general death rate was second only to that of Liverpool, laid claim in the 1870s to an infant mortality rate lower than that of most other cities. Throughout the period there were notorious black spots of both overall and infant mortality, such as Liverpool and Dundee. The high mortality of Liverpool (general death rate 35 per 1,000, infant mortality 269 per 1,000 in 1874) was often ascribed by contemporaries to the poverty and insanitary habits of its large colony of Irish immigrants. But the Irish back home in Ireland enjoyed more favourable mortality rates at nearly all ages than the inhabitants of the rest of Britain. Among the cities of Ireland only Dublin slaughtered its innocents with quite the ferocity of the English and Scottish cities, suggesting perhaps that lack of a main drainage system (not installed in

Dublin till 1906) was a more important determinant of death than either poverty or national character.

As with the birth rate, there was much debate among contemporaries about how mortality statistics should be interpreted. The Edwardian statistician T. A. Welton remarked that the British took a patriotic pride in statistical proofs of progress, and that in nothing was progress more tangibly embodied than a lengthening expectation of life. Medical authorities of the period were generally optimistic about adult death rates, pointing out that for people in the prime of life British mortality tables compared very favourably with those of the rest of Europe. Professional opinion at the end of the nineteenth century ascribed the decline in the death rate mainly to environmental factors: to better sanitation, water supplies, housing renewal and slum clearance. Until the 1890s sanitary theory and practice were dominated by 'Farr's Law', the formula propounded by the Assistant Registrar General Dr William Farr, which posited an exact mathematical relationship between level of mortality and degree of over-crowding. Farr's Law was challenged and disproved in the late 1890s, but its vogue over the previous twenty years had done much to improve the airiness and spaciousness, if not the physical attractiveness, of new working-class housing.

Later authorities, however, have questioned the impact of housing and sanitation on improved levels of mortality, and have shifted the explanation from density to medicine, and more recently from medicine to diet. It has been argued that sanitary reforms were based on false scientific premisses and could in any case only have affected a limited number of water-borne diseases such as cholera and typhus. Instead, attention has turned to the decline in mortality from zymotic diseases,* brought about by inoculation against smallpox and by the isolation of cases of tuberculosis, whooping cough, measles, and scarlet fever. (Deaths from smallpox were virtually eliminated in England and Wales between 1871 and 1905, while deaths from scarlet fever fell from 759 to 126 per million inhabitants; and although tuberculosis remained a great scourge, Edwardian mortality from TB was little over half that of the mid-Victorian years.) More funda-mentally, however, the emphasis in explaining lower death rates has moved away from the specific impact of disease to the more general standard of nutrition. A study undertaken in the 1980s concluded that more than half

---

* Literally, diseases stemming from fermentation and putrefaction. Reflecting the earlier Victorian belief that infection was transmitted by poisonous miasmas, the term was widely used in the later Victorian period to refer to all forms of infectious disease.

the decline in the death rate between 1860 and 1914 must have been accounted for 'by improvements in the standard of living—in particular the consumption of more and better food'. This view coincides with the evidence of rising real wages and rising per capita incomes over most of the period, at least until the 1900s; but it poses a number of problems. If nutrition be the key to improved mortality rates, then it is hard to see why such improvement should have been so much more marked among women than men, since numerous sources confirm that female diets and general living standards were considerably lower than those of men. Similarly, it is difficult to relate improved nutrition to the low mortality prevailing in the countryside, since agricultural wages were notoriously low and, with certain limited home-grown exceptions, fresh food was scarce and dear in most rural areas. (It was one of the many ironies of free trade that condensed milk was so widely consumed in agricultural districts.) Moreover, the point made earlier about the different levels of mortality prevailing in apparently similar economic settings suggests that mortality cannot be reduced to a single predominant causal variable. On the contrary, mortality rates were the product of a whole complex of socio-economic and cultural factors, which included not merely real income, medicine, and sanitation, but less quantifiable influences such as conditions at work, length and flexibility of working hours, high or low alcohol consumption, cigarette smoking (rare in Britain before the 1890s), local access to institutional care, and the strength or weakness of family and community support.

The futility of reductionism is perhaps most apparent in discussing infant mortality, since no observer succeeded at the time and no historian has succeeded ever since in finding a simple clue to that most intransigent of late Victorian social problems. Infant mortality was high in the Lancashire textile towns, which led many authorities to ascribe it to the prevalance of working mothers; and that women's employment—often accompanied by wet-nursing, bottle-feeding, and child-minding—had some connection with high infant death rates seems indisputable. But infant mortality was also high in mining areas, where married women's employment was rare. Moreover, infant mortality fell markedly in the 1900s, a decade when employment of married women was rising. George Newman in his classic study of 1906 ascribed high infant mortality partly to women's employment and partly to low family income; but he failed to make it clear which was the lesser evil of the two—an important omission since, as many Edwardian surveys of family income made clear, the wages of working mothers were often the indispensable buffer between sufficiency and starvation. In fact, as with adult mortality, it seems probable that infant mortality was sensitive to a whole cluster of conditions and factors. As Elizabeth Roberts has observed in her study of Preston, the fall in infant mortality in the 1900s coincided with the replacement of earth privies by water-closets, with the introduction of health visitors and qualified midwives, with a rise in family incomes at least partly occasioned by a rise in married women's employment, and with a marked decline in the rate of zymotic disease.

IV. Society, sickness, and medicine

Sickness and health were more than just statistical phenomena, and more must be said about the wider relation of mortality and morbidity rates to the institutions and ideas of late Victorian and Edwardian society. The late nineteenth and early twentieth-century period was in many respects a unique watershed in the history of health, sickness, and the treatment of disease: it was a period in which economy, society, and population structure were assuming their 'modern' shape, but before modern antibiotic and therapeutic medicine was fully available to treat the pathological side-effects. Huge agglomerations of people lived close to each other in a densely packed urban environment, to an extent that was quite unprecedented in human history; whilst at the same time the growth of heavy industry, mass production, mass retailing, and office employment totally changed the character of the physical and psychological stresses and strains that were imposed upon the human body. Grief at the loss of babies and small children continued to afflict hundreds of thousands of parents every year, a phenomenon that still awaits imaginative historical reconstruction. In spite of rising real incomes, life in great cities went hand in hand with epidemic and infectious disease, and with a great mass of chronic sickness that was related to damp, stress, foul air, contaminated food, and malnutrition (research carried out for the Royal Commission on the Poor Laws in 1905–9 suggested that 49 per cent of working-class women of the period were in permanently poor health).

Moreover, the cauldron of deep structural change generated many new pathological conditions, whose causes and ramifications were only imperfectly understood even by the most advanced forms of contemporary biological knowledge; and the period teemed with competing medical and sociobiological theories, rooted partly in common sense and pragmatism, partly in moral and metaphysical speculation, partly in the gradual accumulation of testable medical science. The late nineteenth-century discoveries of 'germs', 'microbes', and 'spirochaetes' laid the foundation of much future medical advance, but at the same time they created a widespread sense of psychological unease about the sinister invisible undercurrents of modern urban living. Much of what later generations have derided as the Victorian and Edwardian obsession with 'cleanliness' becomes more readily explicable if one recalls the lethal consequences of untreated sewage and contaminated water-supplies, and the very limited facilities for washing and personal hygiene that characterized large numbers of both urban and rural working-class homes well into the twentieth century. Fears about degeneracy and physical deterioration were the expression of an attempt to make sense of the mysterious and often terrifying phenomena of mass urban and industrial concentration and the apparent estrangement of large sectors of society from their 'natural' roots. The fact, or belief, that many diseases were closely linked to dirt, drink, and sexuality gave to sickness and health a strongly moral dimension that was closely intertwined with the growth of medical science. Tuberculosis and syphilis, insanity and imbecility, masturbation and menstruation were all the subjects of periodic moral, social and medical panics that were inseparable from the wider culture of the late Victorian and Edwardian age. In particular, venereal disease, a problem viewed by earlier Victorians with surprising insouciance, became a focus for many psychological fears of the *fin de siècle*, an anxiety fuelled by the discovery that syphilis was transmissible to unborn children and that it was a major cause of sterility, blindness, nervous disorder and the condition known as 'general paralysis of the insane'. A series of official reports between 1904 and 1916 suggested that VD was endemic throughout all classes of the industrial population (only agricultural labourers were relatively unaffected) and that victims included many little girls between the ages of 4 and 14—a fact attributed by the Royal Commission on Venereal Disease 'to the abominable superstition that intercourse with a virgin cures venereal disease in a man'. Thus 'purity' and 'pollution'— and all the widely ramifying fears and taboos that followed from these concepts—were no mere anthropological abstractions: they were inexorable facts of everyday life in the encircling urban and industrial world.

Similar ambivalent points may be made about the role and status of medical practice. Between the mid-nineteenth century and the First World War both medical institutions and medical practitioners profoundly changed their roles in British society. Hospitals for the first time became major agencies for the cure and prevention of disease rather than mere prisons for the deviant and depositories for the dying. Medicine as a science rapidly advanced in status, as medical researchers and practitioners successfully identified bacteria and viruses, developed new forms of drug treatment and painkiller, and improved their techniques of inoculation, vaccination, sterilization, and anaesthesia. Doctors moved from the margin to the mainstream of social life; and, although there were many gradations within the medical profession, by 1914 both specialists and general practitioners were well on the way to acquiring the exalted prestige and high public profile that their profession was to enjoy later in the twentieth century.

Nevertheless, throughout the period the relationship between medicine, sickness, and society was a tense and problematic one. There was no simple, tidy equation between the expansion of population, the advance of biological and chemical knowledge, and the growth of popular access to enhanced medical care. On the contrary, social change constantly ran ahead of (or in contradiction to) scientific understanding; and—particularly in the early stages of mass urbanization—attempts to create a new and more sanitary environment owed as much to engineering and public administration as to medicine and scientific research.* Mid-nineteenth-century advances in practical nursing and hospital care were influenced more by dynamic and imperious social reformers such as Dr Farr and Florence Nightingale (whose theories of infection were scientically false) than by more circumspect practitioners whose medical theories were scientifically correct. Even in the 1890s and 1900s, when bacteriology and pharmacology were rapidly advancing, improvements in medical care were largely based on the better practical management of patients (improved hygiene, more effective isolation of infection, more emphasis on rest, diet, and convalescence) rather than on cure through the administration of drugs. The rise of the orthodox medical profession rested not merely upon its increasing capacity to offer effective diagnosis and cure—though that was clearly an important element—but upon its successful campaign to control medical recruitment, its triumphs over professional rivals (such as sanitary engineers, midwives, pharmacists, and homoeopathists) and, particularly towards the end of the period, upon its ability to influence government and to command public resources. Doctors were increasingly revered, but also widely resented—by other professional groups whose skills they had outlawed or downgraded, as well as by women terrorized by gynaecological inspection, by parents whose children had died from compulsory vaccination, by libertarians opposed to disease notification, and by individuals in

* For example, the body louse that carried typhus, a major killer of the mid-Victorian decades, was not identified until 1909, three years after the elimination of typhus by isolation and improved hygiene and sanitation.

all classes who resisted the creeping 'medicalization' of what had previously been viewed as 'common sense' areas of human life, such as child care, sexuality, physical fitness, diet, and crime.*

The human body (whose image was so often invoked by theorists of the period to throw light upon the workings of human society) paradoxically remained a largely mysterious organism whose laws and inner dynamics were very imperfectly understood, not just by laymen but by the cream of the medical and scientific élite. Ideas about evolution, inheritance, and natural selection invaded medical thought from the 1860s onwards and fuelled continuous debate about the relative impact of heredity and environment, mind and body; but until long after 1914 they did little to explain and much to obscure the nature of many illnesses. The late nineteenth-century treatment of tuberculosis centred partly upon isolation and fresh air, but partly also upon the strengthening of 'moral character' to combat the effect of 'hereditary predisposition' (an interesting concatenation of apparently contradictory ideas that owed a great deal to contemporary social theory, but very little to experimental science). Evidence submitted to the Royal Commission on the Care and Control of the Feeble-Minded in 1904–8 revealed that the medical profession was split down the middle between those convinced that mental deficiency was hereditary and incurable, and those who thought that it was produced by insanitary environment and malnutrition. Both schools of thought persistently identified deafness, dumbness, blindness, epilepsy, squints, left-handedness, aphasia, and sexual precocity with mental retardation, though there was some dawning awareness in the 1900s that cause and effect were less self-evident than was frequently supposed. Throughout the period systematic advances in medical knowledge must be set against the fact that there were large areas of physiological life about which doctors appeared to speak with authority but were in fact almost wholly ignorant: these included the female reproductive cycle, the medical repercussions of sexual intercourse and abstinence, safe conditions of childbirth, the causes of depression and insanity ('moral pathology'), and the nature of hereditary disease.

Similarly, expanding access to both environmental health and personal medical care was governed by a jumble of local, socio-economic, and often purely random factors. The Local Government Board, set up in 1870, continually extended its powers of inspection and control over many humdrum but crucial areas of public hygiene; and the Public Health Act of

---

* There was widespread popular resentment at the growing attribution of certain forms of crime to insanity and mental illness. With few exceptions the late Victorian lower classes preferred to be thought bad rather than mad.

1875 left no part of England or Wales without a local sanitary authority, wielding wide mandatory and discretionary powers with which to regulate water supplies, sewerage, overcrowding, slum clearance, food adulteration, and the notification and isolation of infectious disease. Yet thirty years later there was still massive local variation in the extent to which public health authorities were prepared or could afford to use their powers, a fact which the Interdepartmental Committee on Physical Deterioration identified in 1904 as one of the key variables in the incidence of apparent urban degeneration. Similar variety prevailed in the treatment of individual patients. The growing effectiveness of personal medical care made it an increasingly desirable 'consumer good'; and a regular, fee-paying relationship with a 'family doctor' became more and more common in upper- and middle-class households. The last decades of the nineteenth century also saw a great expansion in both the quantity and quality of Poor Law hospitals, which appear to have been particularly effective in the isolation and prevention of tuberculosis (the chief adult killer disease of the mid-Victorian years). From the start of the period Poor Law medical services were being used in many areas by normally independent citizens, a fact that was recognized by an Act of 1885 which allowed people to receive medical poor-relief without losing the right to vote. In most major cities there were voluntary hospitals financed by fees and charitable subscriptions, which gave free in- and out-patient care to the local population (in some areas to all who needed it, in others to those who could produce a letter from a charitable subscriber vouching for their good character and financial need). Financial provision against personal sickness was an important part of the Victorian thrift movement, and by 1900 probably as many as four million workers were covered by some form of contributory sickness insurance, offered by friendly societies, trade unions, and the newly burgeoning industrial assurance companies. In addition, the friendly societies and trade unions employed 'club doctors': low-paid general practitioners of precarious status, whose job was partly to provide rudimentary medical care for society members, partly to keep a check upon malingering and to prevent misuse of provident funds. The work of all these agencies was supplemented by a wide range of charitable and commercial bodies catering for various aspects of the nation's health. These included provident dispensaries, medical missions, and a growing number of 'Saturday' and 'Sunday' schemes that raised funds for local hospitals; a dwindling but still important residue of herbalism and ancient folk remedies; a large and expanding market for quack remedies and mass-produced patent medicines; and a wide variety of pharmacists, homoeopathists, hydropathists and practitioners of 'fringe' medicine. Jesse Boot, the son of an itinerant Nonconformist herbalist and healer, who was to become the founder of the country's largest chain of retail chemist shops, symbolized the transition from the folk medicine of past eras to the science and consumerism of the new 'modern' age.

For all this gigantic voluntary and commercial enterprise, however, the availability of personal medical care remained arbitrary and patchy. For the very rich and the very poor both general and specialist medical treatment were by the 1900s inestimably superior to what they had been half a century before. In Ireland public medical provision developed largely outside the Poor Law, and in Scotland by the end of the nineteenth century Poor Law medical services were widely catering for the whole of the working class. But for a majority of people in England and Wales, ranging from the 'middling' sections of the middle class through to the unskilled working class, personal medicine was often either an object of stigma or an expensive and unaffordable luxury. In spite of the removal of voting disqualification, many still refused to use the Poor Law doctors; and, in spite of the massive improvement in Poor Law medical care, Poor Law authorities throughout the period were torn between the rival goals of promoting the prevention and cure of sickness, and of fulfilling their statutory obligation to maintain an element of 'deterrence' and 'less eligibility'. A large minority of men, and the vast majority of women and children, were not covered by voluntary provident schemes; and access to specialist treatment depended largely upon the geographical accident of living within the catchment area of one of the great teaching hospitals (whose location often bore no relation to the modern distribution of industrial population).

All these factors meant that the relationship between health, sanitation, medicine and the wider society was increasingly complex and contentious. As scientific knowledge advanced, fatalistic attitudes to sickness and mortality declined, popular expectations of medicine rose, and access to medical resources became increasingly intertwined with political and economic power. Fear of dirt, smallpox, and cholera meant that public health and sanitary science had always burst the bounds of theoretical 'individualism', even in the early Victorian age; and by the turn of the century anxiety about Britain's declining industrial and military efficiency, together with fears about the growth of an underclass of physical 'degenerates', were combining to promote the view that even the *private* health of individuals was a matter of public and national concern. There is little evidence in this period of any widespread popular demand for publicly financed personal medical care; but such a demand became increasingly central to the visions of social reformers, as could be seen in the introduction of public funding for school medical inspection (1907), in the movement for local maternity and child welfare clinics, in Sidney and Beatrice Webb's proposals for a state medical service, and above all in the 1911 National Insurance Act, which provided sickness insurance and rudimentary health care for the whole of the employed working population. Moreover, as doctors advanced in knowledge and status, they sought, or had thrust upon them, an increasingly powerful role that went beyond the treatment of individual patients into the shaping of public policy and morals. Even in the 1860s there were ambitious and visionary doctors like John Simon who saw medicine and sanitary science as central themes of national politics; and by the 1900s there were many doctors who viewed themselves not merely as scientific professionals, but as the moralists, theologians, and political philosophers of the new industrial age. George Newman, shortly to become chief medical officer to the Board of Education, wrote in 1907 that local authority sanitary services were the nucleus of the 'real welfare of a worldwide state'; and he described his book on *The Health of the State* as 'a missionary handbook, sent forth as a reminder that the physical health and fitness of the people is the primary asset of the British Empire and the necessary basis of that social and moral reform which has for its end "the creation of a higher type of man"'.

Health and medicine therefore moved increasingly from the periphery to the centre of social life over the course of the period. By 1914 not merely such intrinsically public spheres as sanitation and the treatment of epidemics, but the continuing personal health of private individuals, were seen in many quarters as matters of crucial public concern. The interdependence of physical health with national and civic well-being was a recurrent theme of Edwardian public debate at all points on the ideological spectrum, conservative, liberal, and socialist; and from the 1860s down to 1914 the human body and its diseases supplied an increasingly potent model and metaphor for the understanding of the wider 'body politic'. The history of health and medicine in this period thus encapsulates many wider trends and movements in the history of society. It demonstrates the growth of new professional élites, the reluctant encroachment of government upon the private sphere, the increasing importance of competition for material resources as a central theme of political life, and the struggle of science and ideology to explain, contain, and regulate the burgeoning forces of unprecedented and unpredictable social, industrial, and demographic change.

3

Family and Household

I. THE 'VICTORIAN' FAMILY

Many foreign visitors to nineteenth-century Britain commented on the widespread passion for family life, and G. M. Young's classic account of the Victorian period pinpointed commitment to the family as one of the few 'vital articles' of a 'common Victorian faith'. Novels, folk memory, albums, and memoirs combine to portray the family in this period as large in size, wide-ranging in kinship networks, close-knit in emotional ties, and patriarchal in moral authority. Yet nineteenth-century social theorists from Marx and Engels through to Le Play and Durkheim predicted the inexorable decline and disintegration of stable family life under the impact of industrialization. In a series of studies published in the 1890s and 1900s the sociological journalist T. H. Escott portrayed British family life and particularly upper- and middle-class family life as in a state of terminal decline—a decline in which the emotional and cultural, as well as the economic, functions of the traditional family were increasingly being transferred to the wider sphere of 'society'. Many Edwardian pressure groups clamoured for state intervention to preserve the family unit at all levels of society from moral, economic, demographic, and racial collapse. And in 1910 Sidney Webb's review of recent social movements for the Cambridge Modern History identified 'the substitution of the individual human being for the family group as the unit of the social order' as the leitmotiv of European social history over the previous hundred years.

More recently, historians and sociologists have disagreed profoundly about the functional and personal significance of the 'Victorian' family. Was it an emotional power-base whose support enabled individuals to cope with traumatic social change, or was it a forcing-ground for psychic tensions and disorders? Were the purposes of the family increasingly confined to affection, sex, and nurture, or did it in certain circumstances retain and even expand its economic role? Did the family buttress or subvert the norms and functions of the wider community? Was the family strong in the mid-nineteenth century, but falling into decay by the early twentieth century—or the other way round? Such questions have been mooted by many recent studies, but reliable answers have been impeded by the scarcity of research into the history of the British family between the Industrial Revolution and the First World War (due partly to the limited availability of unpublished census data). Pioneering case-studies based on oral history have been published by Thea Vigne, Paul Thompson, Elizabeth Roberts, and others, and these provide invaluable benchmarks for wider generalization. But Helen Bosanquet's remark that the history of the family 'is a great work waiting for a great scholar' remains as true for the late Victorian and Edwardian period as it was when she made it in 1906. A provisional, patchwork set of answers can be pieced together from a variety of sources; but much of what follows about the structure, functions, ideology, and social framework of family life rests upon a rather precarious scaffolding of inference and conjecture.

II. FAMILY SIZE AND STRUCTURE

To assemble the bare bones of family structure for the period seems on its face a straightforward task, since in spite of the limited census material there is so much information in published census reports, social surveys, and descriptive and literary sources. Yet this data does not always answer the questions that historians wish to ask. We know for instance that marriage was much more central to the matrix of family life than it had been in the early nineteenth century, but we do not know why. We know that the average number of children born to each marriage between the 1870s and the 1900s declined from just under six to just over three; but we do not know precisely how far contemporary perceptions of 'the family' were limited to parents and children. Census investigations often equated 'family' with 'household' or with 'tenements in separate occupation'; but again this begs the question of how far the 'family' exclusively comprised persons living together under the same roof. The number of such households rose from just over 5 million in 1871 to just under 8 million in 1911. Average household size over the period was about 4.75 persons, rising slightly between 1871 and 1891, and falling to 4.4 persons by 1911. At each decennial census nearly 70 per cent of the population lived in medium-sized households of between three and six people. One-person households were rare throughout the period, though they rose in the 1900s (reflecting partly the new phenomenon of metropolitan bedsitterland and partly the flight of younger people from the countryside, leaving large numbers of the elderly living alone). Two-thirds of households lived in houses or tenements of between four and six rooms. At every census overcrowding was recorded as a serious social problem, but the proportion of individuals living more than two persons to a room declined markedly in the 1900s. By the end of the period nearly half the population lived in households where there was only one occupant or less per room, a figure that pointed tentatively towards new possibilities of individualism and privacy within the family circle: a 'room of one's own', though largely unattainable below the middle classes, was nevertheless increasingly regarded as one of the touchstones of ideal family life.

These bald outlines give some idea of the overall physical shape of the late Victorian and Edwardian family, but little information about its internal structure. In particular they tell us little about how far the typical family of this period was simply a larger version of the twentieth-century nuclear family of parents and young children, or whether it contained elements of more extended networks. Historians of the family have long disposed of the view that the extended family (with several generations and/or wider kin domiciled in the same household) was common in pre-industrial England. And the Census of 1871 had no hesitation in affirming the normality of the nuclear model: 'The natural family is founded by marriage, and consists, in its complete state, of husband, wife and children.' Similarly, the common law obliged a man to support his wife and under-age children, but no wider kin. Other contemporary authorities, however, were not quite so sure. The doyen of family sociologists, Frederic Le Play, whilst acknowledging the growing prevalence of the modern 'unstable' or attenuated family, nevertheless thought that Britain in the 1860s had a higher proportion of traditional, property-centred, inter-generational families than other European societies. The Poor Law (by contrast with the common law) embodied the principle that economically active individuals should be financially responsible not merely for their children, but for their parents, grandparents, and grandchildren; and restrictions on outdoor relief after 1870 may have compelled many aged people who might otherwise have lived alone to move in with younger families. Descriptive sources of the period also present an ambivalent picture of family integration: some turn-of-the-century observers deplored the reluctance of even quite affluent working people to harbour aged parents (or only to do so if they brought with them an income from outdoor relief), whilst others thought that the taking in of grandparents and solitary relatives was an integral feature of working-class life. 'Over and over again one comes upon these joint households among working homes', recorded Lady Bell in her survey of Middlesbrough steelworkers in 1906. 'In nearly every case this difficult question . . . is empirically dealt with and practically solved by the old and enfeebled man being taken in and cared for by his younger children.'

Which of these accounts more accurately reflects contemporary attitudes and behaviour remains unclear. Studies by Michael Anderson of mid-nineteenth-century Lancashire have suggested that industrialization may have strengthened rather than weakened kinship ties and inter-generational co-residence, because of the practical help that resident grandparents could render to working mothers. And Elizabeth Roberts's survey of Preston, Barrow, and Lancaster uncovered the same pattern of close kinship networks, co-residence of grandparents, and mutual exchange of services in the 1890s and 1900s (though Roberts found no evidence to support Anderson's view that help to relatives was based on conscious mutual calculation). In Ireland in 1911, 15 per cent of the population were extended kinsfolk resident in the dwellings of 'stem' families, similar to those described by Le Play fifty years before; and many Irish immigrants lived in extended family structures in Scots and English cities (though whether they did so as a transplant of their ancient culture or simply as a practical means of coping with poverty and immigration is hard to tell). In Scotland multi-generational households were much more common in the crofting economy of the Highlands and Islands than in the market economy of the Lowlands. A conjectural estimate by Richard Wall suggests that 19 per cent of households in England and Wales probably contained kinsfolk other than the basic nucleus of parents and children in 1871; and the fact that mean household size over the ensuing forty years fell more slowly than the mean number of children may indicate a trend towards more shared residence with kin. The demographic combination of declining fertility with increased longevity may have produced more three-generational households by the start of the twentieth century than thirty years before.

Some contemporary sources, however, point to a quite different conclusion. Of the London households analysed by Booth in the 1890s, only 3.07 per cent included grandparents and 0.8 per cent other extended kin. In east London, often cited as the classic heartland of traditional working-class family cohesion, the proportion of families with co-resident grandparents fell to 2.0 per cent.* In Rowntree's 1899 study of York the figure for three-generational households was 1.4 per cent. In the four urban communities sampled by Bowley and Burnett-Hurst in 1912, resident grandparents received only the most cursory mention. And Clementina Black's inquiry into married women's employment in 1909–10 reported on the myth of the supportive grandmother in very jaundiced terms ('widows with young children dependent on them who can hardly afford the fees of a crèche seem to be peculiarly devoid of relatives willing to take charge'). Analysis of the records of rural Poor Law unions has suggested that, although as many as a quarter of elderly widows may have lived with kinsfolk, co-residence declined as the widows grew older and, presumably, more in need of care. Margaret Loane was highly critical of the idealized picture presented by Lady Bell, and stressed the acute intergenerational tensions that often arose when—in a period of rapid cultural transformation—respectable working-class families tried to house elderly relatives (particularly grandfathers) who still retained the coarser manners, speech and sanitary habits of a generation before. Certainly the very high proportion of old people, particularly men, living in institutions in 1911 suggests that, for whatever reason, many failed to find a foothold within a family home.

On the other hand, though Booth and Rowntree found few examples of extended families living under one roof, they found numerous cases of grandparents, brothers, sisters, and other kinsfolk living next door or in the same street. They recorded also the very widespread practice of adult, unmarried, working children living with their parents—a family structure that may count as 'nuclear' but that was nevertheless a very different kind of arrangement from the 'symmetrical' nuclear family of the mid-twentieth century. Numerous studies of the period commented on the pivotal role of mother–daughter relationships, long after the latter had left the parental home. And in families with large numbers of children, the fostering and virtual adoption of one or more children by childless aunts and uncles was common (far more so than more formal fostering through the Poor Law guardians).

Moreover, family networks were not necessarily confined to close kin. Many working-class families took in 'lodgers', a concept that embraced a wide spectrum of social relationships, ranging from purely business

* I have arrived at these rather artificial figures by an analysis of Booth's published material on London households. An analysis of Booth's unpublished data might yield very different, and certainly more reliable, figures.

arrangements through to sexual cohabitation. The fact that among the Reading households studied by Bowley none had resident kin but 20 per cent had resident lodgers suggests that the boundary between lodging and kinship was often ill-defined. At the start of the period even servants sometimes counted as part of a family structure, and the census enumeration of servants in 1871 included large numbers of individuals who were in fact resident kin. The studies of Miss Loane, based on her experience as a district nurse, were very critical of the view that 'a family is necessarily limited to one household', and claimed that there were many communities 'where family life embraced six or more households, and services of all kinds were constantly and freely interchanged'.

Such widely varying observations suggest that although there were several recognizable models of family behaviour in this period there was no standard pattern. Nuclear and extended family arrangements were not mutually exclusive polar opposites, but points on a spectrum along which different families occupied different points at different times. Both external community pressure and internal moral obligation to maintain certain kinds of family structure were strong; but the fact that the harbouring of aged parents increased after the 1908 Old Age Pensions Act points to an element of prudence in family ties, if not necessarily of downright calculation. Furthermore, the very fact of variation implies some element of choice; and choice implies that family life belonged at least in some degree to an open, free, impersonal *Gesellschaft* model of society, rather than a closed, tight-knit *Gemeinschaft* in which roles and structures were predetermined and prescribed. In practice, however, individual families often combined elements of the two. Family structures were powerful, but not all-embracing, as was shown by the fact that many people lived more or less permanently in some kind of institution (nearly half a million on 1 January 1911). And, though institutional life might be an index of family failure, it was not necessarily so. From the 1860s onwards, for example, many 'surplus women' chose to live in institutions (including religious orders) as a positive alternative to living as low-status appendages in the household of a brother. The large numbers of old people, particularly old men, living in workhouses were not always the victims of family neglect: they were also a product of migration, of stern policies on outdoor relief, and of the fact that a relatively high percentage of those born in the 1830s and 1840s, who reached old age at the turn of the century, had never married. A 1908 survey of old people in workhouses found that more than a third simply had no relatives and only 16 per cent had kinsfolk with whom they might conceivably have lived.

Precise identification of different types of family structure therefore remains difficult, partly through lack of exact, microscopic information, but partly because contemporaries themselves were confused and undecided about the proper norms and patterns of family life. The issue is also obscured by the uncertain relationship of family and household. Statistical evidence seems to indicate that few people lived in three-generational households; but more descriptive and idiosyncratic sources suggest that wide and active kin-relationships were in no sense precluded by the fact that grandparents, parents, grandchildren, and cousins did not cohabit under the same roof. A sense of family identity, and of the obligations which this entailed, varied enormously according to local custom and economic circumstance. Contrary to the expectations of most nineteenth-century sociologists, close-knit family structures in England (though not Scotland and Ireland) appear to have been much stronger in urban than in rural areas, a phenomenon partly explained by the fact that family ties were easier to maintain in stable and prosperous communities where relatives lived close by, than in declining communities scattered by migration and emigration. Booth's survey of the aged poor recorded an almost infinite variety of familial norms, ranging from Barking in Essex where 'a very wonderful and beautiful loyalty to parents' was 'shown in many houses', to Richmond in Yorkshire where 'filial duty is at a low ebb'.

III. DOMESTIC ECONOMY

What economic functions were retained by the late nineteenth-century family? The role of the family as an economic institution had been profoundly changed by industrialization, but perhaps less uniformly than is sometimes supposed. The migration of production from home to factory took place patchily in different areas and different industries; and 'homework' in the clothing industry underwent a massive revival in the late nineteenth century with the advent of cheap sewing-machines (though homework might or might not entail family production). The traditional identity of the family as a productive unit survived into the twentieth century among shopkeepers and self-employed artisans (a group that in the 1900s comprised half a million persons). Tenant farming (another quarter of a million) was a combined father-and-son or mother-and-daughter* occupation in most areas; and in some regions, such as Northumberland and Durham and the Scottish Lowlands, whole families of farm labourers were still hired on

---

* There were nearly thirty thousand women tenant farmers.

annual contracts down to the end of the period. Family employment at harvest time was universal in agricultural areas in the 1870s, but was vanishing by 1914.

Elsewhere in the economy, the home had largely ceased to be a centre of production; nevertheless, the family retained many residual economic roles and acquired some new ones. In many walks of life there was a strong tendency for occupations to pass from father to son. In the 1890s, 40 per cent of clergymen and a third of army officers were the sons of fathers in the same professions. Most coalminers first went down the mines as 'company' for their fathers. In the textile industries spinners at the beginning of the period still subcontracted work to their own children; and although this was restricted in the 1880s (after revelations of widespread parental exploitation), a survey of 1911 nevertheless found that textile employment was still a largely hereditary occupation. The same was true of many skilled jobs. Booth in London found that 'boys following the father' was 'everywhere the case above the lowest classes', and particularly common among artisans. In 1912 a quarter of builders and carpenters, a third of miners and metal workers, and half of clerical employees were children of workers in the same occupation. Indeed, as formal apprenticeships declined a family connection became more rather than less important in enabling a boy to enter a trade. Family ties were equally important within the employer class: by 1914 more than 70 per cent of British firms still remained in family ownership, a far higher proportion than in other industrialized countries, where corporate management was increasingly the norm. Many firms remained in the same family for several generations, and even when a transfer of ownership appeared to take place, it was often to a relative or connection by marriage. The absorption of private banks by joint-stock banks concealed the fact that banking families were virtually a hereditary caste. Moreover, as studies of both wealth and poverty at the end of the nineteenth century made clear, individual 'economic man' was largely a meaningless abstraction: it was families who owned, earned, and spent the nation's wealth or fell into destitution.

Not surprisingly, the economic rationale and priorities of families differed widely both between and within different social groups. At the beginning of the period the economic role of landed families remained what it had been for centuries: an important strategy for the conservation of property. The bulk of a landed estate would pass intact to an eldest son, after provision had been made for support of his widowed mother and endowment of his sisters. About 50 per cent of landed property was inherited under some form of settlement which prevented the heir from disposing of real property and provided for the estate to be passed on to some identified successor, normally his own eldest son; younger sons were left to fend for themselves by pursuit of an heiress or a career. If an estate-holder died intestate, the common law prescribed strict primogeniture. The late nineteenth century brought some minor modifications in this system, but settlements and primogeniture remained common until the end of the period, diluted only by the desire of landed families to adopt new strategies for survival in the wake of agricultural collapse.

Among owners of non-landed wealth the political economy of the family was more variable. Just as landed property could be preserved by settle-ments, so personal property could be retained within families by various forms of private trust. The period saw a marked increase in intermarriage between members of landed and non-landed families, and this probably involved some absorption by the latter of aristocratic attitudes towards property. Particularly among bankers and merchants in the City of London, dynastic alliances were as common as among owners of land; and the enormous expansion of the London season acted as a national matrimonial bazaar for old status and new wealth. Most non-landed wealth-holders were, however, much less obsessed with consolidation of property as a prime end of marriage than were the owners of land. Many business and professional men were largely indifferent (and often actively hostile) to the claims of primogeniture, and much more inclined to distribute their property equally among all their children, a fact which at least partially accounts for the surprising paucity of businessmen among the nation's millionaires.* Middle-class marriages rarely involved the hard-nosed haggling over property characteristic of marriages among the aristocracy;† and European visitors noted with amazement both the meagreness of middle-class marriage portions and the apparent indifference of British bridegrooms as to whether their brides were dowered or not. Only in Ireland was a middle- or lower-class bride expected to match her husband's resources with a dowry of equal worth, a practice enhanced by the growth of peasant proprietorship under the Irish Land Acts of 1885 and 1903. The most striking economic aspect of middle-class matrimony was not dynastic strategy but the prolonged postponement of marriage until a certain stan-dard of living had been reached—an attitude that resulted in long engage-

* Discussed more fully in Chapter 4.
† Such marriages evoked a good deal of middle-class derision and contempt. When, for instance, in 1897 the Countess of Desart defended 'commodity marriages', her views were denounced in popular journals as 'hideous to the delicacy of true culture, utterly hideous to the instinct of true cleanliness'.

ments, an increasingly high average age of marriage and a substantial body of middle-class people who never married at all.

Beyond this initial prudence, however, many middle-class families seem to have been surprisingly indifferent to the long-term conservation of wealth. The aim of many a middle-class father was not to provide his sons with an inheritance after his death: it was to provide them with the education, deportment and business connections to establish their independence while he was still alive. In spite of fashionable homilies on the virtues of thrift, the numerous budgets of middle-class households published in periodicals of the 1890s and 1900s suggest that provision for future generations played a relatively small part in bourgeois domestic economy. Most middle-class heads of households insured their lives, as indeed did many of the working class, and professional men increasingly purchased annuities to cover the costs of retirement. But beyond this minimal provision the middle-class family was usually much more concerned with immediate consumption than with long-term saving of accumulation of property. Le Play in 1875 complained that, far from providing a model of thrift, it was precisely the spending habits of the middle classes in Britain that seduced working-class families into emulation and extravagance. And Taine similarly noted that English middle-class families (wholly unlike their French counterparts) sought money in order to spend it—on houses, holidays, servants, fashionable clothing, and ample food and drink. If this was true of the 1870s, all contemporary observers agreed that the ethic of conspicuous consumption had soared to a crescendo by the 1900s. Thrift and deferred gratification remained an important part of middle-class family ideology: the reality had arguably been on the wane for the previous half-century.

Throughout the period it was rare for middle-class households to contain more than one breadwinner. Sons of middle-class parents remained dependent on their fathers for a much longer period than working-class sons, but usually left home and founded a separate establishment once they had entered a profession. Daughters contributed nothing to family income, even the few who were well educated and gainfully employed; and the tiny minority of wives with a professional background almost invariably gave up work on marriage (though by the 1890s some female schoolteachers were experimenting with a new combination of home and career). The contribution of most middle-class wives to the domestic economy was mainly one of management—keeping accounts, direction of servants, dealing with tradesmen, ordering of menus—and even within these limited spheres there were many complaints in the 1900s that middle-class women were increasingly delegating these tasks to their servants. Such complaints were certainly exaggerated, because few middle-class households could afford a wholly idle wife. But the exacting standards of cookery, needlework, hygiene and tidiness that Edwardian female philanthropists prescribed for lower-class housewives were standards that such ladies expected from servants and inferiors: they were rarely skills which they themselves possessed.*

By contrast, the economy of a working-class household was far more likely to be rooted in the collective earnings of father, mother, and children. Indeed, at a material level reciprocal work services were the basis of working-class family life. Classical wage theory postulated as axiomatic that a workman's wages must maintain himself and his dependants at least at subsistence level; but the contours of social reality were always much more uneven than this model supposed. The frequency of households in which adult children lived at home has already been mentioned. Such children would normally hand over a substantial part of their wages packet to the mother (often with great pride, sometimes unwillingly, as memoirs and oral memories of the period reveal). Their contribution to the domestic budget was the single most powerful factor that could raise a working-class family into affluence and comfort; and, at the same time, their own living costs were much lower than if they chose to live in lodgings. Even when children moved away from home, contributions to the family budget were often sent through the post (though migration and emigration inevitably dissolved many kinship ties). In addition there were the earnings of school-age children. An official inquiry of 1901 found 300,000 children in England in regular employment, many of them working more than forty hours a week; and part-time employment of children over 10 continued and even increased in many areas down to 1914. The earnings of such children would have been almost wholly integrated within the family economy. With respect to younger children, much has been written about the loss of income to working-class households brought about by their withdrawal from the labour market into compulsory education. The extent of this impact has almost certainly been exaggerated; though, subjectively, the prospect of earnings foregone may well have been a relevant factor in encouraging parents to limit family size. If this was so, then the long-term consequence was to bring about a marked improvement in household

* 'My mother', recalled Gwen Raverat, granddaughter of Charles Darwin, 'would have told anyone how to do anything: the cook how to skin a rabbit, or the groom how to harness a horse; though of course she had never done, or even observed, these operations herself.'

incomes by reducing the ratio of dependants to wage-earners. Bowley and Burnett Hurst in 1913 identified the reduction of the dependency ratio in working-class households as the single most crucial factor in raising living standards over the previous decade (which had been a period of static or declining real wages for individual workers).

Even more important for most working-class households was the economic contribution made by mothers: as wage-earners, as unpaid domestic servants, and, almost invariably, as managers of the domestic budget. Paid employment of married women outside the home varied widely according to the nature of local industry. Census returns show less than 2 per cent of married women working in mining areas, and as many as 30 per cent in Lancashire, the Potteries, and the jute city of Dundee—a fact that casts some doubt upon the oft-repeated view that it was industrial capitalism that prescribed sexual division of labour and confinement of women to the home. Though some wives worked for 'pin-money' or for 'the excitement and gossip of factory life', most evidence suggests that the vast majority of married women worked for one overwhelming reason: to supplement an inadequate or non-existent male wage. Of the families surveyed by Booth in east London, one-third were dependent on the joint income of two parents for survival. Over the country as a whole there was a gradual decline in married women's employment over the last thirty years of the century, then an increase in the 1900s, probably reflecting the falling cost of living in the earlier period and rise in the latter. In addition, women added to family incomes in numerous informal ways unrecorded by official surveys: by child-minding, fostering, charring, looking after lodgers, gleaning, hopping, dressmaking, and many other forms of casual and temporary employment.

Above all, wives contributed to the household economy by unpaid domestic labour. Recent research has shown that, contrary to what was once believed, the keeping of servants was not just a badge of middle-class status: working people eagerly employed domestic help whenever they could afford to do so. But such help was beyond the reach of most wage-earning families, particularly those with small children; and the life of most working-class mothers was an incessant round of cooking, laundering, child care, ironing, cleaning grates, laying fires, emptying slop-pails, and keeping dirt at bay. Much of this labour was not merely of domestic significance but an essential (if invisible) part of the wider process of industrial production. Miners' wives who prepared daily baths for their husbands, for example, were performing a function that fifty years later would be seen as part of the job of pit-head management; and the South

Wales miners' strike of 1909 was precipitated by a wives' revolt against the new shift system, which threatened to double the daily load of preparing meals. Paradoxically, the burden of domestic labour increased in the late nineteenth century in line with rising incomes and aspirations to order and hygiene (the latter transmitted into working-class homes by the millions of mothers who had worked as domestic servants). Coal ranges, copper boilers, gas mantles, and china sanitary-ware added greatly to standards of hygiene and comfort, but (unlike a later generation of domestic gadgets) they complicated rather than simplified the duties of the housewife; while the filtering downwards of the mid-Victorian fetish for knick-knacks and decorative commodities added immensely to her toil. It was no accident that the word 'housework' entered into everyday speech only towards the end of the nineteenth century.

Finally, the management and expenditure of a working-class family's collective resources fell universally upon the wife. It was she who paid the bills, planned the menus, negotiated credit, traded with pawnbrokers, saved for clubs and holidays and—when all else failed—deprived herself in order to feed her husband and children. Social surveys recorded wide variation in how much of their wage packets husbands kept back for their own pleasures; and some sources suggest that towards the end of the period husbands were retaining an increased proportion of their incomes to spend on commercialized leisure. But observers of family life who could agree on nothing else agreed upon one thing: it was the wife's skill or ineptitude in making ends meet that largely determined the comfort or dereliction of working-class homes.

IV. PATRIARCHALISM

Observers of British society in the 1860s and early 1870s often remarked upon the amazing survival of 'patriarchalism' in family life—amazing because in other contexts British society laid such strong emphasis on individual rights and personal freedom. An English husband* at the beginning of the period had an absolute right of control over his wife's person and, unless constrained by a private settlement, over her property as well. He was solely responsible for the rearing and guardianship of their children, and, although he was legally obliged to maintain his wife and under-age children during his lifetime, the common law gave him absolute freedom

---

* This section deals primarily with English experience. Scots law on divorce, custody and property rights was different throughout the period.

to bequeath his property away from them if he so wished. A wife, by contrast, had no legal duties and no enforceable legal rights: in common law her juridical personality was totally submerged in that of her husband (Blackstone's dictum to this effect was bandied around public houses as 'something more than a stock joke'). She could not hold separate property or enter into contracts; nor could she take proceedings against her husband to enforce her claim to financial support. She had no right to the guardianship of her legitimate children unless specifically appointed by her husband to act as guardian after his death. In disputes over custody mid-Victorian judges almost invariably upheld the rights of a father, however reprobate, against a mother, however virtuous. A similar bias governed legal perceptions of sexuality. Under the Matrimonial Causes Act of 1857 an act of adultery constituted automatic grounds for divorce if committed by a wife, while a husband's adultery counted as an offence only if accompanied by desertion or cruelty. A wife who left her husband's home, for whatever reason, could be forcibly restored to him by an order of the courts.

Children were similarly to a large extent their father's legal property. Heirs to settled estates were under the protection of the Court of Chancery, and the Factory Acts restricted the employment of children under 13; but for the vast majority of children the law of England in no way limited their father's control over their persons and their lives. Acts of violence which would have constituted criminal assault if practised on fellow citizens were perfectly legal if perpetrated by fathers (and indeed by mothers) on their under-age sons and daughters. The structure of parental authority had been largely undented by the rise of legal individualism, and may even have been reinforced by the early nineteenth-century revival of Old Testament fundamentalism. The ideal of fatherhood in the 1860s was one of stern omniscience, that of motherhood the tender and submissive 'angel on the hearth'. For many children daily reality was more brutal. 'It is unhappily to a painful degree apparent . . . that against no persons do children of both sexes need so much protection as against their parents', recorded a Select Committee on the Employment of Children in 1866.

From 1870 onwards, however, the legal framework of family life began to change in a variety of ways. In 1870 and 1882 the Married Women's Property Acts gave to all married women the powers to hold, acquire, manage, and dispose of their own property, which were already enjoyed by rich heiresses under equitable settlements. These acts were clearly limited in their immediate effect to the minority of wives who owned property (including earnings from employment); but the formula embodied in the acts—that henceforth for purposes of ownership married women were to be treated 'as if they were not married'—was potentially of much wider significance in the development of norms about marriage. Changes also occurred in the law relating to the custody and guardianship of infants. An act of 1873 allowed the courts to grant custody to a mother in the case of children under 16. In 1886 a mother was permitted for the first time to appoint guardians, and to act as the guardian of her own children without her husband's express consent; and the courts were empowered to override a father's custody rights where this was deemed conducive to 'the welfare of the child'. From 1895 a woman who had been assaulted by her husband could apply to the county courts for a judicial separation and maintenance.

Such legal intervention in family relationships was initially confined to cases of marriage breakdown, but the law also began to make tentative inroads into the rights of parents generally. Much-publicized cases of 'baby-farming' in the 1860s and 1870s and of parental child abuse in the 1880s led to the formation of Benjamin Waugh's National Society for the Prevention of Cruelty to Children, which publicly campaigned against 'the great, double, indiscriminating national tradition' of 'the sanctity of the home' and 'parental right'. Buccaneering philanthropists like Dr Barnardo increasingly dealt with parents' common-law rights simply by ignoring them. In 1889 the first of a series of Cruelty to Children Acts was passed, under which parental violence beyond certain limits was made a criminal offence, parents of both sexes could be dispossessed of their custody rights, and the legal guardianship of children could be taken over by courts and local authorities. Incest became a civil crime for the first time in 1908; and in the same year the so-called Children's Charter totally reversed the earlier silence of the law by spelling out in meticulous detail the duties of parents on such issues as care, maintenance, medical attention, abstention from cigarettes and alcohol, exclusion of children from public houses, and prevention of injuries and burns.

Within certain clearly defined limits, this long series of statutory and case-law changes brought about a major restructuring of the legal relations between husbands and wives, parents and children, the family and the state. Though parental rights remained extensive and fathers still enjoyed more rights than mothers, legal intervention had by the end of the period largely eroded the absolute paternal rights enshrined in the common law. Only sexual relations between husbands and wives remained largely untouched by legal change. Case-law gradually dismantled a husband's right to detain his wife by force; but there was no formal modification of the 1857 assumption that adultery on the part of a man was an accident, on the part of a woman a premeditated act (though equalization of the law in this respect was unanimously recommended by the Royal Commission on Divorce in 1913). Family law notoriously hinges, however, on cases of family breakdown; and the question remains of just how far values and relationships in the vast majority of families that did not break down were influenced by the changing structure of the law. Was the English family at the beginning of the period as 'patriarchal' in sentiment and practice as the formal letter of the law allowed? Were changes in the law mirrored in personal relationships? And how far did the hierarchy of authority within families depend upon legal structures—or upon other more intangible factors such as custom, ideology, and economic constraint?

Contemporary opinion on these issues varied widely. John Stuart Mill's classic study on *The Subjection of Women*, published in 1869, saw the legal non-existence of women as the key to their subordination in a much wider sphere; while others—such as Le Play, Bagehot, and James Fitzjames Stephen—portrayed the authority of fathers as the moral cement that held English society together. But even at this early date, when the legal predominance of fathers was indisputable, there were some dissenting interpretations of day-to-day social practice. Taine in 1871 was struck not by the moral supremacy of English fathers but by the high proportion of Englishmen whose 'sole contribution to family life is money', leaving all real decisions over consumption, child-rearing and domestic morality to their wives. A few years later T. H. Escott portrayed the middle-class father as increasingly marginal to family life: 'the wife speedily creates for herself a little world of her own, in which the husband only figures as an occasional visitor.' And the sociologist Herbert Spencer claimed to have detected the evolution of a new type of marriage relationship, based not on male dominance but on functional differentiation and ties of ethics and affection. In other words, the legal privileges of men and the legal disabilities of women, even before the onset of statutory reform, were perceived by some as largely irrelevant to the balance of matrimonial power.

Similar diversity of views prevailed a quarter of a century later. The autobiography of Frances Power Cobbe, published in 1898, portrayed the overthrow of the *patria potestas* as the cardinal social change that had occurred in Britain over the previous half-century. Helen Bosanquet concluded in 1906 that the patriarchal family was effectively dead, not merely in Britain but in all parts of Europe except the Russian steppes. Its residual traces were to be found only in ritual observances, such as the Anglican marriage rite; and even for Anglicans religious doctrine now enjoined 'personal freedom and responsibility' in family relationships, rather than dominance and submission. H. G. Wells, ideologically very remote from both Cobbe and Bosanquet, nevertheless reached a similar conclusion: the 'monogamic patriarchal system' was an empty shell. Other turn-of-the-century authorities, however, disagreed. The studies of Mona Caird portrayed the family as still in a state of profound tension between 'sexual feudalism' and 'equal citizen rights'; wives and mothers might have acquired some of the trappings of legal equality, but sexual relations, childbirth, economic dependency, and exclusion from politics left them where they had always been, as clients and vassals of their husbands. And the French social psychologist Émile Boutmy claimed in 1904 that 'up to our own days English family life has retained all the characteristics of an absolute monarchy'. Boutmy acknowledged that major changes had occurred in the legal status of husbands and fathers, but was sceptical about how far these changes had penetrated into popular sentiment and social structure. English life in general, he argued, was much more profoundly conditioned than that of other nations by history and habit, much less susceptible to artificial manipulation by reformatory laws. In particular, in spite of a generation of legal change, the English father retained 'undisputed sovereignty in the interior of his own home'. 'I know of no person in the modern world who puts me in mind of the ancient Roman paterfamilias than the head of an English family . . . He is a monarch reverenced in his own kingdom, almost a monarch by divine right. Compared with him the [French head of a family] seems like a President elected by a critical Parliament.'

Which of these accounts was more correct? Was Taine or Le Play a more perceptive analyst of family life in the 1870s, Boutmy or Bosanquet in the 1900s? Contemporary accounts and more recent studies of matrimonial relationships in this period seem to indicate that patterns of paternal authority were always more varying than is often supposed. There were some sectors of society where, in spite of legal change, patriarchy and division of gender roles may have become *more* deeply entrenched during this period. In York in 1899, for example, Rowntree noted that it was becoming fashionable for affluent workers to confine their wives to decorative idleness, just when such a notion of unoccupied femininity was becoming less fashionable among the professional middle class; and the decline of married women's employment down to 1900 may have meant that in many areas the economic dominance of husbands was being reinforced just as their legal privileges were being dismantled. Throughout the period there were certain tracts of society where patriarchal practices and attitudes were more concentrated than elsewhere, such as mining communities, first-generation Jewish and Irish immigrants, the landed and labour aristocracies, and the 'Puritan' housholds of the northern factory valleys. Even within these groups, however, there was much local variation: Cornish miners, for example, were conspicuously less patriarchal in their home lives than those of Scotland, Northumberland, and Durham. And it may perhaps be doubted how far genuine patriarchy was ever really acknowledged as a predominant norm throughout the social spectrum. There were many women within the lower reaches of the London working class who regarded themselves rather than their (often absentee) husbands as 'heads of households'; and London police court records reveal that in cases of matrimonial violence wives were often as aggressive as their men. Among agricultural labourers 'dogged comradeship' was more commonly recorded than male domination. In the 1900s there were some communities, such as Lady Bell's Middlesbrough and Joseph Chamberlain's Birmingham, where wives occupied a mainly passive and subordinate position, and others, such as Margaret Loane's Portsmouth or the Lancashire communities studied by Elizabeth Roberts, where wives played a much more directive role in family life. In some Edwardian working-class communities, such as Robert Roberts's Salford, masculine involvement in domestic tasks was inconceivable without neighbourhood ridicule and loss of face; but the writings of Miss Loane and Hilda Martindale, and more recent studies of Norfolk fishermen and Lancashire textile workers, suggest that the sharing of child care and household tasks was in some contexts a perfectly routine feature of day-to-day working-class life. In households without access to a main drainage system, men universally performed the task of burying the contents of earth-closets, a function of such privacy and shame that it eludes all written records.

Moreover, deference to a husband's authority was influenced by the nature of a wife's employment *before* marriage: wives who had previously worked in an office or factory, for example, were much more inclined to demand a share in regulating family size or household expenditure than those who had been domestic servants. In all strata of society, from the highest to the lowest, active contacts with relations outside the immediate parent–child nucleus were far more often maintained with the wife's kin than with the husband's. At a more abstract level, patriarchalism as a political philosophy was deeply entrenched within the ancient propertied élites and remained a vigorous force in politics down to 1914. But its impact on upper-class women was always limited by private settlements, and Pat Jalland's study of family relationships within the governing classes suggests that the translation of public theory into private practice was very diverse. At all times there were upper-class wives such as Lady Balfour,

Josephine Butler, and Lawrencina Potter, who got their way by will-power, wealth, superior moral force, or psychological terror.

Patterns of male authority within different households therefore varied widely, and, as with many other aspects of family life in this period, there is scattered evidence of movement in quite contrary directions. One area in which change undoubtedly occurred, however, was the sphere of moral opinion. Much less was written about the role of husbands and fathers than about wives and mothers; but what *was* written suggests that even by the 1870s public endorsement of the autocratic ideal of the earlier Victorian era was in irreversible decline. Handbooks on marriage, even those written by authors with traditionalist views, increasingly emphasized shared responsibility between husbands and wives, including the sharing of child care and domesticity. It was 'as much their duty to rock the cradle, nurse a baby or play with the children as it is the mothers' ', declared an evangelical marriage guidance manual of the early 1870s; and close involvement in the care of children began to be cited as the touchstone of a good husband. Studies of family life from the 1880s onwards also commented on the growing moral diffidence of fathers, their reluctance to engage in ethical and religious instruction, their growing willingness to resign such functions to wives, schoolteachers, Sunday schools, the police, and the state. Such a decline in moral confidence was not confined to a single class; indeed, Edwardian commentators often suggested that moral abdication was more pervasive among upper and middle- than among working-class fathers, because the former were more infected by the rise of relativism in moral and religious belief. Yet even among the Edwardian working class Miss Loane recorded (probably with exaggeration) that fathers were perceived by their children as 'companions', 'protectors' and 'abettors', but virtually never as a source of ultimate moral power:

I doubt if the bare idea of fathers being equal to mothers in authority even enters the mind of any cottage child under the age of sixteen. Father is generally regarded in the light of mother's eldest child, and disobedience in *him* is a far more heinous crime than in them, because 'he'd ought to know better than not to do what mother says!' Fathers are as a rule perfectly satisfied with this position.

V. Motherhood

The roles of wives and mothers also changed, partly in tandem with, partly independently of, those of their menfolk. As indicated by Margaret Loane, there appear to have been many families in which the balance of personal power lay increasingly with mothers. This was not merely a case, however, of maternal authority expanding to fill the moral vacuum left by fathers: it was related to other, more external pressures. The withdrawal of married women from employment, the elaboration of housework and the extension to all classes of a previously very limited conception of 'the home' as a centre of leisure and conspicuous consumption: all these trends conferred on wives an increasingly central role as the stage-managers of one of the most important venues of social life—a venue, moreover, that was constantly lauded and promoted in sermons, speeches, and popular literature as the great progressive alternative to the gutter and the pub. The all-embracing mother bustling over a nest of piety, warmth, cleanliness, and comfort may have been invented by the early Victorians, but it was not until the late Victorian period that such a vision became a tangible reality for a substantial section of the working class.

The changes in housewifery outlined earlier were accompanied by changes in the duties of motherhood. Among the poorer classes the period saw a great extension in the average length of childhood, brought about by compulsory education and the limitation of child employment; and although husbands may have participated in child care to a greater extent than in the past, it was, nevertheless, largely upon mothers that the increased responsibility for nurture lay. Mothers were more directly affected than fathers by relief from the dangers of childbirth and by the greater emotional investment in individual children that a declining birth rate brought in its wake. New ideas about play, discipline, child development, and sex education, which appeared dimly on the horizon in the 1870s and surged into a torrent in the 1890s, were mainly directed at mothers, as were demands of the 1900s that the family should become the breeding and training ground of a new imperial race. Over the period as a whole there was a revolution of rising expectations about the maternal role. Though writers of the 1860s and 1870s had bemoaned the fact that there were many inefficient mothers, mothering had continued to be seen as something that women did naturally or learnt through a process of automatic cultural transmission. Bad motherhood was seen as deplorable in the individual, but not necessarily as damaging to society as a whole. In the 1900s, by contrast, it was widely believed that natural processes and cultural transmission were inadequate: mothering was increasingly seen as an activity of much greater moral, itellectual and technical complexity, that needed to be learned artificially like any other professional skill. Bad mothering was no longer seen merely as a private failure, but as subversive of community, nation, Empire and race.

The effectiveness with which wives and mothers responded to these new challenges predictably varied both between and within different social groups. Since domestic comfort only became an option at a certain level of income, it was unsurprising that squalid domestic arrangements often coincided with poverty and overcrowding. Nevertheless, as observers like Lady Bell pointed out, efficient managers and ineffective sluts were found in every class. Among the middle class, the great surge of publications on household management from the 1860s onwards bears witness to a growing, almost obsessive commitment to domestic efficiency; and oral historians have uncovered widespread evidence of a similar obsessiveness among women of the working class. Foreign observers like Ernst Dueckershoff and Paul de Rousiers thought that English housewives at all levels were less skilful at cooking and ancient household arts than their French and German counterparts, but that their homes were much more comfortable and clean notwithstanding. Many Edwardian moralists bemoaned the fact that much higher standards of domesticity had been possessed by their agricultural forebears, but in fact there is not the slightest evidence to suggest that the wives of agricultural labourers were more domestically accomplished than working women of the towns. (As Miss Loane pointed out, the image of the omnicompetent domestic paragon of the rural past was not derived from the rural poor but from the wives and daughters of substantial tenant farmers.) In 1904 the Interdepartmental Committee on Physical Deterioration severely criticized the average competence of working-class housewives; but the evidence of witnesses to this committee suggested a rather different picture—of generally rising standards with which, for various reasons, a minority of working-class women were unable to keep pace. Moreover, as writers like Anna Martin and Clementina Black pointed out, official inquiries often applied wholly inappropriate criteria to working-class domestic management—looking for standards of long-term economic rationality that would in fact have been *irrational* if applied to precarious incomes that varied from week to week. Though many working-class housewives resented upper-class criticism, however, few questioned the desirability of devotion to domestic duties if it were financially possible; indeed, most working-class women saw confinement to domesticity as a luxury to be sought after rather than an imposition to be shunned. When in the late 1900s voices began for the first time to be raised against the apotheosis of domesticity, they were not working-class voices: the Edwardian rebellion against what Rebecca West called 'the rat-poison of housework' was an almost purely middle-class revolt (and, even so, largely confined to a small intellectual minority).

Standards of motherhood were equally variable, and again were partly, but by no means wholly, related to income, housing, and social class. Among the middle classes tens of thousands of boys, and to a lesser extent girls, were at any one time incarcerated in boarding-schools, where they ran the risk of encountering varying degrees of mental and physical cruelty from teachers and peers. Children of families employed in the Empire were often boarded out with foster-parents, with results graphically described in the memoirs of Rudyard Kipling.* For many middle-class children below school age or educated in day-schools, however, the period was one of rapidly rising standards of physical and material care. Fewer children per family, rising incomes, better medical services, easily available domestic help and a diminishing sense of fatalism about infant mortality meant that an intelligent middle-class mother was able both to excel at and to enjoy motherhood probably to a greater extent than at any previous time in human history. From the 1870s onwards a great proliferation of child-rearing manuals gave detailed advice on such questions as infant-feeding, toilet-training, health, and moral discipline. By the 1900s few middle-class nurseries were unaffected by the new fashions for fresh air, rest, holidays, exercise, and play. Material improvements were accompanied by psychological and emotional change. The formality and rigid discipline of parent–child relationships in the early Victorian period were already beginning to slacken by the 1870s. Twenty years later, writers of traditional views were deploring the fashion for middle-class children to address their mothers by nicknames and Christian names or by such sobriquets as 'old pal'. Freud made little impact in Britain before 1914, but other theorists of child development such as Gabriel Compayré and James Sully were widely read—as were the works of Margaret E. Sangster on *Winsome Womanhood* and *Radiant Motherhood*. The immensely popular 'child-study' movement, which involved thousands of mothers in keeping detailed diaries of their children's behaviour, may have been insignificant in the history of formal psychology, but it greatly enhanced the self-confidence and self-awareness of mothers and aroused popular scientific interest in relations between mother and child.

Among the working classes, patterns of motherhood were more variable and erratic. Undoubtedly there were some working-class mothers who were drunken and negligent, who left their children to 'bring up themselves' on the streets and whose families were not sheltered, like those of negli-

---

* Kipling's account of the 'house of desolation' was no mere fictional extravaganza: my own research on the family of William Beveridge found that the experience of the young Beveridges, left for two years with English guardians while their parents were in India, closely resembled that of Kipling.

gent upper-class mothers, by a protective barrier of nursery servants. Undoubtedly there were those who tranquillized their children with Godfrey's Cordial, or who were unscrupulous beneficiaries of infant life-insurance policies. But accounts by nurses, widwives, and others who worked closely with working-class women suggested that the maternal goals and ideals of the vast majority were remarkably similar to those of more privileged mothers. The problem for many was not 'maternal ignorance' but a continual tension between the aspiration to attain desirable standards of motherhood and the dismal realities of poor health, poor nutrition, and inadequate family income. Public opinion from the 1880s onwards primarily blamed married women's employment for low standards of child care and high infant mortality, and severely censured working-class women who aped the upper classes by paying for their children to be cared for by other people; and there was substantial statistical evidence to support the supposed connection between infant mortality, 'baby farming', and the employment of mothers. However, a survey by Clementina Black found far more 'gossips at doorways' and 'frequenters of public houses' among non-working than among working mothers; and as investigations of the 1900s showed, infant mortality was also closely linked with deficiencies in food and income that often could only be remedied by a mother going out to work. In addition, many mothers had to cope with a crowded, insanitary, and polluted urban environment which posed problems for infant nurture that nothing in the hereditary folklore of child-rearing prepared them to meet. Even the Royal Commission on the Poor Laws, which found very few 'definitely bad mothers' but deplored the prevalence of 'negatively bad mothers', admitted that negative badness was closely linked to chronic maternal ill-health. Undoubtedly, many habits of working-class mothers were harmful (such as feeding babies on skimmed milk and swaddling their lower organs with eight layers of flannel); but the desirable alternatives (fresh pasteurized milk supplies and the towelling nappies that came on to the market in the 1890s) were often not merely financially, but also physically impractical (nappies, for instance, presupposed facilities for laundering and constant supplies of hot water).

Given such difficulties, what is perhaps surprising about late Victorian and Edwardian working-class mothers is not that many failed to keep pace with rising professional norms of maternity, but that many succeeded. Detailed accounts of individual families reveal again and again the immense struggles of working-class mothers to maintain not merely cleanliness, good health, and regular meals, but privacy, modesty, good manners, and the cherished separate identity of each of their children in often grossly overcrowded homes. In spite of the formal exclusion of women from civic life, it was largely mothers who represented the family in the public sphere: to teachers, doctors, social workers, Poor Law inspectors and magistrates. Moreover, there is no evidence to suggest that, in purely emotional terms, working-class mothers in general were more deficient than those of the upper and middle classes—sometimes, in fact, quite the reverse. Some of the most extreme cases of maternal deprivation involved children of the highest social classes, like the infant Winston Churchill and the future Mrs Humphry Ward. Miss Loane claimed that child abuse and maternal coldness were commoner among middle-income groups than among the very poor; parents prosecuted by the NSPCC had a mean income considerably higher than the average working-class wage; and many Edwardian writers commented on a disturbing trend among fashionable upper-class mothers for treating their children as toys, showpieces or objects of decoration. Such examples suggest that inadequate motherhood was not confined to the working classes and—in spite of the undoubted importance of income, nutrition, and environment—in no sense wholly determined by material constraints.

VI. CHILDHOOD

The increasing demands made upon mothers were inseparably linked with changing conceptions of childhood; and in no aspect of family life did attitudes and practices change more extensively than in relation to children. In the early and mid-Victorian period there was much idealized writing about childhood in poetry and novels; but for the vast majority of children 'childhood', if it existed at all, was effectively over by the age of 10. Beyond that age, and often earlier, children within the lower classes were required either to contribute to family income or to maintain themselves. Even children who did not earn a wage worked long hours in the service of their parents and others—at home, in the streets, in fields, and in factories. In many agricultural areas tiny infants worked with their families in the fields from the age of 4. In factory districts full-time employment was prohibited below the age of thirteen, but children over the age of 8 often laboured at work subcontracted to them by those most pressing taskmasters, their own parents. The fifty thousand children living in Poor Law institutions in the late 1860s were expected from the age of 7 to contribute to their own maintenance by tasks of work. For many poor children homelessness or the death or desertion of parents meant that the protective home life idealized by middle-class writers was as remote as the garden of Eden (almost literally so, since pupils at 'ragged schools', when questioned about Paradise, envisaged a large warm room full of ham and sausage rolls). London and other large towns contained a floating population of ragged children, apparently quite detached from any family structure, who slept under railway arches and supported themselves by begging, stealing, and a myriad varieties of marginal and casual labour. Even where parents were alive, overcrowding and large families placed severe strains on home life: public inquiries and personal accounts of working class life regularly reported on the widespread (though unquantified) incidence of incest and sexual abuse of children among both urban and rural poor. In overcrowded slums children witnessed, and tried to copy, acts of sexual intercourse long before the age of puberty. Children of the working class often looked indistinguishable from miniature adults: their clothes were cut-down adult cast-offs, their faces prematurely aged. 'Even the memory of boyhood and young manhood are gloomy', recalled James Keir Hardie, future leader of the Labour movement, born into a poor but not destitute working family in 1853. 'I am one of the unfortunate class who never knew what it was to be a child.'

Amongst upper- and middle-class families childhood was more extended and protected, but even here earlier Enlightenment perceptions of childhood as a time of innocence and freedom had been at least partially eclipsed by fear of childhood as a time of barbarism and depravity. Such notions are often ascribed to evangelicalism but in fact were prevalent in many early Victorian households of every ideological shade—evangelical, High Church, utilitarian, positivist, and secularist. Children were subject to rigid discipline, long hours of brain work, adult standards of rationality and self-control, formality and distance in relations with parents. All discussion of sexual matters was taboo, but sexual curiosity and precocity were severely punished—occasionally by extreme measures of physical and even surgical restraint. 'Play' was strictly limited in duration and scope. There were, of course, exceptions, like the 1860s households described by Edna Lyall, where parents and children were constant companions, nurses told endless stories and toys included a Noah's ark, a doll's pram, a toy farm, and building bricks with coloured glass for making stained-glass windows. But even in the Lyall household children were punished by prolonged confinement in empty rooms, and were forbidden to play 'imaginary games' on Sundays, since imagination was a breach of the Sabbatarian code. Attitudes to child-rearing were deeply enmeshed with both current theology and social and economic aspiration; parents who loved their children dearly forced themselves to treat them severely, lest they should condemn them to failure in this world and damnation in the next.

Such attitudes were not unknown in English families forty years later; and the large number of children living in institutions, ranging from Poor Law cottage-homes to expensive private boarding-schools, must be set against too child-centred an interpretation of Edwardian family life. Nevertheless, from the 1870s onwards recorded perceptions of childhood and the treatment of children began to change in a variety of ways. At a very fundamental level the declining birth rate made children both more valuable and more manageable. Differentiated personal relationships between parents and children were possible in families of three or four that had been difficult or impossible in families of nine or ten. The very fact that by the end of the century many married couples were reputedly 'on strike against parenthood' suggests that those who chose to have children did so more purposively than in earlier generations. For both the middle class and more prosperous sections of the working class, rising real incomes and smaller families made the rearing of children less of an economic and physical burden than it had been in mid-century. As fears of Malthusian crisis faded into folk memory, many of the taboos generated by those fears began slowly to relax.

Change was most extreme and tangible within the middle classes. Among certain sections of the middle class, silence on sexual issues was gradually replaced by the belief that on reaching puberty children should be taught the 'facts of life'. Ideas on sexuality did not become more permissive (if anything the reverse); but the pretence that sex did not exist was replaced by concern to promote a single standard of purity common to young persons of both sexes. New trends detectable in the 1870s were becoming fashionable practice by the 1890s. In many families 'reasoning' with children replaced corporal punishment and learning by rote. Silence at meals was replaced by encouragement of 'conversation'; and 'little people should be seen and not heard' was denounced as a 'stupid saying'. Middleclass parents who whipped their children for spelling mistakes were now seen as 'moral criminals'. Children's clothes, games, books, toys (the latter often reflecting the fashion for Empire) began to be produced for a much wider market. 'Knickerbockers' and then 'knickers' replaced 'frocks' and 'petticoats' for little boys, loose woollen 'combinations' were advocated by doctors for infants of both sexes. Whereas mid-Victorian children, even in wealthy households, had normally slept in communal nurseries, Edwardian middle-class children were now given separate bedrooms. Popular handbooks on child psychology flooded into England from Germany, France, and America. Most of them were couched in a specifically religious frame-work, seeing religious teaching by parents as an essential part of a child's moral and cognitive development; but most had wholly abandoned the common assumption of the earlier Victorian period that the central fact about child psychology was original sin. 'As soon as the child evinces a personality we recognize that innocence is there, mighty yet helpless innocence', declared an Edwardian study of *The Home Training of Children* in 1910. 'Parents will be careful that no tinge of gloom shall colour the child's thoughts of God or of His works. God is Love not fear.' New ideas were accompanied by new fashions in child entertainment and education. Christmas pantomime, hitherto a lewd working-class adult entertainment, now became a spectacle for middle-class children, reaching its apotheosis with *Peter Pan* (1904) and *Where the Rainbow Ends* (1910). In large towns mothers and nurses chaperoned their children to Sesame clubs, gymnasium classes and Montessori kindergartens to learn 'self-expression', 'individuality' and 'creative play'. The result was an 'enhanced sense of the child' through-out middle-class family life. 'Up to now the world of childhood has been an undiscovered or at least an unexplored land', wrote a prominent Harley Street paediatrician in 1910. 'The child is a new discovery.' Childhood was no longer seen merely as a miniature form of adulthood and a brief annexe to grown-up life, but as a complex condition that required special under-standing and treatment and that had its own generic modes of behaviour and perception. Children themselves were increasingly viewed not as their parents' private possessions, but as 'national assets' and as autonomous individuals with status and rights.

Working-class childhood changed too, but at a different pace and to some extent in different ways from childhood among the upper and middle classes. Edwardian cities were full of poor, ragged, and undernourished children, but the gangs of 'street arabs' who had swarmed in London in the 1860s had largely given way to a more docile, disciplined, family-centred child population. In certain respects middle- and working-class notions of child-rearing converged over the period, and drew away from the practices adopted by the very rich at one extreme and the very poor at the other. Rising incomes and more living space meant that at least a section of the working class could now treat its children to toys, holidays, and childrens' clothes in a way that had been inconceivable in the 1860s and 1870s. Both dolls and Christmas trees penetrated the agricultural villages of the southern counties for the first time during the 1900s. Though the ideal of separate bedrooms might be unattainable, increasing emphasis was laid on personal privacy: children might sleep several to a bed, but elaborate routines were worked out to ensure that they never saw each other unclothed. The efforts of working-class mothers to achieve new middle-class standards of physical efficiency have already been noted; and in both middle-class and respectable working-class households intimacy, friendship and mutual confidence between parents and children were valued more highly than three decades before. Edwardian fathers who did not know the names of their own legitimate offspring were found only among aristocrats, university professors, and the casual poor.

In other respects, however, middle- and working-class practices diverged; and part of the changing treatment of working-class children involved the adoption of manners and practices that were dying out among the middle class but had been fashionable in a previous generation. Heavy corporal punishment was largely confined to the roughest sections of the working class (and was less common there than wife-beating); but by the 1900s strict discipline, early bedtimes, silence at meals, and the outlawing of references to sex were being increasingly imposed on working-class children, just as such habits were slackening within the middle class. 'Cheek', 'breakages', 'touching things that don't belong to you' and interrupting grown-up conversation were all viewed in well-ordered working-class families of the 1900s as major crimes. Working-class mothers began to aspire after babies with ample chins and chubby cheeks, just when middle-class mothers were beginning to worry about excess fat. The most fundamental pressure for change in the life of most working-class children, however, was the introduction of compulsory schooling in the 1870s and the gradual extension of the normal school-leaving age to 14. Contemporary critics of elementary education often accused it of 'drying up all the poetry and mystery of child life, all the romance of the unseen'; and modern historians of childhood have criticized the formal curriculum, the displacement of an ancient folklore of childhood by rote-learning, and the dragooning of children into an artificial daily routine. Miss Loane, not normally an ally of state interference, took the opposite point of view. She claimed that school had 'nearly doubled the years of permitted childhood and added incalculably to its interests and pleasures'; and, far from driving out an inherited culture of childhood, it was largely through school that children acquired their knowledge of supposedly archaic folklore, idioms, imaginative rituals, and communal games. Whereas in the 1860s working-class children had been precipitated into adulthood much earlier than middle-class children, by the 1900s the reverse was often the case: now middle-class children were adopting grown-up language and manners from the age of 12 or 13, while working-class children were still immersed in an imaginative world of play and games.

Compulsory schooling reacted upon the status and treatment of children within the family in a variety of ways. By some parents, particularly in the early days, 'school' was seen as an enemy, the embodiment of pressures that were drying up children's earnings and sapping at the roots of parental authority. Throughout the period there were occasional, much-publicized incidents when parents attacked teachers with physical violence. By the 1900s, however, there was growing evidence of an opposite stance: of parents anxious for their children's success, who treated the authority of the teacher often with exaggerated deference. School was increasingly viewed at the very least as an institution that relieved mothers of the sole burden of child care, at best as a force that might fundamentally determine a child's future chances in life. School was also crucially important as a medium for transmitting to working-class parents some of the major new doctrines of the Edwardian era, namely that child-rearing was no longer a purely private matter, that 'the child belonged to both the family and the state' and that there was 'a fundamental unity between the individual and the race'.

VII. SEXUAL RELATIONS

Did the changing patterns of family life find any echo in the sphere of sexual relationships? A firm answer to this question is forever veiled behind the Victorian culture of privacy and reticence; but several recent historians, perhaps in reaction against the romanticized version presented by G. M. Young, have constructed a portrait of late Victorian and Edwardian marriage as cold, emotionally claustrophobic, and sexually repressive. Sexual passion, so it has been argued, was widely sacrificed to the economic imperative of limiting childbirth—an end achieved by a mixed strategy of late marriage, sexual restraint, and resort to mass prostitution. An asexual ideology of marriage was supplied by a battery of powerful authorities: by Ruskin's vision of wifehood in *Sesame and Lilies*, by fashionable physicians who taught that women were incapable of sexual passion, and by the claim of sociologists like Patrick Geddes that sexual desire was being phased out among higher racial types by progressive social evolution. The result, so it has been argued, was widespread sexual repression among both the married and the unmarried; and a study by John Gillis concludes that 'this long era of mandatory matrimony . . . utterly failed to transform the myth of conjugal love into lived reality as far as ordinary people were concerned.'

Such claims remain unproven, however, partly because the evidence cited to support them is highly idiosyncratic, and partly because much of it does not refer to the late Victorian period at all, but to a period several decades before.* Certainly there is no shortage of examples of individual unhappy marriages; and the widespread prevalence of venereal disease (affecting perhaps 10 per cent of the adult male population in 1914) is a standing reminder of the dark undercurrents of Victorian and Edwardian sexual relationships. But at least some of the fragments of evidence relating to late nineteenth-century sexual behaviour point to a rather different conclusion: that sexual expectations within marriage were higher and more central in this period than they had been in the earlier Victorian years. Victorian Englishmen had always endorsed, in theory if not in practice, the ideal of marrying for love; but from the late 1860s onwards the campaign against a 'double standard' in sexual behaviour laid an unprecedented degree of emphasis on the continuing interdependence of sex and marriage. Evangelical writings in morality in the 1870s and 1880s almost invariably emphasized the importance of conjugal sex: 'Love your wife ardently', counselled one such publication of 1870. 'Courting often ends where marriage begins. It should be the very reverse if marriage is to continue.' 'No observing person can doubt that the sexual relations of men and women determine in a great degree their happiness or misery', declared a popular guide to matrimonial relationships published in 1896. When an Anglican bishop suggested that sexual intercourse between married persons should be confined to the procreation of children and abandoned after child-bearing age, he was publicly rebuked by no less a person than Mrs Bramwell Booth, who remarked, 'I have never heard such a view of married life entertained before, and it does seem to me that such a view is not entertained in Scripture.' An American publication, *Dr Foote's Home Encyclopedia*, which sold hundreds of thousands of copies in Edwardian Britain, stated uncompromisingly that 'reciprocity in the sexual passion is *indispensable* to the contentment and happiness of the husband and wife'. Such guides of course prove nothing about actual sexual behaviour, and cannot be used to construct an authoritative picture of marriage in this period. But they were far more widely circulated, and probably more widely read, than the more arcane works of the advocates of marital

* John Gillis's conclusions, for example, are based on the records of families who deposited their children with the Foundling Hospital and the National Children's Home: scarcely a representative cross-section of 'ordinary people'. Peter Cominos's much-quoted study of 'Late-Victorian Sexual Respectability' cites the repressed upbringing of John Stuart Mill as 'an excellent case-study from Victorian reality'. Mill was born in 1806.

celibacy—or of the new 'sexologists' of the 1890s and 1900s who were beginning to advocate experiment with free love.

New views of sex and marriage were closely bound up with new methods of birth control; and, as was suggested in the previous chapter, massive advertising in popular almanacs indicates that birth control devices and 'illustrated Malthusian guides' were readily available to the literate classes from the 1880s onwards. Moreover, the prevalence of such advertising in unsophisticated provincial journals like *Old Moore's Almanac* indicates that, in England at least, the new knowledge was by no means confined to the metropolitan middle classes. By the 1900s studies of modern marriage were declaring, often regretfully, that men and women no longer married to found a dynasty or to perpetuate the race, but for personal self-fulfilment: they married simply 'because they desire the society of a certain person with whom to live out their lives'. Young men contemplating matrimony in the 1900s were advised no longer to look for an angel on the hearth but for 'the wife as lover and friend'. Whether young women shared these new aspirations remains a matter for conjecture, but it seems inconceivable that a generation of women saturated with the novels of Mrs Henry Wood could have believed the doctrine that women were incapable of sexual passion.

Such references prove nothing more than that new conceptions of sexuality were in the air, but they lend little support to the view that marriage in this period was primarily an exercise in economic calculation and emotional repression. Over the period as a whole, and particularly in the 1900s, there was a gradual increase in the proportion of both sexes who chose to remain unmarried; but the fact that the marriage rate was highest and the age of marriage lowest in areas where female employment was most prevalent casts doubt upon the claim of Edwardian feminists that women were forced into marriage because they were trained for nothing else. Divorce also became more common, particularly among the wealthy; and it seems possible that greater emotional expectations and the spread of ideas of 'self-fulfilment' may actually have helped to increase the degree of conscious unhappiness in marriage. The evidence remains patchy and inconclusive, but it suggests that at least some marriages of the period shared in the growing emphasis upon qualitative personal relationships, which was becoming almost imperceptibly one of the definitive characteristics of the modern age.

VIII. FAMILY LIFE

Something remains to be said about the inner dynamics of family life, and about the role of the family within the wider social structure. Beyond a certain point the day-to-day interaction between members of families necessarily eludes the historian; and detailed studies of late Victorian families, such as Barbara Caine's history of the Potter sisters, suggest that, not just within the same social stratum but within a single family, norms of sexual, parental, filial, and sibling behaviour varied so widely as to defy sociological generalization.

Nevertheless, the patchwork evidence of contemporary sources gives some indication of the following general trends. Over the period as a whole, upper- and middle-class families became less cohesive and less self-contained than they had been in the earlier Victorian period. There is little evidence from the late nineteenth century to support the familiar picture of the bourgeois family at the height of the Industrial Revolution, as a secure emotional refuge from the physical and moral horrors of an encircling market economy. On the contrary, the boundaries between family and society at large seem to have become much weaker: family-based religious worship declined, entertainment of visitors from outside the home became more common, and leisure activities—be they religious, literary, musical, or sporting—were now pursued less in the context of the home, and more in society at large. By the end of the century the growth of apartment blocks and service flats, the burgeoning habit of eating in restaurants, and the rise of metropolitan clubland were all cited as signs of the decline of family life; and, for those with the necessary income or connections, weekends at country-house parties or Continental holidays began to replace relaxation in the bosom of the family as the preferred escape route from the pressures of business life. These changes were encouraged by the declining size of families and reinforced by other contemporary social trends, such as changing patterns of religious observance, the gravitational shift from provinces to metropolis, and the rise of psychological (as opposed to economic) individualism. The persistence of family firms and of family business-relationships acted as a brake and counterweight upon such change; but in cases where the domestic economy was largely confined to consumption, personal relationships within families became less pre-determinate, more a matter of private affection and individual moral choice. Such changes were very gradual in impact and, initially at least, limited in scope. Much of the experimentation with new relationships was confined to the younger generation; and, even among the moral avant-garde of Cambridge and Bloomsbury, ties of kinship in the Edwardian period remained surprisingly strong. Nevertheless, there were many late Victorian and Edwardian upper-middle and middle-class families in more or less painful transition from one model of family life to another.

Among lower-middle and working-class families there is evidence to suggest that, in some communities at any rate, trends moved in the opposite direction: that the strengthening of family ties may have reinforced the gulf between home and society, and entailed a withdrawal from the wider community into the bosom of family life. The period saw an apotheosis of home life among the respectable working class—or perhaps it would be truer to say that a well-ordered home life constituted one of the touchstones that made working-class families respectable. This apotheosis was rooted partly in rising living standards, as at least some of the working class achieved the space and privacy that had buttressed middle-class family life a generation earlier; but it was rooted also in a much larger residue of economic and functional ties than was the case with the more affluent classes. For many workers, particularly those in heavy industry like the Middlesbrough steelworkers described by Lady Bell, daily employment would have been well-nigh impossible without the ancillary domestic services supplied by female relatives. In other words, the sexual division of labour was no mere patriarchal aberration, but an arrangement rooted in material necessity. And the very fact that mechanisms of social support outside the family were weak or non-existent inevitably reacted upon family functions and roles. Throughout the period the systematic withdrawal of outdoor relief in many areas, the liability of relatives for support of the destitute, and official prosecutions (about 7,000 a year) of those who failed to fulfil this duty starkly outlined to working people the fact that the family rather than the individual was the basic economic unit of the wider social order. And certainly in the eyes of Poor Law administrators the working-class family in the late nineteenth century was an incomparably stronger institution than it had been in the days of more liberal poor relief fifty years before.

It would be wrong to imply, however, that working-class families were glued together merely by economic scarcity and the constraints of social policy. On the contrary, home for many was a focal point of affection, emotional security, leisure and sociability—often at the expense of wider social sympathies. Contemporary observers noted that, even in areas with a flourishing community life, it was unusual for street sociability to spill over into hospitality in each other's homes: front parlours were for show or funerals or private family celebrations, not for wider entertainment. Communal solidarity in the public sphere (over strikes and unemployment, for example) could coexist with an overwhelming ethic of privacy in the domestic sphere. Few working-class people would interfere with the beating of a neighbour's wife, and there were some communities in which the very fact of marriage was viewed as a licence for violence. The weekly eucharist of working-class social life—the midday Sunday dinner—was a family occasion that virtually never included neighbours or friends. Moreover, much family leisure-time activity was physically located in the home (and, if it were not so, then both middle- and working-class observers felt that something was amiss). By contrast with their French and German counterparts, British working-class families rarely appeared together in public places, a habit influenced by the greater size of their houses, the prevalence of gardens, the rarity of cheap restaurants and the rough masculinity of British pubs. Workers themselves ascribed the difference to the Continental habit of living in flats: it was 'our self-contained cottages which make home sweet home a reality', commented a group of metal-workers from Birmingham on a visit to Berlin in 1906.

Such comments should not lead one to exaggerate the degree of close-knit working-class domestic life. Migration and emigration split families physically, and often led to the severance of close kinship ties. Tens of thousands of children at any one time were in charitable orphanages or Poor Law institutions, a fact which, given the obsession of the Poor Law with family cohesion, implied either the absence of parents or total family breakdown.* Forty thousand of the London children surveyed by Booth went to school hungry, many because of poverty, but many also because of parental neglect. Throughout the period, public and private inquiries emphasized the well-nigh impossible task of sustaining family life in slumland; and, in spite of the housing campaigns of the 1880s onwards, by the end of the period 10 per cent of the population of Britain still lived in slums. The extent of family violence is impossible to quantify, but the emergency sessions of magistrates that always followed bank holidays were an index of the recurrent 'saturnalia of beaten wives'. A study by Clara Collet in the 1890s found many married women in the East End of London who had had 'a marital experience which seems in most cases to have brutalized and degraded them', and that for many life was 'nothing more than procrastination of death'. Widowhood and desertion meant that probably 25 per cent of Edwardian children lived at one time or another in one-parent families, a fact which did not necessarily entail lack of respectability or emotional deprivation, but almost invariably brought dire poverty. Increasing prosperity brought strains for family life as well.

* The fact that a very low proportion of such children ultimately went on to become adult paupers casts some doubt upon the common assumption that close-knit natural families were the necessary cradles of civic virtue and social respectability.

Upward mobility in a working-class family could transform the ethic of privacy into a fetish; and, as noted earlier, there were more reported cases of child cruelty among the affluent working class and lower-middle class than among the poor. Increased disposable income could mean the buttressing of family life, but it could also lead to the growth of interests and habits of consumption outside the home; and there were some signs that this was happening in the Edwardian period (the very same Birmingham metalworkers who rhapsodized about 'home sweet home' were also notorious practitioners of the new masculine culture of commercialized leisure). Family cohesion may also have been affected by demographic change: the combination of later marriages, fewer children and more grandparents meant that families spanned a wider range of age groups than in previous generations, with a consequent growth in age stratification and the formation of social peer groups outside the home. It was no accident that both 'old age' and 'adolescence' come to the fore in the discussion of social relationships in the last few years of the nineteenth century.

Such factors should warn us against accepting the contemporary rhetoric of family life too much at its face value. Unsurprisingly in a large, ramshackle and profoundly custom-based society, the internal histories of families were almost infinitely varying. Clearly there were large-scale demographic, economic and cultural changes at work which threatened far-reaching repercussions for family life, but of which most contemporaries were largely unaware. There is almost no evidence, however, to support the view that the family was dwindling in this period either as a fact of social life or as an ideal of public policy. If anything, the reverse was true, in that, at least among the working classes, settled family life became more feasible than in earlier generations; and in that, as an item of social policy, the family moved from the periphery to the centre of public concerns. The fears of Edwardian reformers about the decline of family life reflected not so much the fact that family life *had* declined as that the moral and practical standards by which families were judged were continually rising. Sidney Webb's diagnosis of 1911, cited in the introduction to this chapter, was therefore false—or, if not false, misleading. It accurately captured something of the new element of psychological individualism that pervaded human relationships in the 1900s; but it bore little relation to trends in the history of social structure over the previous fifty years.

4

Property

Underpinning all other social institutions of late Victorian and Edwardian Britain was the institution of property. Politics, law, morality (even, claimed Lord Salisbury, theology and foreign policy) were deeply intertwined with the rights, privileges, and duties attached to the ownership of property. At the start of the period the rights to vote and to hold public office were still defined largely with reference to the ownership or tenancy of various kinds of property; social status was visibly graphed by access to, or exclusion from, control over property; and rival schools of political thought that could agree on little else concurred in seeing private property rights as the spine of the social order. Yet the very omnipresence of property makes its specific shape and significance peculiarly difficult for the historian to grasp, and contemporaries themselves were often equally confused. Political polemicists spoke of property as though it were a static and seamless entity, corresponding to a single, easily recognizable social and economic interest. In reality, however, nothing was further from being the case: property was a cluster of complex and chameleon-like ideas, governed by a variety of different legal and normative systems. It embraced a wide range of interest groups, often at loggerheads with each other: the Crown, freeholders, leaseholders, tenants, creditors, mortgagees, heirs, and—of growing importance in this period—the claims of the 'public interest'. And, although attitudes to property were often predictable (people who had it wanted to keep it), there were some marked changes of emphasis over the years. Certain perspectives that had belonged to advanced radicalism in the 1860s, for example, had become bulwarks of conservatism by 1914. Ideas and principles that had traditionally been attached to the ownership of land were increasingly transferred to property in general; while, conversely, landownership, which in the past had been seen as *sui generis*, began increasingly to be viewed as indistinguishable from other forms of property. Possession of property, viewed as self-evidently desirable in most mid-Victorian literature, was portrayed in novels of the *fin de siècle* as a potent source of social and psychological disorder (even by writers like Henry James, who had no quarrel with private property as an economic principle). This chapter can do no more than sketch some of the main outlines of the subject; but an attempt will be made to survey what is known about the ownership of property, about the laws and norms which governed property rights, and about the changing role of property in the public life of the nation.

II. THE DISTRIBUTION OF PROPERTY

'Imagination shrinks', wrote the statistician Sir Robert Giffen, 'from the task of framing a catalogue or inventory of the nation's property.' Yet such a catalogue was seen by many as a crucial index of national prosperity, and numerous attempts were made to calculate the volume and distribution of the nation's wealth. Giffen himself, by capitalizing from the annual income-tax returns, estimated in the late 1860s that national property was worth just over £6,000 million; and on the eve of the First World War a senior Inland Revenue official, Sir Josiah Stamp, arrived at a figure of £14,300 million. Other contemporary estimates differed slightly, but concurred in these overall proportions. Nominal wealth per head of population, therefore, increased from about £200 in 1865 to about £318 in 1914 (or to £330 if we take account of the intervening fall in prices). Comparable figures for the immediate pre-war period were £303 per head in France, £240 per head in the German Empire, and £424 per head in the United States.

Bald averages, however, tell us little about the changing character of property and its distribution. A striking feature of the period was a marked shift in the proportions of different types of property, a shift that mirrored wider changes in the economy as a whole. Central to the social history of the period was the absolute and relative decline in the value of land, which rose from £1,800 million in the late 1860s to a peak of over £2,000 million in the late 1870s and then fell steadily to £1,155 million at the outbreak of the First World War. In 1878 land constituted one-quarter, in 1914 less than one-twelfth of national wealth. This overall figure masked an even more dramatic decline in the value of purely agricultural property, since in the face of prolonged depression nearly three million acres went out of cultivation, and throughout the 1880s and 1890s much rural land, particularly in Ireland, was practically unsaleable. By contrast housing and business premises, which had accounted for £1,000 million in 1865, had risen to nearly £3,300 million by 1909. The growth of cities, suburbs, and urban infrastructure greatly inflated the value of land for building and development, and a major political controversy of the period centred upon the windfall profits or 'unearned increment' accruing to the owners of site values in expanding urban areas. The official land valuation carried out at the end of the period underlined the futility of measuring landed wealth purely in terms of acreage, since values varied from £26 per acre in Scotland, £52 in Wales, £73 in the English western counties, and £474 in industrial Lancashire through to £5,197 per acre in London north of the Thames.

Similar shifts occurred in the salience of other forms of property. The value of equities in publicly quoted companies increased fourfold, in spite of a prolonged stagnation in the stock market in the late 1900s. Local authority stock, a negligible sum in 1870, amounted to £425 million in 1905. Bank deposits increased by 300 per cent between 1870 and 1914, while life assurance cover increased from £500 million in 1890 to £1,000 million in 1910. The capitalized value of domestic, industrial and commercial profits on the eve of the First World War was estimated at between £3,400 and £3,800 million. Holdings in transport and public utilities rose from £200 million in the mid-nineteenth century to £1,500 million in 1914. Estimates of property held abroad varied widely and were by their nature peculiarly liable to error, but such holdings probably increased from about £700 million in the mid-1880s to close on £4,000 million at the eve of the First World War.

Some insight into the relative importance of different types of property is given by the breakdown of estates passing at death and subject to probate (i.e. worth a minimum of £100). In 1910–11, around 40 per cent of all such wealth was held in stocks and shares, 14 per cent in housing and business premises, 10 per cent in mortgages and insurance policies, 6 per cent respectively in cash, trade assets and agricultural land, and under 3 per cent in consumer goods, the remaining 15 per cent being unclassified. Over the period as a whole there was a gigantic shift of economic power from landed to non-landed property, from home to overseas investment, from private to institutional forms of saving, and from personal to impersonal ownership of business property—a shift more profound and far-reaching in its impact than many more dramatic and violent epochs of economic change.

Who owned Britain's property, and did the distribution of the national wealth change significantly between 1870 and 1914? Did the emergence of new types of property imply the emergence of new property-owning groups—or did it merely indicate that property owners were shifting their assets from one form of security to another? Was the changing nature of property a cause or a consequence of, or merely coincidental with, other changes in the structure of British society? Such questions are difficult to answer, partly because of imperfect evidence, but also because of logical and conceptual problems entailed in the interpretation of that evidence. 'Public property', for example, owned by central and local government and public charitable corporations increased from under 5 per cent to over 15 per cent of domestic national wealth between 1875 and 1905, and was clearly of importance in the growth of the administrative state. By 1911 municipalities alone owned capital of £22 per head for every inhabitant of the United Kingdom; yet two-thirds of the value of that public property was owed to private creditors, and it is almost impossible to determine to whom it should be allocated in the distribution of national wealth.

Of more interest to contemporaries was the vast residue of national property which remained in private hands, and many attempts were made to plot the personal distribution of private wealth. The New Liberal economist Sir Leo Chiozza Money claimed in 1906 that 87 per cent of private property within the United Kingdom was owned by 882,690 persons (or 4,4000,000 if one included families and dependants): the remaining 13 per cent was shared between 38,600,000 people. These striking contrasts masked even more dramatic polarities at the top and bottom of the property-owning scale, for an inner core of 117,000 property holders owned nearly two-thirds of domestic private wealth, whilst at the other extreme 90 per cent of those who died left no recorded property. The significance of these figures was hotly contested at the time by critics who claimed that Money's calculations took no account of age and family structure, but their overall shape was substantially accepted by Edwardian taxation experts as the most reliable estimate available. More recent estimates, corrected to take account of the fact that property was rarely owned by children, have suggested, if anything, an even more extreme pattern of inequality. Professor Revell's calculations for 1911–13 suggest that among citizens over 25 years of age the wealthiest 1 per cent owned 69 per cent of property, the next 4 per cent owned 18 per cent of property, and the next 5 per cent owned 5 per cent of property; in other words 10 per cent of the mature population owned 92 per cent of the nation's wealth. Figures for other European countries in the same period suggest a similar though slightly less extreme distributional shape: in Prussia in 1908 the richest 10 per cent owned 84 per cent of property, and in France (1909–13) 70 per cent had no property while 10 per cent owned 84 per cent of national wealth.

Such figures suggest that, in terms of access to property, Edwardian Britain was probably more unequal than other comparable European countries, and possibly (though this is more conjectural) more unequal than at any other period in national history. If, as contemporaries believed, the ownership of property was a 'national passion', then it was a passion indulged by remarkably few of the nation's citizens—and this before any account was taken of the impact of overseas investment, itself largely concentrated among the better off. What such estimates do not tell us, however, is who the rich and very rich actually were, whether ownership of wealth was static or constantly changing, and whether disparities in property ownership were increasing or decreasing over a longer period; nor do they tell us how far property ownership was related to other forms of power. Contemporary efforts to answer these questions were largely inspired by the recurrent political debate on the ownership of land; and—perhaps misleadingly—it is for the landed sector of society that we have the most detailed information about patterns, habits and trends in property ownership over the period as a whole.

III. ARISTOCRATIC PROPERTY

Detailed scrutiny of the ownership of land began with the New Domesday survey of 1874–5, an inquiry commissioned by Parliament in response to radical complaints about the continuing decline of small-scale ownership and the monopolistic implications of primogeniture. The inquiry attempted to ascertain the acreage and value of landed hereditaments for the whole of the United Kingdom, excepting only the City and metropolis of London. Its findings were digested and corrected in *The Great Landowners of Britain and Ireland*, published by the Tory land reformer John Bateman in 1877. They revealed a pattern of landownership apparently untouched by a century of industrialization and by half a century of 'popular government' and market economics. Only 15 per cent of land in England and Wales was farmed by owner-occupiers, the rest being let to tenants under various forms of tenure, the most common being a yearly rack-rent. Out of a population of 31 million, slightly fewer than 1 million were owners of freehold land (compared with more than 5 million in both Germany and France). Of that 1 million, 850,000 owned less than an acre, while 7,000 persons owned half the land of the United Kingdom. 'Four thousand five hundred persons held half the area of England and Wales, one thousand seven hundred held nine-tenths of Scotland, a single owner having in his hands more than a million and a quarter acres.' At the centre of the charmed circle were 2,800 'great landowners' (including 400 peers) whom Bateman defined as persons possessing both 3,000 acres in land and a minimum of £3,000 per annum in rent rolls. 'Great landowners' included a small percentage of erstwhile business and professional men, but the majority were members of families who had owned their lands, and whose primary income had been derived from land, since the sixteenth century. Second in importance to the great landowners were 12,000 'squires' and 'greater yeomen', owners of a thousand acres on average, who for over a century had been gaining territory at the expense of a declining class of lesser freeholders and copyholders. The continuity of large estates was maintained by primogeniture and by such devices as strict settlement, which limited the power of a tenant-for-life to sell or alienate any part of a family holding.

Such a pattern of ownership presented a startling challenge to the prevailing image of Britain in the 1870s as the world capital of commerce, advanced liberalism and free competition. In no other European country, with the possible exception of Hungary, were great estates still so concentrated in the hands of the descendants of a feudal and court aristocracy; and in no other country was the majority of citizens more remote from a share in those 'absolute rights' of property which the prevailing political economy of classical liberalism was so concerned to defend.

The findings of the New Domesday defined the terms of both sociological and political debate on landownership over the next half-century; yet striking and significant as these findings were, they were also in certain respects misleading. Wealth estimated from gross annual rental could be wildly inaccurate, as recent monographs on individual late Victorian estates have shown. Both the New Domesday and Bateman tended to give undue weight to sheer acreage, underestimating the enormous local variation in the value of land as a realizable asset. Thousands of acres around Cape Wrath might confer enormous social prestige, but they were not necessarily indicative of economic power; and a recent recalculation of the New Domesday data in terms of values rather than acreage reduces the degree of aristocratic predominance by half. Bateman himself pointed to the absurdity of failing to distinguish between urban and agrarian land, an omission that was to generate much misunderstanding and muddled thinking in political debates on property over the next half-century. Obsessive emphasis on great estates led to relative neglect of lesser land-owners, among whom there was much more evidence of economic openness and upward and downward mobility. Moreover, by concentrating exclusively on landed wealth, the New Domesday gave no indication of the relative importance of land within an individual's total assets, though there was much evidence from other sources to suggest that even in the prosperous 1860s and early 1870s many landowners treated land as a non-economic good which they invisibly subsidized from other sources of income. As Trollope's Archdeacon Grantly remarked, 'Land gives so much more than rent. It gives position and influence and political power, to say nothing of the game.' It was these invisible social assets that explained the 'fancy prices' paid at the beginning of the period for land with meagre rent-rolls, and the willingness of many Victorian landlords to let agricultural properties below an economic price.

The major shortcoming of the New Domesday data, however, was that as sociological evidence it was little more than a death-mask. Its findings continued to be cited virtually without qualification throughout the period (by, for instance, such otherwise reliable texts as Chiozza Money's *Riches and Poverty* and Stamp's *British Incomes and Property*). Yet even before the results of the survey had been fully digested, the situation which it described was being fundamentally transformed by a long series of bad harvests, competition from North American producers, the collapse of agricultural rents, and a massive resurgence of migration to the towns. The late 1870s saw the smashing of an age-old equilibrium in agrarian incomes, whereby bad harvests were offset by rising prices, and by the early 1890s the price of wheat had fallen to its lowest level for a century. The forty years after the New Domesday saw the beginnings of a long-term revolution in the economics, politics and social structure of landed property in the United Kingdom—a revolution that was in some contexts dramatic and highly visible, in other contexts largely imperceptible to the majority of contemporaries. The most obvious arena of change was Ireland, where agrarian rents were subject to statutory control from the early 1870s, and where more than two-thirds of agrarian freehold land was ultimately transferred from landlords to erstwhile tenants under the Land Acts of 1885 and 1903. In England, Wales, and Scotland change was slower and much more variable. Dairy and market gardening areas survived the depression well, benefiting from cheap imported animal foods and expanding urban markets. Nevertheless, over Britain as a whole rent-rolls fell by 20 per cent between the late 1870s and the late 1890s, and in the south of England they fell by 40 per cent. Moreover, land prices fell even where rent-rolls remained high, reflecting both a growing desire among landowners to sell their land and an unprecedented disinclination among the owners of new wealth to buy it. Institutional investors, such as insurance companies, who down to 1875 held the bulk of their funds in mortgages, now began to purchase a much wider range of securities (Standard Life, for example, held 71.62 per cent of its assets in mortgages in 1880, only 10.04 per cent in 1910). Land lost status as well as value: from the 1880s it was no longer a necessary embellishment to a newly acquired peerage, no longer an indispensable appendage to 'social position, territorial influence and legal privileges'. In the 1900s many landed estates were on the market, well before the fiscal panic induced by the 1909 budget (in 1900 half of Scotland was up for sale at the hands of a single Edinburgh lawyer). Tenant farmers in Edwardian England were buying land on an increasing scale (often reluctantly, as many would have preferred to hold their capital in buildings and machinery). By the end of the period two contradictory trends were occurring in the structure of rural landownership in England and Wales: on the one hand, the burden of debt and mortgages was driving many small freeholders into liquidation, thus apparently intensifying aristocratic monopoly, but at the same time widespread tenant-purchase marked a movement in the opposite direction. Agrarian historians have detected in this latter trend the first signs of the break-up of the great estates that was to take place on a far more cataclysmic scale at the end of the First World War.

Did the economic embarrassment of landowners and the undoubted decline in absolute and relative land values signify an equally dramatic shift in the ownership of wealth—or did traditional owners of wealth simply repair their fences by diversifying their investments into other forms of property? As indicated above, land values were virtually halved during a period in which industrial, commercial and institutional assets increased by over 300 per cent; and farmers' capital, an asset shared between tenants and owner-cultivators, fell from £668 million in 1875 to £320 million or less by 1911–13. Although this points to a major reordering of economic structure, however, it was not necessarily indicative of a corresponding shift in personal ownership of wealth. Data about the composition of personal fortunes from the years 1909–14 indicates that landownership formed a disproportionately large component of great fortunes, whereas newer and more buoyant forms of wealth were much more heavily represented among smaller fortunes; and this fact in itself may indicate some kind of narrowing of the gap between the very rich and the not-quite-so-rich that was largely invisible to contemporaries. On the other hand, right down to 1914 the largest personal (non-landed) fortunes bequeathed at death belonged overwhelmingly to landowners, rivalled only by those whose main source of wealth was the City of London. Throughout the Edwardian period the largest blocks of both real and personal property passing through the hands of the Inland Revenue belonged to great landowners (as Treasury records of the period reveal, the death of one octogenarian marquess could tip the balance between surplus and deficit in the nation's annual budget). Such facts may indicate that, though land itself dwindled as an asset, landowners as a wealthy class survived surprisingly well.

Whether such survival was typical or atypical, however, remains to some extent obscure. Research into the fortunes of individual families suggests wide variation according to chance, character, and individual circumstance. On the whole, great landowners survived better than lesser landowners, because their scope for diverting resources into non-landed wealth was more extensive. In some cases the sheer size of a landed estate enabled it to survive as an economic unit in a way that might not have been possible if the same land had been parcelled out among smaller owners. Some landowners were lucky enough to own land with potential for urban development, whilst others found new sources of income in using land for leisure and pleasure (the Dukes of Sutherland, for example, increasingly gained more from commercial sporting rights than from agrarian rents). Mineral rights saved some, although, contrary to radical expectations, the Select Committee on Land Values after the war found that these constituted a minuscule proportion of overall landowning assets. Some landlords, like the Duke of Bedford, put up the capital for the sale of their estates to their tenant-farmers, finding it more profitable to act as mortgagees than as collectors of rent. And for the first time in centuries the British aristocracy became net sellers rather than collectors of art treasures, many great international fine art houses (such as Agnew's and Duveen's) having their origins in this period as brokers between impoverished landowners and the aristocracy of high finance.

Another conspicuous trend of the period was the growing involvement of members of landowning families in other forms of enterprise: as *rentiers*, as governors of dominions and colonies, and as nominal figureheads or active participants in business concerns. Some great landlords had always participated in business enterprise, and younger sons had traditionally engaged in commerce; but from the late 1860s onwards the growth of public companies opened up a multitude of new ways in which this could be done, while maintaining the habits and outlook of a gentleman. The Cokes of Norfolk were an example of a family who successfully shored up their waning agricultural revenues with an active and expanding share portfolio. Trollope in the early 1870s noted that speculative companies were purchasing credibility by appointing indigent peers to their boards of directors; and by the mid-1880s this was becoming quite commonplace even with affluent peers and among the most respectable firms. Scottish Widows, for example, one of the most sober, long-lasting and profitable of life assurance companies, boasted as its President and Vice-Presidents in 1880 a duke, a marquess, two earls, a baron and a High Court judge. The first aristocrat to join the Stock Exchange did so in 1875. By 1896 a quarter of the peerage, and by 1910 a half, were company directors, often of several companies at once.

The coincidence of agricultural depression with the opening up of new forms of overseas investment cemented an alliance between landowners and the financial sector of the British economy that had been gestating throughout the nineteenth century. Scions of some of the great banking and commercial houses, whose fathers in earlier decades had withdrawn from business into country life, now increasingly returned to active employment in the City. Intermarriage between landowning and financial families, never unknown, became increasingly common: by the 1890s, 24 per cent of partners in London's leading merchant banking houses were married to daughters of peers. A study of 1904 remarked that boys at Eton now knew more 'about trusts and contangos than about trochees and caesuras'. An instructive case was that of Loulou Harcourt, heir to an ancient baronetcy and an encumbered Oxfordshire estate, who was an unsuccessful candidate for the chairmanship of the London Stock Exchange and the eventual bridegroom of the niece of Pierpont Morgan. An example in the opposite direction was the financier Sir Ernest Cassel, who married his daughter into the ancient Whig peerage and his granddaughter to a first cousin of King George V. South African mining finance attracted many sons of noblemen into City offices, many of them centred around the Rothschild headquarters in New Court. The Settled Land Act of 1882, which for the first time made it possible for the life tenant of a landed estate to dispose of land like other forms of capital, marked a major symbolic turning-point in the transformation of landownership into simply another form of business enterprise. Legal historians have seen this act as presaging a massive migration away from 'settled land' and into 'trusts of money', whereby family property could be held in a much wider range of securities. The seventy million pounds in compensation paid to landowners by the Exchequer in exchange for ten million unsaleable acres in Ireland almost certainly had the same effect. The detailed story of what Anglo-Irish landlords did with the money remains untold, but much of it was sucked into the late Edwardian boom in overseas investment. Over the period as a whole it seems reasonable to conclude that in so far as great landowners remained landowners their wealth dwindled; they survived by merging their real property with other, more anonymous forms of capital. With certain notable exceptions the best survivors were the greatest landowners, whose property holdings increasingly acquired the rationality, diversity and impersonal management structure of large business corporations.

IV. MIDDLE-CLASS PROPERTY

If our knowledge of landed property is scattered and imperfect, our knowledge of the inner structure of other forms of property is even more so. It is one of the curiosities of modern history that the entity which many historians see as the dynamo of social and economic development— bourgeois private property—remains in its details (as opposed to grand national aggregates) so relatively obscure. Unfortunately for the social historian, no financial or industrial Domesday ever logged the ownership of non-landed capital. All contemporaries agreed that the volume of such capital was growing, but differed between those like Giffen and Leone Levi, who believed that small-scale property ownership was becoming more widespread, and those like J. A. Hobson and Chiozza Money, who believed that business wealth was becoming increasingly concentrated in a few private hands. The growth of public companies and the quotation of securities on the London and provincial stock exchanges meant that the period saw a great increase in the number of middle-class *rentiers* (persons living wholly or partly on income from invested capital). The middle-class 'drone' was a much more prominent figure in Edwardian society and clubland than he had been forty years before, but contemporary estimates of such persons varied widely (the Fabian Society claimed that over 800,000 unoccupied people with 2 million dependants were living on 'private means', while T. A. Welton put the figure at less than 20,000). Share-holders' lists suggest that the largest groups of investors were merchants and manufacturers, followed by 'landowners, soldiers and sailors, clergy-men and a considerable number of women'; but no information is available about the precise distribution of investment between different social groups, nor whether for most investors shareholding was a primary or supplementary source of income. The analysis of business wealth was complicated by the problem of what actually constituted 'property' in a business context: what proportion of a businessman's income was rent on his capital investment and what was simply payment for his entrepreneurial skills? Were such factors as 'goodwill' and scarce professional knowledge (the so-called 'rent of ability') forms of property, and, if so, what was their capital value? Such questions constantly perplexed contemporary observers, and continue to vex historians who venture into the maze of middle-class wealth.

A tentative picture of certain aspects of middle-class property can, however, be pieced together from contemporary estimates, from recent research into probate records and to a lesser extent from business and professional histories. Chiozza Money calculated in 1905 that there were 861,150 people in the United Kingdom owning property worth between £500 and £50,000, a figure that had risen to 916,860 by 1912. This was almost exactly the same number as those recorded in 1911–12 as having professional, salaried, and self-employed annual incomes above the lower income-tax threshold of £160; and although it is impossible to say how far these two groups were identical, it seems reasonable to assume that between then they embraced the bulk of the nation's 'middle class'. The average amount owned by members of this group was just under £5,000, and if one assumed, as Money did, that each property owner represented four dependants, then the per capita wealth of the middle class was just under £1,000 (or three times the mean for the whole population). The median of middle-class per capita wealth was undoubtedly far lower than this; and one of the most striking features of the estimates of national wealth made by Mullhall and Giffen in the 1880s and by Money in the 1900s was the modest size of the vast majority of middle-class fortunes. By far the most numerous group in Money's classification of substantial wealth-holders were the half a million persons (excluding dependants) who owned property worth between £1,000 and £10,000. About one quarter of the wealth of this group consisted of non-agricultural real property, while just over a quarter was held in stocks and shares. They owned a third of the nation's life assurance cover and were substantial owners, though not necessarily occupiers, of private housing (it was not until much later in the twentieth century that owner-occupation became almost a *sine qua non* of middle-class identity). They were also large holders of those uninvested, 'old-sock' savings deplored by later economists as one of the congenital weaknesses of an immature private enterprise economy. Such figures suggest that—whatever may have been the case among the commanding heights of British capitalism—the individual wealth of the bulk of the

Victorian and Edwardian business and professional classes was considerably more modest than is often supposed.

Was the same true not only of the 'middling' and lower-middle classes, but of the *haute bourgeoisie* of the late Victorian and Edwardian economy as well? The pioneering research of W. D. Rubinstein and Harold Perkin into probate records has revealed a number of striking facts about the character and distribution of business and professional wealth. One major point is that, throughout the nineteenth century but particularly from the 1860s, large-scale business wealth had been disproportionately concentrated in London rather than in the heavy industrial heartlands of Lancashire, Yorkshire, the West Midlands and the North East. Measured in terms of personal fortunes, this concentration intensified during the period under review (57 per cent of millionaires who died in Edwardian England were London-based, compared with 38 per cent between 1880 and 1899). A corollary of this was that the greater business fortunes were commercial and financial rather than industrial; and again this characteristic became much more marked after the turn of the century (half of great Edwardian fortunes came from banking and commerce compared with a third in 1880–99). Furthermore, even within the ranks of manufacturers the greatest wealth was not found among the owners of heavy industry but among those producing consumer goods for new mass retail outlets: the brewers, distillers, cigarette manufacturers, and producers of packaged foods.* A third point, stressed earlier, is that, even in the face of prolonged agricultural decline, it was only very slowly that holdings of property derived from business came to rival those embodied in landed wealth: financier millionaires and half-millionaires came to exceed landed millionaires and half-millionaires only after 1900, while large fortunes belonging to persons whose primary occupation was 'landowner' continued to outnumber large fortunes from industry right down to 1914.

Such evidence may be interpreted in many different ways and its implications are by no means self-evident. One possible explanation of the relative poverty of industrialists is that the sheer physical size of manufacturing industry and the human capital that it employed deluded contemporaries and later historians into greatly exaggerating its significance in the structure of national wealth, a point lent some support by the fact that according to the 1907 Census of Production only a third of national income came from manufacturing industry. Another quite different

---

* This point applies only to England and Wales. Industrialists and textile manufacturers were strongly represented among the wealthiest group in Scotland.

possibility is that the apparent imbalance between financial, industrial, and landed property was not so much the product of the relative wealth generated by these sectors, but of the different strategies of inheritance pursued by different economic groups. As was shown in Chapter 3, a deliberate policy of wealth concentration had been pursued by landed families for centuries, through the practice of strict settlement and primogeniture; and it seems likely that similar policies were being employed by London financiers and city merchants during this period, as part of a general process of aristocratic assimilation. By contrast, settlements and primogeniture were viewed as morally obnoxious by many mid-Victorian provincial businessmen, who campaigned for free disposability of property or for equal division of inheritance among all a testator's children. Some leading manufacturers such as the Frys and the Cadburys went so far as to disapprove of inherited wealth altogether, and provided for their sons not by inheritance but by setting them up early in life as independent men of business. Such an attitude was no mere Quaker eccentricity; indeed, Taine in the late 1860s and de Rousiers in the 1890s suggested that it was one of the most distinctive characteristics of the English bourgeoisie, in marked contrast to the attitudes of their European counterparts. Since virtually no great fortunes were the product of one-generational rags-to-riches accumulation, it seems probable that the relative modesty of industrial fortunes—and of middle-class fortunes generally—was at least partly accounted for by a widespread normative preference for partition rather than concentration of family wealth. Towards the end of the nineteenth century these cultural contrasts may have become less marked. As landowners became more capitalistic their obsession with primogeniture relaxed, and the opposite may have been true of gentrified industrialists— though precise evidence on this latter score is lacking. Between the 1880s and 1914 inheritance accounted for a considerably higher proportion of national property-ownership than in the mid-Victorian period or after the First World War; and since such an increase can scarcely have been accounted for by landed property, it suggests that inheritance was beginning to bulk larger in the fortunes of the business classes than in earlier generations.

Beyond these points, middle-class property continues to elude firm generalization. The widening of opportunities for limited liability investment, combined with the growth of life assurance, annuities and pension schemes meant that Giffen's and Levi's prophecy of the 1880s was fulfilled and that the numbers of people owning medium-sized property substantially expanded. At the same time the widening distance between medium-sized fortunes and the greatest fortunes in the business world may indicate that Hobson and Chiozza Money were also right in their diagnosis of increasing plutocratic concentration.

V. WORKING-CLASS PROPERTY

The title of this section would have been seen by early Victorians as a virtual contradiction in terms: lack of property, except in the form of labour power, was precisely what defined both the 'poor' and the 'labouring-classes' (the two terms being used virtually interchangeably). This perception gradually changed, however, with the growth of national wealth and the rise of popular savings institutions; and from the 1860s onwards evidence of working class property-ownership was eagerly sought as a prime indicator of national prosperity. By the end of the nineteenth century the terms 'poor' and 'working-class' were increasingly acquiring different, and sometimes mutually exclusive, connotations.* Nevertheless, major problems surrounded the identification of working-class property. One problem was that little of such property was assessed for taxation or appeared in official records. Another was that much working-class property was 'contingent property': it consisted of the right to claim from certain institutions if misfortune occurred, rather than outright ownership. And a third problem was that of precisely defining the boundaries of the working class, since a definition that made sense in terms of industrial function did not necessarily do so in terms of income, property or social status. Moreover, though the idea of working-class property was no longer inconceivable, the acquisition of property beyond a certain minimal level still tended by its very nature to shift a worker into the ranks of the lower-middle class.

Such problems make the identification of working-class property even more difficult than for the upper and middle classes: again, however, a provisional picture can be patched together from a variety of sources. Giffen, Leone Levi and Chiozza Money, finding it impossible to fix a precise boundary between working and lower-middle classes, sought to measure working-class property by aggregating together the capital owned by working-class thrift institutions—namely, savings banks, building

* Though it is interesting to note that authorities like Alfred Marshall and Helen Bosanquet, who in theory insisted upon the separateness of the 'poor' and the 'working class', in practice often confused the two: a tacit acknowledgement of the fact that in the real world there was a great deal of overlap and migration from one condition to the other throughout the period.

societies, trade unions, co-operatives, and industrial life assurance societies. Their estimates suggested an increase of collective working-class property from about £154 million in the mid-1880s to about £450 million in the mid-1900s, giving an average at the latter date of £29 per head. Booth in the 1890s thought that aggregate working-class savings would soon be large enough to finance the whole of domestic investment (leaving the rich to concentrate on more speculative investment abroad). A critique of such estimates by Paul Johnson has suggested, however, that although working-class people may have formed the bulk of the depositors in these institutions, they were not necessarily the owners of the bulk of the capital and that probably 70 per cent of savings banks' funds and 90 per cent of building society funds were owned by depositors from ranks above the working class. When this factor is taken into account, it appears that adult working-class institutional savings amounted to no more than £8.8 per head in 1901, rising to £11.2 per head in 1911.

These averages of course concealed wide variations between different sectors of the working class and between different regions and levels of income. The culture of 'thrift' varied widely between different communities, by no means necessarily in relation to affluence. Membership of building societies flourished in small Lancashire towns, but was rare among workers in large industrial cities (among the latter, Leeds was famous for providence, Sheffield for gambling and sport). Co-operative societies were often too expensive for the lower-paid, unless they flouted the fundamental ethos of the co-operative movement by allowing purchases 'on tick'. Friendly society sick funds (by far the biggest working-class financial institutions) were largely confined to skilled and semi-skilled workers, and seemed by 1900 to have reached the limits of their natural growth. Only industrial life assurance—based on weekly collection of premiums by door-to-door collecting agents—attracted a large clientele from all sections of the working class, including the very poor. In addition there were a myriad informal, unregistered, often transient savings institutions in the form of sick clubs, clothing clubs, tontines, and corner-shop Christmas Clubs, whose functions were deeply woven into the financial and cultural fabric of working-class homes. Both their numbers and their holdings are incalculable, but almost certainly they declined during the 1900s as Post Office savings accounts became more liquid and accessible and as peripatetic commercial insurance agents began to penetrate every level of working-class life.

The 1890s and 1900s also saw the emergence of a new form of contingent property rights in the form of social welfare entitlements created by the state. Even the Poor Law was sometimes paradoxically portrayed as a species of property right (radicals from William Cobbett through to Keir Hardie claimed that poor relief should be viewed as compensation to the poor for the past expropriation of common land and monastic charity by the rich). The introduction of workmen's compensation in 1897, old-age pensions in 1908 and national insurance in 1911 were sometimes viewed in this light by contemporaries. And in form and substance they were just as much genuine property rights as the voluntary savings institutions mentioned above, which economic analysts of the period treated as the most reliable index of the wealth of the working class.

What of other, more personalized, less collective forms of property among the working class? As with other social groups the historian is thrust back upon a bewildering variety of fragmentary and often contradictory contemporary records. Though dwindling as an element in total industrial production, there were still 329,000 self-employed craftsmen in Britain in 1911, and, although the class position of such craftsmen may have been ambiguous, it seems reasonable to assume that a substantial number should be classified as workers. A master toolmaker in Birmingham, interviewed by the French sociologist Paul de Rousiers in the 1890s, owned £2,800 in business and domestic capital, an estate which he proposed to divide equally among his six children at death (thus, as with the middle-class property-holders noted above, tending to minimize the long-term impact of capital accumulation). This case was clearly atypical, but was nevertheless indicative of the high degree of property-ownership that could be attained while retaining some kind of 'working-class' identity. No other worker recorded by de Rousiers owned so much, but several had substantial possessions in the form of houses and household goods. In *The Classic Slum* Robert Roberts recorded that his mill-worker mother had shared in a family inheritance of £900, £40 of which was used to purchase his father's shop. Elizabeth Roberts's oral history of Lancaster uncovered the case of an illiterate widow who made a fortune buying houses and other items at auctions. In the south of England a dwindling residue of rural smallholders still held a life interest in pockets of land granted to them under enclosure schemes earlier in the century. And in the north of Scotland the Crofters' Commission of 1884 found families holding twelve-to twenty-acre plots in return for an annual quota of quasi-feudal day labour. Working-class shareholding was not unknown, several Lancashire spinning-mills being owned and managed by working-class joint-stock companies. The manufacturing co-operative movement of the 1870s was largely a failure, but Beatrice Webb discovered 112 such co-operatives still existing in 1892, with an annual turnover of more than a million pounds.

A few years later David Schloss recorded that 'workmen usually preferred to hold shares in a mill in which they themselves were not employed' and that 'of recent years the shares in these companies have been more and more passing into the hands of middle-class capitalists.'

Another area of working-class property was house-ownership. No reliable estimates exist of owner-occupation of housing during this period (the figures usually cited are 10 to 15 per cent of national housing stock), but there is some evidence to suggest that house-ownership was more prevalent among working people in the 1870s than by 1914. Certainly building societies, which had sprung up earlier in the nineteenth century as face-to-face associations designed to enable working men actually to build their own homes, had been transformed by the 1900s into impersonal financial institutions mainly serving the new suburban lower-middle class. Birmingham was estimated to have 13,000 owner-occupiers in the early 1870s, but far fewer by 1914. In central London the Artisans' Dwellings movement of the 1860s and 1870s began with the aim of financing owner-occupation, but was forced to switch into letting because so many clients could not keep up their mortgage repayments. Booth's survey of London in the 1890s cited many examples of house-ownership among 'class E' (artisans and shopkeepers) but virtually none in the classes below. Rowntree in 1899 found that 6 per cent of houses in York had working-class owners—many of them not industrial heads of household but retired spinsters who had sunk their life savings into what appeared to be secure investments. The Amalgamated Society of Engineers—most aristocratic of the old craft unions—was mortgagee to over ten thousand members in the years just before the First World War.

The major areas of working-class house-ownership were one-class towns like Oldham and Jarrow or industrial suburbs like Woolwich and Plumstead, where more than a third of the housing stock was in owner-occupation. In some industrial villages in South Wales the figure was as high as 60 per cent, considerably higher than for the middle-class suburbs of Cardiff. In Oldham in the 1890s a two-up, two-down terraced house could be bought for £150–180. And many workers were not merely owners but landlords to their neighbours as well. In the 1860s and 1870s working-class landlordship was an eagerly studied and much praised phenomenon, apparently exemplifying the growth of thrift and the blurring of the barriers between capital and labour. But over the next few decades perspectives changed. High local authority rates, an excess of speculative building and the downturn of real wages in the 1900s combined to depress the return on rented accommodation, and the depression was most severe among the poorest class of housing. 'As safe as houses' remained a familiar proverb, but landlords great and small found that working-class housing was no longer the modestly sound investment that it had seemed thirty years before. Moreover, progressive opinion turned against the working-class landlord, who was far less able than his richer brethren to maintain adequate repairs or to forgo an economic rent in the face of rising costs. The 1886 Royal Commission on Housing found that the smaller the landlord the worse the accommodation; and in the 1890s no less a person than the Fabian socialist Sidney Webb compared working-class landlords unfavourably with London's great landlord-dukes, whom he saw as a necessary phase in an eventual transition to municipal collectivism.

Working-class capitalists who housed or employed other workers were clearly a small minority of the working class as a whole. Their significance was more than purely idiosyncratic, in that they demonstrated both the many-tiered character of the working class and its economic diversity. But among most working-class people, property-ownership was of an entirely different order and consisted mainly of 'household goods'. Of all types of property, household goods were the most difficult to quantify and formed the most speculative element in the various estimates of national wealth; Stamp, for example, in 1914 suggested a global figure of £450 million, his Inland Revenue colleague Bernard Mallet more than twice as much. Both of these figures were wild guesses, designed to do little more than tidy up the balance sheet of national bookkeeping, and probably no more reliable estimate can ever be made. Nor is anything known about the distribution of household goods, beyond the self-evident fact that a disproportionate share was owned by the better off. Something must be said, however, about the cultural role of household goods within the working-class domestic economy. Public inquiries and social surveys of the period dwelt in voyeuristic detail upon the dwellings of working men, frequently deploring the lack of anything but rags and a few sticks of furniture. Often, however, the comment was of the opposite kind: that working-class homes were crowded with an immense variety of apparently superfluous consumer goods, often bought on credit from the 'tally man', the 'gombeen man' or, by the 1900s, through the rapidly developing system of hire purchase. 'Luxury articles most longed for were pianos,' recalled Robert Roberts, 'but one would settle happily for a banjo, sewing-machines . . . bicycles, gramophones, gold lockets and watches and chairs . . . fireside objects in brass and copper . . . Bedding and underclothes in good condition were anxiously sought after, since on washing day they would have to be hung to dry across the street.' Margaret Loane frequently remarked upon the absence of adequate cleaning and washing utensils, even among the affluent working class; yet, even in 'the poorest houses . . . there are almost invariably photographs, vases and ornaments in abundance . . . jugs in the handsome toilet sets are filled with paper instead of water, while the proud owners still go downstairs unwashed and perform their unwilling ablutions in the sink.'

Such pretentious acquisitiveness among the working classes—often at the expense of wholesome food, house repairs, and saving for the future—was condemned by Edwardian sociologists in terms very reminiscent of the moral scorn which Marx in the 1860s had poured upon the 'commodity fetishism' of the bourgeoisie. Particularly deplored was purchase on credit, which at best involved purchasers in very high rates of interest, at worst made them liable to county court summonses and possible imprisonment for refusal or inability to pay their debts. Yet such property was by no means always so functionless as its critics supposed. At an intangible level decorative objects were often the outward and visible signs of inner dignity and self-respect. They were important badges of status in a society riddled with status differentials. And on a more utilitarian plane they were pledges of credit with the pawnbroker in times of need (the very fact of running into debt was in itself a sign of a certain minimal degree of affluence, since credit was never given to the wholly possessionless class). Nor were the coveted objects in themselves necessarily pointless. Bicycles and sewing-machines made an obvious practical contribution to day-to-day economic life; and the widespread possession of musical instruments bore witness to a popular musicality that was more widely diffused than in any other period in the history of Britain. Furniture and photographs were both practical and symbolic embodiments of the centrality of family and home noted in earlier chapters: a point made by Lady Bell, who remarked that social observers were in danger of condemning among working men precisely the kind of comfortable domesticity that was seen among the better off as morally imperative. This comment underlines one of the most striking features of working-class attitudes to property-ownership: namely, that where such ownership *was* attainable, the preferences and aspirations of many working people were remarkably similar to those of the class above them. 'Their desires are for better clothes, more amusements, better furniture and better opportunities for their children', admitted Miss Loane in *From Their Point of View*, published in 1908. And in 1893 Octavia Hill had told the Royal Commission on the Aged Poor that 'the working classes do not buy annuities . . . They prefer educating their children well and getting them to better positions, or buying a small business or having a little home or a quantity of furniture.' Both these remarks were meant to explain why working-class people so rarely conformed to rational expectations of economic behaviour; yet both of them exactly echoed the remarks made by Taine, de Rousiers, St John Brodrick and others about the attitudes to property that appeared to be quintessentially characteristic of the British middle classes.

VI. PROPERTY AND POLITICS

Property has been discussed so far largely as a question of who owned how much or how little. Yet property was much more than that: it was deeply interwoven with ideas, values, politics, class relationships, and the shifting boundaries of public and private life. The local distribution of leasehold and freehold property was a major determinant of the economic life and social structure of most Victorian towns and cities, often at least as important as more obvious factors such as access to markets, raw materials and supplies of labour. A shared sense of proprietorship was an important element in a shared sense of social class; and the blurring of the distinction between different types of property (particularly land and investment capital) was an important element in the reformulation of class identity in late nineteenth-century Britain. The laws relating to property had an important bearing on personal and family ties, and upon an individual's relationship to the community and the state. A vision of property as the first prerequisite of civic virtue lay at the heart of the ancient political system that was under siege in Britain between 1870 and 1914; and new forms of property right which emerged during the period—often in the form of a statutory claim upon the state—were subtly transforming the character of British society and the balance of power between different social groups. Work itself was often viewed as a species of property right, both explicitly in the Labour Party's 1908 Right to Work bill and, more diffusely, in the view of many a worker that 'a job is, as it were, his property . . . he must hold it against all comers.' Beliefs about property were never uncontroversial, but attitudes to property that in 1870 had been widely accepted as axiomatic were by the 1900s highly contentious and the focal point of national political debate.

What were the main areas of change, and how and why did such changes come about? One area in which change was remarkably limited (remarkable in view of the wider changes occurring in society at large) was the formal structure of private property law. In 1914 as in 1870 personal property continued to be largely governed by freedom of contract, real property by a mixture of free contract and more archaic, quasi-feudal principles. Throughout the period there were spasmodic demands for technical reforms such as registration of title, the assimilation of real and personal property law and the simplification of conveyancing, but these largely foundered on the hostility or apathy of the legal profession. By the 1880s the earlier, utilitarian impulse for law reform had largely spent itself, leaving the law to settle into a more conservative mould. This is not to say that legal authorities always endorsed politically conservative causes: on the contrary, there were some striking examples of clashes of judicial opinion, and of case-law endorsing a radical point of view. In the debate on the licensing laws, for example, judges refused to endorse the claim that publicans' licences were a form of absolute property right. And in the famous case of *Bradford Corporation* v. *Pickles* (often seen as the apogee of judicial support for private property rights), the Court of Appeal clearly supported the claims of the community *against* the individual owner—before the rights of property were reasserted by the House of Lords. By contrast with the early Victorian period, however, law followed rather than created the movement of public opinion. As Dicey remarked in 1905, it was a standing paradox that land and housing in an advanced industrial, urban and democratic society remained subject to a cluster of rules and practices largely inherited from an aristocratic, pre-industrial age.

Pressure for change did not come from within the law, but from wider political, intellectual, and structural changes within British society. Perhaps the most fundamental change was the gradual severance of property, and particularly of landed property, from its age-old connection with political rights. This effectively began with the Representation of the People Act 1867, which conferred the parliamentary vote in English borough constituencies on male heads of household and certain categories of lodger. As was argued in Chapter 1, this act was originally conceived as a highly traditional measure. Its provisions were confined to those who had sufficient stake in their dwelling-places to pay their own rates; and it was designed to graft on to the ancient constitution the mid-nineteenth-century virtues of 'economic independence' and 'good character' as honorary forms of property. Such a compromise proved highly unstable, however, and by the early 1870s a series of largely arbitrary legal decisions was opening up the franchise to many elements in society who were neither ratepayers nor householders in the sense envisaged in 1867. The same franchise was extended to all parts of the United Kingdom in 1884; and shifts in the same direction were evident in the lifting of the franchise disqualification from recipients of Poor Law medical relief in 1885, in the extension of the lodger vote to Poor Law and local government in 1894, and in the introduction of salaries for MPs in 1912. The process was not complete until after the First World War, and throughout the period ownership or tenancy of property continued to be an indispensable qualification for many forms of public office.* Fear of the erosion of property rights—and fear also of a takeover of politics by political adventurers—formed a powerful barrier to the introduction of a straightforward universal suffrage, which would have tripled the size of the working-class electorate. Nevertheless, a powerful wedge had been driven into the largely axiomatic assumption that defence of property rights was the prime purpose and function of the British constitution and of organized political life. A major consequence of this change was a slow transformation of the personnel of British politics. In 1870 and indeed right down to the early 1900s high politics was still dominated by aristocratic statesmen who saw political life as an appendage of and justification for the ownership of land. Such men were still prominent in both major parties in 1914, but in both they were being ousted, not so much by industrialists and entrepreneurs as by the men who relied on public office as a form of professional income. After centuries of amateur rule by 'an aristocracy of independent gentlemen', British government at the end of the period was beginning to exhibit many features of the system of 'politics as a vocation', identified a few years later by Max Weber as one of the touchstones of the modern age.

Linked with these trends was a metamorphosis in the part played by property in political conflict. Property had of course never been far from the centre of debate throughout Britain's political history. Early Victorian disputes on such issues as free trade, currency, and Church reform had all involved competing conceptions of property rights. Down to 1870, however, few within the mainstream of British politics would have questioned the absolute legitimacy of private property; differences had centred instead upon the degree of priority to be given to different forms of property (land versus capital) and upon whether a 'natural' distribution was best achieved by inheritance and historic entitlement or by a competitive market. Conservative opinion tended towards the former principle, radical-liberal opinion towards the latter—the division being exemplified by the Cobdenite-utilitarian campaign to smash aristocratic privilege by 'free trade in land'. Attack on aristocratic monopoly continued to be a live, indeed burning, issue in radical politics right down to 1914; but from the late

* Municipal corporation and county councillors, for example, had to own real or personal property worth £1,000, or be liable for rates on property with a rateable value of £30 a year.

1860s onwards other aspects of the property debate began to jump around upon the political compass. As early as 1865 the usually *laissez-faire* economist Henry Fawcett called for state intervention to prevent the 'anti-social' use of land and to promote small proprietorship. The rationalization of outdated charities by the Charity Commissioners—a favourite progressive cause of the 1830s—was by the 1870s increasingly viewed by radical opinion as a middle-class usurpation of the property rights of the poor. A select committee of 1869 bore witness to a growing Liberal disenchantment with the enclosure movement, which had too often lacked 'a full and accurate knowledge of the wants and wishes of the labouring poor'. And early in the 1870s J. S. Mill's denunciation of enclosure (a cause previously much favoured by utilitarian theorists) signalled a marked shift of radical opinion away from individual property rights towards a more communitarian perspective. Such sentiments gathered momentum with the advance of Birmingham-style municipal socialism, and with Henry George's claim that 'site-values' were wholly the creation of the surrounding community rather than of individual proprietors. On a broader front later editions of Mill's *Principles of Political Economy* moved from attacking hereditary privilege towards questioning the justice and efficiency of a purely market-based distribution of resources. The 'New Liberal' philosophy which emerged at the turn of the century enunciated two distinct doctrines on the subject of property-ownership: on the one hand all human beings needed a basic minimum of private property, as an indispensable medium of 'self-realization'; on the other hand, all property (not just land) included a substantial input of communal production and was therefore subject to the overarching claims of the community and the state. Such shifts of opinion graphed the transformation of the Liberal Party in the 1890s and 1900s into the party of 'redistribution', critical of extremes of both poverty and wealth.

Conservatism meanwhile moved in a different direction, increasingly becoming the creed not merely of landed and hereditary property but of absolute property rights in whatever form. As part of this process 'freedom of contract crossed the floor of the House', and in Conservative polemic of the 1890s large landed estates were increasingly defended in terms of a rational allocation of market resources rather than the principle of heredity. Such was the central thesis of conservative intellectuals such as W. H. Mallock and the Duke of Argyll, and of right-wing pressure groups like the Liberty and Property Defence League. Simultaneously, and not altogether consistently, Conservative opinion increasingly emphasized the value of property less as an economic than as a social principle, the widespread diffusion of small proprietorship being seen as the most effective 'rampart' against democratic spoliation. Such an impulse could be seen in Bateman's critique of primogeniture, in Lord Randolph Churchill's espousal of leasehold enfranchisement in the early 1880s and, shortly before the First World War, in the enthusiasm of the Tory Social Reform Group for state-subsidized home-ownership. In this respect, no less than in support for freedom of contract and a free market, late Victorian and Edwardian Conservatism inherited a view of property originally espoused by radical Liberalism half a century before.

Unsurprisingly, the interaction of ideas about property with day-to-day politics was more complex and less unilinear than political theory or polemic might suggest. Throughout the period there were social, economic, and administrative pressures operating upon all governments that largely constrained public attitudes to property and blurred the distinctive perspectives of the different political parties. Moreover, it was a period in which fluidity of political thought was matched by fluidity of political allegiance. Joseph Chamberlain, who in the 1880s had even-handedly attacked both hereditary privilege and freedom of contract ('the convenient cant of selfish wealth'), could find himself a decade later in alliance with the owners of vast ground-rents; whilst in the 1900s a sprig of the landed aristocracy like Winston Churchill could find himself at the spearhead of advanced liberalism. It was a Conservative government that in 1875 first conferred upon local councils the right of compulsory purchase in the interests of public health, though as Sir Assheton Cross told the House of Commons in introducing this measure, 'I do not suppose that any Hon. Member will think that town councils should have the power of taking other people's property without compensation.' Similarly, it was a Conservative enactment—the 1897 Workmen's Compensation Act—that began the process of creating new contingent property rights through the medium of statutory social welfare. And it was a Conservative government that in 1899 shocked orthodox legal opinion by allowing the trustees of settled property to sell land at less than the market price, provided that such land was used to build housing for the working classes. By contrast there were certain Liberal policies of the period that strongly reinforced the traditional view that individual claims to property had precedence over those of the community, a principle seen most clearly in tax remissions for life assurance premiums (a legacy from the 1850s), for landlords' repairs (1894), and for support of dependent children (1909). Members of both parties supported the principle of tax relief for mortgage interest payments, introduced by the Conservatives in 1899. Within the Labour movement attitudes to property were equally ambivalent. Labour opinion in the late 1900s strongly opposed any suggestion that land reform in England should proceed on the lines adopted in Ireland, on the ground that small proprietorship would subvert the ultimate goal of land nationalization; but a few years earlier part at least of the Labour movement's case against the Taff Vale decision had centred upon defence of the property rights embodied in trade union funds. Such attitudes and policies confound any attempt to confine the social history of property within strict party or ideological lines.

Nevertheless, throughout the period contemporaries perceived a gradually widening gap between the underlying attitudes to property held by the two major parties. More than any other single factor the lurking suspicion that the Liberals were no longer 'sound' on defence of property rights accounted for the continual haemorrhage of large, medium and small property-owners out of Liberalism and into Conservatism between 1867 and 1914. For the most part, substantive Conservative policies in defence of property were cautious and passive; they consisted mainly in adhering to positions which many had believed to be common ground between the two parties in the mid-Victorian years. Certain measures were introduced to defend the landed interest, such as the partial de-rating of agricultural land in 1897; and within the rank and file of the Conservative party there was much support for reciprocal tariffs and a bimetallic currency (both of which would have entailed state intervention to devalue some species of property and to upgrade others). But, in spite of much diehard discontent, there was nothing to parallel the massive social and fiscal 'aristocratic reaction' that occurred in many Continental countries as a response to the agricultural depression. Until the abortive movement for tariff reform in the mid-1900s Conservative orthodoxy largely defined itself as a critique of Liberal heresy and a warding off of radical attack.

By comparison, Liberal policies were more innovative and aggressive. From the 1860s onwards Liberal espousal of Irish tenant-right, embodied in the principles of fair rent, free sale and fixity of tenure, threatened a two-pronged attack upon both residual feudal privilege and the more modern, positivistic principle of 'absolute' rights of ownership. The Irish Land Acts of 1870 and 1881, which imposed statutory rent control and compelled landlords to compensate tenants for improvements, were seen as tantamount to expropriation—which, given the subsequent unsaleability of Irish land, was what in fact they were. Similar principles were perceived in the expansionist and high-spending policies pursued by Liberal and Progressive local authorities, in the extension of powers of compulsory purchase under the Allotments Acts, in Liberal attacks on mineral rights and game preserves and, above all, in the evolution of Liberal policies towards direct taxation. Only a minority of Liberals supported the radical and socialist campaign for land nationalization, but by the 1900s the vast majority supported taxation of site values, a principle which denied any validity to the concept of 'mere ownership' of land. On a broader front, the introduction of 'graduation' into death duties (1894) and income tax (1907) seemed to extend the challenge to property rights from landed property to property in general. The two strands of Liberal taxation theory came together in the Budget of 1909, which introduced a supertax on incomes over £5,000 and a new succession duty on estates passing at death, and proposed the compulsory assessment of site values. The result was the rejection of the Budget by the peers, two general elections resulting in two hung Parliaments, and the eventual passage of the Parliament Act of 1911, which severely curtailed the powers of the House of Lords. Competing conceptions of property and anxiety over property rights thus lay at the heart of the most severe political and constitutional crisis of the late Victorian and Edwardian age.

5

Work

I. WORK AND GENTILITY

Addiction to work has often been portrayed as the most characteristic of
Victorian attitudes and values, and certainly there is no lack of evidence about
the centrality of work in many Victorian lives. Economists viewed it as the
ultimate source of wealth, moralists as diverse as Ruskin and Samuel Smiles
prescribed it as man's highest earthly calling, and for the vast majority of men
and women it was an indispensable prerequisite of physical survival. In the
1900s no less than in the 1870s or the 1840s, having a foothold in the labour
market was for most people a far more powerful determinant of economic
viability and social status than any other factor in their lives (far more
important than possession of property or access to the vote). Though the hours
worked by women and children were limited by statute, the freedom of an
adult male to work as hard and as long as he wished was viewed for most of the
nineteenth century as a cardinal tenet of civil liberty; and at all levels of society
from Mr Gladstone down to the humblest labourer examples could be found of
men and women who regularly worked for eighteen hours a day. 'One more
day's work for Jesus', sang the little matchbox girls in *The Bitter Cry of Outcast
London* in 1883. *Blessed be Drudgery* proclaimed the title-page of one of the
most widely circulated volumes of Victorian sermons, originally delivered in
the 1850s but reissued nearly every year until the 1880s and still in print in
1903. And for many, work was not merely an economic imperative and a
moral duty but an all-absorbing psychological passion. 'The majority of
Englishmen have no life but their work', commented Mill in the 1860s. 'That
alone stands between them and their *ennui*.'

Yet, paradoxically, work was also frequently viewed in a very different light, either as merely instrumental to some other goal or as tainted with inferiority, bondage and lack of access to culture, status, and power. Social theorists who stressed the 'perpetual dignity and nobleness' of work (Carlyle's phrase) were nevertheless uneasily troubled by the utilitarian suspicion that human beings would *not* work unless it was in their interest to do so—unless spurred on by marginal advantage or by shame and fear of starvation. No less paradoxically, the glorification of work was always in latent conflict with the counter-attractions of leisure, education and gentility. In what Marx had ironically called 'capitalist anthropology', men were exhorted to work to the limits of their capacity and yet were held in low esteem for being able to do nothing else. 'We feel and regret that work, instead of being honoured as noble, is too often looked down upon as degrading', recorded the Working Ladies' Guild, a body that struggled to open up what had hitherto been seen as exclusively masculine occupations to impoverished gentlewomen and women of the lower-middle class. A study in 1895 deplored the persistence of the 'old stigma attaching to the workman or the factory hand', and numerous contemporary reports bore witness to the fact that the most toil-ridden occupations were those of most menial status. Not until the 1890s was there any serious questioning of the view, clearly spelt out in the writings of Austin and Bagehot and central to the old aristocratic theory of the constitution, that active engagement in earning a living (either as an employer or as a labourer) was a positive disqualification for public life; and right down to 1914 there was widespread belief in the need for a leisured class to fulfil the political and ceremonial functions of the nation.

Such attitudes were pervasive at all levels of society. Throughout the later nineteenth century, affluent working men, who would have thought it shameful not to work themselves, were registering their new-found prosperity by withdrawing their wives and daughters from the labour market. A journeyman who completed an apprenticeship would regard it as a first charge upon his income 'to make his mother comfortable . . . and relieve her from any further necessity of labour for hire'. And among the middle classes—reputedly the *locus classicus* of the work ideal—puritanical addiction to work increasingly competed with expanding private incomes, fears about loss of status, the opening up of 'high society', and increasing opportunities for fashion, travel, cultivation, and pleasure. The titanic endeavours of Samuel Smiles's engineers must be set against the attitudes of bankers like Lord Rothschild, who feared that too strenuous a commitment to business duties might erode the confidence of aristocratic clients. Unlike Mill, Taine in 1870 believed that most Englishmen worked not as an end in itself but as a means of purchasing entertainment and comfort. In the late Victorian factory, dreams of 'windfalls' that would enable the dreamers to 'get out of the shop' and 'set themselves up' or 'go upon the turf' were no less common than they were a century later. Snobbish disdain for work was not unknown even among the very poor: when Beatrice Webb investigated London's sweated trades she found many grossly overworked and ill-paid women who insisted that they worked for pin-money and not from necessity. Pride in *not* working, or in not being 'obliged to work', were just as much variants of Victorian culture as moral exhortation to work and work as a psychological obsession.

Such an odd conjunction of contradictory attitudes suggests that there was no such thing as a homogeneous Victorian 'work ethic': on the contrary, outlook and practice varied enormously between different classes, different sectors and strata of workers, different industrial communities, and different individuals within the same workplace. Generalizations which may have held good for the 1840s (when average per capita incomes were still barely above subsistence) were not necessarily true of the 1870s, and still less so of the period down to 1914. Analysts who tried to construct a general sociology of work—such as Marx in the 1860s, Charles Booth and the Webbs in the 1890s—all foundered upon a patchwork quilt of almost infinite variety. Within a single occupation, hours of work, practical techniques, methods of recruitment, physical hazards, and division of labour between the skilled and unskilled—the whole custom, language and philosophy of working life—could vary profoundly, as in the contrasting cultures of the coalmining communities of South Wales and of Northumberland and Durham. Agricultural labourers who in the south of England were a profoundly depressed and poverty-stricken class, in the north were a much more independent and affluent group, jauntily conscious of their market value. Women's work was governed by different norms and traditions from that of men, and again varied widely in apparently similar settings. In weaving, for example, women were often highly skilled workers in their own right, whereas in cotton-spinning they were usually unskilled appendages to a male labour aristocracy. The most important aspect of women's work—housework—was scarcely acknowledged as genuine work at all until just before the end of the period, though it was the nation's largest single occupation.

Such variety may imply that a wholly adequate history of work can be written, if at all, only at the level of the individual farm, factory, home, office, or workshop. Yet the very centrality of work as a pillar of social, economic, and moral life makes it imperative to fit the conditions and experience of work into some wider social context. Contemporary observers between 1870 and 1914 continually puzzled and wrangled over the problems posed by the interaction of 'life and labour', problems which have vexed and divided historians of labour ever since. Was labour the sole source of wealth (and therefore the object of continuous expropriation) or was it symbiotic with capital? Did the advance of machinery and organization enhance or diminish personal skills and human freedom? Was British labour increasing, decreasing, or stagnating in output and efficiency? Was the degree of a person's skill, or some other factor, the main determinant of income, class, and status? Was work in the eyes of workers merely instrumental to gaining a living, or was it inextricably bound up with personal and social identity? This chapter will review the structure and evolution of work in Britain between 1870 and 1914, concentrating particularly on the context and organization of work; on evidence of popular attitudes to work; on changing patterns of employer–worker relations; and on the interaction of work with class and social structure.

II. STRUCTURE, SKILL, AND ORGANIZATION

The last three decades of the nineteenth century are sometimes portrayed as the period of the 'second industrial revolution': a period in which advanced technology, heavy capitalization, mass-production techniques, and large-scale organization of work increasingly encroached upon the relatively simple and small-scale processes of the Industrial Revolution proper. As a social and physical phenomenon manufacturing industry reached its flood-tide, a higher proportion of the labour force being engaged in manufacture in 1901 than at any earlier or later date. The horsepower of British industry increased from 2 million in 1870 to 10 million in 1907. Manufacture of textiles—the 'leading sector' of earlier industrialization—was rapidly outstripped by the much more heavily capitalized mining and metallurgical industries and heavy engineering. Although family ownership of firms remained common, there was from the 1860s a continual growth in limited liability companies, often employing professional managers; and the 1890s saw a wave of 'amalgamations' in British industry, designed to achieve monopolistic control of markets and economies of scale. In many industries the highly personalized craft skills employed by the early stages of industrialization were giving way to electrically powered tools, production lines, machine-minding, and semi-skilled employment; and from the 1880s onwards the growing cost-consciousness of employers in the face of rising international competition led to increased emphasis on output, productivity, scientific incentive schemes, and managerial supervision. State regulation of safety and conditions at work—previously confinèd to coalmines and textile factories—was extended in 1878 to all establishments employing mechanical power, and in 1891 to small workshops and (tentatively) to outworkers. Simultaneously the growth of cities, communications, Empire, and international trade generated whole new areas of 'service' employment, of a kind that had scarcely existed in the earlier stages of industrialization. Between 1871 and 1911 employment in transport, clerical, commercial, and retail occupations increased fourfold, transport alone constituting the country's second largest male employment sector by the turn of the century. While gross national product increased by 150 per cent, the financial services sector increased by 1,100 per cent. In nearly all spheres the penetration of market forces at the expense of custom was far more rapid and all-embracing than it had been half a century earlier. Provincial towns which in the 1870s were still largely dealing in the goods of their agricultural hinterland were by 1914 exchanging the produce of the globe. Local fluctuations in demand for labour had progressively gelled into national and international cycles of boom and depression, the latter accompanied by the newly conceptualized problem of 'unemployment'. Free trade had won its political triumphs in the 1840s and 1850s; but in economic, social, and cultural terms its full impact on British society was not felt until more than a generation after the epic Corn Law repeal of 1846.

What impact did such changes make upon the day-to-day organization of work and the structure of employment? At a superficial level many of the changes wrought by advanced industrialization were surprisingly limited and slow. Agriculture and domestic service continued throughout the period to be the two largest sectors of employment (though both of them dwindled as a percentage of the workforce). In spite of the growth in the size of firms, the gigantic industrial complexes envisaged by Marx in 1866 remained wholly untypical of British industry. Only six industrial firms employed more than 10,000 workers in the year 1900, and most of these were scattered among numerous small factories and workshops. Moreover, large firms grew in tandem with rather than at the expense of small workshops, many of the latter newly emerging in the last quarter of the nineteenth century to supply accessories and unfinished goods to larger establishments. Coal companies often employed thousands of men, but within those companies the typical individual colliery employed about 300. Smallness of size was often accompanied by archaic and piecemeal methods of organization. Throughout the period the most usual contract of employment in all trades except agriculture and domestic service was terminable at a week's notice or less. Hiring fairs waned in the 1870s and 1880s, while employment bureaux flourished in the 1890s and 1900s. At all times, however, the commonest methods of finding work were customary and idiosyncratic: private tip-offs, employer patronage, favouritism from foremen, trade union and family connections, personal application at the factory gate.

Technological change, for all its far-reaching extent, was variable and patchy. In textiles, for example, there was very limited technical innovation after the 1880s, when the last substantial residue of hand-loom weavers was sucked into factory production. In the Potteries some potbanks were revolutionized by the introduction of the 'jolly' and the 'jigger', which led to the substitution of unskilled women for skilled men; but others remained almost wholly unmechanized. In printing, linotype machines were first introduced in the 1880s, but were not in general use until just before 1914. In the Edwardian mining industry, collieries employing electrically powered drills and lifts existed side by side, often at the same coalface, with collieries still reliant on rope, pony, pick and shovel. In some industries, such as Sheffield steel, advanced machine tools were simply grafted on to a highly archaic workshop organization. In the clothing industry the arrival of the sewing-machine gave a massive new lease of life to small-scale production in both workshop and home.

Moreover, despite continual concern about the debasement of skills and the decline of apprenticeships, skilled employment in the economy as a whole was, if anything, considerably more prevalent at the end of the period than at the beginning. Over 40 per cent of male manual workers were classed as skilled in 1911, compared with one-seventh in the later 1860s; while those with intermediate skills declined from one-half to 43 per cent, and the unskilled from 36 per cent to 15 per cent. Throughout the period British industry in nearly all sectors was remarkably 'skill intensive' and invested a much higher proportion of its resources in 'human capital' than its American and Continental rivals. In spite of the growth of machinery the 1907 Census of Production revealed that many functions both skilled and unskilled were still being performed by hand that could in principle have been done by machinery: the practice of 'washing the coals' in the mining and coking industries was a striking example. Though there were wide variations in different sectors, average pay differentials between skilled and unskilled workers did not markedly change between 1870 and 1914. Throughout the period function and status within occupational groups remained rigidly hierarchical. A study of the 1880s suggested that an unskilled workman would scarcely dare to converse with a skilled tradesman, far less to encroach upon his sphere of work. This sense of hierarchy was strongly conveyed by witnesses to the Royal Commission on Labour in 1893; and towards the end of the period Alfred Williams's description of the exclusiveness and status gradations among workers in the Great Western Railway works replicated almost exactly the account given of the 'inner life of the workshop' by Thomas Wright, the famous journeyman engineer, nearly fifty years before.

Such apparent continuities, however, masked some extensive and profound changes in industrial practice and occupational structure, though the nature of these changes varied in different trades. Although plant size remained small, over the period as a whole the factory replaced the work-shop as the typical and predominant unit of industrial production. Apparent statistical continuities in production concealed a great deal of underlying change and instability. Hours of work and levels of output fluctuated wildly, and the average life-span of firms was very short. The growth of production-line processes and of white-collar and retail employment precipitated what was at first an almost imperceptible change in the gender composition of the workforce. The proportion of women in full-time work declined by about 10 per cent between 1871 and 1901, and then began slowly to rise; but these overall figures masked a dramatic decline in agricultural work and a big increase in women's employment in factories, offices, and retail trades. Clerical employment for both men and women grew from an insignificant 100,000 workers in 1861 to a rapidly burgeoning three-quarters of a million in 1911; and office work, together with teaching, largely replaced small-scale ownership of capital as the main lift-shaft of upward social mobility. At the same time a complex conjunction of invisible social forces increasingly distinguished 'work' from the rest of social life. For those in regular employment, hours and con-ditions of work became much more regular and 'routinized'; whilst 'unemployment', seasonally endemic for all workers in a pre-industrial setting, became much more concentrated upon a (fluctuating) minority of the labour force. Growth in both the size of the workplace and the urban environment meant that the physical cleavage between work and home grew much wider. Few workers in 1914 enjoyed what many in 1870 took for granted: a home near their place of work (though this was partially compensated for by the arrival of the bus and the bicycle). Work also became much more age-specific: what protective legislation did for young children, increasing longevity and intensified machine-production did for the elderly by beginning to drive them out of the labour force. Though initially confined only to a minority of workers, the end of the century saw the emergence of the concept of 'retirement' as a new epoch in human life between work and death.

More immediately visible to contemporaries was the social impact of economic change upon particular industries and modes of employment. Throughout the period there were examples of formerly flourishing trades falling into decay under the impact of declining demand, shifting world trade routes, foreign tariffs, or international competition; such were the Thames shipbuilding industry in the 1860s and 1870s, the Welsh tin-plate industry in the 1890s, and the sugar-refining and glass-blowing industries in the 1900s. The London unemployment crisis of the 1880s was at least partly generated by the painful transition of London's small-scale engineering, clothing, leather goods, and furniture industries from craft to mass production. Case-studies of urban pauperism, casual labour and applications for unemployment relief nearly always found a significant minority of previously skilled workers who had been pressed downwards and outwards by the obsolescence of their former trades. The social composition of the London docks was a vivid graph of the incessant process of change and decay wrought by advanced capitalism. Most dramatic and far-reaching was the change in the scope and character of agricultural employment—not merely in the crude shrinkage of numbers employed, but in the whole culture and environment of work on the land. At the start of the period agriculture was still a predominantly familial occupation, much of the most routine work being performed by gangs of women and children. Though officially classed as 'unskilled', many agricultural tasks involved a wide range of archaic skills that were part of the residue of an earlier peasant economy. By 1914, however, women in agricultural areas had largely been sucked into suburban domestic service; family employment survived mainly in the form of casual work at harvest time and the annual exodus of East Londoners to the hopfields of Kent. Many farmers had either gone out of business or become increasingly gentrified and managerial. The traditional skills of the farm labourer had not wholly vanished, but they had been massively eroded by the piecemeal advance of machinery, the shift of acreage from cultivation to sport, and the growth of a mass retail food industry which made such practices as cider-pressing, gleaning, and pig- and beekeeping seem economically irrational and futile. As many Edwardian investigators discovered, in no other occupation was the destruction of custom and the proletarianization of the worker more relentless and total than among agricultural labourers, a fact reflected by their low status in the sight of the rest of the working class. 'They were called every sort of name', recalled a farm worker from Norfolk—'Jony Hodges, Clod Hoppers, Louts, any other low term that came to their tongues, by the rest of the Workers and the Town People.'

In most occupations, however, change in the character of work was more gradual and incremental, and it often took the form not of absolute de-skilling but of the substitution of new skills for old ones. In an industrial context there was still a 'labour aristocracy' in the 1900s, but its com-position and mental outlook was not identical to that of the 1860s, and in many trades the meaning and definition of skill had perceptibly changed. In 1867 a high proportion of skilled workers were men who had worked a seven-year indentured apprenticeship and who applied to an industrial setting a wide range of pre-industrial skills. Such men often made and mended their own tools and draughted their own designs, personally bridging the technological gap between the blacksmith's forge and the factory. But traditional apprenticeship was in decline from the early 1870s onwards, if not before—initially because journeymen found that they could command high wages without completing their training, later because the widespread application of machine tools rendered their skills increasingly redundant. A survey of 1895 recorded that only 'archaeological evidence' remained of many ancient trades. In many traditional crafts, such as cabinet-making, joinery, stonemasonry, and bookbinding, the work of the craftsman was increasingly reduced to fitting and 'finishing' a factory-made article; and by the 1900s owners of small workshops in these trades were more often small businessmen rather than the superior master-craftsmen of the previous generation. In a factory setting the skilled worker of the 1900s learned a 'process' rather than a 'trade': he performed a more limited and specialist range of functions, often after a shorter period of training, than his predecessor in the 1860s. Such a change did not necessarily involve a diminution of skill so much as a transformation of its character: the machine-tool maker, boiler-maker, riveter, and pattern-maker increasingly replaced the ex-blacksmith and generalist engineer of earlier phases of factory production. The changing structure of the economy also brought to the fore a new class of workers who were undoubtedly skilled, and who shared much of the craft pride and exclusiveness of the labour aristo-crat, and yet whose work did not require a formal apprenticeship: the work of miners, transport workers, and of many in the heavy metal-lurgical industries were examples. Where apprenticeship survived, it often did so not because it was intrinsically necessary but because it was fiercely defended by workers with obsolete skills as a means of enhancing their control over work processes and limiting entry to a trade.

Parallel changes occurred at other levels of skill and organization. Among the new class of Edwardian clerical workers only a small minority were engaged in the work of the 'confidential clerk' characteristic of the 1850s and 1860s, many more being engaged in routine processes of copying, shorthand and stenography. Among manual workers the 'less skilled' worker of the 1860s and 1870s was often a multifaceted handyman who could 'turn his hand to anything', whereas from the 1880s onwards he was usually a 'semi-skilled' worker who performed a single routine function on a mechanized production line. 'It requires no violent stretch of the imagination to conceive that in the near future there will be little work other than machine-making and machine-minding', commented a report on the engineering industry in 1895. Semi-skilled work was also prevalent in the new public utilities, where many workers migrated from unskilled to semi-skilled status, not because they had acquired new skills but because their work became more regular and carried an element of responsibility: railway guards, gas stokers, and bus conductors fell into this group. Jo the crossing-sweeper in Dickens's *Bleak House* would by 1900 have been a semi-skilled sanitary worker employed by the Holborn Borough Council or the Metropolitan Board of Works. The boundaries between semi-skilled and unskilled work were always blurred, and by the 1900s the latter term was being widely used to imply not so much lack of skill as lack of 'organization'—lack of regularity in methods of recruitment, in managerial and trade union control, and in hours of work. Stevedores and wharfingers, whose work was specialized, exclusive and organized, were classed as skilled or semi-skilled workers, while dock labourers, whose work was irregular and open to all comers, were perceived as the archetypal 'unskilled' class.

At the bottom of the occupational heap were many sweated and home workers who at first glance seem indistinguishable from those interviewed by Mayhew for the *Morning Chronicle* in the 1850s. But the studies of Beatrice Webb, David Schloss, and other turn-of-the-century investigators suggest that the semblance of continuity is in part a false one. Mayhew's rag-pickers, fur pullers, and street criers were largely self-employed survivors from the pre-industrial system, whereas the chain makers, box makers, and garment workers of the 1900s were more typically working for a petty capitalist on a mechanized or routinized process. They were making either cheap consumer goods for a mass retail market or 'unfinished' component parts for more advanced industrial production: in either case their work was essentially 'modern' rather than archaic. The same was true of casual dock labourers, porters, carriers, and others who eked out a precarious living by casual engagements: they were the marginal workers in a modern market economy rather than anachronistic survivals from an earlier economic age.

'Organization', a keyword in the social vocabulary of the Edwardian period, was symptomatic of another dimension of change, even—and indeed especially—among workers whose skills were preserved, enhanced, or created by technical innovation. Mass production and the large capital sums involved in heavy machinery together greatly intensified the premium upon good timekeeping, discipline, and regularity of work that had been characteristic of factory production since the start of the Industrial Revolution. Giant blast-furnaces and gas-coking ovens that could never be allowed to cool greatly extended the previously limited practice of working in shifts. The sheer noise of modern machinery curtailed much of the badinage, conviviality, and debate on topics high and low that had punctuated life in the workshop of the 1860s. What later became known as 'Taylorism' was relatively rare in British industry before 1914; even so, routinized processes generated a previously unknown degree of managerial direction and supervision. The role of the foreman—the worker promoted from the ranks to superintend the work of others—became increasingly important and socially problematic. Skilled craftsmen at the beginning of the period were sublimely unconscious of costs ('as remote as political economy in Saturn' commented one small businessman, George Bourne), but the low profit-margins of the 1880s made employers increasingly concerned with 'productivity' (a neologism of that decade). Throughout the period methods of calculating wages were so complex and variable as to defy generalization, but there was a general drift from time-rates to piece-rates, and a growth of the 'premium bonus' system, which tried to combine the two. Most of the new mechanized labour aristocrats were piece-workers at the time of the Census of Production in 1907.

Organizational change itself generated further changes in occupational structure. In the 1860s it was rare for any but the largest firms to employ more than a single double-entry bookkeeper, but by the end of the period many had acquired a white-collar establishment which performed the routine tasks of lower industrial management: record-keeping, calculation of wages, checking out stores, and (from 1912) deduction of contributions for National Insurance. Many areas of expertise that were crucial to business management and advanced industrial production—such as accountancy, surveying, and mechanical and structural engineering—became increasingly 'professionalized' during the period (Professor Harold Perkin has identified no fewer than seventy new professional organizations that were first set up between 1870 and 1918). At higher levels of management, organizational change was variable, and many economic historians have emphasized that limited liability, corporate ownership, and structural amalgamation often masked the continuance of small units of production, traditional rule-of-thumb methods, and family control. There can be no doubt, however, that although the average size of industrial plant remained quite small, an increasing proportion of the workforce was employed in large-scale organizations in which direct contact with employers and managers was virtually non-existent. Even in quite small workshops uneasy awareness of marginal costs was much more acute and pervasive in the Edwardian period than it had been forty years before.

III. Alienation, leisure, and the work ethic

How did changing patterns of work affect the social and mental life of working people? Popular comment in the 1860s and 1870s often portrayed the English worker as emotionally besotted with work, and as immensely more productive and industrious than his foreign rivals. Great ironmasters and railway promoters like Lowthian Bell and Thomas Brassey—major figures in European as well as British heavy industry of the period—found that the 'uniform accuracy of the English, their intelligence, their consummate mastery of all details of their art, and their resources in every difficulty have entirely established their superiority.' In skilled workshops working men set standards of excellence that were often higher than those of their masters. 'The only chance for me to make more profit would have been by lowering the quality of the output,' wrote one small businessman, 'and this the temper of the men made out of the question.' As late as 1899 a socialist journalist writing about Lancashire textile workers complained that their mental horizons were entirely confined to the world of work— 'they do not see that work is but a means to life.'

By contrast, much popular comment by the turn of the century was beginning to tell a very different story, a story of high labour costs, artificial restrictions on output, psychological estrangement from work— and the progressive dethronement of commitment to work by a burgeoning rival culture of commercialized leisure. Comparative studies of productivity, which in the early 1880s found that British workers still excelled their rivals in nearly all fields, found by the early 1890s that the gap was rapidly narrowing and that in some heavy industries (notably Yorkshire weaving and the South Wales coalfield) output per worker was actually lower than it had been twenty years before. Numerous Edwardian studies compared the apathy, absenteeism, and sports mania of the British workman with his Continental counterparts. 'The workman here is generally speaking of a much lower order than the foreigner and is accordingly less efficient', complained an employer to the 1906 Tariff Commission. 'He is less thrifty, takes less interest in his work, is fonder of outdoor amusements, is more addicted to drink and is altogether a less educated man than the foreigner . . . the average British workman . . . generally is more interested in the next football match and the nearest public house than he is in his work . . . some trades suffer much from St Monday.'

Contemporaries who sought an explanation for this putative change looked partly to the advance of trade-unionism (restrictive practices and the gearing of the standard rate to mediocre workers) and partly to the alienating pressures of modern industrial production. Numerous studies from the 1890s onwards emphasized the 'vulgarizing and stultifying' effect of mechanized production lines, the impersonal character of limited liability ownership, the stress induced by the premium bonus system, and the harassing impact of detailed managerial control. Workers themselves complained that employers would no longer permit them 'to do their best work, but compel them to take out the finish, smoothness and beauty, in order that they can get into the market cheap'. 'Can there be any wonder', asked a representative of the Amalgamated Society of Engineers in 1895, 'if they turn their attention, for the sake of a little excitement, to the ginshop, to gambling or horseracing and to all kinds of vice and folly?' George Bourne described the divided consciousness of the mechanized agricultural labourer, which he saw as no different from that of the desk-bound clerk: 'Between the two processes (work and play) a sharp line of division is drawn; and it is not until the clock strikes, and the leisure begins, that a man may remember he is a man and try to make a success of living.' Alfred Williams's classic study of the Swindon railway works drew a detailed picture of the 'deathlike vacuity' of work in large-scale manufacturing industry on the eve of the First World War: a picture of remote and insensitive management, bullying and officious foremen, a skiving workforce, hideous and insanitary surroundings, deafening noise, debased technical standards—and an almost total collapse of the intense workshop camaraderie of a generation before. Moreover, material and organizational change had wrought profound change in human relationships in the workplace. 'Many of those who remain have altered to such an extent under new conditions that I have sometimes wondered whether they are really the same who worked the night shift and jested with us in the years ago. So striking is the change that has taken place, not only in the administration, but in the very life and temper of the factory during the past decade.'

Such comment was so prevalent after the turn of the century as to suggest that some major transformation had indeed occurred—that the circumstances observed by Mill had given way to those prophesied by Marx, and that mid-Victorian addiction to work had been superseded by widespread apathy and alienation. The fractious condition of industrial relations in the period before the First World War might be taken as a pointer in the same direction. Dr Stedman Jones's study of London during the late Victorian period suggests that from 1870 onwards there was a rapid eclipse of an old, work-centred, artisan culture by a new, consumerist, working-class culture, focused not upon the workshop but upon the bookmaker, the music-hall and the pub. John Burnett's survey of working-class biographies concludes that, although there was little decline in the actual number of hours worked after the late 1870s, interest in work was becoming marginal in most working-class lives.

Other evidence, however, presents a more ambivalent picture, suggesting that attitudes to work were as variable as material conditions of work, and that the former were not always directly determined by the latter. Certain features of industrial life that were identified by Edwardian writers as of peculiarly recent growth had in fact been commonplace fifty years before. 'Lushingtons' and 'hard bargains' (i.e. heavy drinkers and layabouts) were no less common in the workshops of the 1860s than in the routinized factory system of the 1900s, while Edwardian worship of St Monday was a pale shadow of a practice that had been common in many sectors of the workforce at the start of the Victorian era. 'Getting disenchanted' was part of the industrial education of the indentured apprentice no less than of the semi-skilled machine operative. The labour force was not an undifferentiated national mass, but a jigsaw of local communities and trades with peculiar traditions of skill, discipline, initiative, and wider culture. Over the period as a whole both subjective responses to work discipline and objectively measured productivity varied widely in different communities (and sometimes in very similar ones, as could be seen in evidence to the Royal Commission on Labour, where employers in the coal industry gave diametrically opposite accounts of whether their men were more or less industrious and disciplined than thirty years before). In some industries the introduction of a Saturday half-holiday in the late 1860s and the nine-hour day in the 1870s had largely mopped up the problem of absenteeism; whereas in other industries shorter hours and greater opportunities for leisure merely compounded irregular attendance at work.

Similarly, in some communities higher real wages tended to enhance output, whereas in others it was a 'matter of earning just as much as will keep him per week, anything above that he spends in lost time.'

Moreover, not all international comparisons of quality and productivity in the latter half of the period told against British workers: British ship-builders in the 1890s were 30 per cent more productive than their French rivals, and a study of 1910 reported that, in German steelworks, three men were doing tasks that in England would have been done by one. Further-more, change over time was by no means unilinear. Complaints about the declining quality of workmanship were common in the 1860s and 1870s; British performance at international exhibitions of technology was more successful in the 1890s than in the 1860s; while a recent study of house-building suggests that (contrary to the oft-cited testimony of Robert Tressall's *The Ragged Trousered Philanthropists*) standards of workmanship among both craftsmen and labourers in the building industry were largely undiminished down to 1914. Even at the beginning of the period there were many Continental contractors who found that the Englishman's legendary appetite for work was more than outweighed by his obstreperous distaste for discipline and his 'intemperate and imprudent habits'. And—in spite of Edwardian diatribes against drink—drunkenness at work and the smuggling of alcohol on to industrial premises were far less common at the end of the period than they had been fifty years before.

Even within the minds of individual workers attitudes to work were often highly dualistic. The evidence of workers to the Royal Commission on Labour gave no hint of psychological estrangement from work, but if anything the contrary: an obsessive immersion in the minute technical details of work processes and workshop practice so narrowly focused as to preclude any wider grasp of the economics of industrial life. Restrictions on output often stemmed not from distaste for work but from its opposite: fear of unemployment and de-skilling and strong emotional attachment to well-tried industrial practices. Trade-unionists were often accused of limiting levels of output and 'keeping back smart men'; yet both formal trade-union rules and informal shop-floor practice were unsentimentally severe on men who failed to pull their weight. 'Ca'canny' and 'go-slows' were grass-roots protests against high standards imposed by trade unions no less often than against the exactions of employers. A major problem for would-be reformers of casual labour was not how to maintain incentives to work, but how to persuade casuals to forgo the extreme alternations of overwork and idleness characteristic of more archaic work practices, in favour of the more limited but regular work required by modern organizations. Among women workers there was a widespread desire to escape from paid employment into the home; but there were many significant exceptions to this rule—among them women who appeared to be some of the most exploited workers in the country. A report of 1904 on women in the Potteries commented on their passionate addiction 'to all the excitement and gossip of factory life . . . it is impossible not to be impressed by the universal preference among the women for factory over domestic life; and how depressed and out of health they became if they were obliged to remain at home.'

Moreover, not all workers regarded machinery as oppressive. On the contrary there were many who found it as exciting and addictive as older forms of technology; many who saw it as enhancing rather than detracting from their status, skills and earning power; and many who 'fondled and patted' their machines, endowing them with human qualities and Christian names. Craft resistance to production-line processes centred, nearly always, not upon machinery *per se* but upon the question of who should man and control it. Pride in personal skill took various and sometimes bizarre forms: in weaving, for example, there were workers who boasted of being able to complete all their tasks efficiently while reading a newspaper. Not all workers resented piecework and premium bonuses; indeed, David Schloss's studies of 1892−8 found that many groups of workers positively welcomed piecework as giving them greater freedom from supervision than timework, watched over by 'speeds and feedsmen'. The same was true of large-scale limited liability ownership: there was much nostalgic talk of the dwindling of personal contacts with masters, but many workers preferred the better physical conditions and diminished paternalism of the large-scale, impersonal factory.

Throughout the period there was undoubtedly a great expansion of commercially organized leisure, but again this interacted with work, community, and personal life in many different ways. Taine's comment on the mid-Victorians—that they worked excessively hard so as to get more out of their leisure—has already been noted. Subsequent foreign observers such as de Rousiers and Schulze-Gaevernitz portrayed leisure not as subversive of the work ethic but as an active ingredient in a work-centred culture. ('As an Englishman, Brown believes that in order to work well one must know how to amuse oneself from time to time', recorded de Rousiers of a Birmingham artisan.) The impact of mass leisure on the social structure of great cities was different from its impact in industrial villages and small towns. Whereas in the former it was one among many influences tending to dissolve community ties, in the latter—particularly in towns dominated by a single industry—it may well have helped to reinforce them. The studies of Patrick Joyce and Ross McKibbin have suggested that, far from dividing workers from their place of work, leisure pursuits were often closely connected with paid occupations. In many industrial towns football clubs, brass bands, works outings, and church-going were all part of a densely woven culture centring on the local pit or factory. A Newcastle collier recalled that the comradeship forged by 'terrible conditions' at work could be the seedbed of a highly active and integrated leisure culture. 'Down the pit appearing to be demonic, up above other qualities came out of them. The churches and chapels were full, the organs giving forth delightful music.' Even Alfred Williams, who constantly stressed the alienating impact of modern industrial production, found many examples of men whose occupational skill was also their chief domestic hobby (railway-carriage upholsterers, for example, spent all their spare time repairing furniture). Olive Malvery noted in the 1900s that no factory—even those employing only young girls—was without its 'starting-price bookmaker', and a common passion for sport and gambling was a central feature of the collective life of the workplace in many trades.

This intermingling of work and pleasure was often blamed by social investigators for Britain's waning industrial supremacy; but again there was little real evidence to support the view that productivity was inversely related to an interest in football and gambling. The opposite may even have been the case. The 1907 Census of Production found that the 'value added' by workers to the total industrial product was greatest in the south of England, where the penetration of commercial leisure was deepest, and lowest in Scotland, where the impact of the new leisure culture was comparatively weak. Puritanical addiction to work and exclusive absorption in the concerns of the workplace were often most pronounced in certain traditional industries where productivity was stagnant or declining. Conversely, two of the industries with the highest levels of productivity—the electrical goods industry and the armaments industry—were also those where employers complained most bitterly about high levels of absenteeism and the distractions of leisure and sport. It was perhaps no coincidence that the workers in Woolwich Arsenal—a plant characterized by extreme division of labour, high absenteeism, *and* high productivity—also produced what became the most famous southern football team of the Edwardian period.

IV. INDUSTRIAL RELATIONS

Patterns of work were integrally bound up with relationships between employers and employed; and although such relationships were highly variable and fragmented, this was a key area of social structure in which it is possible to identify several strands of dynamic and far-reaching change. At the start of the period the relation between employer and employed was seen as belonging essentially to the private domain. Except when industrial conflicts erupted into violence and civil disorder, 'the State had no interest in upholding the one at the expense of the other', affirmed the Royal Commission on the Law of Master and Servant in 1874. In the early 1870s only 4 per cent of the labour force (covering perhaps one-tenth of skilled workers) belonged to trade unions, and many of these were unstable and transient associations unrecognized by employers. Trade-unionism as such had been legal since 1824, but throughout the early and mid-Victorian period many of the practices by which unions pursued their generic ends—such as strikes, picketing, and the exclusion of non-members—had fallen foul of the laws against restraint of trade and civil conspiracy. By 1870 collective bargaining was beginning to emerge in a few trades, but by and large the process of hammering out wages and conditions of work was localized, customary, and rule-of-thumb. A few trade-unionists still harboured Chartist visions of a more synoptic role for labour, but the vast majority largely accepted capitalism on its own terms and sought merely to work the market system for the benefit of the skilled worker.

Since the 1850s, employers had also been joining together in shadowy combinations; but at all levels of industry the role of the typical mid-Victorian employer was a highly personalized and idiosyncratic one. Great charismatic entrepreneurs like Joseph Whitworth and Thomas Brassey often acted as their own site or works managers; whilst at the other end of the scale the proprietors of small workshops laboured side by side with their own employees. In a rural context the novels of Thomas Hardy accurately recorded the close-knit and fluid relationship that often obtained between masters and their superior workers in agriculture and in small country towns. Relations between such men and their employees were often rough and harsh (more so than later in the century), but, culturally if not financially, the social space between them was narrow: they spoke with the same regional accents, shared the same highly localized provincial identity, worshipped at the same chapels, and often addressed each other by Christian names. Opportunities for upward mobility from worker to employer varied widely from region to region and from industry to industry, and were possibly greater in the boom of the early 1870s than at any time earlier or later in the nineteenth century. The inflated demand of those years also gave rise to a rash of workers' co-operatives and profit-sharing schemes, few of which survived the depression of the 1880s.

Outright ownership of capital, however, was only one among many of the flying buttresses that linked workers to the central edifice of private capitalism, and throughout the mid-Victorian period the aspirations of the bulk of workers were not geared to wider control over the means of production but to control over the immediate circumstances of their own work. In nearly all branches of the manufacturing, extractive, and construction industries 'subcontracting' in one form or another was almost universal—an arrangement which (according to one recent study) gave to many workers a personal independence, experience of management, and sense of identification with the whole manufacturing process that they could never have hoped to acquire from formal ownership. In certain major industries, such as Lancashire textiles in the 1860s and the Durham coalfield in the 1880s, workers and employers forged a close relationship of mutual dependence and obligation that presented a striking contrast to the industrial anomie and conflict described by Engels and Disraeli a generation before. Fiercely negotiated industrial disputes were fought out by a semi-ritual process, in which both employers and workers tacitly connived at the goals of the other side. Contemporaries identified this new relationship as a form of industrial 'feudalism', and feudal it indeed was in the limited but literal sense that, within the wider constraints imposed by the market, workers had transformed the shop-floor into a largely self-governing fief. Within this fief skilled workers enjoyed a high degree of productive autonomy and day-to-day control over wages and the workload: they regulated entry to a trade, trained apprentices and adolescent recruits, prescribed the division of labour between skilled and unskilled, frequently nominated their own foremen, and—in some extreme cases—refused to perform any part of their work in the presence of an owner or manager. Similar freedoms were claimed, and often obtained, even in less paternalist and less highly organized trades, like building. Such limited but powerful autonomy formed the bedrock of what many historians have seen as the mid-Victorian 'bargain' between capital and labour. Clearly it was a limited bargain in that it excluded the majority of the workforce (the unskilled, casuals, women, and juveniles) and was predicated upon historically unique conditions of unchallenged industrial supremacy. But it was of crucial importance in determining the character both of attitudes to work and of wider industrial relations over many subsequent decades.

Many features of this mid-Victorian bargain survived in recognizable and even expanded form down to 1914. The new labour aristocracy of the early twentieth century was no less committed than its more archaic predecessor to workshop autonomy, control over recruitment, and freedom from managerial control. With a few notable exceptions on both sides, workers and employers shared a common prejudice against formal technical education of the kind increasingly common on the Continent; a preference for 'learning on the job' and 'getting one's hands dirty on the shop-floor' was far more characteristic of industrial culture in this period than any decline in the national 'industrial spirit'. With the advance of limited liability ownership, personal employer paternalism dwindled but was replaced in many instances by a new form of corporate paternalism, which saw security of employment and company welfare schemes as an integral part of modern industrial management. Though subcontracting probably declined from the 1880s, it was still widespread in the 1900s—officially condemned, but generally acquiesced in, by the trade unions. Legislation of the 1870s freed the unions from the charge of being 'in restraint of trade', protected their funds from actions in tort, legalized strikes and peaceful picketing, and generally buttressed the unions' position as a normal and legitimate feature of social and industrial structure. The 1880s and 1890s saw a widespread growth of voluntary arbitration agreements (reinforced by the Conciliation Act of 1896) and of sliding-scale agreements, whereby the unions agreed to wage adjustments in accordance with the state of trade and the prevailing level of prices. German observers such as Paul Duckershöff and Dr Schulze-Gaevernitz, writing in the 1890s, were forcibly struck by the relative tranquillity of British industrial relations, by the common culture and shared perspectives of employers and workers, and by the detachment of industrial disputes from wider political conflict. 'Several thousand pitmen were present but no police', wrote Duckershöff in evident amazement after attending a miners' gala in Newcastle. And a marxian study of 1904, which compared the life of British workers with that of their French counterparts, concluded that Britain was much more socially divided than France in domestic life and in the public sphere, but that British workers enjoyed much more autonomy and status in the context of daily work. The growth of organized collective-bargaining arrangements (which by 1911 covered a quarter of the labour force) and sliding-scale agreements, and the spread of conciliation and arbitration arrangements may all be seen as evidence of the continuing symbiotic relationship between capital and labour initially forged in the mid-Victorian years.

From the 1870s onwards, however, the mid-Victorian bargain was under pressure, both from changing external circumstances and from its own inherent limitations. The increased scale of production and of social organization, the relative decline of local and provincial community life, the creeping gentrification of certain sections of the manufacturing class and the spread of institutions that tended to formalize class divisions—all tended to erode the somewhat rough-and-ready cultural and functional proximity of employer and worker in the mid-Victorian years. The economic boom and high money wages of the early 1870s, followed by the recession and growing international competition of the 1880s, constituted fertile ground for industrial conflict. Some of the fiercest disputes of the late Victorian period were triggered off not by pressure for wage advances but by worker resistance to wage cuts in the face of falling prices (such as the cotton lockout of 1887 and the coal strike of 1893). The new technology of the 1880s and, even more, new methods of managing that technology constituted a major challenge to the self-regulating workshop of the 1860s, an issue which lay at the heart of such disputes as the engineers' lockout of 1897. Some employers bought industrial peace either by eschewing technological change altogether or by conceding to workers who operated the new system the same privileges and status as they had enjoyed under the old; but in many industries the employers' 'right to manage' became an endemic, if often ill-acknowledged, flashpoint in the evolution of industrial relations.

Union recognition was another potent source of industrial disputes. The Royal Commission on Labour in the early 1890s found that most employers now accepted trade-unions in skilled trades and indeed welcomed their co-operation in recruitment, training, work discipline, and general promotion of industrial stability. But the 'new unionism' among unskilled workers which had come to the fore with the Great London Dock Strike of 1889 was another matter. Combination among the unskilled seemed to many employers to be nothing more than an artificial creation of scarcity—a scarcity, moreover, which rested on no intrinsic skill and could therefore be defended only by intimidation and mass picketing. It was to break combinations among the unskilled that some employers launched in the 1890s what became known as the 'employers' offensive', a strategy based on the setting up of powerful employers' federations, the hiring of 'free labour' to break strikes, and challenge through the courts to picketing, the closed shop and ultimately (in the Taff Vale case of 1901) to the immunity of trade union funds.

These conflicts were accompanied by a widespread explosion in the sheer size and scope of potential industrial confrontation. The enormous growth of the labour force in mining, transport, and public utilities meant that strikes in these sectors could bring the rest of the economy to a halt in a way that had never been envisaged in the mid-Victorian era. The growth of scale also affected institutional aspects of employer–worker relations: the formation of powerful employers' federations in a number of key industries from the early 1890s was the counterpoint to growing structural amalgamation within the trade union movement (the Cardroom Weavers' Amalgamation of 1886, the Miners' Federation of 1889, the Transport Workers' Federation of 1911). Trade union amalgamations were nearly always confined to workers within a single grade of skill, but within these limits they increasingly sought to shift the locus of wage-bargaining from the district to the regional or even national level, regardless of local prices or the profitability of individual firms. In the 1900s a majority of trade unions were still very market-oriented; but some trade-unionists had moved beyond trying to exact the maximum that could be squeezed out of the market, towards asserting the view that wages should be a 'first charge' on industry, regardless of market conditions. Such a view was implicit in the Edwardian campaign against 'sweating', in the demand of the Miners' Federation for a minimum wage, and in the textile strikes of 1910, when spinners sought to terminate the 1893 Brooklands sliding-scale agreement even though most mills during the depression of the late 1900s were running at a substantial loss.

In the process industrial relations moved slowly but inexorably out of the private and into the public domain, a transition regretfully but far-sightedly acknowledged by Gladstone during the labour troubles of 1893. From the mid-1880s onwards the government through the medium of the Board of Trade began to collect far-reaching statistical data about industrial conflicts, and a publicly funded arbitration service was set up by the Conservative government's Conciliation Act of 1896. In 1897 Joseph Chamberlain's Workmen's Compensation Act effected a major breach in the private contractarian tradition by making employers wholly liable for accidents at work and requiring them to make payments to injured workmen over and above their common-law obligations. Skilled workers who travelled in the Empire, as many did in the 1890s, brought back with them knowledge of the experiments in minimum wage legislation, statutory hours limitation, and state mediation of trade disputes that had been introduced in New Zealand and South Australia. In the late 1900s Liberal ministers—particularly Lloyd George as President of the Board of Trade and later as Chancellor of the Exchequer—began to make regular personal forays into the settlement of large-scale strikes. Legislation for a miners' eight-hour day (1908), a miners' minimum wage (1912), and wages boards in low-paid industries (1909 and 1913) brought an unprecedented degree of public intervention into industrial relations and the contractual conditions of employment. As Lloyd George himself acknowledged, these acts—though limited in practical effect—constituted a deathblow to the old-fashioned Liberal view that relations between worker and employer lay wholly within the realm of private civil society. It was a curious and anachronistic paradox that the centrepiece of industrial legislation during the period—the Trades Disputes Act of 1906—should have entrenched the wholly private and non-corporate identity of trade unions just at a time when the concerns of trade unions were becoming deeply enmeshed in the wider concerns of society and the state.

V. WORK AND THE 'WORKING CLASS'

As was suggested in Chapter 1, many historians have identified during this period a crystallization and hardening of British class-relationships—a process within which the hitherto amorphous mass of heterogeneous working people became for the first time a coherent 'working class', united by common experience, institutions, and culture. How far did changes in the character and organization of work contribute to this growth of a uniform class identity? Did the erosion of archaic skills and the advance of routine and rationality provide the catalysts that transformed working people into a single homogeneous class? Did 'work', as ordinary language might suggest, create the British working class, or was class-identity forged by other factors?

At first glance it seems inherently likely that the downgrading of archaic skills and the advance in status of the unskilled—both of which were a corollary of advancing industrialization—*would* have produced a convergence of the outer boundaries of the working class and thus a greater sense of class solidarity and common class-identity. There is, however, very little empirical evidence to suggest that this did in fact occur. On the contrary, throughout the period, wage differentials remained static and work in all different settings was riddled with status differentials. Work was often the focal point of very intense interpersonal loyalty and camaraderie, but in very few settings (mainly single-industry villages) did this loyalty spontaneously metamorphose into a wider sense of unity across the barriers of occupation, income, status, and skill. Indeed, in many industries privileged workers systematically protected their position by exploiting and even expropriating weaker workers (even when, as was often the case in factory employment, the latter were their own wives and children). In the spinning mills, for example, 'minders' deliberately excluded the inferior 'piecers' from the acquisition of skills, blocked their road to advancement, controlled their wages and compelled them to form a separate union (subscriptions to which were deducted by the minders from the piecers' weekly wage). In printing, the maintenance of a wholly artificial seven-year apprenticeship system meant that employers got fully competent apprentices on the cheap and were thus able to subsidize the wages of adult labour. Numerous inquiries into sweated labour found that 'sweating' was often practised by microscopic capitalists whose incomes were no greater than those whom they employed. Even in mining, where the sheer physical interdependence of workers was highly conducive to group consciousness, there were many clashes of interest between coalface and surface workers and between hewers and trainees. Mining communities, legendary for their class solidarity, were no less ridden with personal snobberies than other late Victorian communities; and contemporary observers noted profound differences between those miners' families whose occupational horizons were wholly bounded by mining, and neighbouring families which pursued collective strategies to get at least some of their children 'out of the pit'. A small minority of working women, mostly weavers, got equal pay and status with men; but far more often women workers were viewed as members of a rival or subordinate sex rather than fellow members of the same class and workforce. Moreover, women themselves were no less prone to occupational snobbery than men. Robert Roberts remarked upon the great divide between 'hat girls' and 'shawl girls' in the Lancashire mill-towns; whilst Olive Malvery's studies of working girls in London found that factory girls, costermongers, and domestic servants viewed each other 'with as much mutual contempt as a belle of New York and a Chicago heiress'.

Such differences of status, sex, and social experience were only very imperfectly transcended by trade-unionism. Virtually no skilled union opened its membership to unskilled or semi-skilled workers—even though the general unions were weak and unstable for a generation after 1889 and would always have been willing to merge their identity with that of the older élite unions. Though some individual trade-unionists tried to foster the recruitment of women, the main thrust of union policy was towards excluding women from all but the lowest-status occupations and en-suring that their pay-scales were well below those of men. The Women's Industrial Council, founded in 1894 to promote female trade-unionism, secured some co-operation from working men on local trades councils, but was largely led and organized by middle-class 'social feminists'. When skilled workers *did* involve themselves in the concerns of the unskilled—as in the Great London Dock Strike—it was usually for ideological reasons (in this case, commitment to socialism) and not as an expression of pre-existing class solidarity. Moreover, the trade unions themselves frequently clashed with the workers whom they claimed to represent, over such issues as levels of output, discipline and safety; and the labour unrest of 1910–14 was splintered down the middle by unofficial action on the part of workers repudiating their official trade union negotiators. The 1890s saw the emergence in some industries, notably engineering, of unofficial shop-floor leaders whom a later generation dubbed 'shop stewards'. These new leaders often invoked the language of class solidarity, and even of industrial syndicalism, but their policies were nearly always the traditional ones of sectoral self-protection, exclusion of unskilled workers, and the main-tenance of craft control.

Indeed, it is difficult to escape the conclusion that, outside the imme-diate work group, work was often a source of division and hierarchy within the working class, and of immense cultural diversity among workers in different trades and localities. The growth in the size of the factory and in trade union organization helped to broaden the immediate reference group, but it was a far cry from this to generalized working class consciousness. What is most striking about the social response to technological change in the period is not the uniformity that mass production induced—though there were some pressures in that direction—but the immense variety of the forms of adaptation and the ingenuity with which many workers managed to graft new processes on to an older workshop culture. Even the rise of unemployment—itself partly a product of more advanced organization—reacted upon class identity in a highly ambivalent way, since on the one hand it reinforced the moral economy of 'the lump of labour' (workers must not steal jobs from one another), but at the same time it strengthened the sense, noted in the previous chapter, of 'work as a species of property right, to be defended against all comers'.

VI. CULTURE AND CONTEXT

The social experience of work cannot therefore be seen as responsible in itself for that massive consolidation of the British working class that historians perceive as occurring during this period. Clearly the advance of industrialization created the raw material for the growth of a working class, in the form of an employed population of which more than 80 per cent were manual workers. But the sources of a unifying class-consciousness must be sought elsewhere: in ideology, in political movements, in exogenous economic pressures, in the leadership of minority organizations. To this extent traditional historians have probably been right in seeking the collective history of the 'working class' in formal institutions such as trade unions and co-operatives rather than in the experience of the shop-floor. The history of work cannot, however, be reduced simply to the history of the working class; work was the central reality of social life for the vast majority of people, while coherent 'working-class consciousness' was a phenomenon whose distinctive identity ebbed and flowed according to context and circumstance. The sheer variety of attitudes, interests, and behaviour among working people during this period recalls Lenin's famous lament that English workers were incapable of seeing political economy in global terms or of generalizing to the universal from the particular. Such a narrow perspective could be found again and again in the very localized frame of reference of working men and women, in their often emotional attachment to individual items of machinery and to detailed technical processes, and in their unwillingness to translate particular conflicts with specific employers into a general onslaught upon the whole edifice of capital.

On the other hand, the history of work lends little support to Lenin's other claim, that English workers were profoundly 'economistic' (that is, concerned only with short-term material gain). Though a majority of strikes may have concerned wages, throughout the length and breadth of industry personal and group freedom and collective control of the workplace were primary concerns (often to the detriment, in purely material terms, of the well-being of the workers involved). Such control centred partly upon the maintenance of privilege (limitation of entry, defence of apprenticeship, exclusion of the unskilled) and partly upon a residual defence of the structural intermingling of work and play inherited from a pre-industrial culture (expressed through absenteeism, horseplay, meal and smoking breaks, and resistance to working under supervision). The former practices were by their nature confined to craft trades, but the latter were found no less among casual dock labourers and female jam-packers than among skilled engineers and miners. Towards the end of the period such practices increasingly competed with the introduction of modern 'rational' organization and with 'best-practice technology'. Employers responded sometimes by simply failing to innovate, sometimes by trading more disciplined and directed conditions of work for more extensive leisure and welfare facilities, and sometimes by an uneasy and fractious compromise between the two. Each of these responses could be invoked by Edwardian critics to lend substance to the charges mentioned above: that having been in the past the most industrious and productive workers in the world, British workers had become obstructionist and pleasure-loving. Probably there *was* an absolute decline in the value attached to work, as real incomes rose, as some tasks became more boring and as the option of leisure became less costly. But what most markedly changed was not the inner culture of work but its wider material context. Habits of extreme independence, personal ingenuity and inventiveness, small-group solidarity and dislike of authority, all of which had been highly functional to the pioneering days of early machine production, became increasingly ill adapted to the era of stereotyped production-line processes. It was this idiosyncratic attachment to personal freedom, rather than devotion to a disembodied work-ethic, that most characterized British attitudes to work from the high Victorian period down to the outbreak of war in 1914.

6

Religion

I. THE ISSUE OF 'SECULARIZATION'

Both folk memory and history books recall the early Victorians as devout and churchgoing, the later Victorians as rent by doubt but still churchgoing, and their Edwardian successors as agnostic, materialist, and increasingly given over to secular pleasures. In numerous memoirs of the period the Sabbatarian Sunday of the 1850s and 1860s appears to have given way by the reign of Edward VII to the 'English weekend', in which churchgoing was either conspicuous by its absence or reduced to the mainly sartorial ritual of the Sunday parade. G. M. Young, drawing partly from personal recollection, portrayed the late Victorian era as one of relentless transition from evangelicalism to agnosticism; while R. C. K. Ensor noted the almost complete disappearance after 1870 of earlier talismans of Christian piety such as daily Bible-reading and family prayers. Later writers have portrayed a similar picture. As small-scale cohesive communities declined, so it is argued, religion lost its traditional role as a medium of social control and social cohesion. Religious matters progressively withdrew from the centre to the periphery of public life, and national and local politics were realigned around the axis of social class. As an intellectual system religion was eroded by the advance of science, while its pastoral functions were taken over by the growth of social welfare and commercialized leisure. The language of religious belief, deeply rooted in pre-industrial codes of life and thought, was increasingly estranged from the day-to-day material realities of man-made environments and mass production. Even the spectacular religious 'revivals' of the period (the Moody and Sankey campaign of the 1870s, the evangelical 'holiness movement' and the Welsh revival of the early 1900s) are perceived as more artificial, transient and socially marginal, less powerfully geared to the mainstream of social and cultural life than their predecessors earlier in the century. Historians have disagreed widely about how and why these changes occurred, but most have agreed that the period was one of advancing 'secularization'.

Such impressions convey an authentic flavour of certain powerful trends in late Victorian and Edwardian Britain, but any close analysis of religious practice and belief and their interaction with other social phenomena soon dissolves the picture in many different directions. In no sphere of social life was a contemporary sense of change more pressing, yet contemporaries were profoundly divided about the nature of that change and its overall direction. Some, like Matthew Arnold, saw Christian faith as inexorably upon the ebb tide, whereas others, like Sir Henry Maine, were much more struck by its post-Enlightenment survival and revival. Though some deplored (or welcomed) the rise of secular values, there were many others who hoped (or feared) the exact opposite: that 'modernity' and 'mass society' would lead not to de-Christianization but to a massive renewal of popular and possibly fanatical religious zeal. From the 1860s onwards there was a marked decline in candidates for holy orders, particularly in the Anglican Church, but Britain in the 1880s still had more clerics of one kind and another than any other European country except Spain and Italy. Throughout the period churchmen of all denominations puzzled over the gulf between the churches and the working class; to informed foreign visitors, however, it appeared that the ordinary people of Britain were among the most Christianized in Europe (in marked contrast to foreign impressions of the British a century before). Most historians have treated the predominantly 'middle-class' character of Victorian churchgoing as a symptom of weakness; but to observers at the time—particularly surprised visitors from France and Germany—the fact that religion flourished among the educated and 'progressive' classes rather than the poor and ignorant classes was a sign of life and strength. To many people religious commitment was increasingly a matter of personal choice and private taste; but to many others it was intimately concerned with, and even embodied in, certain quintessentially public movements, such as the advance of democracy, social reform, the global march of the British Empire or the assertion of national and cultural identity (English, Scots, Welsh, or Irish). In some quarters sectarian enthusiasm was becoming blurred by relativism, ecumenism, and fading theological certainty; while elsewhere in the religious landscape mid-Victorian disputes about doctrine, ritual, authority, and relations with the state burned with unabated, sometimes even renewed, vigour right down to 1914. Moreover, the sense of change, though widespread, was by no means universal. While some felt that the very nature of religious consciousness was being transformed by science, history, and moral pluralism, others laid claim to an essential continuity of religious identity and experience, rooted in the English Civil War, the Reformation, the Middle Ages or the Fathers of the Church. The Archbishops' Committee on Church and State, coming at the very end of the period, was marked by an acute sense of contemporary social change—but also by a sense of unbroken, though often stormy, national religious tradition stretching back to the withdrawal of the Roman Empire in the second century AD.

Disentangling the forces behind these conflicting trends and opinions to a certain extent transcends the sphere of social history. However, religion or reaction against it permeated the lives, language, institutions and moral imaginations of large numbers of people living in Britain in the late nineteenth and early twentieth centuries. Many visualized themselves as belonging to a 'Christian nation' in some public and collective sense; and although the formal dismantling of Church–State relationships was well under way by 1870, organized religious bodies continued to play a major role in public life, particularly in the sphere of education. From the disestablishment of the Irish Church in 1869 through to the disestablishment of the Welsh Church in 1914–19, the question of State–Church relationships continued to be a fiercely contested issue (the partial reunion of the Scots Presbyterian churches in 1902–4 took up far more administrative and parliamentary time than other, better remembered issues of the post-Boer War era, such as physical deterioration, unemployment and the restructuring of national defence). Both religious solidarity and religious aggression were major determinants of political identity down to 1914. Indeed, support among English and Welsh Nonconformists for the Protestant minority in Ireland was a major factor in eroding the popular base of a Liberal party committed to Irish Home Rule. Membership of religious bodies and participation in religious ceremonies remained by far the most widespread form of associational culture. Even for those who had no worshipping connection with any church, religious organizations performed many functions and supplied many services that a hundred years later would emanate from the market, the mass media or the welfare state.

Though many of these functions had changed in character by 1914, it is by no means self-evident that the process of change in this period was a simple unilinear movement from the sacred to the secular—or that the two were necessarily at opposite poles from each other. The problem is further confused by the erratic quality of much of the historical evidence.

Quantitative data relating to external religious observance may be an unreliable guide to internal religious conviction; while descriptive accounts of religious behaviour were often caricatures derived from hostile sources (Nonconformists portrayed Anglicans as plutocratic careerists, Anglicans portrayed Nonconformists as vulgar philistines, while both portrayed Roman Catholics as the seditious fellow-travellers of a hostile foreign power). This chapter will review what is known about changing patterns of religious practice and affiliation. It will examine the role of churches, chapels, missions, and synagogues as social and cultural institutions. And it will also attempt to penetrate the ways in which the substance of religious belief changed, and to relate changing perceptions of transcendental truth to more mundane changes in social structure and organization.

II. THE SOCIOLOGY OF CHURCH ATTENDANCE

Who went to which churches and for what reasons? Information about religious observance may be gleaned from a variety of sources. Trends over time may be detected from church membership figures, from marriage, baptism, and burial returns, and from subscriptions, pew rents, and numbers taking Communion. More precise, but more transient, snapshot impressions can be derived from the 1851 religious census of England and Wales, and from more limited and local surveys of church attendance such as those carried out by the *British Weekly* in 1886, by Charles Booth in the 1890s, by the *Daily News* in 1903–4, and by the Royal Commission on the Church in Wales in 1910. All these sources are imperfect in coverage and contentious in their implications; but they enable some kind of general picture of church affiliation and attendance to be constructed for different parts of the country and over the period as a whole.

The religious census of 1851 had found that slightly more than 50 per cent of the adult population attended a place of worship on the Census Sunday; but other sources suggest that active and regular membership of church congregations at mid-century amounted to little more than half that figure.* Over the next fifty years regular church affiliation ebbed and flowed at around one quarter of the adult population of England, Wales, Scotland, and Ulster.† A low point of church membership was reached about 1880,

---

* No attempt has been made here to review the large historical literature that has criticized the methodology and findings of the religious census.

† Ireland outside Ulster was a different matter. Throughout the period nearly 90 per cent of the population in what later became the Irish Free State claimed membership of the Roman Catholic Church.

at a time when the crusading zeal and public clamour of the Nonconformist conscience might have led one to expect that Christian conviction and organization were at their height. Twenty years later, during the supposedly decadent *fin de siècle*, a higher proportion of British people were active members of religious denominations than at any earlier time during Queen Victoria's reign. There was some slight contraction during the Edwardian decade; but even so, as a proportion of the adult population the combined membership in 1910 of the established churches of England and Scotland and of the Protestant Nonconformist churches was still 3 per cent higher than it had been in 1860 (even though societal pressures to secure religious conformity were certainly much stronger at the earlier date). Over the same period membership of the Roman Catholic Church in England, Wales, and Scotland doubled (largely but not wholly due to Irish immigration), while membership of Jewish congregations increased by 1,000 per cent. Many other numerical indices tell a similar story. Though many Nonconformist groups in the late 1900s were failing to keep pace with demographic growth, the Anglican Church in the Edwardian period was attracting a higher proportion of the population as Easter communicants than at any time in the previous century. Attendance at Sunday schools (formerly a 'secular' institution now become much more specifically religious in character) nearly trebled between the 1860s and 1906. Membership of Bands of Hope, Boys' Brigades, Men's Societies, the Girls' Friendly Society and the Young Men's and Women's Christian Associations (all of them late Victorian foundations) ran into many millions. Moreover, the fact that family size was diminishing while the number of separate families was increasing suggests that the continuance of religious practice was more than just the perpetuation of inherited family tradition: it must have been, to some extent at least, the product of conversion and successful missionary endeavour.

Such figures lend little support to the stereotypes of advancing secularization mentioned at the beginning of this chapter. They are a useful reminder that, even at the height of the Victorian era, a substantial minority, and possibly a majority, of the population was largely detached from formal contact with organized religion. But more surprisingly, they also suggest that, measured in terms of active membership of worshipping bodies, the British people constituted a rather *more* religious society in the Edwardian period than they had done half a century before. Bald aggregates, however, tell us little about the day-to-day practice of religion among different social groups or about the salience of religion in wider society. Victorian and Edwardian religion was never wholly reducible to sociological categories;

nevertheless, throughout the period the map of religious observance was closely linked to such factors as historic and ethnic identity, gender, region and class. Anglicanism was strongest in the south-east of England, Primitive Methodism in the south-west and north-west, Wesleyanism in Lancashire and Yorkshire, 'old dissent' (Presbyterianism and Congregationalism) in Scotland, Ulster, and the old Cromwellian counties of the English East Midlands. Over three-quarters of the Irish living in Ireland were Roman Catholic; and everywhere Catholicism followed in the wake of Irish immigration, most conspicuously in Lancashire and the west coast of Scotland. Nonconformist pluralism flourished in Wales, where communities of a few hundred often boasted a dozen different chapels, many of them Welsh-speaking and fiercely protective of Welsh national culture (though, contrary to Nonconformist claims, the Established Church in Wales was also actively engaged from the 1880s onwards in protecting the native language). In all congregations except Jewish ones, females outnumbered males in public worship, the imbalance being, paradoxically, greatest where women had least institutional power. Thus the proportion of male worshippers was highest among Congregationalists, where women might be preachers and ministers, lowest among Anglicans, where women were excluded even from electoral rolls for the new parochial councils set up after 1894.

Religion was also closely intertwined with social status and class; and the Census for 1851 had loosely identified Anglicanism with the gentry and the rural poor, Nonconformity with the commercial and provincial lower-middle class, and 'irreligion' with the urban working classes. These stereotypes, and to a certain extent the realities behind them, persisted throughout the period. Yet the relation of class and religion was a complex, even tautological, one, because religious behaviour and affiliations were important components of what contemporary perceptions of class and status entailed. Thus many economically successful Nonconformists—particularly at the start of the period—preferred to identify themselves through chapel membership with a lower class and status group than their economic position would otherwise have implied (the tensions implicit in such a choice were a crucial thread in the social history of the period). Conversely, as John Wesley had discovered a century earlier, personal religious commitment—bringing in its train 'sobriety' and 'character'—could set a man or woman inexorably upon the ladder of upward social mobility without any formal change in his or her economic function. An added complexity came from the fact that the religious affinities of different social groups differed over time and in different contexts, often in unexpected ways. The Church of England by the end of the nineteenth century had lost much of its hold upon the rural poor, and the reform of private patronage was undermining its links with the landed classes; but it had established a foothold in the slums of great cities, and was positively booming in the new clerk and commuter suburbs. The rural labouring piety of the 1850s crumbled in the 1870s and 1880s, not because of 'irreligion' or 'secularization' *per se*, but because of the enforced migration and collapse of archaic community structures brought about by agricultural depression. Falling land values also eroded the status and social prestige of the Anglican clergy who—always a more precarious group than their critics imagined— were from the 1880s sliding inexorably downwards from the lesser ranks of the landed gentry into the urban lower-middle class.

Mid-Victorian Nonconformity, as already indicated, had occupied a crucial and ambiguous position within the emerging industrial class structure. In the 1860s and 1870s hostility to the Established Church was at least as potent a rallying cry for advanced radicalism as hostility to land or capital; and there were still powerful traces of this sentiment in the politics of Asquith and Lloyd George. In certain social contexts, particularly remote agricultural and mining villages without a resident employer, religious dissent—shading off frequently into anticlericalism, less often into secularism and millenarianism—was a focal point of lower-class consciousness, and continued to be so right down to 1914. In other contexts, however, such as Birmingham and the Lancashire mill towns, dissent was a powerful force for reconciling and transcending social class divisions; as many historians have shown, the stability and inter-class harmony of the 1860s and 1870s was closely interwoven with the community life of the Nonconformist chapels. This was still important in the 1890s and 1900s; but by the turn of the century there were distinct signs that the integrative function of Nonconformity was waning, as economic tensions rose, and as issues like Empire, feminism, and Irish Home Rule split Nonconformists into rival political allegiances. Moreover, the lower-middle classes who were the backbone of Nonconformity were themselves changing in character; and there was a world of difference between the religious outlook of the superior artisans and small shopkeepers of the mid-Victorian era and the office-workers of the 1900s. For the former, religion was often an expression of solidarity with the local community; for the latter it was often an expression of separateness and difference, and increasingly likely to take the form, if not of Anglicanism, then of a more refined and anonymous suburban Nonconformity than had been common forty years before (the transition was symbolized by the migration of a famous body of Leeds Congregationalists from inner-city 'Salem chapel' to suburban 'Trinity church').

Roman Catholics were also divided on class lines, between a small group of mainly upper-class converts and hereditary Catholics, anxious to emphasize the loyalty, respectability, and 'Englishness' of their confession, and an increasing majority of Irish immigrants and families of Irish descent, for whom Roman Catholicism was an important medium of both Celtic and proletarian culture. The Roman Catholic working class of this period were no more regular in their churchgoing (outside Ireland) than the Protestant working class; but Catholic priests—often themselves of working-class origin—were conspicuously more successful than most of their Protestant counterparts in maintaining a pastoral presence in poor areas and in preserving a sense of continuing Catholic identity. The Salvation Army, founded by General Booth in the late 1870s, specifically targeted both its proselytizing mission and its social work upon the very poor; but the bulk of its officers and converts appears to have come from the new urban lower-middle class (often dissatisfied migrants from other Protestant evangelical organizations).

The religious habits of the lower orders vexed and puzzled Victorian and Edwardian observers, and have continued for different reasons to vex and puzzle social historians a century later. Since the 1820s massive resources had been poured by all major denominations into the Christianization of workers in industrial cities. Thousands of new churches and chapels had been built, and thousands of old ones had been opened up and reinvigorated by the evangelical and High Church revivals. The Anglican Church in particular had devoted the funds and administrative machinery of a great department of state into stretching the new industrial Britain upon the procrustean bed of the old parochial system. By the 1870s all groups and denominations were diversifying their labours into social welfare schemes: orphanages, industrial schools, ragged schools, rescue homes, shelters, and soup kitchens for the very poor; mothers' meetings, men's clubs, youth clubs, and a host of self-help and savings clubs for the more regular and respectable working class. The idea that churches should save bodies as well as souls, reputedly discovered by General Booth in the late 1880s, was a commonplace among parish priests, dissenting ministers, and city missioners in London at the start of the 1870s (indeed, Annie Macpherson, pioneer of emigration schemes for abandoned children, was criticized by other social evangelicals for her prime emphasis on spiritual regeneration).

Moreover, though some church- and chapel-goers never crossed the class divide, many others devoted themselves to charitable visiting: in the 1880s it was estimated that there were no less than half a million 'parish visitors' and something like 80,000 'bible women' attached to the various Protestant denominations.

Such efforts bore fruit in a variety of ways. The active hostility of some working-class communities to organized religion, frequently encountered in the 1840s and 1850s, had virtually vanished by the end of the nineteenth century. Observers from all quarters, including those hostile to religion, agreed that working-class atheism was virtually unknown outside a very limited circle of mainly London-based radical republicans. Recent studies in oral history have suggested that contemporary surveys probably underestimated the piety of the poor, and that outside London as many as 20 per cent of the Edwardian working class may have attended churches on a more or less regular basis. The millions of children attending Sunday schools were overwhelmingly working class;* and the working class generally continued to use churches and chapels for the major rites of passage. Civil marriage, for example, declined in the 1860s and 1870s and was only slowly rising at the end of the period; while irregular liaisons and 'common-law' marriages were far less common than they had been in the first half of the nineteenth century. The 'churching' of women after childbirth was common down to 1914, and working people flocked to many of the newly invented religious ceremonies of the period, such as watch-night services, Mothering Sundays, and harvest festivals. The elaborate pomp of working-class funerals (at a time when funerals in other classes were becoming simpler and more private), popular resistance to the spread of cremation, and the universal fear of a pauper's grave (with its bitter concomitants of social stigma and medical vivisection) suggested no lack of interest in the resurrection of the body and the prospect of a life hereafter. By the 1900s belief in hell-fire and everlasting judgement was probably stronger among working-class people who did not go to church than among middle-class people who did. The nascent labour movement in all its aspects—trade unions, co-ops, socialist societies, Lib-Labists—was full of men and women who were either active members of Christian churches or who were searching for some more literal and tangible embodiment of the Sermon on the Mount. 'It is due to the religious customs of the country that the avarice of the capitalist has been kept in check', declared the president of the Trades Union Congress in 1892; this was in striking

* Paradoxically, attendance at Sunday school, deemed a badge of respectability by the working class, was viewed as 'not respectable' by many middle-class parents.

contrast to the outlook of organized labour in other industrialized European countries of this period, where working-class movements were much more commonly atheistic, materialist, and militantly anticlerical.

For all their relative benevolence towards organized religion, however, a majority of working-class people, particularly in great cities, refused to do what their betters wanted them to do, which was to go to church regularly on Sundays. In certain peculiar circumstances—in small, close-knit, single-occupation industrial communities, or in congregations with an outstandingly saintly or charismatic minister or priest—organized religion and local working-class culture, and even working-class militancy, might converge.* This appears to have happened, for example, among Wesleyans and Primitive Methodists in the Durham coalfields, and in certain famous Anglo-Catholic parishes in London, Portsmouth, Leeds and Sheffield. Working-class enthusiasm could often be mobilized, too, when religion bisected with ethnic and tribal loyalties, as was shown by the existence of large congregations, both Protestant and Catholic, in Liverpool and Glasgow. But in most contexts, and particularly in the great anonymous metropolitan agglomerations, institutional religion appeared to contemporary observers to be largely irrelevant or marginal to the lives of the majority of working-class citizens. The reasons for this paradox—of a predominantly 'Christian' population, in a self-consciously 'Christian nation', declining to take part in religious organization and worship—were and remain a matter for conjecture. The Census of 1851, mapping the 'dingy territories of this alienated nation', had blamed ignorance of Christianity and lack of 'aggressive' missionary endeavour. This can scarcely have been the whole story, though, since by the end of the nineteenth century large sectors of the working class were almost certainly better instructed in the rudiments of Christianity—through Sunday schools, denominational schools and the compulsory religious teaching of the post-1870 board schools—than at any other period in British history. As one disconsolate evangelist remarked, the problem was less one of 'ignorance' than of 'saturation' and 'over-exposure'. Other commentators throughout the period blamed the repellently 'class' character of much organized religion: the pew rents, the wearing of Sunday clothes, the use of theology to buttress inequality and orthodox economics, and the 'middle-class' deportment of congregations and clergy. But though such factors may explain

* One of the two miners shot by troops in the famous Featherstone Colliery riot of 1893 was 'James Gibb, a respectable young man, a Sunday school teacher at Normanton . . . who was also a member of a young man's class taught by the clergyman in charge of Normanton Church'.

working-class estrangement from the Established Church, they can scarcely explain the relative failure of radical Nonconformity (and, as Thomas Wright had shown in the 1870s, there was plenty of wearing of Sunday clothes among well-off working men who would never have dreamed of setting foot inside a place of worship). More recent analysts have emphasized the rise in the 1890s of a mass, secular culture of newspapers, sport, clubs, and music-halls, which weaned working people away from religious belief and practice; and expanding opportunities for leisure were certainly of central importance in the social history of late Victorian working-class life. But they can scarcely explain working-class 'irreligion', which had long antedated the rise of this new mass culture; moreover, as will be shown in more detail below, the churches themselves were often to the forefront in promoting many aspects of the new leisure activities.*

A further possibility, hinted at in a number of recent studies, is that there was in fact a great deal of informal and unstructured working-class religious activity which has largely escaped the eyes of historians because it took place outside the boundaries of formal churchgoing and left little in the way of conventional written records. The large gap between occasional church attendance figures and actual church membership suggests that there was at all times a substantial floating population of persons interested in religion for a variety of reasons—intellectual, social, emotional, spiritual, or merely inquisitive—who were not prepared to attach themselves formally to any religious organization. Oral historians have shown that large numbers of women who did not go to church on Sundays (when they had to shop in street markets and cook Sunday dinners) regularly attended mothers' meetings on the following Mondays; and in the 1900s many working men who avoided matins and Eucharists on Sunday mornings attended discussion groups and prayer meetings later in the day. A great deal of late nineteenth-century evangelical worship took place not at conventional church or chapel services, but at revivalist rallies, Bible studies, 'house churches', and 'tea-and-experience meetings', which by their nature have left little trace in written records. Charles Davies's eyewitness accounts of London religion in the 1870s indicate that there was a teeming mass of 'unorthodox' and 'heterodox' popular religious and quasi-religious activity, that embraced millenarianism, mesmerism, transcendentalism, Seventh-Day Adventism, pantheism, spiritualism, occultism, and the humdrum quest for day-to-day brotherly love, much of which had only the sketchiest

---

* A more potent factor may have been the churches' attitude to work and play in previous eras, and the cumulative impact of several centuries of rationalizing puritanism, that had severed the archaic ties between work, worship, and pleasure.

connection with any of the institutional churches. Father Dolling's work in London and Portsmouth led him to conclude that there was 'a vast body of unattached Christians, or of laymen with their hearts aflame with the love of souls', who shunned ecclesiastical connections. Even secularism itself had an unexpected religious dimension, in that secularist orators often invoked the 'independent' dissenting tradition of the seventeenth century, and the heavenly visions of John Bunyan and William Blake. The 'Labour Church Movement' of the late 1890s and early 1900s, which substituted ethical socialism for orthodox Christian doctrine, drew heavily upon this tradition of intense but informal, this-worldly, working-class religiosity. Such activities—often lay in origin and idiosyncratic in theology—fell far outside the conventional boundaries of ecclesiastical history, but were an important part of subterranean popular culture. They are no less a part of the social history of the period than more formal religious organizations or the more material realms of family, leisure and work.

III. THE CHURCHES AND CIVIC CULTURE

Though only a minority worshipped in churches or belonged to church congregations, churches themselves were major social institutions of the period and more must be said about their role in the wider ordering of society. As we have seen, there is little evidence of a dramatic shift in the level of church affiliation in this period. Is the same true of the wider organic relationship between the churches and the nation's social, political, and ethical life? Already by 1870 the Church of England had lost its earlier position as the sole spiritual expression of the secular state. It was in process of losing its control over the ancient universities (through secularization of fellowships) and was about to lose control over the administration of canon law (through the setting up of new secular courts under the Judicature Act of 1874). Nevertheless, the Anglican Church at the beginning of the period was still the major public institution in the sphere of civil society, and it still enjoyed a great deal of both formal and informal legal and corporate power. It was geographically omnipresent throughout England and Wales, and its representatives were still overwhelmingly prominent in a wide range of public institutions (in cabinets, Parliament, Poor Law, hospital, and prison administration, and in a wide range of voluntary movements and learned societies). North of the border the same was even more true of the Presbyterian Established Church of Scotland. At the same time the Nonconformist churches, though not incorporated within the state, were an aggressive and dynamic cultural and political force whose concerns—articulated nationally through the Lancashire-based 'Liberation Society'—determined much of the agenda of public life throughout the 1860s and 1870s. Both national and local political allegiances were closely correlated with religious affiliation, and religious rioting was a regular ritual accompaniment to both general and local elections. Churches, chapels, and other organs of religious life dominated—indeed, to a large extent *were*—the mass media of mid-Victorian Britain. Church and chapel life was a major forum not merely for piety, but for sociability, snobbery, finding work, borrowing money, choosing a marriage partner, and conducting business relationships. Furthermore, clergy were major dispensers of charity (a particularly important function at a time when orthodox Poor Law theorists were trying to limit the social expenditure of the secular state). God and Providence were frequently invoked in public discourse and parliamentary debate as familiar actors in the life of the nation; and the particular style of politics associated with Mr Gladstone was a constant reminder that the vision of a godly nation need not necessarily be limited within the narrow confines of an Established Church.

The imprint of the churches was still everywhere visible in the Edwardian era. Indeed, far from dwindling in the face of modernity and secularization, the corporate activities of nearly all denominations appeared more vigorous, varied and voluminous than they had been half a century before. Though some forms of group activity, such as the Wesleyan class meeting, had declined, they had been replaced or supplemented by many new forms of associational life—including, in the case of the Anglican Church, the establishment of church congresses, parochial councils, and lay houses of convocation to represent the laity in church policy and government. The period had seen a massive growth of 'home missions' and of parish- and congregation-based clubs and societies, offering a vast range of religious, secular, and intermediate activities ranging from prayer to pugilism and from gymnastics to choral singing. From the 1880s onwards evangelical feminism was at the spearhead of many major reform movements; and between 1870 and 1903 the Established Church built over six thousand new schools. Far from being outflanked by the new culture of mass leisure, many churches at the turn of the century were energetic pioneers of new popular pastimes (in striking contrast to early and mid-Victorian Britain, when clerics were more often engaged in 'rationalizing' or repressing the archaic pleasures of the poor). Weekend football was widely promoted as a wholesome alternative to drink, and many football teams that were later to grow into famous professional clubs owed their origins to late nineteenth-century clerical sponsorship. Father Osborne Jay, the celebrated Anglo-Catholic vicar of Shoreditch (who himself looked like a prizefighter) was a leading patron of working-class boxing in the East End, while W. T. Stead, the Congregationalist editor of the *Pall Mall Gazette* and the *Review of Reviews*, was an often controversial promoter of the new mass-circulation 'sensational' journalism. In the 1900s many of the films being shown at the new silent cinemas were about religious and biblical themes. Moreover, in all denominations congregational religion was being increasingly supplemented by large-scale national organizations, set up to defend religious interests or to promote a religious perspective in social and public life. The Church of England Men's Society, the Mothers' Union, the Girls' Friendly Society and the Boys' Brigade—all of them London-based societies with hundreds if not thousands of federated local branches—were prominent examples of these new social growths; and parallel developments were taking place among Roman Catholics, Jews, and most branches of Nonconformity.

Similar growths were occurring, or had already occurred, in the field of social welfare. The pastoral work of parishes and individual congregations was being buttressed in the 1900s by large-scale national philanthropic organizations on a far more massive scale than forty years before. The foundation of such bodies as Dr Barnardo's, the Church Army, the 'social wing' of the Salvation Army, the Jewish Board of Guardians, the Catholic Federation, and the Society of St Vincent de Paul—all bore witness to the increasing engagement of churches with social problems, and to a new perception of those problems as far transcending the traditional face-to-face charity of individual Christian congregations. All these bodies acted both as direct dispensers of charitable resources and as pressure groups for social action by local authorities and the state. At the same time representatives of churches were becoming more involved in the promotion of undenominational and secular social welfare schemes, such as hospital funds, provident dispensaries, savings clubs, friendly societies, Boy Scouts and Girl Guides, and, increasingly in the 1900s, the provision of professional social-work training. Individual churchmen and churchwomen were very much to the fore, too, in the burgeoning civic reform movements of the Edwardian era, which in all major cities were organizing neighbourbood visiting schemes, pressing for Poor Law reform and searching for a new definition of 'community' rooted in 'ethical consciousness' and 'organic solidarity' rather than in traditional geographical units. Such activities were particularly attractive to Christian socialists and radical Nonconformists, but were by no means confined to those groups. Roman Catholics in Edwardian Lancashire, for example, were being urged by their bishop to take part in secular social work, to serve the 'commonwealth' and 'to accept the duties of citizenship as well as its fruits and not to be content with merely Catholic activities'.

Religious influences were no less pervasive and prominent in the sphere of Edwardian politics. In spite of the formal admission of atheists to Parliament in 1884, party political identity continued to be closely linked to confessional and sectarian origins. The Liberal majority of 1906 contained the highest-ever proportion of Nonconformist MPs (many of them enthusiastic 'new Liberals'), while Conservative members of the Opposition were 90 per cent Anglican. The Liberal cabinets of 1905–14 included a substantial group of politicians (including the Prime Minister, H. H. Asquith) who had built their early careers upon militant Nonconformity; and the culmination of their social reformist programme was to be the disestablishment and partial expropriation of the episcopal Church of Wales. The political scene in Ireland at the end of the period was much more starkly divided on Catholic–Protestant lines than had been the case in the 1870s and 1880s. And the 1900s saw spasmodic, quasi-political, sectarian street violence in many parts of Britain, provoked by such issues as Jewish immigration, Eucharistic processions, Orange Day parades, and over-zealous denominational missions. Rate support for denominational education, which had been rejected in 1870, was introduced for the first time by the Education Act of 1902; and Nonconformist outrage at this measure, which subsidized mainly Anglican and Roman Catholic schools, showed that peaceful mass mobilization of religious opinion could still be a formidable political force. The accession of George V was racked by controversy over demands from ultra-Protestants for reform of the Coronation oath. In all denominations there were some critics of imperialism, but many more who viewed the extension of the British Empire as a vehicle for self-sacrifice, an antidote to materialism and a manifest expression of God's purpose in the world (there was striking unanimity on these issues in the sermons of otherwise unlikely theological bedfellows, such as the Farm Street Jesuit, Father Bernard Vaughan, the Anglican Broad Churchman, Dean Farrar, and the arch-modernist minister of the City Temple, the Reverend R. J. Campbell).* On a rather different level the decline of

---

* Religious attitudes to Empire were often complex, and deserve more careful analysis than they often receive. Apparently simple and self-explanatory positions were often not so. The Church Missionary Society, for example, strongly supported expansion of the British Empire, and for that reason has often been viewed as a tool of white supremacy; yet the main, if misguided, concern of the CMS was to forestall colonization by France and the subsequent conversion of colonized peoples to Roman Catholicism. Far from being 'white

establishment made little difference throughout the period to the willingness of Parliament to legislate on religiously sponsored moral issues, as was shown by the Licensing Act of 1883, the Inebriates Act of 1899 and the reassertion in the 1900s of the laws on Sunday trading. With the sole exception of the 1907 Deceased Wife's Sister Act (which itself raised a storm of religious protest) statutory endorsement of canon law in the Edwardian era remained virtually unchanged from the time, three-quarters of a century earlier, when Britain had been legally and constitutionally an Anglican confessional state.

All these factors might appear to indicate that the corporate life of religious denominations, both as 'reactionary' organs of sectarian rivalry and as 'progressive' agencies of public service, was no less pivotal in Edwardian Britain than it had been forty years before. Yet most historians have concluded that this was not in fact the case, and that—for all their social, political, and missionary activism—the churches at the start of the twentieth century were ceasing to be a dominant social force. They had become in Hobsbawm's term 'recessive': a group of institutions which, though still numerically powerful, was nevertheless outside the mainstream of the fast-flowing historic currents of the age. Is this an accurate perception, or is it distorted by trends that only occurred later in the twentieth century? What explains the seeming paradox of buoyant church membership, booming social and evangelizing activity, aggressive political mobilization—and the sense among historians that organized religion was becoming increasingly marginal to the nation's communal life?

The case for the churches' dwindling significance hinges largely upon the view that they failed to come to terms with changing social structure and were unable to adapt to the new social forces of materialism, democracy, mass organization, and segregation by social class. This critique undoubtedly pinpoints certain chronic anxieties of intelligent churchmen of all denominations throughout the late Victorian and Edwardian age. In all religious groups there were severe tensions between spiritual and material pressures, between tradition and modernity, between belief in 'individualism' and acknowledgement of the mass reality of social class. Such tensions were, however, scarcely peculiar to religious bodies; and, as has been suggested above, it would be hard to accuse the churches in this period of turning their backs *en masse* upon the material, institutional, and organizational world. On the contrary, from the 1870s onwards Anglicans, Non-

supremacist', the CMS from its inception strove to prevent the creation of 'colonist' churches and to promote indigenous church structures with native priests and bishops—a useful reminder of the sheer diversity of goals and values in an apparently homogenous age.

conformists, Roman Catholics, and Jews were increasingly caught up in material concerns, and in all churches there were spectacular developments in large-scale social organization—often in advance of such developments in the secular sphere.

The same point may be made about democracy. It is true that among Anglicans democracy was often feared as the antechamber to disestablishment; but religious groups outside the Established Church were often at the spearhead of movements for political reform, and the internal structure of Wesleyanism was a powerful model for the formation of caucuses and mass secular parties. Moreover, even the Anglican Church was in process of reorganizing itself on more democratic lines (and the limited, gender-based character of those reforms was no more than a reflection of current limitations in the secular sphere). Some of the most virulent opponents of feminism were found among members of churches, chapels, and synagogues; but at the same time large numbers of both social and political feminists rooted their campaigns for purity, temperance, and sexual equality in orthodox Christian doctrine. In the field of mass culture, there were certainly aspects of the new culture of the 1890s that were largely indifferent to religion (such as working-men's clubs, music-halls, and the underground market for salacious literature), but there were many other aspects in which religious bodies were innovators and pioneers. In other words, far from being inherently estranged from the new social forces, churches and religious organizations were often promoters and carriers of the new ideas and institutions that were supposedly bringing about their inexorable decline.

Such points suggest a need to look more closely at the exact nature of the decline of religion in public life and the causes that lay behind it. That there *was* a change in the relation between religion and society in this period is undeniable; but its character was of a different kind from what is often supposed. The causes of the change lay at least as much in the changing character of religion itself as in the external structure of society; and religious bodies were often active mediators of societal change rather than mere passive victims. As was shown above, churches were important agents in the shift of public life from small-scale community associations to large-scale national organizations. In spite of their theoretical commitment to maintaining family and community, they were also active promoters of a new kind of associational life based on division of social groups according to ages and genders (with long-term unintended consequences for social stratification that were only to become manifest later in the twentieth century). The most crucial immediate areas of change lay, however, in politics and public administration. Though religion remained prominent in political life, by the 1900s political commitment was far less reducible to religious belief than had been the case in 1870. Though parties in Parliament still replicated traditional religious stereotypes, this was far less true among rank-and-file supporters of these parties and among the nation at large. As already noted, disputes over Irish Home Rule and (slightly later) state social welfare policies snapped the earlier, almost axiomatic link between Nonconformity and Liberalism; while the sustained virulence of Edwardian Conservative pamphleteers on the theme of wet radical parsons suggests that the same kind of breach was occurring between Toryism and Anglicanism. In other words, the relationship between religion and politics was becoming much more complex, individualized and indeterminate; the symmetry of belief, self-interest and political ideology was nothing like as strong as it had been a generation before.

Although, as we have seen, religion continued to bisect public issues at many (often unexpected) points, a new approach to public policy was clearly emerging, one that was overtly neutral on matters of belief and that assumed the existence of areas of public life in which religion had no competence. This implicitly 'secular' view horrified Nonconformists when it was articulated by Disraeli in the sphere of foreign policy in the late 1870s. Yet it was precisely this principle that Nonconformists themselves were actively promoting throughout the period in such spheres as education and social welfare. This view had almost no connection with 'secularism' as a system of anti-religious belief. It stemmed, rather, from the intensity of competition between different religious groups, which almost accidentally forced the state to act as an impartial umpire. And, perhaps more fundamentally, it stemmed from the claim of many pious Victorian Christians that religion should be a matter of conscience rather than of convention, and that it was therefore morally wrong to prop up a certain set of beliefs by too close a connection with state power. Such a view lay at the heart of the riotous pluralism of Victorian religion, and of the sustained attacks by Nonconformists upon the privileges of the Anglican Church (attacks that were often supported by 'catholic' Anglicans, anxious that the Church should clearly rest upon divine rather than secular authority). It was closely linked to a view increasingly being expressed at the end of the nineteenth century, that although religious individuals could and should involve themselves in the political domain, the churches as institutions should refrain from corporate involvement. Paradoxically, therefore, the marginalization of the churches and the carving out of an expanding area of secularized neutrality in public life was the achievement, not so much of secular forces *per se*, but of many of the most zealous and dedicated religious believers. Far from being designed to weaken religion, it was intended to strengthen and purify religious institutions and to remove corruption and privilege from public life. To many late Victorian Christians who held this view, secularization was not the antithesis but the practical fulfilment of Christianity, in that it would make all religious organization 'voluntary' and reduce all religious commitment to a pure matter of private conscience.

Such views were of immense importance in late nineteenth-century religious culture and in the wider civic culture of the nation. They help to explain the seeming paradox of the enormous expansion of secular activity on the part of the late Victorian churches and their increasing confinement to the periphery of affairs in the secular world. Not all religious people were happy with this trend, as recurrent battles over church schools and disestablishment showed; but by the end of the nineteenth century there were few churchmen of any denomination prepared to defend the principle of a return to a unitary confessional state. Even in the sphere of education, where religion and policy were still closely enmeshed, the claims of Anglicans and Roman Catholics to provide sectarian education for those who wanted it were quite different from the monopolistic claims of the Establishment in the early nineteenth century. The Anglican Church still viewed itself as the spiritual guardian of the nation, not just of the churchgoing faithful; but in practical terms most Anglicans at the beginning of the twentieth century had acquiesced in the assertion of their Nonconformist rivals that the Established Church was one among many voluntary associations offering goods and services in a context of religious free competition. In 1910–14 the rearguard defence of the Established Church in Wales centred primarily upon resistance to expropriation of church property rather than upon the principle of a state church. The Welsh Disestablishment Act of 1914 saw the apogee of the voluntaristic principle that Nonconformists had been inseminating into British society since the beginning of Queen Victoria's reign. As with other religious issues in the post-Victorian period, however, the Act involved some unexpected shifts in the traditional moral kaleidoscope, in that a substantial minority of Welsh Nonconformists actively *opposed* disestablishment of the Welsh national church because they 'disliked the prospect of disendowing religion in an age of growing secularism'. There was a dawning understanding here, at the very end of the period, that secularization in a modern society might bring in its train something very different from what secularizing Christians had imagined over the previous fifty years.

IV. The structure of belief

The changing role of the churches in late Victorian and Edwardian Britain stemmed, therefore, at least in part from the nature of contemporary religious belief; and more must be said about the inner content of belief and its interaction with society must be further examined. The early Victorians had inherited the assumption, handed down by generations of Christian history, that religion was more than just a private metaphysic: it was a theory of knowledge, a moral philosophy, and a clue to the understanding of the secular world. This assumption had been under attack from new forms of knowledge for over a century; but in the context of British (as opposed to Continental) history, the disruptive impact of the philosophies of the Enlightenment had been remarkably slight. In spite of the theological controversies of the 1830s and 1840s, one of the hallmarks of intellectual life in the early part of Queen Victoria's reign had been the continued coexistence of natural and social science with Christian theology. Far from dwindling in the face of new secular knowledge, traditional Christian doctrine had been firmly restated, first by the late eighteenth-century evangelical revival and then in the 1830s and 1840s by the Tractarians. Few early Victorian Christians were quite the crass fundamentalists parodied by their positivist critics, and many were active participants in new scientific movements; but in all branches of Christianity there was at that time widespread acceptance of the verbal inspiration of the Bible and of orthodox Christian dogma as set out in the creeds: Creation, the Fall, the Incarnation and Divinity of Christ, the Atonement and the Resurrection. There were some differences of opinion about 'sources of authority' and 'means of grace' (election or conversion, sacraments or the inner light) and some residual eighteenth-century scepticism about the ethical implications of the Atonement and the doctrine of the Trinity. Unitarianism was strong among northern, provincial, middle-class intellectuals (as it would continue to be throughout the nineteenth century). But many educated believers in the 1830s and 1840s lived in a state of desperate search for personal salvation and daily expectation of the second coming of Christ. It is unclear how many early Victorian Christians should be classed as 'evangelicals'; but evangelical styles of worship and behaviour transcended divisions between Establishment and dissent, and between High, Low and Broad Church. Sermons were long, ceremony austere, musical embellishment confined to psalms, sabbath observance mandatory, Bible-reading and daily prayer common. In many spheres a rigid dualism divided this world from the next, while perceptions of the Deity were awesome, punitive and transcendent. There was no lack of evangelical pastoral and social concern, but—with certain notable exceptions—this stemmed primarily from the promptings of private conscience rather than from a sense of Christianity as a corporate social philosophy. Protestantism as a public creed was seen as inextricably entwined with the constitution of the British state and the historic identity of the British nation; aside from that, however, Christian belief was overwhelmingly viewed as a guide to personal moral behaviour and as an internal psychological mechanism for the salvation of individual souls.

This style of religious practice and belief was still powerfully present in the Britain of 1870; but since just before the start of Queen Victoria's reign there had been many rivulets of change, some of which were swelling by the 1870s into mighty torrents. The opening up of the constitution to Roman Catholics, Nonconformists and subsequently Jews had fundamentally changed both the status of the Church of England and the religious identity of the state—leading some, as already shown, to demand complete disestablishment, some to press for a broader and more comprehensive state religion, and others to look for a new, more spiritual definition of Anglican Christianity, rooted not in historic expediency but in ancient 'catholic' truth. Both inside and outside the Anglican Church the theology of conversion and personal salvation was still strong in the mid-Victorian age; but it was increasingly being challenged and supplemented by other styles of religious thought, by a growing emphasis on sacraments and by a growing perception of the material world as an integral part of 'The Kingdom of Christ'. And beneath the surface of changing fashions in theology lay other, more deep-seated issues: the challenges presented to the whole content and structure of traditional belief by developments in the areas of history and natural science.

The first such challenge came at the start of the Victorian era from discoveries in geology, which showed that the world was much older than suggested by a literal reading of the Book of Genesis—a claim that most churchmen took with equanimity, though it clearly cast doubt upon the extent to which the Bible in all its aspects was divinely inspired. More disturbing was to be the gradual percolation into Britain of new modes of German historical scholarship, which questioned the historicity of many parts of the Bible and in particular emphasized the temporal and human limitations of the person of Jesus Christ. Finally, between 1859 and 1871 there came the series of biological hypotheses associated with the name of Darwin: the evolution and mutability of species, creation as a process not of 'divine Providence' but of 'random selection', the descent of man not from Adam but from the apes. Holding all these discoveries together was a gradually emerging new secular philosophy of the natural and social worlds as provinces governed by immutable and self-sustaining natural laws, in which will and personality, be they human or divine, played no part. It was a philosophy that in the eyes of many anxious contemporaries left little ultimate space for morality and meaning of any kind, let alone for such quintessentially religious categories as miracles, revelation, salvation and grace.

These events in intellectual history, many of them occurring before 1870, form an essential backcloth to the history of changing patterns of religious belief in Britain between 1870 and 1914. They help to explain both the vast proliferation of religious pluralism in this period and the increasing uncertainty with which many people viewed the relation of religion to the secular world. Nevertheless, while it is hard to exaggerate the extent of this change, it is easy to mistake its nature. Throughout the period there were some dramatic and famous crises of faith, particularly among intellectuals (Henry Sidgwick, Leslie Stephen, Beatrice Webb, Mrs Humphry Ward's *Robert Elsmere*, and many others). Some transferred their allegiance to the 'Unknowable Absolute' predicated by Herbert Spencer, or to the 'Religion of Humanity' preached by the disciples of Auguste Comte. There was also much lapsing into a frankly relieved indifference (as in Samuel Butler's autobiographical novel *The Way of All Flesh*). A more common response, however, was not outright loss of faith but dilution, adjustment, or diversification of religious belief into something that was often much more nuanced and nebulous than had been common in the early Victorian age.

This transformation of religious ideas took many forms and occurred at many levels. For some it took the form of a doctrinal reassertion of orthodox belief—Protestant, Catholic, or Jewish—as a sphere of consciousness wholly different and separate from the sphere of secular knowledge; while for others it took the form of embracing and sacramentalizing evolutionary principles as a proof of the interdependence of natural and divine law. For some believers adjustment took the form of rationalization of religious belief and the shedding of all vestiges of the miraculous and supernatural (an approach aided and expressed by the ethical movement of the 1890s and by the widespread currency of both academic and popular 'philosophical idealism'). For many evangelicals it involved a retreat from emphasis on penal substitution into private camaraderie and the cult of 'personal holiness' (popularized from the mid-1870s by the annual Keswick conventions); and even revivalist crusades' increasingly shifted the emphasis of their message from Christ's sacrificial atonement to the less complex and less awesome message of 'Jesus as saviour and friend'. Other responses took the form of increasing emphasis on religion as a form of 'social service' (common among Nonconformists and Broad Churchmen); a collapse of formal dogma into a kind of non-doctrinal, Wordsworthian sub-pantheism that gradually permeated all denominations; and the redefinition of the Devil as 'the principle of injustice, hypocrisy, ugliness and ignorance' and of Hell as 'nothing else than this earth in its present social order or disorder'. Instead of 'meditating on the sufferings or Crucifixion of Christ', remarked a lecturer on the psychology of religion (recorded by Evelyn Underhill in 1912), Christians in the future 'would give all their attention to making the world the sort of place where such an episode would be impossible'.

This growing cacophony of inner belief was accompanied by increasing diversity of outward forms of worship. Liberal Nonconformists as well as Low and Broad Church Anglicans began to experiment with ceremonies, vestments, and decoration previously associated with High Churchmen; while many Anglo-Catholic parishes abandoned parts or all of the prayer-book and rubrics of 1662, in favour of confession, incense, wafers, invocation of the Virgin and Saints, and various idiosyncratic adaptations of the Roman missal. Such experiments were throughout the period a recurring flashpoint of theological controversy, and led to the prosecution and imprisonment of several prominent ritualist clergymen under the Public Worship Regulation Act of 1874; but attempts by bodies such as the Church Association and the Protestant Truth Society to secure Anglican uniformity proved in the long run a dismal failure, serving merely to create martyrs for the pluralist (and thus inadvertently for the secularist) cause. Similar diversity prevailed among the Nonconformist churches, reaching a *reductio ad absurdum* in congregations where participants in the Lord's Supper split into conscientious takers of fermented and unfermented wine. In all branches of rank-and-file religion there was a tendency upon the part of worshippers to ignore the claims of authority and to shop around among denominations and individual churches until they found the mixture of liturgy and theology that suited them best. In all Protestant denominations there was a progressive decline in church discipline, a growing distaste for credal orthodoxy and hell-fire sermons, and a growing preference for hymns, choirs, flowers, and forms of worship that were aesthetically pleasing rather than theologically precise. In all but the poorest classes weddings gradually replaced funerals as the most lavishly celebrated rite of passage;

and even funerals became much more cheerful, with white flowers, meat teas and 'refreshments' replacing the traditional 'black crêpe, scarves, hatbands, cakes and wine'. Contentious statements of doctrine were often sung rather than said, and expressions of religious belief became more bland and polite than in the early Victorian era. The Revised Standard Version of the Bible, which omitted all references to carnal acts, first came to Britain from America in 1870 and rapidly became popular among evangelicals; while squeamish Broad Churchmen began to press for the deletion of sex from the Book of Common Prayer ('those expressions in the marriage service which shock the more refined feelings of the present time').

Moreover, though fierce rearguard actions raged on behalf of biblical fundamentalism, prayer-book orthodoxy and primitive catholicity, both systematic theology and semi-official pronouncements on doctrine were increasingly penetrated by 'modernist' thought. A Royal Commission of 1870 resisted liberal demands for abandonment of the Athanasian creed, but agreed that its anathemas should be read merely as a 'solemn warning' rather than as a serious threat of damnation. From the 1880s onwards a new generation of biblical scholars, headed by Professor William Robertson Smith of the Free Church of Scotland, began to propose a 'hermeneutic' approach to the study of Scripture, which was to be treated as a sacred text of inspired but symbolic meaning rather than as an accurate historical and scientific record. In 1889 *Lux Mundi*, a group of essays by moderate High Churchmen, introduced to a popular audience some of the central themes of the new higher criticism, including the 'theology of the Incarnation', which proclaimed the immanence of God in the material and secular world. Over the next twenty years there was a great outpouring of 'modernist' writing in the Anglican and Nonconformist churches and among dissident Roman Catholics, all of which emphasized the unity of the sacred and profane spheres, the non-contradiction between theology and science, the mundane and existential character of the gospel of Christ, and the growing severance of modern religious experience (and indeed of modern experience in general) from traditional ecclesiastical language, concepts, and structures. In intellectual circles studies of antiquity and social anthropology opened up new perspectives on the deity as genderless, androgynous or female, perspectives which provoked much discomfort among a generation of men reared on Christian manliness, but were of great interest to religious-minded feminists. The Edwardian decade also brought a rising tide of interest in mystical religion, a tide that flowed partly inside and partly outside the orthodox churches, partly in tandem with and partly as a reaction against the prevailing modernist currents. Popular and periodical literature of the late 1900s swarmed with contributions from or about Bergsonian vitalists, Hindu and Buddhist gurus, theosophists, transcendentalists, neo-paganists, and practitioners of orthodox Christian contemplative life—to such a degree that the religious correspondent of *The Times* on the eve of the First World War was commenting with some bewilderment on the 'spiritual renaissance' and 'mystical revival' that was unexpectedly exploding around him. 'For the first time since the great metaphysical period of ecclesiastical dogma, philosophy is tending once more to become a doctrine of redemption and the old cry, "What must I do to be saved?" is whispering itself once more to the restless heart of a . . . wearied age, and to the churning mind of an experimental and adventurous generation.'

All these shifts and changes of belief and worship were accomplished, as was shown earlier, without any notable quantitative decline in popular religious practice; and it may well have been the case that some people actually found it easier to accept the ill-defined benevolent deity of the Edwardian era than the God of wrath who had presided over the early days of Queen Victoria. As with the spheres of social, political, and pastoral life, the evolution of belief during this period suggests no lack of willingness on the part of many believers to come to terms with social and intellectual change and to adjust their tenets accordingly. By the 1900s there were still fundamentalist chapels in which no breath of Darwin ever entered; and the papal interdict on modernism was reiterated for orthodox Roman Catholics in 1907. But elsewhere on the religious spectrum (including dissident Catholics who defied the papal edict) there was widespread adjustment to new secular ideas, to such an extent that in many branches of Christianity the religion of the 1900s was scarcely recognizable as the same belief-system as that of half a century before. Judged by secular standards, theological ideas in many spheres were much more attractive and plausible in the 1900s than they had been in the 1860s: they were more ethical, more rational, more socially concerned, more sensitive to metaphor and ambiguity, more consistent with modern history and science. By contrast with the atonement theology of the early Victorian era, Edwardian incarnational theology was deeply committed to applying Christian principles to all spheres and layers of human existence; and among Jewish congregations 'liberal' Judaic theology was developing traditional Jewish thought along very similar lines.

Why then was religious belief felt by many contemporaries to be of declining significance in the life of the modern world? How can the historian explain the fact that the more theologians sought to apply religious doctrines to the mundane and material facts of everyday life, the more the gulf between the religious and secular spheres appeared to be growing? To some contemporaries the obvious answer lay in the fact that religious truth had been exploded by the advance of modern science and that belief was a mere 'survival' from the 'childhood of the race' (a view exhaustively argued in Sir James Frazer's *The Golden Bough*, the first edition of which was published in 1890). This message was the central theme of the secularist mission to working men conducted by Robert Blatchford and J. M. Robertson in the early 1900s and was to be of some significance in the long-term formation of a popular secularized culture. But in the Edwardian period, outright scientific positivism was less common than either simple agnosticism or the search for new forms of religion more relevant to modern experience and thought. To some observers, however, the explanation for the declining power of belief lay precisely in that search for modern relevance. In the view of Samuel Barnett, founder of the universities' settlement at Toynbee Hall, and a man at the heart of many late Victorian 'progressive' causes, religion had ceased to have meaning because it had lost its vision of eternal verities: it had ceased to be engaged with the deepest psychological realities of life and had given up its sense of sin. And certainly there was some truth in the view that the religion of the 1900s was less morally and psychologically compelling than that of the 1840s: social service, personal holiness, and even meditation and mysticism were less all-enveloping and traumatizing than the deadly and inexorable pressures of heaven and hell. None the less, this again can scarcely have been the whole story, since moral repugnance for the older religion of damnation had been a major stumbling-block for many would-be believers earlier in the nineteenth century. Another prominent churchman, J. N. Figgis of the Community of the Resurrection, blamed the obeisance of the churches to plutocracy and Mammon; and undoubtedly, as was shown earlier, the gulf between rich and poor was a major barrier to popular religious practice, if not to actual belief. But it was not a new problem in the history of the Christian churches, and organized Christianity in the Edwardian era was more critical of economic and social injustice, more actively engaged in trying to transcend class-barriers, than it had been for many generations before.

The answer lay much more in the increasing vagueness and indeterminacy of religious belief, and in its disorderly pluralism. By the 1900s the boundaries of 'belief' and 'unbelief' had become much more blurred and imprecise than they had been even two decades before. 'Christian agnosticism' had become much more common among active members of religious congregations; while at the same time many people with transcendental or supernatural beliefs were choosing not to attach themselves to the corporate life of any of the Churches. Vagueness was encouraged by the ever-increasing variety of religious belief and by the apparent absence of any external canons of authority. Furthermore, in spite of the efforts of modernism and incarnational theology, the period saw an increasing operational cleavage between systematic religious doctrine and other spheres of intellectual and material existence. Unbelief and agnosticism had not been uncommon among intellectuals long before 1870; and the separation of religion from other spheres of systematic thought—law, economics, political thought—had been gestating for centuries. What was new at the end of the nineteenth century was that many men and women who were privately 'believers' were practising the new secular disciplines—physics and chemistry, history and anthropology, medicine and biology—with no overt reference whatsoever to the sphere of religious thought. The same was true of many other areas of material life. Cleavage between religion and business activity was no new phenomenon; but the period saw a great accentuation of the tendency to treat religion as a Sunday hobby, functionally and theoretically divorced from the practice of weekday affairs.

These changes underlined the fact that, despite the active social engagement of the churches, religion was fast becoming a much more private matter than it had been in previous generations. It was increasingly determined, not by inescapable membership of a given corporate and geographical community, but by private conviction and personal taste. Such a trend was demonstrated by widespread evidence of the breakdown of the parish system, particularly in great cities. As localities grew in size, as transport opened up geographical mobility, as churches and chapels grew more elaborate and diverse in forms of liturgy, so increasing numbers of people worshipped in the congregation of their choice rather than in their own local community. The exercise of such choice might be deeply serious (motivated, as in the case of the large 'gathered' evangelical congregations described by Charles Booth, by the quest for higher truth). Or it might be largely frivolous (as in the case of a Wimbledon solicitor who told the 1875 Select Committee on Public Worship that 'after being hard at work all the week in London' he did not want his Sundays spoiled by dreary and lugubrious sermons: he wanted entertainment, elegance, good music, and a surpliced choir). In both cases religion was becoming more anonymous, 'consumerist' and private; it was closely linked to notions of personal morality, but it was largely detached from the wider constraints of neighbourhood, work and community life. Such changes in the climate of belief powerfully reinforced what J. H. Newman described as the 'Englishman's prerogative to be his own master in all things and to profess what he pleases asking no one's leave . . . to take up any or no religion, and to be an impartial critic of each of them'. Such an attitude both exemplified and reinforced the powerful current of psychological individualism—often running in tandem with, rather than in opposition to, social and institutional collectivism—that has been noted in this period in many other spheres.

V. RELIGION AND SOCIETY

These trends in the practice, organization, and theoretical underpinning of religion in the late Victorian and Edwardian periods suggest that the revolution in religious life during this period was one of kind rather than degree. Religion continued to play an important part in politics, society, and culture, but—outside certain specific sectarian contexts—it was more as an individual, and less as a collective, force. No fewer people, and possibly more, were engaged in the pursuit of religious truth (at least in its outward forms) in the Edwardian period than in the early Victorian period, but the quest was now a less urgent one. It had become, for many people, more of a part-time interest, less of a consuming fire; more of a guide to good citizenship and decent behaviour, less of a passport to eternal life. Communal religion continued to be a collective social force in certain cohesive, close-knit communities (often working-class ones); but in great cities religious practice was increasingly one among many private activities in an ever more differentiated, impersonal cosmopolitan *Gesellschaft* (this was perhaps one reason why—contrary to what many people expected in 1870—the Anglican Church survived the transition to 'modernity' better than most Nonconformist churches). Organized religion continued to erupt from time to time into the political arena, but it was no longer the keystone of politics that it had been in the mid-nineteenth century. And although some religious groups continued to organize themselves into factions, others increasingly emphasized the individual duty of Christian or Jewish citizenship rather than the role of religion as a collective or institutional force.

As a cultural influence religion was more widely but more thinly diffused than it had been half a century earlier. The churches maintained their hold upon the major rites of passage (though declining birth and death rates meant that the impingement of such rituals upon family life was less frequent than in the past). The 1870 Education Act entrenched both denominational and non-denominational Christian teaching within the popular culture, and made a generalized Christian morality more nearly universal than ever before or since (only a few thousand parents exercised their right to withdraw children from such teaching over a period of forty years). The slightly greater volume of regular churchgoing, and particularly Anglican churchgoing, in the 1900s than in the 1880s may reflect the influence of religion taught in school. For the majority, however, school religion did not lead to greater adult involvement in the life of the churches, and may indeed have had the opposite effect, either by encouraging the view that religion was 'for the children' or by persuading people that school was a substitute for church. The threat to organized religion from the new recreational culture of the 1880s and 1890s has probably been exaggerated by historians (though it was clearly to be of much greater importance later in the twentieth century). As shown above, the churches themselves were leading purveyors of this new culture; and, even where they were not, many aspects of the new culture—such as cinema, mass circulation newspapers, and organized sport—were rarely overtly hostile to religion, and were often imbued with its precepts. Edwardian observance of the 'quiet Sunday' was much more universal than the mid-Victorian sabbath, though its religious character was much more muted and its inner core was often not churchgoing but family, home, and the Sunday dinner. (Its much more overtly secular cousin, the notorious Edwardian 'country house weekend' was confined to a tiny, albeit trend-setting, minority of the shooting, bridge-playing, motoring rich.)

The cultivation of family cohesion and sociability was often idealized by contemporary preachers as the prime forum of religious life; and throughout the period mothers were key transmitters of religious morality and practice, alike in Protestant, Catholic and Jewish cultures. Women were generally more successful than men in preserving a spiritual dimension to modern life—possibly because the home was less exposed than the workplace to the pressures of materialism and competition, possibly also because the shift of emphasis from God as a judgemental patriarch to God as an incarnate 'suffering servant' was more attuned to female spirituality than to male. Except among orthodox Jews and a tiny minority of intensely fervent Christians, though, it is doubtful how far the home was really an important medium of formal religious doctrine. Even in the 1860s and 1870s there was a widespread expectation among parents that the rudiments of religious faith would not be taught by themselves, but by day-schools and Sunday schools; and by the 1900s observers could find little outward difference in the language and religious knowledge of children from churchgoing and non-churchgoing families. Moreover, the liberalization of theology and the nuancing of many previously bald and straightforward concepts made religious language and communication more difficult than they had been in the past; and by the end of the period there were many signs that talk about religion was joining (or replacing) talk about sex as the major taboo of the British people, even among those living in devout Christian homes.

Many of these changes came about, either directly or indirectly, because of wider (often only partially visible) changes in the character and organization of society at large. Demographic trends, migration, changing family and class structure, the mass organization of work, a more cosmopolitan frame of reference—all conspired to abet the shift from a religion that was strongly community-based to a religion that was increasingly internalized and private. Such a change occurred even though the most powerful currents of theology moved in the opposite direction, away from a religion of personal salvation and towards an attempt to 'sanctify' the wider structures of material life. Yet religion was not merely the passive victim of wider social forces: there were factors within religion itself which powerfully influenced both the status of the churches in British society and the wider impact of supernatural belief. The most important of these factors was pluralism. Pluralism of organization increasingly challenged and eroded the long-standing relations of Church and State, and this necessarily generated a new secularized civil polity (a polity that, at least initially, was warmly welcomed by large sectors of the religious population). At the same time, pluralism of belief gradually undermined the traditional authoritative role of religion in determining the character of politics, ethics, and culture. The result was increasing vagueness in private conviction and a growing reticence about all reference to religion in public and professional life. It was the diversity and privatization of religion, rather than unbelief or 'secularization' *per se*, that led almost accidentally during this period to the growing emergence of a secular society and the secular state.

7

Society and the State

I. THE SOCIAL BASES OF THE STATE

It was claimed by Philip Abrams that the British people in this period had no conception of the 'social basis of the state'—a claim that seems almost perversely misplaced in view of the highly fraught debates about which status, class and gender groups should have access to the constitution, debates that simmered in British politics throughout the period 1867 to 1914. Between these two dates British politics moved from a very limited notion of citizen rights to a much more comprehensive one, but, as was suggested in Chapter 1, this was by no means a simple, unilinear transition. Throughout the period there was a profound tension between an older vision of the national polity as a narrowly self-contained sphere occupied by the possessors of property, education, independence, and civic virtue, and a newer vision of the national polity as coterminous with all adult members of British society, regardless of economic standing, gender, character or class. With whiggish hindsight it may appear obvious that the former vision was bound to give way to the latter, but this was by no means self-evident at the time. The 1867 Reform Act is often hailed as the harbinger of the new democracy, but the reform debates of the 1860s were full of resonances of the older-style polity; and the Act of 1867 was specifically framed to embrace a class of working men who possessed moral character and economic independence, and to exclude a 'residuum' deemed to be lacking in these attributes of civic virtue. Many promoters of the 'new democracy', from Gladstone and Bright in the 1860s through to Sidney Webb and Ramsay MacDonald in the 1900s, shared the view of older-style politicians that the character of a state was intrinsically bound up with the character of its citizens. This concern took on a new urgency from the 1880s as British politics became increasingly caught up in the politics of Empire, and as British citizens both male and female were viewed as the raw material of a new imperial race. Such concerns lay at the heart of many apparently pragmatic debates about the extent of the franchise and the composition of the electorate. Far from ignoring the issue, late Victorian and Edwardian political thought was continuously and often obsessively preoccupied with the 'social basis' of political power.

What is true, however, is that there was widespread disagreement about the nature and purposes of the state and about the relation of governing institutions to economy and society. To many mid-Victorians the very word 'state' was a distasteful concept, redolent of foreign tyranny and ill-fitted to describe the historical, evolutionary, and empirical character of government in Britain. Popular discussion of what political theorists called the state commonly invoked Crown, ministers, Parliament, law, and the Established Church rather than more abstract and analytical terms. There was a tradition of nineteenth-century social thought, represented by Coleridge, Ruskin, Arnold, and some Anglican churchmen, which sometimes spoke of the state as though it were coterminous with society and embodied the whole material, cultural, and spiritual life of the nation; but in a British context this was an arcane view. A more common perspective was one which saw the state in much more finite terms, as a set of useful but limited institutions that were functionally quite separate from society at large. This view was both reflected in and fostered by the relatively narrow practical scope of mid-Victorian government—government whose main overt purpose was not to shape the character and destiny of British society, but to provide a framework of law, liberty, and sound finance within which 'society' and autonomous social institutions could largely govern and develop themselves.

This very finite perception of the relationship between state and society remained common in Britain down to 1914. Yet from the 1860s onwards there were many movements and pressures—economic, social, political, and intellectual—conspiring to alter the character of the British state and to promote a wider conception of its role. The changing nature and increasing scale of economic organization meant that local and voluntary provision was increasingly inadequate to provide a social infrastructure for economic life—a problem greatly exacerbated by the collapse of land values, large-scale migration and the fact that demographic growth and economic opportunities were increasingly out of kilter with archaic community structures. The advance of 'market' relationships, far from consolidating the private domain, had many unforeseen social consequences and side-effects that precipitated increasing public intervention in many private spheres. The shrinking of the formal role of the Established Churches created a vacuum in many areas of social life—legal, educational, and material—that other institutions had to fill; and as was shown in the previous chapter, the sheer plurality of late nineteenth-century religious and cultural affiliations almost accidentally generated an arena for state expansion into what had previously been private and voluntary affairs. The restructuring of the legal system in the early 1870s did not change the substantive character of English law, but the unification of the ancient common-law and equity jurisdictions under a single High Court gave legal institutions and procedures a much more formal and systematic character than in times past, a character which coincided with the perception of most nineteenth-century political theorists that law was a quintessential part of the rational-bureaucratic structure of the modern unitary state.

Similar changes occurred in many other contexts. The extension of the franchise, the creation of new, popularly elected local government institutions, and the long-term shifts towards large-scale production and international finance—all brought to the fore new social groups with untraditional expectations about the uses of political power. Both Ireland and the Empire presented problems and made demands upon the British government at Westminster that could not be contained within traditional constitutional forms; and in the late 1880s both radicals and imperialists were pressing for the adoption of a more 'federal' and 'republican' constitution on the American model. At the same time the emerging rivalry of Continental states with more dynamic and interventionist governments—particularly Imperial Germany—led many to demand that the British government also should develop a directive social, economic, and technological role. Inner forces within government itself—particularly the growing administrative, financial, and expert competence of a reformed bureaucracy—began slowly to point in the same direction. Various forms of socialism began to make an impact, often less as a positive programme than as a negative critique of existing governmental methods. From the late 1870s onwards the emergence of a prominent school of philosophical idealism gave a powerful intellectual fillip to older 'organic' theories of the state, and strongly emphasized both the fundamental unity of state and society and the participation of private citizens in the larger social whole. Even those who clung to more traditional theories, based on utilitarianism or private contract, often recast those theories in a more collectivist, more societal, and in some instances more authoritarian mould.

The result was a continually evolving relationship between British society and its organs of government. That relationship was perhaps intrinsically no closer in 1914 than it had been in 1870. At both dates most inhabitants of Britain clung to the idea of a sphere of 'natural liberty', a dimension of private existence that was prior to and beyond the reach of state control. At both dates visiting Europeans were amazed at the relative absence or invisibility of the hand of police and bureaucracy in the details of everyday life; but over the intervening period there had been increasing acknowledgement of the interest of the state in certain key spheres of social activity, an interest that was tangibly embodied in new representative and administrative bodies, juridical institutions, and specialist government departments. Active partnership between the state and private organizations—educational, philanthropic, moral, scientific, or punitive—was much more acceptable in the Edwardian era than it had been half a century before, and interest groups which aimed to influence public policy were ceasing to be viewed as automatically 'sinister'. The Edwardian state was compelled to recognize and collaborate with the economic power of both capital and labour to a far greater extent than the mid-Victorian state had been. The whole perception of the 'public sphere', and of its dramatis personae, was changing. The full story of these changes cannot be told in detail here; but this chapter will review certain elements in the process of change that bore most closely upon the character and structure of British society. It will analyse the shifting 'social basis' of the state, and the involvement of the state in such spheres as taxation, social policy, public order and crime.

II. The mid-Victorian state

A tacit ideal of mid-Victorian politics was that the state should stand above and apart from 'society'. A long series of institutional reforms had dismantled or was in process of dismantling the legacy of the 'patronage' state inherited from the eighteenth century. Royal government had given way to 'parliamentary' government; aristocratic, clerical, and corporate privilege had been eroded; the 'bloody code' of the eighteenth-century criminal law had been rationalized and humanized; and mercantilism and monopolies were being progressively displaced by competition and free trade. The sphere of civil society—family, work, property, religion, and membership of voluntary associations—was seen as largely independent of the public sphere and defined by private rather than by public law; and where private and public did coincide—as in the Established Church, the role of hereditary peers or the laws which limited free combination—there were large and vocal pressure-groups in the 1860s and 1870s campaigning for their abolition. The aim of the political culture inherited from Sir Robert Peel was to create a neutral, passive, almost apolitical state, standing above and apart from the fast-moving, chaotic, and open-ended evolution of mid-Victorian society. Much of the work of Gladstone's first period as Prime Minister (1868–74) was devoted to this end—to reforms of the Church, civil service, army, legal system, and ancient universities that were designed to purge the state of past entanglements with particularist interest-groups, and to enable ministers and civil servants, in Gladstone's words, 'to endeavour to forget the parts in the whole'.

Just how far Gladstone and his disciples were successful in attaining their administrative and governmental vision will be considered in more detail below; but in its social aspects the vision was never even remotely attainable at any time during the mid-Victorian years. On the contrary, politics and public administration remained deeply enmeshed in the specific character of mid-Victorian social and economic structure. Participation in public life continued to be universally linked to such factors as property, family, education, gender, and social class; and although most religious barriers to citizenship had been formally swept away, political life at all levels was closely intertwined with sectarian commitment. Women in the 1860s were excluded from all forms of public office except the Crown, and from all political rights except the Poor Law franchise (and even here their legal standing was precarious and ill-defined). In both national and local society the holding of public office conferred not merely political power, but prestige, social position, and often material reward. Ministers of the Crown, drawn largely from the landed classes, were the fashionable apex of the nation's social life—far more so than the dull and dowdy court of Queen Victoria, or the 'smart set' who dined with the Prince of Wales at Marlborough House. Victorian newspaper readers were far more interested in the private doings of politicians than of princesses, a taste that lingered even after the rise of the mass-circulation dailies in the last decade of the nineteenth century. Membership of the House of Commons was an obvious prerequisite for those seeking political office, but for many more it was the ultimate badge of social status, alike in local communities and in the more cosmopolitan society of London. Parliament might be the awesome seat of national sovereignty, but it was also, in T. H. Escott's words, a 'brilliant club', whose late hours and long recesses were exactly tailored, not to the practical needs of modern 'democratic' government, but to the nocturnal habits of fashionable men-about-town of sixty years before. Parliamentary life might be deeply divided on political issues, but socially and convivially it was bipartisan. Members of rival political factions (scarcely parties in the later sense of that term) regularly dined together, gossiped together and visited each other's homes. Gladstone himself, for example, weekended far more often with the future Conservative leader, Lord Salisbury, at Hatfield than with any of his own Liberal supporters. The intimate social life of the House of Commons in the 1860s and 1870s was sealed by the fact that, despite thirty years of middle-class enfranchisement, members of all political persuasions continued to be drawn predominantly from the landed classes. Even in 1868, at the first general election after the granting of the urban household franchise, a quarter of MPs returned were sons of peers and over 80 per cent had landed connections. Less than a tenth came directly from industry and commerce, almost all of whom had ceased to be active in business. The same landed bias was found to a more modest extent in the civil service. Benthamite 'open competition' had begun to penetrate some of the lower-status public offices like the Education Department; but in the 1860s, first-division posts in the civil service, together with diplomacy, Royal Commissions, and government inspectorates, were still largely manned by the younger sons of landed families. Where middle-class 'experts' did succeed in obtaining posts or influencing policy, it was often through the patronage of reformist aristocrats (mediated through member-ship of such bodies as the Royal Statistical Society and the National Association for the Promotion of Social Science).

Politics and élite society similarly intermingled in the context of local communities, although the social structure of local government was widely variable. Aristocratic politicians showed little interest in the government of London, which was largely run by seventy-three shopkeeper-dominated vestries—in theory reformed and democratized in 1855, but in practice elected on a £25 ratepayer franchise that excluded all below the substantial middle classes. The City of London Corporation, regarded by radicals as a living museum of old corruption, had largely escaped the age of reform and was still dominated by the guilds and livery companies of the later Middle Ages; erstwhile goldsmiths, skinners, leather sellers, and fishmongers, of whom a few still practised their ancient trades but a majority had evolved into a patrician *haute bourgeoisie*, largely engaged in administering lucrative charitable trusts. Outside London, both antique parish-pump institutions and newly incorporated boroughs provided a political platform for shop-keepers, manufacturers, and artisans; and mid-Victorian local government was a tumultuous cockpit of sectarian and partisan conflict across a wide range of issues, from education and drains to cholera and church rates. Such conflicts generated in many cities a very dynamic local and provincial culture, headed by an ambitious, dedicated, and sometimes highly intellectual urban middle class, who acted to some extent as a counterweight to aristocratic dominance of national society. The 1860s also saw the burgeoning of various forms of 'industrial feudalism', particularly strong in Lancashire textile towns, whereby workers living in factory-owned housing were expected to vote for the candidate of their employer's choice. But many provincial towns and all counties were still dominated by the traditional 'men of metal and many acres'; and, far from being crowded out of county government by the reform era, the gentry and aristocracy since 1832 had in many areas re-emerged and reconsolidated their power— on boards of guardians and quarter sessions, as organizers of the local militia, as patrons of philanthropy and even to some extent as members of borough corporations (Leeds, Birmingham, and Manchester all had an active landowning element in city politics down to the 1880s). The posts of High Sheriff and Lord Lieutenant, generally viewed as the leaders of county society, were still universally held by the owners of landed estates; and non-landowners neither sought nor were deemed suitable for the ceremonial and supra-political functions attached to these roles.

Such landowning predominance in an age of industrial capitalism and 'popular' politics was continually denounced by radicals as a residue of corruption and privilege, and to a certain extent it undoubtedly was just that. Many seats in the reformed House of Commons continued to be informal family fiefs. Many elections were uncontested, or went to the candidate with the longest purse. Certain territorial areas, such as Tory Lancashire and Liberal Northamptonshire, were still (and continued to be down to the end of the century) the political latifundia of great landed magnates. Yet there was more to landed dominance than mere material coercion. Many middle-class electors were happy to vote for aristocratic candidates, not necessarily out of 'deference', but because they viewed the whole purpose of an aristocracy as being to supply political leadership on the cheap (or not, at any rate, at the expense of the electorate). Electoral pressures in the pre-ballot era came from sideways and below as well as from above, and were often viewed not as corruption but as a normal part of the representation process. The distinctive hallmark of mid-Victorian community politics was not deference or corruption or coercion *per se* (though there was much of all three): it was a process of continuous social and cultural incorporation, whereby the different strata of society both contained and influenced other strata (usually those below, but sometimes those above).

Moreover, although landed persons occupied positions of power out of all proportion to their numbers, they did not do so as a coherent and homogeneous class. The interests of different sectors of the landed classes were rarely identical, and even when they were so they did not necessarily determine the character of landed politics. On the contrary, the landed interest was predominant in both major parties; and in nearly all political conflicts of the mid-Victorian era, landowners were to the fore on either side of the divide. Such divisions may be partly explained by the varied nature of their non-landowning interests; but they were also linked to the fact that at least some of the landed classes viewed landownership not merely in material terms, but as the basis for an Aristotelian ethic of disinterested public service. This ethic spanned both Liberalism and Conservatism, and was found among both high-minded parvenus like Peel and Gladstone and the heirs of great aristocratic houses. Bertrand Russell, for example, recalled that his grandfather, Lord John Russell, had presided in the early 1870s over a household of 'Spartan simplicity' and 'puritan piety and austerity' in which all personal interests were sacrificed to the public weal. Lord John himself, even when First Minister of the Crown, had practised 'a kind of theoretic republicanism which was prepared to tolerate a monarch so long as he recognized that he was an employee of the people and subject to dismissal if he proved unsatisfactory'.

III. CHANGING POLITICAL CULTURE

Certain aspects of the social edifice of mid-Victorian politics and government survived in recognizable form down to 1914. As was shown in Chapter 6, the sectarian identity of Members of Parliament was even more sharply accentuated and polarized in the Edwardian period than in 1870. Landed aristocrats and their relations formed a majority in nearly all British cabinets down to 1905, and still played a conspicuous part in the reformist Liberal ministries of 1906–14. MPs drawn from the landed classes formed the largest occupational group in the House of Commons until 1900, when they were overtaken by those with interests in finance (many of whom doubtless also had landed connections).* Not only in Britain but throughout the Empire there were many dignified and ceremonial functions for

---

* Significantly, the shift from land to finance occurred simultaneously in all four parties in the House of Commons—Conservative, Liberal, Liberal-Unionist and Irish Nationalist— a fact that underlines the continuing social homogeneity of Parliament. It has been estimated, however, that the average personal wealth of Conservative MPs in the 1890s was almost exactly twice that of the Liberal MPs.

which the main qualifications continued to be birth and title (in 1892 a young Whig grandee reluctantly turned down such a post, proffered by Sir William Harcourt on behalf of a Liberal government, on the ground that he could scarcely read or write). Aristocratic figureheads were if anything more eagerly sought after by local government, philanthropic institutions, universities, and reformist pressure groups during the 1900s than they had been a quarter of a century before. Similarly, in the administrative sphere, patronage went on operating side by side with 'open competition'. The Edwardian Foreign and Colonial Offices remained bureaucratic enclaves of the landed aristocracy; and even in the more mundane domestic departments, officials were still frequently recruited not by examination but through personal contacts with aristocratic politicians. (Some of the most dynamic and innovative Edwardian administrators, such as Robert Morant, Hubert Llewellyn Smith, and William Beveridge, were recruited in this way, just like their Utilitarian predecessors half a century before.) Most parts of the political nation and most forms of public office remained closed to women. Parliament throughout the Edwardian period retained the habits and atmosphere of a fashionable West End club;* and high politics maintained its intimate cross-bench conviviality, nurtured by dinner parties, house parties, fashionable salons, and boudoir intrigues. The Balfour–Asquith era was remarkable for the prevalence of close personal relationships between politicians who were sworn political enemies. When at the very end of the period Asquith as Prime Minister was faced with the problem of treasonable conspiracy in Ulster, he was faced also with the fact that several of the leading conspirators were his wife's ex-suitors and his own personal friends—a situation that might have stepped straight out of a novel by Anthony Trollope fifty years before.

The mask of continuity was, however, in many respects misleading. Even in the 1860s forces were at work that were remoulding the character and identity of the political nation, changes that were to be accelerated by extensions of the franchise and by the economic transformation that set in during the 1870s. At the start of the period there were already signs that the landed classes were losing their monopoly on the leadership of public life and that landed attitudes to politics were subtly changing. The Parliament of 1868 was notorious, not for its defence of either aristocratic or democratic interests, but for the wheeling and dealing activities of a small

---

* An atmosphere that was often hostile and threatening, not only to the small group of MPs from working-class backgrounds, but to certain dull provincial businessmen, inarticulate army officers and prosy colonials, who made little headway in the Edwardian House of Commons.

group of 'business' MPs, who made an impact in such areas as debt, bankruptcy and railway legislation out of all proportion to their numbers. Popular Liberalism in the late 1860s and early 1870s had a largely urban mass following, mobilized through Nonconformist chapels and radical clubs, that idolized Gladstone and John Bright but was otherwise very remote from the mainly aristocratic Liberal leadership. Indeed, the chief expectation of that mass following was that political power should be used to expel the remnants of aristocratic privilege throughout the kingdom from all public aspects of both Church and State.

The result was a marked decline in the willingness of landowners to accept public office, and a gradual retreat of those who did so into an inward-looking defence of purely landed interests. Even in the Conservative party, where landed leadership remained strong (and was indeed strengthened by refugees from Liberalism), party organization and administrative matters were increasingly taken over by a new Conservative middle class. Over the next thirty years the legal undermining of landownership in Ireland, the rise of agricultural trade-unionism, the decline of land values from the 1880s, and increasing attacks by radicals and socialists upon the economics of private landlordism all combined to sap both the social basis and the moral legitimacy of aristocratic power. The process of erosion was a slow one, and for many landowners partial absorption into other economic sectors cushioned the shock of change. Many were content to withdraw from their ancient public roles into plutocracy and private citizenship; and a few, like the third Lord Carrington, were still managing after the turn of the century to marry up aristocratic paternalism with 'progressive' social policies. The House of Lords as the upper chamber of Parliament more and more confined itself to the promotion of private bills, often of an uncontentious 'business' nature.

Beginning in the 1880s, however, there was an increasingly militant group of landowners (often 'radicals' in other spheres) who sought to resist both the plutocratic and the democratic embrace. This minority fought a long-drawn-out rearguard action to revive and reassert the primacy of landownership as the practical and moral basis of the nation's public life. Commitment to land as more than just a private, vested interest—as the veritable cradle of civic virtue—was deeply interwoven with aristocratic involvement in a long chain of revanchist social issues: bimetallism and agricultural derating in the 1890s, tariff reform in the 1900s, and resistance to the 1909 Budget and to reform of the House of Lords. To at least some of its protagonists pursuit of this vision appeared to be identical with the wider interests of the political nation; but to many contemporaries it seemed increasingly like simple defence of class power. As was suggested in Chapter 4, the gradual expulsion of land from the 'high ground of national identity' to the defensive periphery was central both to late Victorian and Edwardian high politics and to the history of the wider social structure of the age.

There was more, however, to the social revolution in politics than mere aristocratic retreat and collapse. The Reform Acts of 1867 and 1884 (which enfranchised urban and then rural male householders, together with certain limited categories of lodger) fell far short of universal suffrage; but they brought something much closer to popular democracy than had been dreamt of only a few years before (particularly since the vagaries of electoral law soon began to let in a much more precarious and impoverished class than had originally been intended by the franchise legislation).* Moreover, the Act of 1884 brought into existence for the first time a large bloc of Irish voters, many of whom did not share the English vision of the historic working relationship between nation and constitution, society and the state. The Reform Acts were accompanied and followed by a series of measures, often apparently trivial in themselves, that chiselled away at ancient constitutional principles and together reconstructed both the framework of politics and the invisible social undercarriage of political power. In 1869 Parliament restored to unmarried female ratepayers a right which they had enjoyed until 1835, that of voting in local government elections; by 1900 there were more than a million women on county, borough, and Poor Law electoral registers—a female Trojan Horse within a still overwhelmingly masculine national constitution. The Ballot Act of 1872 freed electors from the more obvious forms of political influence and coercion, emanating from workmates, neighbours and wives as well as from social superiors; but at the same time the secret ballot nourished the growing notion of the franchise as an individual rather than a communitarian right. The Redistribution Act of 1885 broke up the multiple representation of ancient communities, replacing it in many cases with single representation for smaller, often socially homogeneous suburbs—thus powerfully reinforcing the stratification of politics into blocs based on social class.† This was followed by the removal of franchise disqualification

---

* In 1915 about 60 per cent of the 10,250,000 adult males in England and Wales were on the parliamentary register. A bias towards property remained in the fact that there were about 450,000 plural voters. But the research of Duncan Tanner has corrected the view that those unregistered were mainly composed of the poorest sector of the working class.

† Though this by no means automatically led to the rise of working-class politics. To labour leaders at the time it seemed that redistribution closed the door upon working-class

from applicants for purely 'medical' poor relief—a seemingly minuscule measure, but one that nevertheless breached the hallowed constitutional principle that voting rights should never be exercised by those without independent means of support. And in 1894 the extension of the 'lodger' vote to elections for Poor Law guardians was widely seen as opening up control over the Poor Law to a class indistinguishable from recipients of poor relief.

These extensions of the voting system were accompanied by the piecemeal creation of a new network of local government institutions, which transferred to local communities large areas of social life that had previously been under aristocratic, oligarchic or clerical control. The Education Act of 1870 provided for management of public elementary schools by popularly elected local school boards (boards for which women were for the first time eligible to stand as candidates, schooling being deemed part of the legitimate female sphere). The Public Health Act of 1875 erected district councils in many urban areas; and in 1888 the Local Government Act swept away the Elizabethan quarter sessions (for three centuries the institutional stronghold of the landed gentry), replacing them with new ratepayer-elected county and county borough councils. The non-ecclesiastical functions of churchwardens were transferred to secular parish councils (open to women as both voters and candidates) in 1894; and the new structure of local government was completed by the abolition of the London vestries (except for the City Corporation) and their replacement by metropolitan borough councils in 1899.

This series of electoral and institutional reforms called into being a massive new constituency of lower-middle- and working-class voters, who had to be contained and absorbed within both national and local political life. The process of absorption had social and cultural implications as well as political ones; and the late Victorian and Edwardian period saw a great proliferation of sub-political institutions and techniques, designed to expand, inform, educate, and manipulate the new political nation. The introduction of universal (and subsequently compulsory and free) elementary schooling in the 1870s and 1880s was very explicitly linked to the civilizing of future citizens; and throughout the period education for citizenship took far greater priority in nearly all quarters of the education system than education for economic efficiency. Both major parties hoped that their different models of Irish land reform would not merely redress agrarian

representation, because local electors who were willing to adopt a working man as one of several candidates were much more reluctant to consider him as their sole representative.

grievances but would create a politically integrated Irish peasantry on the model of the French. In the aftermath of the Second Reform Act there was much upper-class involvement, both Liberal and Conservative, in the founding or sponsorship of popular political clubs, designed not merely to win votes but to initiate the new electorate into the tenets and practices of constitutional behaviour. Clubs proved limited in scope and difficult to control, however, and although they remained important as venues of popular culture, the focus of political activists rapidly shifted to other, more far-reaching and theatrical modes of political management. Caucuses, paid agents, public meetings, mass demonstrations, claqueurs and brass bands (all of them to some extent in evidence well before 1867) now became part of the standard paraphernalia of urban party politics, together with the more humdrum processes of registering and canvassing a largely uncommitted electorate. Similar techniques on a more limited scale were extended to rural constituencies from the mid-1880s (after an initial lacuna during which landowners falsely assumed that 'Hodge' would 'vote with his masters'). Election expenses were in theory severely curtailed by the Corrupt Practices Act of 1883, but, nevertheless, political finance assumed increasing importance as one of the vital tap-roots of party power. Party 'programmes' and extra-parliamentary promises to electors (viewed by many earlier Victorians as unconstitutional violations of parliamentary sovereignty) gradually invaded day-to-day political practice. The rise of consumerism, imperialism, and the late Victorian cult of monarchy (the latter tangibly embodied in increasingly spectacular jubilees, coronations, funerals, state visits, and durbars) all accentuated the drift towards a more mass-produced, spectator-sport style of political life. Above all, political oratory became the indispensable medium of the age, replacing the role of the sermon only a few years earlier—oratory that might be delivered to crowds of thousands, but that was also increasingly addressed to shorthand-taking journalists for instant telegraphic transmission to the mass-circulation dailies. From Gladstone to Lloyd George the public theatre of British politics was dominated by virtuosi on the human voice, esteemed for their capacity to reduce strong men to tears and to tame rough audiences into submission. 'At the first sound of his voice they became as one man', recorded Beatrice Webb of a speech addressed by Joseph Chamberlain to the massed citizens of Birmingham. 'Every thought, every feeling, the slightest intonation of irony and contempt was reflected on the face of the crowd. It might have been a woman listening to the words of her lover!'

It is important to stress, however, that the mass-manipulation model of politics never wholly prevailed over the ideal of citizen-participation; and to many they were not rival techniques, but complementary ones. Gladstone's Midlothian campaign of 1879 demonstrated how dramatic use of the mass media could be combined in a high degree with politics as a form of moral education. And the most successful mass political agency of the period—the Tory party's mock-feudal, quasi-masonic Primrose League—was designed *both* as a vote-catching machine *and* as an organ for disseminating traditional constitutional principles. On a more limited scale, progressive Liberalism, Ulster Unionism, and the Independent Labour Party all made use of musical evenings, discussion groups, young men's guilds, and informal patronage networks, not simply to win votes but to engender a wider socio-political culture of a kind thought to be favourable to their particular creeds. The mainstream of the women's movement, under the leadership of Josephine Butler and Millicent Fawcett, placed great emphasis on the political education of women and on the redefinition of 'good citizenship' to include such traditionally private and 'feminine' issues as personal morality, child care, health, and home. In many areas 'local parliaments' were founded, loosely modelled on the Oxford Union, that were designed to initiate literate lower-class electors into the skills and mysteries of political debate. And such otherwise dissimilar groups as Robert Blatchford's Clarion Clubs, Baden Powell's Boy Scouts, the Fabian Society's summer schools, and the Edwardian 'Guild of Help' and 'Social Service' movements: all had in common the aims of promoting active citizenship and inseminating ancient civic virtue into modern mass democracy.

Such movements were often organized by the upper and middle classes for the improvement of the working class; but manipulation from above was far from being the only strand in the new political culture. Throughout Britain in the 1890s and 1900s working people above the level of the very poor were involved in a richly variegated, autonomous, and self-governing associational culture, expressed through trade unions, friendly societies, co-ops, chapels, and political and social clubs. These bodies were identified by numerous observers both domestic and foreign as cradles of citizenship, independence, mutual assistance, and social reform—and as holding the key to the unique mixture of libertarianism, public order, and self-control that distinguished British society in this period from neighbouring societies on the Continent. Through this unique culture, wrote Paul de Rousiers in 1894, 'Great Britain is training up generations of capable citizens, and thus is putting herself in a position to meet the political changes in store without violent revolution.'

The result was the first mass political culture in British history—a culture that in part was to be further transformed by the First World War, but many elements of which were to survive for the next half-century. As already indicated the visible impact of this new culture upon many outward forms of public life was limited; and right down to 1914 both high politics and high society still glistened with the patina of aristocratic power. Beneath the surface, however, there were many fundamental changes in the social basis of politics, some of them predictable, others more surprising. One important feature of the period was a growing divergence between activity in politics and the possession of wealth, accompanied by a rapid decline of the older view that ownership of property necessarily entailed some kind of participation in the public life of the nation. Another was the rise of a class of 'professional' politicians, functionally detached from specific community and class interests, and often imposed on constituencies by central party offices, who increasingly sought to make their name in politics by action, innovation and reformist legislation. Although businessmen dominated the new organs of local government and were increasingly numerous in Parliament, neither industrial nor financial capital ever successfully captured the 'high ground' of politics formerly held by land. The mantle of representing the 'national interest' appeared to pass rather to the new administrative class, recruited after 1870 mainly by 'open competition', who by the 1900s increasingly dominated the domestic departments of state. It was these civil servants in Edwardian Whitehall rather than ministers and Members of Parliament who most piously pursued the Peelite tradition of an 'impartial state', standing aloof from the competing interests of economy and society.*

Within the country at large the subdivision of ancient constituencies and the increasing individuation of the franchise tended to reinforce the crystalisation of class division in many spheres of social life. Politics was increasingly invaded by the language of class, expressed throughout the period by radical attacks on landownership and by socialist claims that the real class enemy was not land and aristocracy but industrial capital or middle-class plutocracy. The growth of a class dimension in politics was visibly embodied in the formation of the Independent Labour Party in 1893, the Labour Representation Committee in 1900 and the Labour Party in 1906—all of them specifically committed to securing direct working-

---

* This is not, of course, to claim that they were always successful in their aim. Reports of the Local Government Board reveal how deeply many of its inspectors were immersed in the ideology of the 1834 Poor Law; while the Board of Trade was widely regarded as 'an annexe of the Reform Club'. The vision of an 'impartial state' was nevertheless an active and not wholly meaningless ingredient in Edwardian administrative culture.

class representation in Parliament without the assistance of patrons from other parties. Class division was not an inexorable process, however, and much recent research on Edwardian politics has emphasized the almost infinite variety of class mutations that could be found in local party struggles and alignments. The endemic class war in parts of urban Yorkshire, for example, must be compared with the Nonconformist progressivism that united much of middle- and working-class Lancashire. Party alignments that appeared to be naturally rooted in 'class' were often the product not of spontaneous class loyalty but of intense organizational activity by party agents: Protestant farmers in Ulster, for example, were by no means the conditioned-reflex supporters of Unionism that the historian might expect. Local government was an important forum of working-class politics, and in many areas 'Labour' established itself as an independent force on councils and boards of guardians at a time when labour representation in national politics was still heavily dependent on co-operation with the liberals. But Labour representatives, even in such strongholds of working-class activism as Poplar and West Ham, were often no less committed than other progressive groups to 'community', 'citizenship', 'self-discipline', and 'organic' moral obligation; and many members of the Edwardian labour movement were as fearful as Liberals and Tories about the lurking threat of an uncivilized urban 'residuum'. Furthermore, many of the new local authorities were successful in either perpetuating or creating a cross-class community spirit, that survived in many localities until long after 1914; and numerous key areas of local conflict, such as sectarian education, Jewish immigration, and the Edwardian ratepayers' revolt against high municipal expenditure, were only partly reducible to battles about class power. A supra-class, 'public service' approach to local politics was further strengthened in many areas by the admission of women. In 1870 only three women held elected public office throughout the length of Britain; but over the next forty-four years more than three thousand gradually gained access to school boards, boards of guardians, and municipal, district, parish, and county councils, where they were particularly active in promoting a 'moral' rather than 'class' approach to educational and social needs.

The fears of some prophets in 1867 that franchise extension would be followed by the proletarianization of national political culture were, therefore, nowhere fulfilled; and indeed what needs to be explained is not the speed but the slowness with which assertion of specifically working-class interests caught up with the formal reality of working-class power. Late Victorian intellectuals often deplored the debasement of reasoned political argument by unthinking popular sentiment; and there was much patronizing mockery even in progressive circles of the foibles of 'Arry and 'Arriet (two stereotypes invented by George Gissing to symbolize the ignorant vulgarity that now reigned in public life). But the historian who reviews the political debates of the period—in newspapers, journals, public inquiries, and conference reports—may well be struck by the opposite point: by the surpringly high standards of information, literacy and grasp of principle with which popular discussion of social, economic, and constitutional issues were often sustained, right across the political spectrum. The popular constituency for serious discussion of politics in Edwardian Britain was probably larger in proportion to population than at any time before or since—a fact that should be set alongside the more familiar images of music-halls and 'mafficking', monarchy-worship and jingo crowds.*

IV. CONTRACTION AND EXPANSION

The expansion of the political nation in this period was paralleled by far-reaching changes in the practical role of the state, and it is tempting to see the one as the direct consequence of the other—to see the revival and expansion of paternalist government as what Sidney Webb called 'the economic obverse of democracy'. In fact, popular attitudes to state intervention were widely varying and ambivalent; and it is perhaps more accurate to see the extension of popular politics and the growth of the administrative state as twin responses to the same wider pressures for change—social, economic, and ideological. It is important also not to draw the contrast between the 1860s and the 1900s too strongly: as many historians have shown, the mid-Victorian state was never quite so 'minimal' as either its defenders or its detractors believed. Economic *laissez-faire* did not necessarily entail moral *laissez-faire*, and many mid-Victorian social policies were explicitly designed to reward or punish certain kinds of rational moral behaviour on the part of individuals. Both the compulsory vaccination of young children (which under an act of 1867 included draconian powers of legal enforcement against parents) and the compulsory inspection of prostitutes (introduced on medical and military advice by the Contagious Diseases Act of 1866) are useful reminders of the extent to

* An exception was the tariff reform campaign, whose popular propaganda introduced a strident and vulgarian note into Edwardian politics that strikingly jars with the high-minded tone characteristic of other areas of reform; but the very limited popular success of the tariff reform movement lends support to the point which I have made.

which perceptions of public safety might override private autonomy, even in a self-consciously libertarian age.

There was nevertheless a widespread sense in the 1850s and 1860s that, at least in the economic sphere, the fundamental principles of public policy had been fixed for all time by an earlier political generation. Social, monetary and economic policy were believed to have been largely 'taken out of politics' by the 1834 Poor Law, the Bank Charter Act of 1844, and the repeal of the Corn Laws in 1846. Each of these measures was perceived not merely as a passing political triumph, but as the embodiment of certain supra-historical universal laws. Beyond these three spheres, state intervention was by no means positively forbidden; but it was widely perceived as justified only to help those too weak to help themselves (mainly women and children) or in cases involving what political economists defined as 'public goods', that could not safely or profitably be left to private initiative (such as public health, water supplies, police, and public order).

This vision of the role of the state was shared by nearly all mid-Victorian politicians and was perceived by many less as a matter of ideological preference than as a fact of life. Throughout the 1850s and 1860s there was a good deal of piecemeal Poor Law and public health legislation, but this largely took the form of refining and regulating the existing duties of local government. Large areas of social life, from business enterprise and industrial employment through to inheritance, education, housing, medicine, and food consumption, were regulated solely by common law and private contract, the only interest of government being in the maintenance and enforcement of the law. Ministers and officials reacted with insouciant scorn to occasional suggestions in the press that they should control immigration into Britain, issue passports or monitor the activities of visiting revolutionaries and members of the First International. Only in the sphere of industrial safety was there conspicuous growth in central government inspection, and even here the boundaries of the public and private spheres were continually contested. The most powerful and dynamic area of mid-Victorian central government was public finance; and here all the energies of ministers and officials were devoted to limiting rather than expanding the public sphere, and to dismantling the last residues of fiscal protection. Public expenditure was stable or falling for most of the 1860s and early 1870s, and for a time during Gladstone's first ministry the major channel of central government revenue—the income tax—seemed on the verge of abolition. Taxation was for the most part strictly confined to the raising of revenue rather than reallocation of the 'natural' pattern of economic resources; and the aim of the annual Budget was to produce an exact and finely tuned balance between national revenue and expenditure. Downward 'redistribution' was largely confined to indoor and outdoor poor relief, disbursed from the local rates and in strict legality payable only to those who were totally destitute. Public expenditure on direct relief to the poor fell dramatically in the late 1860s and 1870s as central government pursued a campaign of promoting the stricter and more literal enforcement of the 'principles of 1834'. Formal provision for law and order was equally limited. The home army was no bigger than it had been at the end of the seventeenth century, when the population was one-sixth of its level in 1871. Expenditure by the new, local police forces rose rapidly in the 1860s, but still barely kept pace with population growth; and in many areas prevention and detection of crime remained largely dependent on the traditional duty of citizens to raise a hue and cry. The result was a strong but strictly limited and largely invisible apparatus of state power. The inactivity and invisibility of governments in the 1860s was aptly (if accidentally) symbolized by the person of Queen Victoria, who for more than a decade withdrew into widowhood and virtually vanished from the theatre of public life.

The shift to a different style of government and to more interventionist forms of social policy came about very gradually; and throughout the period there were many spheres in which politicians and departments of state were simultaneously moving in both directions. The Local Government Board in the 1870s, for example, was vigorously trying to limit and privatize relief to individual paupers whilst at the same time greatly expanding bureaucratic control over sanitation and public health. Thirty years later the Board of Trade was still trying to establish an effective free-market framework for insurance, patents and bankruptcy, just as it was beginning to limit the operations of the market in the spheres of industrial relations and sweated labour. Throughout the period individuals and pressure groups who sought state intervention in one sphere often opposed it in others. Herbert Spencer, for example, the great critic of state intervention in the sphere of social welfare, constantly berated governments for their non-intervention in the spheres of law enforcement and punishment of crime. The United Kingdom Alliance, which lobbied for legislation to restrict or outlaw the sale of alcohol, was overwhelmingly composed of supporters of free trade and administrative *laissez-faire*. The campaign to end Britain's open-door policy on alien immigration—which culminated in refusal of entry to diseased, pauper, and criminal aliens under the Aliens Act of 1905—mobilized both supporters and opponents of market economics. The ethos of private contract—and indeed many other aspects of mid-

Victorian governmental philosophy—remained persistently powerful; and there were many areas of social policy (ranging from education in 1870 through to National Insurance in 1911) in which a main concern of state intervention was to protect or incorporate the private sector and to stimulate and reward continuing voluntary effort.

Nevertheless, from the start of the period there was continuous piecemeal expansion in the sphere of social policy at both local and central levels, and continuous redefinition, both pragmatic and theoretical, of the nature of 'public goods'. Sir Assheton Cross, introducing the Housing of the Working Classes bill in 1875, laid it down as an 'axiom' that the state had no duty to provide citizens with 'the necessities of life'; but he conceded that the state *did* have an interest in promoting health, because 'health is actually wealth'. Such an approach, which permitted a very elastic interpretation of legitimate public action, became a keynote of the new administrative age. Local govenment growth 'took off' in the late 1860s and early 1870s, fuelled by legislation which allowed local authorities to borrow in the market and issue their own stock. Headed by Leeds and Birmingham, many enterprising local authorities launched into the era of 'gas and water' socialism, transforming the physical and environmental infrastructure of urban Britain. At the same time parliamentary legislation began to heap upon local authorities a great mass of new reponsibilities for social arrangements, far wider in scope than their very limited sanitary and poor relief functions of the mid-Victorian years—responsibilities which were often defended on the ground that they would not negate but lubricate an autonomous, self-governing pluralistic society and free-market economy.

The most far-reaching of these new, centrally imposed local government obligations was the provision of primary and secondary schooling under the Education Acts of 1870 and 1902, provision that was largely financed from the local rates but subject to a continuous process of central government direction and inspection. Compulsory education, introduced nationally in 1876 and enforced by a network of 'school attendance officers', brought into the schools large numbers of children whose most urgent needs were physical and social rather than educational; and from the 1880s onwards there was continuous if uneven expansion in local authority provision not merely for the mass of the nation's children but for those with special needs: the blind, deaf and dumb, epileptic, feeble-minded, and the merely 'backward' and 'dull'. Concurrently, the urban crisis of the last quarter of the century generated a long series of new economic and environmental duties for local authorities; duties which were introduced in a largely pragmatic and piecemeal fashion, but together revolutionized the scope and underlying principles of local social administration. Powers over slum clearance and rehousing were tentatively introduced in 1875, and extended in 1892 and 1900. From the early 1890s instructions from central government to local Poor Law guardians gradually relaxed the deterrent conditions attached to poor relief and allowed relieving officers to 'disregard' annuities, friendly benefits and other forms of private saving, thus significantly blurring the 1834 principle of absolute separation between poor relief and the private market.* Powers to purchase land for the provision of smallholdings were first introduced in 1892. And in 1886 and 1893 the Local Government Board issued circulars to local authorities, encouraging them to provide work for the unemployed, a policy that was eventually promoted throughout the country by the Unemployed Workmen Act of 1905.

Initially such powers were eagerly sought after by the new urban élites, confident of their capacity to mould a new urban civilization. There were many spheres, such as technical education, civic universities, free school meals, municipal milk supplies, free libraries, and promotion of 'model conditions of employment', in which radical and dynamic local authorities such as the corporations of Bradford and Birmingham and the London County Council ran far ahead of central government in their thinking—and often far outside the legal limits of their statutory financial powers. 'High rates and healthy cities' was the slogan invented by Sidney Webb for the Progressive alliance that dominated the early days of the LCC. By the 1900s many of the great provincial centres were swallowing up lesser authorities in their surrounding areas and evolving into metropolitan 'city-states', a process exemplified by passage of the Greater Birmingham Act of 1911. Around the turn of the century, however, there were signs of a certain loss of momentum and confidence in local government growth, a mood that was linked to the underlying structural shift away from locality towards nation and Empire that was noted in Chapter 1. By the 1900s many local authorities, large and small, were in serious financial trouble. Educational costs had risen to become the biggest single item of domestic public expenditure, second in the national balance sheet only to the armed services. Poor Law expenditure was growing throughout the 1890s, and shot dramatically upwards in the severe economic depression that followed

* This principle was of course more honoured in the breach than the observance. Throughout the Victorian era Poor Law guardians, particularly in rural areas, had defied central government directives by unofficially supplementing pensions, low wages and family support. But the circulars of the 1890s represented an important change of direction in official Poor Law thought.

the Boer War. In many urban areas during the early 1900s local authorities were faced with turbulent demands for public works from mass demonstrations of the unemployed. As charges on the rates continually expanded, the discrepancies between rich local authorities with few social problems and desperately poor local authorities with many came pressingly to the fore; ratepayers, often themselves quite poor, were in vocal revolt against the cost of the new social services. Local elections between 1902 and 1907 returned rising numbers of right-wing candidates (at a time when Parliament was moving markedly to the left). In many cities the ambitious and free-spending businessmen who had manned the corporations of the 1870s were replaced by a much more cautious and economical generation, to whom high rates were yet another ingredient in the problem of marginal costs (believed to be eroding Britain's competitiveness in international trade). The result was increasing political conflict over provision of local services—and growing demands for retrenchment and for relief to local authorities from the national exchequer. Such pressures were a major cause of the marked shift of emphasis that occurred in the 1900s away from provision of services by local authorities towards national, bureacratic, tax-financed provision by central departments of state.

V. Finance, bureaucracy, and social policy

The growth of central government was a more complex process than that of local government, and at least one of its major propellants—namely, Britain's defence requirements in Europe and the Empire—lies far outside the history of domestic society. Nevertheless, social factors cannot be entirely separated from external and strategic ones, particularly in an age that increasingly linked health, education, citizenship, taxation, and welfare to imperial expansion and defence. Moreover, it was rising defence and particularly naval expenditure that was initially responsible for a latent financial crisis in the late Victorian state. From the 1880s onwards the Treasury and Inland Revenue were casting around for new sources of national revenue, a concern that coincided with the emergence of new groups in British politics, who challenged orthodox mid-Victorian conceptions of central government taxation. Disciples of the American reformer Henry George supported a 'single-tax' on the increment value of landed estates; while Fabian socialists and advanced liberals began to put forward ideas about 'redistribution' and 'taxation according to ability to pay', based on progressive graduation of different levels of income. Faced with prolonged depression and increasing foreign competition, 'fair-traders' began to argue for a revival of tariffs on imported food and manufactures. And there was much sympathy in orthodox 'constitutionalist' circles for the view that extension of the franchise should automatically be accompanied by a 'broadening of the basis of taxation' (on the ground that citizenship and taxation traditionally went hand in hand).* All these groups contributed to a prolonged and often highly dramatized debate about the sources, scope and underlying philosophy of national taxation, that over the course of two decades was to transform the fiscal structure of the British state.

A new approach to revenue was first tentatively heralded by Sir William Harcourt's budget of 1894, which introduced graduated death duties on large landed estates. Five years later, in the midst of the Boer War, a Conservative Chancellor, Sir Michael Hicks Beach, aimed to offset the impact of high wartime income tax by allowing abatements on lower incomes and tax relief for house purchase (both initially very minor measures, but which were destined to loom much larger in fiscal politics later in the twentieth century). The war left a legacy of greatly inflated public debt, which Hicks Beach tried to meet by imposing a tax on imported corn: the first tax on the people's bread for more than half a century. The hidden agenda behind this tax was not to reintroduce 'protection' but rather to promote the 'constitutionalist' principle of incorporating a much larger section of the British citizenry into the taxpaying classes. Nevertheless, it provoked Joseph Chamberlain into launching his tariff reform campaign, which called into question the whole inheritance of 'free-trade' fiscal thought, and put forward an alternative programme of social reform, imperial federation and defence of British industry—to be financed by protective tariffs on imported food and manufactures. The challenge of tariff reform in turn provoked Liberal fiscal experts to look for new sources of revenue consistent with free trade—and thus to commit themselves ever more firmly to 'progressive' direct taxation. This concern became a keystone of public finance, and of wider social and economic policy, when the Liberals were returned to office in 1906. 'Differentiation' between earned and unearned incomes was introduced for

---

* Such constitutionalist views were particularly strongly expressed by Sir Edward Hamilton, the Treasury official chiefly responsible in the 1880s and 1890s for taxation matters, and from 1904–6 permanent secretary. Hamilton's papers and diaries are full of the view that 'no representation without taxation' was a corollary of the principle 'no taxation without representation'. There are obvious affinities between this view and the traditional theory of citizenship, whose continuing importance I have noted at many points in this study.

the first time by the Budget of 1907, tax allowances for dependent children in 1908, and a 'supertax' on higher incomes by Lloyd George's 'People's Budget' of 1909. Taken all together this long sequence of measures enormously increased both the potential income of central government and its power over the allocation of resources in British society—in striking contrast to both France and Imperial Germany, where over the same period reformist ministers tried and largely failed to introduce some form of centralized progressive taxation on incomes and wealth. The result was that, for all its relative invisibility, the British state in 1914 was by far the strongest financial power in Europe. And, for all the revolt of the House of Lords over the 1909 Budget, by the end of the period the owners of large-scale private wealth in Britain were subject far more effectively than elsewhere to some degree of public fiscal control.

Reconstruction of the financial core of central government was paralleled and fuelled by administrative growth in many other spheres. Part of this growth stemmed simply from the inner momentum of bureaucracy itself. Few civil servants in this period were in any sense ideologically committed to an expansion of state power as an end in itself, and many were deeply imbued with the more passive public doctrines of the mid-Victorian era. But the sheer complexity of modern urban and industrial civilization meant that conscientious officials in Whitehall departments were continually expanding their fields of action, not simply by legislation but by use of administrative orders and 'quasi judicial' powers. Advanced mass production, for example, together with 'expert' pressure from its own inspectorate, forced the late nineteenth-century Home Office to take a progressively more interventionist approach to safety at work and legal compensation for accidents. Several Whitehall departments set up 'research' branches, which provided not financial support but information and advisory services for the development of science and technology by private enterprise. Similar internal and external administrative pressures generated the creeping extension of government controls over such spheres as food adulteration, contaminated water-supplies, shipping, roads and railways, and the general area of public health.

The inner momentum of bureaucratic growth is not by itself, however, an adequate explanation for central government expansion, since there were many spheres of policy in which public officials were indifferent or actively hostile to the extension of state power. Of growing and sometimes overriding importance was the external demand for state action from numerous economic, philanthropic, parliamentary, and sectarian pressure groups. By far the most successful of such groups were the Irish nationalists and the

Anglo-Irish landlords, who over the whole period provoked state intervention in Irish social and economic affairs to a degree quite unparalleled in the rest of the United Kingdom. Between 1870 and 1914 both Liberal and Conservative governments at Westminster promoted legislation and provided funds for public projects in Ireland that in England, Scotland, and Wales continued to be seen as belonging largely to the private and contractual sphere—among them tenant-right, land-purchase, agricultural co-operatives and marketing schemes, and the founding of a national university. Even in England, however, the depression of the 1880s began to subvert earlier belief in the existence of a natural, self-sustaining economic 'equilibrium', and led to demands from employers and from chambers of commerce and agriculture for various forms of state economic aid—ranging from bounties and subsidized freight rates to a 'bimetallic' currency and public investment in technological education. These demands were paralleled by a shift of emphasis within the trade union movement away from exclusive reliance on free collective bargaining towards increasing interest in political action and social legislation. The 1880s was also a very active decade for a large body of moral reform groups, who successfully lobbied for more effective state intervention on such issues as licensing reform, the restriction of Sunday trading, the criminalization of homosexuality, the raising of the age of sexual consent, and the prevention of cruelty to children. In the social welfare sphere the depression called into being a wide range of new charitable and reformist organizations which vigorously campaigned for new government policies on housing, land reform and relief of unemployment (in striking contrast to philanthropic experiments of the 1860s, whose main rationale had been to avert rather than to solicit intervention by the state).

Such organized pressures were accompanied by a gradual transformation of more widely diffused popular attitudes towards poverty and public relief—attitudes that moved simultaneously in two quite different directions. On the one hand, violent mass demonstrations in the mid-1880s sharply reinforced earlier fears about the parasitic menace of a feckless and degenerate urban 'residuum'; on the other hand, it became more and more apparent that mass unemployment was afflicting not merely the residuum but large numbers of regular, organized, and often highly skilled workers, whose industries were vulnerable to international fluctuations of trade. The much publicized researches of Charles Booth in London and Seebohm Rowntree in York endorsed the view that there was a small inner core of poverty which was wilfully self-imposed through drink and bad character— and a large outer mass of poverty caused by sickness, low wages, and poor environment, which was largely beyond the scope of individual control. These perspectives were increasingly reflected in public debate. From the 1880s onwards there were recurrent proposals for more stringent 'state sternness' towards deviants and social derelicts. At the same time there was a growing demand from both reformist pressure groups and the organized working class that the 'genuine unemployed'—together with the respectable majority of the sick, disabled and elderly poor—should no longer be consigned to a deterrent and stigmatic system of localized poor relief.

Central government responses to these social pressures came in various ways. Except in the context of Ireland, there is little evidence of direct central government reaction to the threat of popular disorder at any time down to 1914; and response to pressures from more organized interest groups was in many respects more limited than is often assumed. Throughout the period suggestions from English, Welsh, and Scots radicals that the Irish model of land reform might be extended elsewhere in Britain were either rejected or diluted beyond all recognition. Even where there was an apparent causal relationship between pressure-group politics and government growth—in, for example, the campaigns for liquor licensing, free school meals, old-age pensions, and provision for the unemployed—it was very often the case that ministers and officials constructed a new policy on very different lines from those canvassed by its popular supporters. Nevertheless, from 1870 onwards there was a continual growth of specialist government departments which—splitting off from the traditional multi-purpose Home Office and Privy Council—reflected the ever-proliferating variety of functions and interests in a modern urban and industrial society. The Local Government Board was set up in 1870, a Commercial, Labour and Statistical Department within the Board of Trade between 1886 and 1893, a Board of Agriculture in 1894, and a Board of Education in 1899. In all domestic departments new bureaucratic structures and 'managerial' procedures began slowly to emerge from the chrysalis of patronage, idiosyncrasy, and circumlocution that had continued to dominate many areas of public administration in the mid-Victorian years.

Substantive change in the actual content of social policy came haltingly at first, and, as was stressed above, much innovatory legislation of the 1870s was justified as being merely an extension to public health and therefore generically within the legitimate public sphere. From the 1880s onwards, however, central government policies in Britain as well as Ireland gradually encroached upon both the personal concerns of individuals and the sphere of the private market to an extent that redrew many of the conventional boundaries between society and the state. The Local Government Board circulars on public works tacitly challenged the premise of orthodox political economy that artificial creation of public employment merely sucked labour and capital away from the private sector. The Workmen's Compensation Act of 1897 for the first time compelled employers to take responsibility for accidents to their employees, regardless of the extent of their liability at common law. The growing pressure on central government to relieve the financial burdens of the localities has already been mentioned. State subventions to local services—in the form first of 'assigned revenues' and later of 'grants-in-aid'—were growing steadily from the late 1880s; and in 1899 Treasury officials who gave evidence to the Royal Commission on Local Taxation proposed a large additional transfer of social expenditure from local to central government. The 1902 Education Act greatly increased central financial support for elementary and secondary education, and for the first time compelled local authorities to give public subsidies to denominational schools. A further decisive swing in the fulcrum of central–local relationships came in the aftermath of the Boer War, with the Report of the 1904 Interdepartmental Committee on Physical Deterioration. This committee rejected the suggestion from some quarters that large sections of the British population were in a state of irreversible physical and 'racial' decline, but it reported that throughout urban Britain there was widespread physical unfitness, caused by poverty, malnutrition, environmental pollution, and bad personal habits; and it hinted strongly that the sheer scale of the problem and the resources required to deal with it now went far beyond the scope of even the largest local authorities. Such findings chimed with the views of the cross-party 'national efficiency' movement which, in the wake of the disasters of the Boer War, launched an all-out attack on the parochial, amateur, and libertarian traditions of British government and proposed widespread 'professional' restructuring of imperial government, social services, and national defence. A year later, in recognition of the crisis in many local areas, the outgoing Conservative government appointed a powerful Royal Commission to inquire into the working of the Poor Law and relief to the unemployed. From 1905 to 1909, and for some years thereafter, members of this commission orchestrated a massive public debate on the underlying principles of government, citizenship, and social welfare—a debate which constituted a perhaps unique episode in the history of the relationship between British society and the various administrative organs of the state.

All these factors help to account for the dramatic shift of emphasis from local to central government, from rates to national taxation, and from limited provision of public goods to more extensive provision of personal services that was apparent in the social policies of the reformist Liberal government after 1906. From 1907 onwards Liberal ministers in the Treasury, Board of Trade and Home Office were engaged in framing or implementing a long series of social policy measures, that in both administrative structure and the treatment of individual citizens moved far away from the governmental ideas and practices of the late nineteenth century. The earliest of these measures—the Acts of 1906 and 1907 which enabled local authorities to provide free school meals and school medical inspection—were very limited and permissive in form; but in substance they constituted what many saw as an unprecedented public interference in the rights and duties of parents, without the civic penalties attached to poor relief. They were followed by the much more substantial Old Age Pensions Act of 1908, which introduced pensions for citizens over 70, to be administered by the Post Office and financed out of central taxation—pensions which, though subject to a means test, were to be payable as a statutory right without social stigma or civil disability.* In the same year the Home Office introduced the Children Act, which codified earlier legislation for the protection of children, gave central government subsidies to local authority reformatories, and set up juvenile courts and remand homes directly administered by the Home Office and financed out of Treasury grants. A year later the Board of Trade introduced the Labour Exchanges Act and the Trade Boards Act, both of which wholly bypassed the local government sector. The Labour Exchanges Act established throughout the country a network of agencies to find work for the unemployed, which was to be regionally administered by centrally recruited 'managers'; while the Trade Boards Act set up 'panels' of representative employers and workers to impose minimum wages in (mainly female) sweated industries. The 1909 Budget made provision for the setting up of two new central government offices—a Development Commission and a Road Board—which were empowered to use public funds to stimulate employment and to encourage public authorities to concentrate their capital works into times of cyclical depression. Two years later the National Insurance Act introduced compulsory health and sickness insurance for workers in most industrial employments—a scheme that was to be administered by a centralized National Health Insurance Commission working in co-operation with voluntary 'approved societies'. Under the same act compulsory unemployment insurance was set up for workers in the engineering,

---

* The pensions were initially denied to recent recipients of poor relief, but this condition was abolished in 1911—a change whose significance was discussed in Chapter 1.

shipbuilding, and construction industries, to be managed locally by the labour exchanges and centrally by the Board of Trade. Legislation of 1908 and 1912 also introduced a statutory eight-hour day and a national minimum wage in the mining industry—both of them measures which fundamentally breached the Victorian convention that public policy should never interfere with the private economic choices of adult males. Finally, the Mental Deficiency Act of 1913 codified provision for lunatics and mental defectives, and introduced for the first time powers of compulsory detention over that section of the population defined as 'feeble-minded' (namely, those not certifiable as lunatics, but nevertheless deemed unable to support and look after themselves in the wider community).*

VI. CRIME LAW, AND POLICE

So far this discussion of the social history of the state has concentrated mainly upon responses by government institutions to the mounting complexities of a modern market society and to the changing contours of citizenship and social class. Little has been said, however, about the state in its most ancient and fundamental domestic role: the maintenance of public order and the detection and punishment of crime. Crime and public order shared no less than other social spheres in the powerful reformist and rationalizing instincts of the late Victorian and Edwardian age. The transportation of the last boatload of convicts to Australia in 1867 and the last public hanging in 1868 were the dramatic culmination of a much more long-drawn-out shift of emphasis in penal policy that had been taking place over several decades. Private prosecution of offenders, not uncommon in the early Victorian period, was rare by 1914, a transition symbolized by the creation in 1879 of a Director of Public Prosecutions appointed by the Secretary of State. There were important practical and procedural changes in the criminal law, notably the introduction of probation in 1899 and of legal aid in 1903, the setting up of a Court of Criminal Appeal in 1907, the continuous clarification of the laws of evidence, and a gradual shift of policy from flat-rate to graduated sentencing (the latter designed to impose more severe punishment on hardened 'professional' criminals). The prison system, which in the early Victorian period had comprised an array of central, local, and semi-private institutions, was unified under centralized

---

* This act did not, as has recently been claimed, provide that any unmarried mother should be liable to certification as feeble-minded and subject to permanent detention. It provided that women already diagnosed as feeble-minded and living on Poor Law relief should be permanently detained if they became pregnant.

Home Office control in 1877 and was steadily extended to include specialist remand centres, Borstals, and prison 'hospitals' for the criminally insane. Throughout the period pressure from social and moral reform groups resulted in the progressive criminalization of many and varied forms of human activity that had previously been more or less unknown to the law: parental failure to send a child to school became an offence in 1876, living off immoral earnings in 1884, sexual intercourse with under-16s, and private male homosexual behaviour in 1885, theatrical performances by children in 1888, off-course betting in 1906, incest and the sale of cigarettes and alcohol to children in 1908. Unemployed demonstrations in the 1880s and suffragette and syndicalist violence in the 1900s provoked much public alarm and several major public inquiries into problems of law and order. Throughout the earlier part of the period there were spasmodic outbreaks of intimidation and terrorism in Ireland; and in 1913–14 the government was faced with army mutiny, treasonable conspiracy, and mass illegal drilling among Loyalists in Ulster, as a response to the prospect of Irish Home Rule.

All these developments might suggest that late Victorian and Edwardian Britain was a society beleaguered by crime and civil unrest. In fact, almost the opposite is true. One of the most striking features of British society between the 1860s and the First World War was its continually diminishing rate of recorded crime, a phenomenon that was historically quite unusual by comparison both with earlier and later periods in British society and with the experience of other industrializing societies in the latter half of the nineteenth century. In spite of increasing concentration on imprisonment as the sole form of punishment for serious crime, the prison population in all parts of the United Kingdom was proportionally much smaller in 1914 than it had been in the 1860s, while sentences for penal servitude were one-fifth of the level of fifty years before. Recorded crime and conviction rates are clearly a somewhat elastic measure of actual criminal behaviour, and public definitions of what constituted 'crime' were no less fluid in this epoch than in any other. But as legislators throughout the period were constantly *extending* the boundaries of crime and as police were increasingly *active* in its apprehension, it seems scarcely credible that *falling* crime rates can be ascribed to mere transient social perceptions.*

* This point could be demonstrated much more forcefully than I have space for here; but the point should be made that a very high proportion of Edwardian convicts were in prison for offences that would have been much more lightly treated or wholly disregarded by law enforcers in the late twentieth century. In 1912–13, for example, one quarter of males aged 16 to 21 who were imprisoned in the metropolitan area of London were serving seven-day

In fact it seems clear from a wide variety of sources, descriptive as well as statistical, that in terms of both serious and lesser crimes Britain was a much more ordered and law-observing society in the 1900s than it had been half a century before. The early Victorian period had been wracked by very high levels of theft, homicide, violence, and public disorder. Public discussion of crime in the 1840s had frequently assumed that it was widely endemic among the working population, and indeed that the categories of criminal, pauper, and labouring poor, if not absolutely identical, were part of an interlocking social continuum. Crime rates began to fall, however, in the 1850s and 1860s, and plummeted after 1870. Homicides, woundings, and non-violent crimes against property reported to the police fell by more than half between 1870 and 1914. Juvenile crime was high in the 1870s but fell rapidly thereafter. Offences linked with drunkenness were high in the 1870s and 1880s, but then fell continuously down to the outbreak of the First World War. Theft from places of employment was still widespread in 1914, but on a far smaller scale than forty years earlier. Physical attacks on policemen remained common and were part of everyday street culture in many poor areas; but even so the overall rate of recorded assaults on the police declined by nearly two-thirds over the whole period. Large areas of London and other large cities that in the 1850s had been the sovereign republics of armed gang-land had been converted by the 1900s into peaceful and well-patrolled, if not necessarily honest and affluent, suburbs. Only the relatively small categories of burglary and robbery with violence went against the general trend by rising sharply in the last few years of the period, a phenomenon which was widely interpreted by contemporaries to mean, not that popular honesty was once again on the wane, but that serious crime was now confined to a small class of professional criminals. A prominent police criminologist, Dr Robert Anderson, argued in 1901 that crime in Britain could be permanently abolished within a decade if seventy habitual criminals known to the police could simply be locked up for life and separated from all contact with the rest of the community.

Rioting and public disorder declined in a similar fashion. There were, of course, some gigantic mass demonstrations over the course of the period, some of which ended in death and attacks on property—the most dramatic being the Black Monday and Bloody Sunday riots of 1886 and 1887, which

sentences for offences which included drunkenness, 'playing games in the street', riding a bicycle without lights, gaming, obscene language, and sleeping rough. If late twentieth-century standards of policing and sentencing had been applied in Edwardian Britain, then prisons would have been virtually empty; conversely, if Edwardian standards were applied in the 1990s then most of the youth of Britain would be in gaol.

led to the banning of public meetings in the centre of London for the following five years (and to the rather limited and low-key character of Queen Victoria's golden jubilee). The backlash against trade-unionism and rise of the 'free labour' movement in the 1890s, and the spread of anarcho-syndicalism in the late 1900s, meant that 'peaceful picketing' sometimes ended in violent confrontations with the police, and on rare occasions with the summoning of the armed forces. There were periodic outbreaks of violence connected with religion, such as the attacks organized by brewers on the Salvation Army and by ultra-Protestants on Roman and Anglo-Catholic Eucharistic processions. Nevertheless, the endemic popular disorder and disruptions of the peace that prevailed in many areas in the 1840s had markedly declined by the 1870s and had almost vanished by the 1900s. The ritual 'reading of the Riot Act' which was an everyday occurrence at the start of Victoria's reign was most uncommon by the end; indeed, a man charged with failing to observe the reading of the Riot Act during the famous Featherstone Colliery riot of 1893 defended himself by claiming that he had never heard of the Riot Act and did not know what its reading meant. Crowd harassment of the police—and, conversely, police harassment of assembled crowds—certainly occurred in the 1890s and 1900s, but was sufficiently unusual to attract much public criticism and comment. The scenes of drunken violence common to all classes, that had accompanied sporting events such as Derby Day in the 1850s and 1860s, had been replaced in the 1900s by sober and self-disciplined gatherings such as the Cup Final and the Lord Mayor's Show, where crowds of more than a hundred thousand were shepherded by a mere handful of uniformed constables (many of whom were weekend 'specials'). The new sense of order was symbolized by the Great London Dock strike of 1889, when tens of thousands of banner-bearing workers marched through the streets of London 'giving the appearance of a great church parade', and twelve thousand pickets gave rise to only twenty arrests. An international survey on prostitution published in 1914 found that for safety, decorum, and public order London resembled a gigantic 'open-air cathedral', in stark comparison both with the other capital cities of Europe and with London itself some forty years before.

Both the reasons for, and the meaning of, these dramatic changes in popular behaviour remain a matter of historical debate. Some historians and criminologists have linked the decline of crime simply to the numerical growth and increasing efficiency of borough and county police forces: bodies which—after a patchy and localized start in early Victorian Britain—covered all parts of the country by the late 1870s. Such an argument chimes with the perception of many contemporaries: Charles Booth, for example, ascribed the tranquillity of east London almost entirely to the physical presence of the Metropolitan Police. But it does not wholly account for the fact that there were wide local variations in the incidence of crime, which did not always correlate with the strength of local constabularies. Others have pointed to the changing physical shape of British society in this period, the trend towards geographical segregation of property from poverty, and the lack of transport facilities for quick getaways from one class 'ghetto' to another. Such an interpretation may fit the case of giant cities, but it ignores the fact that there were many smaller urban communities in which the poor and better-off still lived side by side; and it fails to explain why even in the metropolis such vulnerable areas as the underground railway system were virtually free from both violent and petty crime. Some have emphasized the functional role of all forces of law and order—not just police, but magistrates, judiciary, Poor Law and the social policy 'inspectorate'—in regulating the poor and buttressing the existence of property and capital. That protection of property was a major priority of the legal system is undeniable; but this priority was no greater in 1900 than it had been in 1840, and it cannot therefore wholly account for so profound and far-reaching a shift in popular attitudes and habits. Moreover, throughout the period the bulk of police and courtroom time was taken up with offences related to drunkenness, soliciting, truancy, and thefts of property worth less than £1—scarcely in themselves crimes that threatened the ramparts of property and capital. Other historians have focused upon the theme of 'social control' and the invisible moral incorporation of working-class communities into middle-class standards and values, not via the iron fist of law and police but via the velvet glove of education, religion, charitable exhortation, and 'rational recreation'. Such strategies were a central theme of nineteenth-century reformist liberalism, and most progressive-minded people throughout the period 1870 to 1914 not merely believed, but gloried in the belief, that disorderly elements in British society could be tamed rather than battered into social integration. Social control, though, was a horizontal as well as a vertical process, and some of the most law-abiding and disciplined communities in Edwardian England were those which were most contemptuous of upper-class patronage, most fiercely loyal to the autonomous culture and institutions of the independent working class. Still further explanations for the decline of crime hinge upon the growth of working-class prosperity after the desperate subsistence crises of the 1830s and 1840s; and certainly evidence about the social background of late Victorian convicts suggests that they were not drawn from the regular and prosperous working class but overwhelmingly from an unskilled and illiterate residuum.* By the turn of the century, however, short-term fluctuations in criminality had become correlated with upturns rather than downturns of the business cycle, thus perhaps foreshadowing the emergence of a new pattern of criminal behaviour that was linked to affluence and high wages rather than deprivation and desperation among the very poor.

All these interpretations—administrative, geographical, structural, and economic—have some validity; but none by itself is wholly adequate to account for the fundamental and far-reaching change in the underlying relationship between crime and society that occurred in Britain between the mid-nineteenth century and 1914. The whole area of crime and public order in this period seems to require more detailed and localized study than it has so far received, with more focus not merely upon national statistics and legislation but upon the interaction of law, morality, crime, and police with different communities, social institutions, personal value-systems, and places of work. More specifically, the diminution of crime needs to be set in the context of a changing social and political culture, to discover whether declining crime, expanding citizenship, widespread participation in voluntary institutions and the growth of popular politics were unrelated movements or different facets of a complex but homogeneous social trend.

Certainly such evidence as is available suggests that both the commission and the repression of crime were not independent variables, but were closely linked to wider socio-political and cultural change. Much has been written about the alienation of the working class in this period from law, police, judiciary, and court procedures; but, as was suggested in Chapter 1, there is only limited support for this view to be found in working-class sources, particularly among that growing sector of the working class who were organized in independent, self-governing associations. Throughout the period both leaders and the rank-and-file within the Labour movement criticized the criminal and civil law for their more flagrant class biases; but there is almost no evidence of working-class rejection of 'law' as an abstract reified principle, culturally divorced from working-class ways of thought. On the contrary, working-class no less than middle-class reformers wanted the law to become *more* abstract, *more* professionalized, *more* detached from traditional social structures (there was universal dislike of untrained lay JPs

---

* In 1898, 19.3 per cent of the inmates of prisons in England and Wales could neither read nor write, while 75.2 per cent were only semi-literate.

and widespread demand for their replacement by professionally qualified stipendiary magistrates). The vast majority of independent working-class associations—trade unions, friendly societies, and working-men's clubs—were themselves extremely severe on breaches of the law, and frequently expelled or prosecuted members found guilty of fraud or dishonesty. In marked contrast to popular attitudes to the workhouse, most working people viewed prisons not as illegitimate agencies of popular control but as neccessary institutions 'where genuine offenders were to be punished'. Vandalism and attacks on public property were virtually unknown, in striking contrast to nineteenth-century France, a fact ascribed by Taine at the start of the period to the growth of 'a state of affairs in which every man is his own constable, until at last none other is required'. Furthermore, there was widespread dislike among working-class people of medico-psychological attempts to soften up the definition of crime and to identify certain types of crime as forms of 'mental' or 'moral' pathology. It seems intuitively probable that many of the most prominent characteristics of mainstream working-class life in this period—community solidarity, parental authority, family integration, and mass membership of a wide range of self-governing associations—were at least as important as deterrence, police, and upper-class paternalism in explaining popular acceptance of the law and the apparent diminution and marginalization of crime in nearly all sectors of British society.

All these points should not be taken to suggest that there was universal, unqualified support for the forces of law and order. On the contrary, throughout the period there were residual but often closely knit communities in which petty crime and dishonesty were forms not of deviance but of day-to-day social convention. There was chronic suspicion among all levels of the working class (as indeed there was among many sections of the middle class) of officious police interference. The detection of crime and the conviction of offenders were chronically hampered, both by the unwillingness of individuals to give evidence against their fellow citizens and by the libertarian traditions of the common law (again in marked contrast to contemporary France, where prosecution and conviction rates were much higher than in England and Wales). Throughout the period campaigns to extend and strengthen the criminal law were countered by widespread concern for civil liberties, a concern that was powerfully entrenched within the legal profession itself, and that spanned both old-fashioned 'natural libertarians' and newer protagonists of more pluralistic sexual, moral and behavioural modes. Numerous archival sources and autobiographies of the period reveal that well-dressed, decorous persons of both sexes who strayed into territorial no-man's-land were liable to be not necessarily physically molested, but harassed and hooted at by casual gangs of roughs. Very little is known about white-collar and upper-class crime, but recent research into Edwardian political and financial scandals suggests that occasional prosecutions and exposures may have been merely the tip of a much larger iceberg. And certainly there was a great deal of upper- and middle-class male juvenile violence and disorder that was never statistically recorded as crime, simply because it was not perceived or registered as such by magistrates and the police.

Policemen themselves enjoyed ambiguous social status; usually drawn from and living among the working classes, yet often viewed as alien agents of the classes above them. Police relationships with the public varied widely, both over time and in different local communities. Gillis's study of juvenile delinquency in late Victorian Oxford, for example, found that crime fell when police methods became less crudely punitive and more communitarian. Popular resentment against the police was often greater in supposedly 'deferential' rural communities than in more 'democratic' urban ones. Most police forces interpreted the law with a degree of flexibility that amounted occasionally to outright corruption, more frequently to tacit connivance at the pettier forms of criminal offence. Prostitution, vagrancy, and off-course betting all operated under a more or less tolerant police umbrella, punctuated by occasional 'cleaning-up' operations or by the activities of ambitious young constables anxious to fill their quota of arrests. A study by Sir Henry Jones published in 1911 concluded that the reduction of crime in Britain had now reached its outer limits and that what remained consisted of an irreducible criminal or semi-criminal culture, which should not be seen as pathological but as a necessary minimum of disease in an organic body politic. The relationship of the police with that criminal culture was one of curious interdependence rather than antagonism: 'The officers of the law and the criminals knew each other as familiarly as opponents in a game of chess and were on not less friendly terms. And the rules of the game were thoroughly understood on both sides.'

VII. AMBIGUITIES OF POWER

This long catalogue of legislative change and institutional growth transformed many aspects of the relationship between state and society in Britain in the decades before the First World War. By 1914 the roles of central government, local government, voluntary associations, families, and private citizens had become much more closely intertwined than in the mid-Victorian years. Many areas of social life—such as education, thrift, child care, sexual relations, mental deficiency, medicine, immigration, alcohol consumption, employment, and the search for work—which in the 1860s had belonged wholly to the private sphere now involved some element of compulsion, prescription, licensing, or monitoring by agencies of law and central government. In the 1860s the visible face of state power in Britain was largely confined to police, magistrates, Poor Law guardians and a small handful of factory inspectors; by 1914 a far more numerous body of public officials—school-attendance officers, asylum managers, official 'foster-parents', labour-exchange officials, health visitors, probation officers, and 'inspectors' of many different kinds—had become a permanent presence in the day-to-day working of society, and an influential 'expert' interest group in their own right. The only major area of private life that was *less* closely entwined with the state in 1914 than in the 1860s was the practice of religion; and even in the religious sphere churches and denominations that were engaged in secular good works were more likely to be receiving state aid and co-operation at the end of the period than half a century before.

These changes occurred with very little conscious attempt to expand or transform or exalt the functions of the state. By comparison with most Continental countries there were still many key areas of social life—such as higher education and scientific research—in which state involvement continued to be minimal to the point of non-existence (in 1905 public expenditure on all forms of higher education was £100,000—equivalent to the running cost of one naval frigate). Throughout the period there was overwhelming popular hostility to any form of compulsory military service; and demands after the Boer War from such bodies as the National Service League for universal military training and conscription resulted in nothing more than the purely voluntary Territorial Army (formed by the Liberal War Minister R. B. Haldane in 1908). Moreover, as feminists like Millicent Fawcett and Maud Pember Reeves pointed out, with certain very limited exceptions the organs of political power still added up to the exclusively 'masculine state' inherited from the early nineteenth century.

Nevertheless, by 1914 it appeared to many contemporaries that there had been some kind of quantum leap in the very nature of the state—that it was no longer merely a useful tool for the protection of order and property, but had become the predicate and arbiter of large areas of private existence. The 'decentralized patrimonialism' that Max Weber identified as uniquely characteristic of the British tradition of government was being supplemented and in some cases displaced by more 'rational–bureaucratic' forms of administrative control. Historians have attempted to explain this change in many different ways: as a response to the pressures of mass democracy, as a consequence of Empire, as an attempt to buttress free-market capitalism, as a shift of emphasis from 'negative' to 'positive' liberty, and as part of an inexorable process of institutional modernization. Each of these explanations has some bearing upon the changing social character of late Victorian law and government. Popular pressures *were* an important influence upon the activities and perceptions of ministers and officials, although—as was demonstrated above—by no means always a direct or simple one. Consciousness of Britain's imperial role *was* a continuing element in the growth of the domestic state (though a far less preeminent one than the great imperial proconsuls—Lords Cromer, Milner, Curzon, and their disciples—would have wished). Strengthening and streamlining market forces *was* a major motivation of many social and administrative reforms: from the Goschen circular of 1869 through to the National Insurance Act of 1911, the question of who should absorb the 'costs' of economic progress was a central theme of social policy debate. Changing conceptions of liberty *were* an important feature of the culture of the age, as will be shown more fully in the following chapter. And throughout the period demands for reform in the structure of government—from 'open competition' in the 1870s to 'National Efficiency' in the 1900s—*were* intertwined with the rhetoric of administrative rationality and political modernization.

By no means all changes in law and government during this period are explicable in these terms, however. As was noted above, one of the most dynamic areas of state expansion from the 1870s through to the 1900s was the public control of private morals, a sphere that bore no obvious relation to the efficiency of private capitalism, nor to what later generations would come to think of as 'modernization'. The vast majority of politically active late Victorians and Edwardians, including many feminists and many critics of private capitalism, regarded the 'moral' identity of the state as a fundamental reality that was simply not reducible to economic or political power (though it was conceded that the moral character of the state might have important secondary implications for these other spheres). This moral perspective was by no means confined to high-minded members of the upper and middle classes, but was shared by many members of the Labour movement. 'The great political and social measure of the session is undoubtedly the licensing bill', reported the president of the Trades Union Congress in 1908—a year which brought the introduction of statutory old-age pensions, the Children Act, and the sharpest contraction in real wages for more than half a century.

Moreover, the practical process by which change occurred was a largely piecemeal and unsystematic one, involving many ambiguities and inconsistencies in public policy and many attempts to harness together and reconcile social principles that were seemingly in tension. The Old Age Pensions Act, for example, was based on means-tested benefits financed out of general taxation; whereas three years later the Treasury—alarmed at the sheer cost of non-contributory pensions—firmly switched its allegiance to the principle of contractual social insurance (thus almost by accident committing the British state to two wholly different prototypes of citizenship and social welfare for the rest of the twentieth century). Ministers influenced by 'new liberal' ideas about redistribution and collective provision were equally concerned with buttressing 'old liberal' ideas about independence and personal saving, a juxtaposition that could be clearly seen in the terms of the National Insurance Act, which encouraged voluntary thrift organizations to share in the management of the state schemes and gave generous subsidies to supplementary private insurance. The state's 'incorporation' of trade unions and friendly societies for purposes of social insurance may be compared with the embodiment of the exactly opposite principle in the 1906 Trade Disputes Act, which reaffirmed the status of trade unions as mere associations of individuals, belonging exclusively to the private sphere. The Census of 1911 recorded a higher proportion of the British people as living in various forms of state institution than at any time before or since; yet such a figure masks the fact that official thinking about institutions was moving simultaneously in quite contrary directions—that, for instance, alcoholics, vagrants and the 'feeble-minded' were being pressed into institutional care, just as orphans, juveniles and petty criminals began to be catered for in other ways. Expansion in the scope of the criminal law was accompanied by continual technical and procedural changes in the laws of evidence, designed to protect even the most habitual offenders from miscarriages of justice and wrongful arrest. Throughout the period the structure of the 1834 Poor Law remained intact and continued to operate side by side with the new social services, partly because, in many spheres, the Poor Law was doing useful work, and partly because—for all the new concern with organic and environmental perceptions of poverty—ministers, officials, and public opinion continued to accept the basic validity of the 'principles of 1834'. Such ambiguities should not be seen as in any way surprising. On the contrary, they accurately reflect the many countervailing social forces that were operating upon law and government in a highly complex and diverse society during a period of widespread structural and ideological change.

8

Society and Social Theory

I. THE PROBLEM OF 'SOCIETY'

A French study published in the 1870s calculated that a large majority of the adult population of Britain belonged on average to between five and six voluntary associations: trade unions, friendly societies, literary, scientific and philosophical societies, savings clubs, co-ops, and innumerable other greater or lesser associations set up for a multitude of purposes. In France, by contrast, participation in voluntary associations was confined to a tiny minority.* This finding coincided with a widespread British perception that the French had been 'macadamized' into uniformity by several centuries of aggressive centralized government, to a point where spontaneous free association of the Anglo-Saxon kind had virtually ceased to exist. Similar observations were made half a century later in numerous surveys that contrasted the British with the Germans. Germany, it was conceded, had a dense network of 'social organization', but it was organization that largely emanated from and was closely regulated by imperial and state governments. Autochthonous self-governing associations of the kind that characterized all functions, all localities and nearly all levels of society in Britain were virtually unknown.

As was shown in the previous chapter, Britain between 1870 and 1914 shifted to a certain extent in the direction of the 'Continental' model of government, and many areas of previously voluntary activity came partially within the state's embrace. Even so, Britain in 1914 remained a society in which private, pluralistic, and self-regulating social relationships—includ-

* The study was carried out by Martin Nadaud, a veteran of 1848 and disciple of Louis Blanc.

ing market relationships—bulked much larger in everyday life and national culture than relationships determined by organs of central government. Observers as diverse as the Australian Empire-federationist Frank Fox, the German sociologist Ferdinand Tönnies, and the black American social scientist Booker T. Washington thought that the very facts of Britain's modernity—the estrangement of the vast bulk of her people from life on the land, the growth of ultra-specialized occupations, and the lack of self-sufficiency which these entailed—all engendered a sense of individual dependence upon and immersion in 'society' to a far greater extent than anywhere else in the world. It was, nevertheless, a society which, even in the face of powerful centralizing and Anglicizing forces, still embodied four distinct traditions of national identity and culture, which in turn harboured many tenacious local loyalties and ways of life. Finally, Britain's role as the pivot of free trade and of an expanding Empire exposed British institutions and citizens to a multiplicity of political, economic, social, and military relationships throughout the world.

How were such powerfully opposing forces reconciled? What turned such a conglomeration of global, national, and parish-pump elements into a 'society'? In all Western cultures during the latter half of the nineteenth century there was a great burgeoning of interest in the question of what held society together, and indeed what a 'society' actually was. Not merely in Britain but throughout Europe and North America there were numerous optimistic attempts to discover laws of social behaviour, comparable in precision and certainty with those that governed the natural world. The sheer complexity and diversity of British society in this period might have been expected to provoke a very powerful school of sociological theory, particularly in view of the fact that associations of citizens dedicated to the study of social institutions were a very prominent and active feature of Victorian and Edwardian voluntarist culture; yet on the whole historians have concluded that this was not the case. British social theorizing in this period and later has been disparagingly compared with the powerful new schools of sociological analysis that were being generated on the Continent by theorists such as Max Weber, Émile Durkheim, Vilfredo Pareto, and their disciples. By contrast with these great systematic schools, so it is often argued, British attempts to understand the nature of society and the dynamics of social relationships were shallow, eclectic, and methodologically naïve; and detached social analysis was always harnessed to and distorted by the British impulse towards moralism and social reform. Whereas Continental theorists of this period are perceived as standing outside or on the margins of the societies which they sought to understand, their British counterparts have been portrayed as fatally immersed within the toils of domestic and imperial public administration. And, paradoxically, although late nineteenth-century Britain was so remarkable for its densely packed culture of self-governing associations, British social science and sociological theory have been depicted as persistently wedded to a conception of the isolated 'rational individual' and largely indifferent to the existence and behaviour of collective social groups.

How far these judgements are in fact justified lies to some extent outside the scope of this study. Naïve or not, however, the attempt by individuals to comprehend both the specific character of their own society and the nature of 'society' in general was a central feature of national culture in the late Victorian period. From self-educated working men through to university professors, from the National Association for the Promotion of Social Science in the 1870s through to the Sociological Society of the 1900s, both individuals and wider groups of citizens were engaged in a continuous process of enquiry and speculation about how society and its constituent relationships actually worked. Social analysis and observation was a major forum of intellectual life for many intelligent women, excluded as they largely were from more formal and institutionalized disciplines such as economics, philosophy, and anthropology. Such enquiry was more than simply an aspect of intellectual history (though of course it was that too): it was part of a wider process whereby people reflected in an often rather episodic and piecemeal fashion about personal identity, class and gender relationships, national character, ethics, and social change—a process that in turn interacted with beliefs, behaviour, art, social structure, and public policy. If it be true that late Victorian and Edwardian social theory was inseparably linked to the desire for practical reform, then that in itself is an important aspect of the social history of the period, worthy of further scrutiny and comment. Similarly, if it be true that, even in the face of the ever-increasing scale of organizational structures, British intellectuals* clung to a notion of the irreducible autonomy of separate human beings, then that again is a notable feature of the culture of the age. Earlier chapters of this book have tried to suggest that ideas about certain key areas of life—such as the family, property, work, religion, and the state—were more than just reified abstractions: they were sociological periscopes that help the historian to uncover and explain the day-to-day working of social

---

* I have used the term 'intellectual' in this chapter to include anyone—from authors of academic treatises on philosophy and sociology through to quite obscure private citizens of all classes—who reflected about the nature and working of social institutions. I am aware of the unsatisfactory nature of the term, but cannot think of a better one.

processes and institutions. This chapter will review changing ideas about the nature and meaning of 'society' in this period, both in the writings of philosophers, social scientists, and political theorists, and in the more informal language of day-to-day life. It will analyse, too, the changing construction of certain specific social forces and phenomena, such as poverty and unemployment, heredity and environment, national identity, race, and class.

II. ATOMISM, ORGANICISM, AND SOCIAL EVOLUTION

Writers on social questions in the 1830s and 1840s had often used the term 'society', but it was not a powerful organizing concept in the thought of the early Victorian age. Macaulay in his *History of England* had used the word mainly to imply 'polite society', or even quite simply convivial company; while Thomas Carlyle had portrayed the organic, hierarchic 'old Christian society' of past eras as in a state of wholesale fragmentation and decline. The late eighteenth-century 'Scottish enlightenment' vision of social life—as a sphere intertwined with, but distinguishable from, political and economic activity—appeared to be largely in eclipse; and political economy, evangelical theology, and strict utilitarianism all allowed little scope for social arrangements that were not reducible to the functions and free choices of rational individuals. More 'organic' views of society were expressed mainly in terms either of old-fashioned High Church Anglicanism, or of the historic development of the British constitution from Anglo-Saxon and Norman times down to the present day. Popular parlance in the early Victorian period frequently spoke of 'society' as largely synonymous with the 'public sphere', and as though such basic arenas of human association as families, education, child care, work, and private philanthropy were the very antithesis of social life rather than its vital constituent parts. Even disciples of Robert Owen, who believed that individual psychology was totally dependent upon the constraining influences of society, were hard put to it to explain what the fundamental category of 'society' actually meant.

This lurking uncertainty about the meaning and status of 'social' action remained characteristic of much British political, economic, and sociological thought up to 1914, and beyond. Throughout the late Victorian and Edwardian period certain key areas of intellectual life remained resolutely attached to what a later generation would term 'methodological individualism'. The mainstream of British political economy continued to focus upon the behaviour of rational individuals; and indeed the effect of 'marginal

223

utility' (conceptualized in the 1870s by W. S. Jevons) was to make the analytical structure of economic thought *more* rather than *less* atomistic than it had been a generation before. Even economists like Marshall and Pigou, who were very conscious of the social and cultural determinants of real-life economic behaviour, ultimately failed to integrate 'society' into their theoretical schemes. British jurisprudence remained largely resistant to the 'corporatist' ideas that were fashionable in Germany and the United States. Atomistic and even anarchic perceptions of private liberty were vehemently defended by such bodies as the Liberty and Property Defence League and the Anti-Socialist Union. As was suggested in Chapter 1, the ancient ideal of politics as an association of free, property-owning, independent, masculine individuals—the vision of virtuous citizens in a virtuous republic, powerfully conjured up in W. T. Stead's *Review of Reviews*—remained a compelling idiom in many areas of public life. And throughout the period there was a powerful culture of hard-headed, no-nonsense, Anglo-Saxon empiricism—strongly represented in many quarters of political, legal, imperial, and academic life—which dismissed all talk of group identity or social action as bogus rhetoric (what James Fitzjames Stephen in 1873 had called a mere 'bag of words').

From the mid-nineteenth century, however, many counter-currents of social thought were attempting to re-interpret both individual and collective human behaviour in more structural and organic terms. The writings of Ruskin and Carlyle kept up a sustained, if somewhat erratic, critique of theoretical individualism, and unfavourably compared the fragmented social philosophy of industrial capitalism with the guild-based communities of the later Middle Ages. The novels of Dickens and George Eliot portrayed individuals as fatally caught up, often far beyond the range of their own understanding, in a myriad counter-currents of encircling social life. Both Broad Church and, slightly later, 'incarnational' theology shifted the emphasis of religious thought away from individual salvation towards a more corporate and immanentist vision of an earthly 'kingdom of Christ'. British disciples of the French sociologist Auguste Comte began to preach the idea of a 'science of society', comparable in precision and predictive power with the physical sciences; and throughout the country numerous mid-Victorian social science associations compiled great masses of statistical and descriptive data about the workings of British society and its institutions. The writings of John Stuart Mill did not clarify the issue of how society should be defined, but they left readers in no doubt of society's omnipresent existence—an existence that Mill's *On Liberty* viewed somewhat ambivalently as both the precondition of freedom and civilization, and as a latent form of psychological tyranny, 'penetrating . . . deeply into the details of life and enslaving the soul itself'.

This shift towards greater awareness of the collective identity of society was reinforced by material and structural change: by the increasing scale of urban life and productive processes, by the rise of mass political organization, by the spread of compulsory education and mass-circulation newspapers, and by the gradual emergence of a trade cycle of national and international economic activity that appeared to be largely outside the scope of rational human control. The sheer accumulation of statistical facts—itself the product of early Victorian interest in the behaviour of individuals—revealed that there were many inexorable regularities in patterns of social and demographic behaviour that appeared to bypass the motions of individual human wills. And the expansion of knowledge about history and anthropology introduced the Victorian reading public to many societies and cultures other than their own, in which social structure and solidarity rather than personal identity seemed to be all-important.

Perhaps the most decisive change in the character of social thought came, however, with the great mid-century explosion of 'evolutionary' ideas, an explosion of which Darwin's *On the Origin of Species* was merely the most famous spark. From the early 1850s Darwin's contemporary Herbert Spencer was setting out his own account of evolution and natural selection in the sphere not of botany and zoology but of organized human groups. Unlike Darwin, Spencer believed that the trigger mechanism of evolution in both individuals and communities was not random mutation but functional adaptation to the pressures of natural and social environment. In a long series of works on 'systematic sociology' he claimed that human nature was not static but constantly evolving, that 'social science' was concerned with establishing the same kind of laws as the physical sciences, and that human societies were living organisms, subject like the rest of the natural world to competition, selection, survival and decay. Within this framework 'progressive' societies were to be identified simply by the fact that, like higher organisms, their members practised a very high degree of division of labour and functional specialization, held together and harmonized by a dense network of voluntary co-operation. Such a process depended on the existence of a strong governing authority to ensure that evolutionary laws were observed; but beyond this minimal level of strict law-enforcement Spencer decisively shifted the emphasis of social analysis away from states and governments and on to the autonomous processes of society itself.

Evolutionary models and metaphors began to invade many aspects of social thought in the 1860s, and by the 1880s had become part of the dominant intellectual paradigm of the age. Spencer's influence upon the language and imagery of the social sciences was all-pervasive, even though the majority of those who used his concepts rejected his equation between social evolution and political *laissez-faire*. Among political economists the 'perpetualism' and 'cosmopolitanism' of Ricardo's *Principles* were widely attacked by those who claimed that economics should become a much more historical, cultural, evolutionary and relativistic discipline. The controversy between Sir Henry Maine and J. F. Maclennan about whether civilization had evolved out of patriarchy or matriarchy was of more than mere academic interest to a new generation of intellectual women, who discovered for the first time the at least hypothetical possibility of historic societies based on female rather than male domination. The 1870s brought a great flowering of interest in the study of primitive cultures; and anthropologists increasingly viewed the habits of tribal societies in Spencerian terms, as indications of what 'civilized' societies must have been like at an earlier historical stage. The sense of British peculiarity and uniqueness, which had been such a marked feature of earlier historical consciousness, did not fade away, but it was at least partially replaced by the view that Britain had reached a higher stage on a common evolutionary staircase, up which all progressive societies were destined to travel. The proceedings of the National Association for the Promotion of Social Science became flavoured with organic and evolutionary references; and although the association collapsed in the mid-1880s, the same emphasis was apparent in the great upsurge of empirical enquiry into practical social problems that dominated British social thought over the next twenty years. Charles Booth's *Life and Labour*, Beatrice Potter's studies of sweating, David Schloss's review of wages, Seebohm Rowntree's analysis of poverty, and the writings of Llewellyn Smith and Beveridge on unemployment and casual labour are often seen as establishing a predominantly descriptive and untheoretical approach to the study of social questions that was to be characteristic of British sociology for much of the twentieth century. Yet all these works were deeply grounded in the view that society was a living organism, that social practices and institutions were either progressive or recessive, and that social efficiency and survival were determined by structural 'organization' and capacity for adaptation to external social change.

III. HISTORICISM AND IDEALISM

The model of evolution was perhaps the most potent theoretical influence in pushing late nineteenth-century intellectuals towards a much greater awareness of, and emphasis upon, impersonal social forces. There were, however, other intellectual movements at work, which were linked to the vogue for evolutionary thought but not entirely reducible to it. Some of the economic and historical writings of Karl Marx began to appear in English in the 1870s and 1880s; and although Marxist economic thought was widely dismissed as yet another variant of a now outmoded classicism, Marx's historical studies attracted much interest and were reviewed by such respectable authorities as the *English Historical Review*. A liberal churchman, exposing the errors of *Das Kapital* in the *Church Quarterly Review* for 1879, conceded that 'at the root of it all there is, as we all must feel, an element of truth which gives the whole indictment a semblance of justice'. Such a sentiment soon found expression, not simply in the conversion of the small handful of radical republicans and Marxist theoreticians who founded the Social Democratic Federation and the Socialist League, but in the gradual growth of a much more widely pervasive sense that social relations were the product not of nature or divine ordinance or personal character, but of an all-encompassing, historical 'social system'—a system, moreover, in which many elements were unstable and pathological. Among many Liberals and Conservatives, as well as among socialist thinkers, there was a noticeable shift from the 1880s onwards in perceptions of social 'class', a term that was increasingly used, not simply in a passive sense to denote different groups of economic functions, but in a much more active sense to denote conflict of interest and structural inequality at the very heart of organized economic life.

Certain aspects of Marxism therefore coincided with rather than negated the inclination of many students of social processes in late nineteenth-century Britain to view society in more organic and systematic terms. Echoes of Marxist thought could be found in many quarters: in Fabian socialism, in the trade union movement, in the largely Conservative school of 'historical' economists, and in certain features of Edwardian New Liberalism. Much more immediately influential than Marxism, however, was the late nineteenth-century upsurge of 'idealist' social thought, an upsurge that partly rivalled and partly dovetailed with the widespread interest in organicism and social evolution. There had been undercurrents of Kantian idealism—of the view that the external world was unknowable without certain a priori categories—in British philosophy and theology throughout the nineteenth century. Kant, Hegel, and other German philosophers began to be more widely studied in English and Scottish universities in the 1870s, a move that coincided with a great revival of academic interest in classical idealism and particularly in the works of

Plato. Numerous late nineteenth-century philosophical works not merely proposed an idealist methodology but reiterated the ancient Greek belief that state and society were logically prior to the individual, and that the goal of human association was not mere private satisfaction, but pursuit of the public good.

It is unlikely, however, that this upsurge of philosophical idealism would have spilt over quite so potently into the study of contemporary society if it had not coincided with both the social dislocations of the 1880s and the widespread (albeit temporary) collapse of confidence in the doctrines of classical economics. At Oxford in the early 1880s the historian Arnold Toynbee lectured to large audiences on the social evils wrought by the 'Industrial Revolution' (a concept newly invented by Toynbee at this time) and on the falsity of the mechanistic equation between public and private interests proclaimed by Adam Smith. Toynbee's teaching led many of his hearers very easily into the orbit of the idealist system of political philosophy taught by the Balliol philosopher T. H. Green. Green, like Herbert Spencer, viewed society as an 'organism', and like Spencer he believed that the true arena of social progress lay in voluntaristic co-operation among human beings rather than in direction by the state. Unlike Spencer, though, he saw the 'organic' character of society as rational and purposive rather than natural and predetermined, and the true sphere of rights and laws as being not nature but human consciousness and will. A fully organic 'society' was a group of interdependent rational beings with a common moral purpose, embodied in a 'general will'. Only in 'society' could human beings find true freedom or 'moral liberation'; and morality did not consist merely in private acts of virtue, but in the bringing of the individual will into conformity with the rules and well-being of the wider organic whole.

It might be expected that two such different modes of thought as social evolution and philosophical idealism—the one based on inexorable material law, the other on conscious will and rational purpose—would have been viewed as fundamentally in conflict with each other; and certainly there were prominent voices in late Victorian society who made precisely this point. Spencer himself constantly argued that collective schemes for the common good were a 'monstrous cruelty to future generations'; and T. H. Huxley's Romanes lecture of 1893 specifically warned his listeners against the fallacy that physiological progress was the same as social and moral progress. On the contrary, in Huxley's view the central paradox of modern civilization was that the moral purposes of society (which increasingly promoted health, security, co-operation, and protection of the weak) were in many respects incompatible with nature's iron laws. Anxiety on this account was a continuous undercurrent of late Victorian and Edwardian debates on social reform, and was expressed most clearly and crudely in the claim of 'social Darwinist' writers like Arnold White and Karl Pearson, that societies which flouted evolutionary laws were doomed to self-destruction. Such a view was never, however, predominant in British social thought at this time, and a much more common perspective among both academic theorists and the educated public at large was that ethical norms and evolutionary theory could ultimately be harmonized with each other. The Scottish philosopher and Fabian, D. G. Ritchie, argued that the rational will of society—embodied in political and social institutions—was perfectly capable of formulating and enforcing social laws that were consistent with the precepts of natural science. T. H. Green's pupil Bernard Bosanquet denied that idealism implied any underlying separation between the natural and the ethical worlds; on the contrary, the true subject of all thought was neither 'mind' nor 'matter' but 'the real world organized by mind'. The 'general will' of society in Bosanquet's view was no mere reified abstraction: it was a synthesis of the day-by-day working out of all different aspects of the culture of the nation-state. An even more 'idealized' view of social institutions was put forward by a man who was to become one of Bosanquet's leading critics, the New Liberal theorist and sociologist Leonard Hobhouse. Hobhouse argued that the true sphere of evolution was in any case mental and moral rather than natural and material: the aim of social policy and 'social progress' was not to strengthen natural forces but to impose rationality and order upon the amoral and inefficient chaos of the natural world.

Discussion of such themes was widespread throughout late Victorian and Edwardian intellectual life. Not simply the major universities, but the Ethical movement, the universities extension movement, the British Association, and numerous religious, reformist, and philanthropic groups all engaged in continuous debate about the interrelationship between purposive 'social philosophy' and deterministic 'social evolution'. Some feminist writers, like Mona Caird, looked with suspicion upon the centrality of reproduction in the Darwinian model of evolution; but others, like Frances Power Cobbe and Millicent Fawcett, re-interpreted the maternal role as the evolutionary tap-root of 'social sentiment' and 'altruism' within the modern state. Many branches of late Victorian theology—and many of the moral and doctrinal precepts taught in both state and public schools—became deeply intertwined with both evolutionary and idealist social thought. British psychology, which for much of the nineteenth century had been strongly committed to empiricism and rationalistic hedonism, was steadily invaded by theories about 'social purpose' and 'group mind', and by the belief that the inner psyche of each individual man and woman 'recapitulated' the atavistic experiences of the whole human race. Even hard-nosed Cambridge utilitarians toyed with notions of harmonizing private self-interest with collective 'social welfare' (a neologism imported from the United States early in the 1900s). The Sociological Society, which was founded in 1904 and included a very wide cross-section of different schools of social thought, committed itself to discovering the 'underlying laws of society'—but to do so by studying 'mind' and 'purpose' as well as the 'statistical regularities' of social life. Patrick Geddes, doyen of the British town planning movement, incorporated both evolutionary biology and Hellenistic idealism into his designs for a rational, organic, cosmopolitan 'Eutopia'. Such a conjunction of apparently conflicting perspectives was a common feature of many disparate intellectual groups: it was shared, for example, by many Fabians, New Liberals and members of the Charity Organization Society, groups which were often hotly opposed to each other on practical issues of policy; it was clearly expressed by many witnesses before the great Edwardian public inquiries into physical deterioration, mental deficiency, and the Poor Law; and it was deeply entrenched in the new departments for the study of the social sciences that were set up in many British universities during the first two decades of the twentieth century.

IV. Social theory and the 'social problem'

How far was the new emphasis upon the collective identity of 'society' in the realm of theory reflected in political practice and in the analysis of social problems? As was shown in earlier chapters, a new perception of family breakdown, illiteracy, and disease as conditions that were harmful to the organic welfare of society, quite apart from their impact on the well-being of individuals, was an increasingly important element in late Victorian social policy. From the 1880s onwards growing international trade rivalry and the shifting balance of world power generated much anxious criticism of Britain's libertarian social and economic traditions, criticism in which arguments based on natural selection and the collective interests of society played a conspicuous part. Both evolutionary and idealist arguments were pressed into support of imperial expansion; and even people who had no great enthusiasm for Empire appear to have been moved by the argument that 'advanced' and 'progressive' nations had a duty to promote rational organization among the backward and decayed. During the years after the Boer War the cross-party 'national efficiency' movement injected a powerfully organic tone into military, educational, and administrative debate and eulogized the principles of 'collective mind', 'social organization', and 'the German belief in the state as a creative and moral agency'. The political theories of both Fabianism and New Liberalism were predicated on the view that 'society' as a collectivity contributed a major element to productive processes and wealth creation, the fruits of which society was therefore entitled to recover in the form of 'rent', or taxation for public purposes. Within the Charity Organisation Society—a body often typecast as the last bastion of *laissez-faire* individualism—there was in fact a striking contrast between the atomistic philosophy of older members like Thomas Mackay and a younger generation who supported the organic 'social collectivism' preached by Bernard and Helen Bosanquet and Thomas Hancock Nunn. A comparable shift of emphasis could be detected in the trade union movement, less perhaps in the adoption by some trade-unionists of doctrinal socialism than in the gradual transition from the mainly legal and procedural reforms sought by the older unions to the much more ambitious substantive and structural reforms demanded by a new generation of trade-unionists in the 1890s and 1900s. Within local government and the public health movement, such traditionally private and microscopic issues as child care, nutrition, physical exercise and personal hygiene were increasingly perceived as part of the public and macroscopic concerns of society, nation, Empire, and race. And on all points of the political spectrum the concept of 'social organization' was a constantly recurring leitmotif of the Edwardian age.

The increasing emphasis upon 'society' in late Victorian and Edwardian social thought should not, however, be confused with automatic support for political or administrative 'collectivism'. Many exponents of evolutionary and idealist views did in fact support policies of state control and intervention, but by no means invariably so. Sir John Simon in the 1860s and 1870s and William Beveridge in the 1900s were examples of evolutionary reformists who thought that public policies could accelerate and reinforce societal 'natural selection'; but, as was noted above, others like Herbert Spencer, Octavia Hill, and—in her younger days—Beatrice Webb maintained exactly the opposite point of view. In the 1890s and 1900s there was much anxious discussion among doctors, education experts, nutritionists, and criminologists of 'physical deterioration' and 'racial degeneracy'; and in all these fields expert opinion was deeply divided between a small but embattled minority who detected signs of irreversible organic decline in the

British race, and a majority who thought that symptoms of decay could be treated and cured by political intervention and environmental improvements. Such controversies found expression in the Edwardian eugenics movement, whose adherents included some who supported ameliorative social reforms, some who favoured benign (or malign) neglect, and others who favoured positive policies of selective breeding and sterilization of the unfit.

Similarly, attachment to idealist notions of a group mind or a transcendent state had no automatic connection with promotion of, or opposition to, interventionist state action. The Liberal statesman and Germanophile R. B. Haldane portrayed such policies as progressive income tax and statutory old-age pensions as a tangible embodiment of the Hegelian conception of the state; but other leading exponents of philosophical idealism, such as the Bosanquets—who, like Haldane, saw 'state' and 'society' as predicates of human existence—were nevertheless hostile to most forms of direct government intervention. Conversely, some leading exponents of state intervention, such as Sidney Webb and many members of the trade union movement, still viewed 'society' in old-fashioned utilitarian terms as little more than a structureless heap of individuals. Indeed, Bosanquet frequently accused Webb and other administrative collectivists of excessive 'individualism', on the ground that they had no conception of the harm which 'mechanistic' state action might inflict upon the 'sinews of society' and 'organic communal life'. In the 1900s the industrial syndicalist and guild socialist movements drew heavily upon the ideas of corporate group identity propounded by F. W. Maitland and J. N. Figgis; but they specifically rejected the idea of a transcendent and all-embracing 'sovereign' state, and emphasized instead a conception of society as not one but many interlocking corporations, each with its own limited autonomous functions, be they political, economic, artistic, or religious.

The weakness of the relationship between holistic conceptions of 'society' and holistic conceptions of social policy is a useful reminder that social theorizing was no less diverse and multifaceted than other aspects of British social life. Since much has been written, however, about the close connection between ideology and policy in this period, more must be said about the interaction between different schools of thought and the discovery and interpretation of certain specific social phenomena. Between the 1860s and 1914 the perception not merely of 'society' in general but of what contemporaries often called 'the social problem' changed in many ways. Certain social contingencies that had loomed like a prolonged nightmare in early Victorian Britain—most notably the spectre of over-population—had by 1870 virtually vanished from the scene. Conversely, some conditions that earlier in the century had been seen by many people as inescapable features of the natural order—such as disease, poverty, and premature death—were beginning to be diagnosed as problematic and pathological. Other conditions, like unemployment, appeared to emerge for the first time as a structural feature of advancing industrialization (though whether they were really new, or simply newly visible, was in itself part of the substance of social debate). And there was a further category of problems—such as crime, alcohol, venereal disease, and illegitimacy—which were perceived at all times as social evils, but whose wider implications for the health and well-being of society were viewed in the 1900s in terms very different from those of a generation before. Concern about alcohol abuse, for example, was a constant reference point in all Victorian and Edwardian analyses of social questions; but there was a marked contrast between the early Victorian approach, which viewed 'drink' as a potent cause of personal sin and suffering, and the late Victorian approach, which viewed excessive alcohol consumption as a major barrier to overall national efficiency. The same point may be made about venereal disease, which moved out of the closet of private morality into the arena of public discussion about organic racial decline. A further important area of change, which has been touched upon at many points in this study, lay in perceptions of the nature of 'personality', 'character', and 'individuality'. As ideas about society and social context grew more important, belief in the significance of the individual did not evaporate; but for many people, by 1914, individualism and 'personal identity' meant something quite different from what they had meant fifty years before.

V. THE LANGUAGE OF RACE

Both the broad contours and the more subtle nuances of intellectual change may be demonstrated more fully in the history of attitudes to such issues as race, poverty and physical 'degeneration'. Ideas about race and 'national character' were omnipresent in the early and mid-Victorian era, but they had only the sketchiest of roots in biological thought and were largely expressed in terms of constitutional tradition and political culture. It was widely assumed in the 1850s that the English and Scots were quintessentially 'Germanic' peoples, as opposed to the largely 'Celtic' Irish and Welsh; and it was also widely assumed that the former were generally superior to the latter.* However, the predominance of the English, and to a lesser extent of the Scots, was far more often ascribed to their good fortune in the inheritance of Anglo-Saxon freedom and Protestant religion than to any innate mental or physical traits. 'It is idle, in fact it is almost wicked,' declared a Cambridge professor in 1865, 'to explain Ireland's misfortunes by saying that the Celtic is naturally inferior to the Saxon race.' The same was true of English (and British) attitudes to races beyond the British Isles. Endemic xenophobia towards the Continent of Europe, and particularly towards the French, was clothed in the traditional forms of anti-Catholicism, anti-atheism, and anti-Napoleonic despotism, rather than of explicit racial consciousness. Even in the Indian Empire the assumed backwardness or decadence of the Indian peoples was widely ascribed to their unfortunate religious and cultural traditions rather than to any inherent racial characteristics; indeed, Indian administrators of the generation of Macaulay were amazingly optimistic about the ease and speed with which India—with its massive and ancient diversity of belief and custom—could be sanitized into conformity with Anglo-Saxon modernity. Mid-Victorian politicians of all complexions resisted the idea that there should be any legal restriction upon movement of peoples between different parts of the Empire; and the liberal economist Henry Fawcett looked forward with insouciance to the possibility that Britain's declining birth rate and rising affluence would one day lead to massive immigration from Asia: 'The lot of the whole human race might be improved if inferior races were gradually enlightened and elevated, by bringing them into contact with the ideas and institutions of a high civilization.'

The sense of racial identity as a primarily cultural and historical rather than biological phenomenon persisted in Britain right down to the end of the period. From the 1860s onwards, however, the concept of race as a medium of common cultural inheritance was gradually rivalled by and intermingled with a sense of race as a deterministic biological force. Both the Indian Mutiny of 1858 and the Governor Eyre controversy that raged throughout the 1860s tended to erode earlier, optimistic beliefs about the brotherhood of man; while mid-Victorian science, and particularly the Darwinian revolution, generated a great deal of heated controversy about

---

* Mid-Victorian social inquiries, such as census reports, Poor Law inspectors' reports, and the proceedings of the National Association for the Promotion of Social Science, were full of racial stereotypes, often of a rather surprising kind. The Scots, for example, were portrayed on occasion as feckless and extravagant, the Welsh as prone to sexual promiscuity, the Irish as provident and austere. Such wild generalizations were no mere peculiarity of the English: the pioneers of Continental sociology, such as Comte, Le Play, Taine, and Durkheim, likewise saw the identification of 'national character' as one of the primary tasks of modern social science.

the unity and diversity of the races of mankind. Most expert anthropological opinion in Britain continued to resist the idea that there were any innately inferior races;* but, as was mentioned above, anthropologists increasingly endorsed the view that there was an immense evolutionary gulf between the 'backward' and 'advanced' races, which the former could only cross by following in the footsteps of the latter. The sheer expansion of Empire involved growing numbers of Britons in a master–servant relationship with members of foreign races in a way that fostered crude notions of innate superiority; and even former radical critics of Empire began to view British ascendancy in more explicitly biological terms. 'Breed is breed in men and horses', wrote one disillusioned Anglo-Indian philanthropist in 1884. 'The real fact is—the substance of England in India—that race for race superiority is on our side.'

Similar biological perceptions of race gradually penetrated the arena of domestic social policy in the late Victorian and Edwardian years. As we have seen at many points in earlier chapters, attitudes to health, education, motherhood, and infant mortality were increasingly suffused with concern about whether conditions of life in urban Britain were adequate for the physical nurture of a modern imperial race. Anxiety about the very poor physical standard of recruits to the British army had been endemic in military circles since the Crimean War, if not before; yet it only became a matter of serious public concern in the post-Boer War period, when stoked by fears of congenital racial decline. Edwardian unease about the spread of contraception and the precipitate decline in the birth rate was closely linked to latent fears about the global eclipse of higher races by lower ones; the optimism of Fawcett on this issue in 1864 may be compared with the misgivings of Sidney Webb in a Fabian survey of 1907, which predicted with alarm that 'the ultimate future of this country may be to the Chinese!' The language of the 'national efficiency' and 'duty-and-discipline' movements constantly invoked competitive racial terminology—less with reference to the non-white races of the world than to Britain's European rivals, particularly the people of Imperial Germany. Moreover, racial metaphors of a biological kind were increasingly applied by some social commentators to the inhabitants of Britain themselves. From 1870 down to 1914 popular discussion of the problems of the very poor frequently referred to them in biological and anthropological terms as 'a backward people' and 'a race

---

* There were of course exceptions to this. Professor Ray Lankester in his evidence to the Royal Commission on the Feeble-Minded in the 1900s maintained that some primitive races, and particularly aboriginals, were in a permanent state of 'amentia'; but Lankester was a psychologist, not an anthropologist.

apart'. At a meeting of the Social Science Association in 1884, a spokesman for the London Working Men's Association protested against the fashion for 'talking of the working classes as though they were some new-found race or extinct animal'. The high proportion of Roman Catholics in industrial and reformatory schools was described by Cardinal Vaughan as 'largely a racial question . . . they were mainly Irish and a residuum of the Irish . . . the cases who had not "wing enough" when they left Ireland to carry them across the Atlantic, but simply fluttered down'. And a black American academic who visited Britain in the 1900s observed that 'racial' segregation between rich and poor in London was more profound than anywhere else in the world, including the southern United States.

Such comments suggest that 'race' as a category in British social theory and practice was much more prominent in the late nineteenth and early twentieth centuries than it had been a generation or two before; and this impression is undoubtedly in many respects correct. It needs, however, some qualification. Although racial concepts steadily infiltrated the language of social science and public administration, they did not invariably have the specifically ethnic and exclusionary connotations that a later generation might suppose. Though crude Anglo-Saxon 'racism' (to use an anachronistic term) *was* a powerful strain in Edwardian social thought, the use of racial language was often merely part of the wider organic metaphor, and was frequently used as such even by the small handful of ethical socialists and liberal internationalists who were in principle opposed to all forms of 'racist' differentiation. Thus the terms 'racial progress' or 'racial decline' *might* refer to some ethnic preconception about the superiority and separateness of the Anglo-Saxon or British people;* but they were just as likely to refer simply to the rate of reproduction or the state of public health. The word 'racial' was frequently used as a synonym for 'physiological', and sometimes even for 'sexual'. The sinister-sounding phrase 'racial hygiene', for example, was a favourite Edwardian euphemism for habits of sexual intercourse and family planning. Many of the leading exponents of improved 'racial hygiene' were Jewish doctors and progressive rabbis, from whom advice and information was being eagerly sought by public inquiries at the end of the period, without any shadow of a 'racist' tinge. And in all quarters of the Edwardian women's movement suffragists and suffragettes continually referred to measures for ending the sexual and economic ex-

---

* They might also refer to the predominance of some race other than the English or British. Edwardian visions of an alternative future 'master race' included the Germans, the Jews, the Japanese, and the Parsees.

ploitation of women in terms of 'racial efficiency', 'racial purity', or the 'elevation of the race'.

Furthermore, for all the sound and fury of political rhetoric, the element of biological determinism in even the crudest specimens of Anglocentric thought was often more limited than one might expect. The numerous drafts of the famous will of Cecil Rhodes, for example, make it quite clear that the great white imperialist saw no fundamental obstacle to the ultimate emergence of black 'Anglo-Saxons'. A militant 'British race patriot' like Lord Milner grounded his patriotism in defence of an ancient vision of the British constitution rather than in an exclusive ethnic chauvinism. Even Benjamin Kidd—whose book on *Social Evolution* (1894) is often cited as the intellectual apogee of British social Darwinism— denied that there were any significant mental or physical differences between different racial groups, and portrayed racial competition in very traditional terms as a contest between rival ideas, customs, institutions, and cultures. Much turn-of-the-century anti-Semitism inveighed against Jewish immigrants, not on quintessentially ethnic grounds, but because Jews were perceived as exemplifying the early Victorian virtues of capitalist accumulation rather than the late Victorian virtues of patriotism and public spirit. Throughout the late Victorian and Edwardian periods there were many social commentators who used the images of 'racial progress' or 'racial decline' in a very loose and metaphorical way, to refer to nothing more than the social well-being of the aggregate of people who happened to live in the United Kingdom, without regard to ethnic division. It is not hard, either, to find specimens of apparently emotive Edwardian racial language which on closer inspection prove to be referring to nothing less than the nature and condition of the whole human species.

VI. PERCEPTIONS OF POVERTY

Similar shifting layers of meaning may be discerned in the history of ideas about and attitudes towards poverty. Throughout the nineteenth century many different schools of interpretation had constantly warred for possession of this most contentious of words, and at no stage can the historian precisely pinpoint a universally accepted usage. Poor Law theorists of the early Victorian era, however, had largely concurred in insisting that poverty was not a social 'problem'; on the contrary, it was a normal and inevitable condition of all whose incomes were dependent on wage labour, a condition regulated not by politics but by natural economic laws. 'Pauperism', on the other hand, was the legal status of those whose incomes had for one reason or another failed, and who therefore applied to the Poor Law authorities for public relief. As is well known, a basic premise of the 1834 New Poor Law was that—at least in the case of able-bodied clients—pauperism was primarily a 'voluntary' condition, brought about by the fact that the rewards of poor relief were perceived as superior to the rewards offered by the market for labour; hence the central principle of the New Poor Law, that relief should only be given to those who proved the authenticity of their need by willingness to enter a deterrent workhouse.

This very simple and abstract view of both poverty and pauperism—the one the product of natural laws, the other of individual human will—continued to be a major parameter of social policy in Britain throughout the late Victorian and Edwardian years. The spectre of the so-called Speenhamland system—the belief that lax Poor Law administration *before* 1834 had brought the nation to the brink of bankruptcy, over-population, and moral ruin—was a living object-lesson in official Poor Law thinking right down to 1914. The official view of poverty was never wholly acceptable, however, to many sectors of popular opinion. Throughout the earlier part of the Victorian period local guardians persisted in giving out-relief to many categories of the poor, and in subsidizing low wages; and from the 1860s orthodox Poor Law theory was continually challenged or modified by a wide range of constantly evolving alternative views. The rapidly rising real wages of mid-Victorian Britain meant that it was increasingly implausible to assume that poverty was the inevitable lot of all working people, with the result that social and political commentators began increasingly to emphasize the distinction between 'the poor' and the 'working classes'. At the same time the emergence of periodic booms and depressions—what writers in the 1860s and 1870s called 'flushes and crashes'—began to erode the official belief that those who applied for poor relief had in some sense voluntarily 'chosen' destitution. The famous Goschen circular of 1869 reaffirmed the hedonistic ethic of the Poor Law by urging guardians to relieve paupers only inside the workhouse; but at the same time the circular advised guardians to discriminate between reputable and disreputable applicants for relief, thus tacitly admitting for the first time that pauperism might be the product of external social circumstance rather than individual will.

This circular set the scene for a debate on pauperism and poverty that was to last for the next half-century. In terms of its immediate objectives the Goschen circular proved to be dramatically effective. Such was the popular horror of strict enforcement of the 'workhouse test' that the Poor Law virtually ceased to be a major source of support for all but a tiny margin of 'able-bodied' adults for the next sixty years. Throughout the period bodies like the Charity Organization Society pursued the theme of distinguishing between 'deserving' and 'undeserving' applicants for relief—the latter to be left to a punitive Poor Law, the former to be helped by sympathetic casework to regain their independence. The very fact, however, that some applicants for poor relief were now admitted to be victims of uncontrollable social forces was an unexploded time bomb ticking away inside the structure of the New Poor Law. The exclusion from the Poor Law of the able-bodied (believed to be the most obviously wilful 'voluntary' pauper class) unleashed sympathetic attention for the more helpless groups who were still within it: the sick, orphans, maltreated children, and the aged poor. At the same time the fact that respectable working men and women could no longer get poor relief except within the confines of the workhouse generated growing concern for a more widely disseminated problem of 'poverty' within society at large.

These paradoxes were greatly reinforced by the deflation and depression of the 1880s, which brought rapidly rising living standards for the mass of the working class, but increased insecurity and unemployment for a large minority. Poverty began to be viewed, by some orthodox economists as well as by reformers and philanthropists, no longer as the normal condition of the working population but as a 'problem' that was concentrated upon specific social groups and social misfortunes. It was a problem, moreover, that was increasingly perceived as affecting the wider body politic as well as the individual. Alfred Marshall in his evidence to the Royal Commision on the Aged Poor in 1893 portrayed the whole economy as depressed by lack of effective demand among the poorest classes, and suggested that abolition of the socio-economic phenomenon of poverty rather than the legal phenomenon of pauperism should become the first priority of social reform. Beatrice Webb, Clara Collet, and others drew attention to the prevalence of sweated labour in households headed by women, and to the connection between below-subsistence-level wages and high infant and child mortality. J. A. Hobson's study of unemployment claimed that 'under-consumption' among the poor was indirectly impoverishing the whole of society, by generating 'idle balances' alike in land, labour and capital. Charles Booth's survey of London likewise concluded that the 'very poor' (only a minority of whom were actual paupers) were dragging down the overall standard of national life, not so much by virtue of their own poverty as by the fact that they competed unfairly with the more efficient classes above them. Rowntree's study of York in 1899 challenged orthodox economic thought by suggesting that—contrary to the axioms of classical wage theory—the largest single cause of 'absolute want' was not sickness or lack of work or loss of the main breadwinner, but wages that were too low for sheer physical efficiency. At the same time, however, Rowntree to some extent reaffirmed the earlier Victorian view that the poor were not a 'class apart' but were deeply intertwined with the rest of the working class. 'Poverty' and 'comfort' were not mutually exclusive cultural conditions: they were cyclical phases that most working people might expect to pass through at some stage in their lives.

Marshall, Hobson, Booth, Rowntree, and Beatrice Webb all drew attention to the structural and organic effects of poverty, as well as its implications for the poor individual. This emphasis was strongly reaffirmed by the Committee on Physical Deterioration in 1904, whose report combined censorious condemnation of the habits of the poor with clinical analysis of poverty as a form of organic social disease. It found its clearest and most ambitious expression, however, in the Majority and Minority Reports of the Royal Commission on the Poor Laws, which appeared in 1909. The Poor Law Commission embraced a wide range of economic and political opinion, including—in Beatrice Webb and Helen Bosanquet—two of the most powerful contemporary analysts of social theory and social structure. It surveyed the history of poverty since 1834, and brought under a giant microscope many of the social and intellectual cross-currents of the Edwardian age. The Majority Report, which represented the views of Helen Bosanquet and the advanced sector of 'Charity Organization' thought, endorsed the traditional individualist view that pauperism was fundamentally a moral condition and that 'self-caused poverty is a crime'. But at the same time the Majority Report came to the conclusions that 'something in our social organization is seriously wrong', that poverty was 'a discredit and a peril to the whole community', and that there were sectors of British society in which it was both morally and practically impossible to make the 'moral exertions' which the avoidance of poverty required. The aims of 'public assistance' in the future should be both 'organic' and 'individualist' (the latter in both the old and the new senses of that term). Social policy towards public dependants should be 'preventive, curative and restorative' rather than crudely deterrent; treatment should be 'adapted to the needs of the individual'; and at the same time 'every effort should be made to foster the instincts of independence and self-maintenance among those assisted'. The Minority Report, drafted by Beatrice and Sidney Webb, shared no less than the Majority in the view that much poverty and destitution were linked to bad moral character. Unlike the Majority, however, the authors of the Minority Report saw bad moral character as a consequence rather than a cause of the wider issue of 'social disorganization', a disorganization which they diagnosed as extending far beyond the confines of poor relief into all areas of economic life and public administration. The solution of the Minority was not more humane and restorative treatment of those specifically defined as poor, but a network of comprehensive public services dealing with health, child care, education, and employment; services which would be equally available for (and equally imposed upon) all classes of the community—rich and poor, healthy and unhealthy, dependent and independent alike. The Minority programme was explicitly defended by Sidney Webb as applying 'the lessons which political economy has learnt from biology and from Darwinism', as embodying a new conception of mass citizenship, and as completing the transition from the 'atomism' of the early Victorian era to the new 'organic' age.

VII. DECAY AND DEGENERATION

Much recent writing on late Victorian social thought, which has explored the rise of organic metaphors in this period, has concluded that the very use of such language signifies a retreat from earlier dreams of human autonomy and progress into nightmare visions of social 'degeneration' and inexorable racial decline. The initial belief that the model of 'natural selection' offered a powerful social weapon against hereditary privilege and corruption rapidly gave way, so it has been argued, to a pessimistic determinism that vetoed all purposive efforts at human betterment and social reform. This *fin de siècle* Darwinian pessimism has been seen as embodied in a variety of forms. It has been detected in the widespread reference by late nineteenth-century social theorists to the existence of a 'residuum' of irredeemable social incompetents, and in the enthusiasm of many reformers, including Marshall, Booth, and Beveridge, for segregating the residuum in disciplinary labour colonies, away from all contact with the rest of the social organism. It has been identified in the spread of 'progressive' criminological ideas, imported from the Italian theorist Lombroso, which increasingly ascribed deviance and criminality not to wilful utilitarian calculation but to inherited mental or physical pathology. And it has been found above all in the Edwardian vogue for 'eugenic' ideas, and in the growing alarm about the possibility of widespread congenital decline among the urban poor, an alarm that found its clearest expression in the debate surrounding the Physical Deterioration inquiry of 1904.

How prevalent were fears of social 'degeneration' and 'decay' in this period, and what was their social meaning? That such fears existed is undeniable: they can be found in a massive range of late Victorian and Edwardian sources, ranging from treatises on the constitution and the future of Empire through to discussion of unemployment, pauperism, venereal disease, and tuberculosis. They were part of a recurrent literary idiom, particularly prominent in the writings of self-educated authors with a penchant for speculative philosophy, such as Thomas Hardy, George Sturt, George Gissing, and Stephen Reynolds. They form a familiar undercurrent in the writings of conservative intellectuals like Salisbury and Balfour, liberals like Hobson and Beveridge, socialists like H. M. Hyndman and Sidney Webb. Much opposition to the 'new woman' was couched in terms of the threat of collective 'race suicide', as was criticism of the Edwardian vogue for conspicuous consumption and pleasure. The authors of the Majority and Minority Reports on the Poor Laws were at one in the belief that there were savage tribes 'lurking at the bottom of our civilization', which if not tamed and disciplined would ultimately overthrow it. And no one who reads Edwardian philanthropic sources can fail to be struck by the long-drawn-out retreat from the earlier belief that the very poor were the rational masters of their own fates; a change that was symbolized within the Charity Organization Society by reluctant abandonment of the categories of 'deserving' and 'underserving', and their gradual replacement, first by 'helpable' and 'unhelpable', and then at the very end of the period by the concept of the 'problem family'.

What is questionable, however, is not whether fears of degeneration and decline existed, but what their wider implications were, and how far they constituted a dominant theme in the ideas and practices of the late Victorian and Edwardian age. As was indicated above, very few social evolutionists in Britain were strict 'social Darwinists', committed to a model of exclusive biological inheritance and of change only through an unpredictable process of random selection.* On the contrary, in so far as social evolution was more than just a vague metaphor for progress, most British social-evolutionary theorists followed the models suggested by Herbert Spencer and by the French biologist Lamarck, both of whom believed that organisms adapted directly to their environment and that offspring inherited the characteristics acquired by their parents. This view was widely grafted on to a long-standing environmentalist tradition inherited from Robert Owen and John Stuart Mill. It followed therefore that, although the effects of drink,

---

* Darwin himself gave only qualified support to such a model: the discussion here relates not primarily to Darwin's own ideas but to the tradition of sociobiological thought commonly identified as 'social Darwinism'.

pollution, malnutrition and disease *were* perceived as hereditary, they were also seen as reversible by wise social policies—and the effects of the latter were seen as in turn transmissible to future generations.

The predominance of an environmentalist model of social thought, even within the Edwardian eugenics movement, has already been noted; and the same point may be made in many other contexts. Booth, Marshall, and the Webbs—all of whom from time to time used 'degenerationist' language—ascribed the existence of a residuum to bad social and industrial organization rather than biological inheritance; and they agreed that, although the current generation of 'incompetents' might be beyond recall, there was no reason whatsoever why their offspring should not be trained and reclaimed. When William Beveridge in 1905 gave a paper to the Sociological Society proposing that the residuum be permanently confined in segregated institutions, he found himself in a minority of one (whereat he rapidly abandoned his youthful flirtation with social Darwinism, never to return). The public health movement in Britain, though strongly imbued with evolutionary styles of thought, at all times resisted, and indeed ridiculed, what one Medical Officer of Health dismissed as the 'tired Malthusianism' of degenerationist ideas. 'If you would give me a free hand in feeding during infancy and from ten to eighteen years of age,' declared one prominent physician to the Royal Commission on the Feeble-Minded, 'I would guarantee to give you quite a satisfactory race as a result.' Lombroso's theories about innate criminal physiognomy were widely discussed by British doctors and social scientists, as they were throughout Europe; but they were conspicuous for their *lack* of influence on the treatment of British criminals (and were largely dismissed by British reviewers as an amusing expression of the Italian picaresque, on a par with organ-grinders and macaroni).

Similarly, although the Physical Deterioration Committee and the Poor Law Commission aired many degenerationist fears, the vast majority of witnesses before these inquiries came down in favour of an environmentalist point of view. Both the Majority and Minority of the Poor Law Commission undoubtedly believed that a decayed and predatory underclass was battening upon and dragging down the rest of the social system; but both sides expressed quite amazing optimism about the prospects for social and moral reclamation. Even the National Birth-Rate Commission of 1912–16, which was overwhelmingly composed of people who were apprehensive about national decay and decline, ultimately rejected the view that the poorest class was composed of hereditary biological degenerates. It is true that this Commission deplored the declining fertility of the highest classes and believed that 'the physical and mental inferiority of the most fertile strata is indisputable'. But it concluded that

the greater part of this class inferiority is probably due to bad environment . . . The commission does not of course seek to deny the inheritance of both mental and physical characteristics . . . but it cannot accept the hypothesis that the broad distinctions between social classes are but the effects of germinal variations, and is satisfied that environmental factors which cannot be sensibly modified by individuals exposed to them, however gifted, often prevent the utilization of natural talents.

This assertion by the National Birth-Rate Commission demonstrates very clearly how widely pervasive were environmentalist and ameliorist ideas, even in circles that were predisposed towards social pessimism and evolutionary determinism. There was, however, one exception to this rule, and that was the sphere of what became known as 'feeble-mindedness' or mental deficiency. The concept of feeble-mindedness, as opposed to certifiable lunacy, only emerged in the late 1880s—partly as a result of the movement of rural people to cities, but more specifically as a by-product of compulsory education, which first drew the existence of backward and handicapped children to the notice of public authorities. In the 1900s concern about the feeble-minded focused sharply upon sexual reproduction: the fear that the feeble-minded were far more fertile than the rest of the population, and that in many parts of the country women of feeble intellect were giving birth to hereditary imbeciles, who were being kept alive in large numbers by modern medicine and maintained at the public expense. Throughout the period medical diagnosis of the problem of feeble-mindedness was highly tendentious and erratic. Left-handedness, word-blindness, dumbness and aphasia were often listed together with mongolism, cretinism, and hydrocephaly as symptoms of the condition; and contemporary medical reports suggest that large numbers of deaf, blind, and epileptic adults and children were undoubtedly wrongly diagnosed over the course of the period as 'feeble-minded', 'mentally backward', or 'morally defective'.

Edwardian doctors, psychologists, social workers, and social theorists differed widely about the precise causes and symptoms of feeble-mindedness; but, in striking contrast to the optimism which prevailed in nearly all other socio-medical spheres, they were virtually unanimous in their belief that the condition was largely incurable.* Moreover, in spite of the

---

* The one major exception was Dr Alfred Eichholz, a Cambridge and St Bartholomew's-trained physician, who was the Board of Education's main inspector of special schools.

concern about feeble-minded mothers who fell upon the Poor Law, the vast majority saw the phenomenon of feeble-mindedness as one that randomly afflicted all classes of society rather than only the very poor. This came out very strongly in the Royal Commission on the Feeble-Minded between 1904 and 1908, a commission on which—alone of the great Edwardian public inquiries—both members and witnesses gave overwhelming support to biological rather than cultural notions of inheritance, and to random mutation rather than adaptation. Lombroso's notions of physiognomy, which as we have seen were given fairly short shrift by British criminologists, acquired a new lease of life when applied to the 'mentally defective', 'backward', and 'dull'. Witnesses of all complexions—male and female, doctors and laymen, public officials and charitable volunteers—supported the compulsory segregation of the feeble-minded and stern limitation of their rights to marry and bear children. Such policies were viewed by the overwhelming majority of Edwardians of all political leanings as 'progressive' and 'humane', as opposed to the reactionary and neglectful policies of allowing them to 'reproduce themselves' and 'roam the streets'. Quite why the perception of feeble-mindedness differed so markedly from that of other early twentieth-century social problems merits closer investigation than it can be given here. What is clear, however, is that many Edwardian social theorists and reformers who were normally wholehearted supporters of either moral or environmental reform—such as J. A. Hobson and Sidney Webb, Lloyd George and Winston Churchill, the Bosanquets and C. S. Loch—joined the opposite camp on the issue of feeble-mindedness. It was here, rather than upon the wider spectrum of Edwardian social thought, that one finds in concentrated form the link between Darwinian beliefs about biological inheritance and random mutation, and the spectre of social degeneration and national decay.

VIII. Society, liberty, and character: Echoes of Greece and Rome

Evolutionary, idealist, socialist, corporatist, and historicist thought all broke decisively with earlier traditions of nineteenth-century social theory,

---

Throughout the Edwardian period Eichholz kept up a passionate public defence of medical environmentalism, and played a key role in bringing the 1904 Physical Deterioration Committee down upon the environmentalist side. He was largely isolated, however, in his environmental interpretation of mental defect. It may be noted in passing that his policy proposals for dealing with the feeble-minded were considerably more draconian than those of many supporters of the eugenics school.

in that each of them in their different ways viewed 'individuals' as constituent parts of a wider social whole. Furthermore, in marked contrast to perspectives that were common earlier in the nineteenth century, each of them treated small-scale units of human association as inextricably bound up with the wider processes of society, rather than as belonging to an intrinsically private sphere. As we have seen in earlier chapters, family life, education, industrial relations, private morals, and the distribution of wealth were all increasingly seen not as independent variables but as part and parcel of overall social structure; and this changing approach to concrete social institutions and processes closely coincided with the changing emphasis of more systematic and speculative social thought. Such perceptions were commonplace in late nineteenth-century social discourse, even among people who were not explicitly either evolutionists, idealists or socialists and who still clung to a belief in the irreducible autonomy of the individual private *persona*. Growing consciousness of the inescapably 'social' context of life and thought was apparent in many spheres, some of them quite remote from social science and social theory. Much late Victorian and Edwardian art, literature, and drama, for example, was overwhelmingly social in content, and not until the very end of the period were there signs of a serious aesthetic revolt in favour of more abstract and less programmatic themes. Daily and evening mass-circulation newspapers—more numerous in the Edwardian period than ever before or since—increasingly mirrored, not just the commanding heights of Court, constitution, and Empire or the parochial news of a particular locality, but the all-enveloping panoply of national life: gossip and gardening, fashion and football, crime and county cricket, marital dramas and sudden deaths. The invasion of the 'social' into the most abstruse realms of philosophy and theology may be traced in the discussions of two key intellectual coteries of the period, the Metaphysical Society of the 1870s and the Synthetic Society of the 1900s (both of them bodies which brought together some of the foremost minds of the age). The former used 'social' concepts only on the rare occasions when members discussed 'social problems', whereas the latter continually invoked social terminology, even when discussing mind, miracles, epistemology, and the existence of God.

As was emphasized earlier, however, there was no coherent march of mind in a unilinear direction. A more traditional ontology, which cherished the autonomy and separateness of the individual, remained powerful in many quarters—including quarters which embraced many aspects of the new 'social' styles of thought. Idealist visions of the general will and 'positive liberty' coexisted, often in the same person, with the view that 'liberty' meant leaving the private citizen largely free to do what he or she liked; Winston Churchill and William Beveridge were examples of two Edwardian Englishmen who held both views in tandem. Even people who favoured a more explicitly collectivist vision of society—such as J. A. Hobson and Sidney Webb—often defended their vision on the ground that a strengthening of 'society' would positively strengthen the expression of individual freedom and personality. The founders of the Sociological Society in 1904 hoped that the spread of 'the sociological habit of mind' would help to promote a new era of public spirit and citizen-consciousness. Nevertheless, Edwardian social investigators constantly came across large tracts of social life that were seemingly untouched by the new ways of thought. Within the working-class communities surveyed by Margaret Loane, the vision of what constituted 'society' was largely confined to a small handful of families living in the same street (though within those narrow limits Miss Loane claimed to have found many miniature examples of what in the wider world would have passed for altruism and devoted public service). Women writers like Olive Malvery and Millicent Fawcett found, not surprisingly, an almost universal lack of 'state-consciousness' among the vast mass of unenfranchised women. And, in spite of the strength of Britain's self-governing voluntary institutions, most women (and indeed large numbers of unskilled working men) were wholly excluded from that far-famed democratic self-help culture until the statutory creation of 'approved societies' under the National Insurance Act of 1911.

Within the complex tapestry of late Victorian and Edwardian social thought there were many alternative strands that have been ignored or only touched upon in passing here, which deserve further enquiry and comment. Some mention has been made of Greek political thought, and much more might be said about the influence of other classical models, which throughout the period supplied a framework no less potent than evolution itself for interpreting and passing judgement upon society in modern Britain. The most famous of these classical models was Matthew Arnold's championship of humanistic 'Hellenism' at the expense of Nonconformist 'Hebraism', set out in *Culture and Anarchy* in 1867—an account which symptomized, if it did not cause, the waning credibility of old Puritan virtues among the educated classes over the succeeding fifty years. Hellenistic ideals were widely invoked to legitimize and dignify a vast range of social activities and institutions of the period, including boarding-schools, civic architecture, homosexual relationships, organized charity, mystical religion, and women's rights. A rival model, favoured by many contemporaries though less noticed by historians, was the invocation of the rise and fall of Rome as a constantly recurring reference point for British virtue, the British Empire, and future British decline. Such images were in no sense the monopoly of the old Etonians who manned the front benches in Parliament. On the contrary, they were part of the stock-in-trade of the popular press and of the organized working class. The opening address to one of the founding conferences of the Labour Representation Committee in 1902, for example, cited Macaulay's account of the ancient Roman republic as a moral pattern for the Labour movement in the early twentieth century. The sense that Britain during the late Victorian and Edwardian years was re-enacting the Roman drama of republican collapse and imperial *coup d'état* was expressed by numerous commentators, particularly those with roots in the provinces and in old dissent. Such apprehensions were linked to fear of the newly enfranchised masses, and of those still outside the gates of the constitution who were waiting to come in; but they were also linked to a widespread belief that the propertied classes themselves were undergoing a process of civic and financial corruption, comparable with that of the Augustan era in ancient Rome. A 'kind of moral dislocation' was perceived as 'even now destroying, in the higher ranks, much of the duty-loving character bequeathed to our Anglo-Saxon race by our Puritan fathers'.

The role of moral character in late Victorian and Edwardian social thought has been almost universally noted by interpreters of the period, but has rarely received the kind of scrutiny that its historical importance seems to require. It has often been assumed that the explanatory emphasis on character was simply a hangover from the era of evangelicalism, individualism and the New Poor Law, and that by the late nineteenth century it was being systematically displaced by the growth of objective social science. It is also frequently taken for granted that the concept of character was exclusively a 'class' weapon, whereby the rich passed moral judgement upon the suppliant poor. All these assumptions are, however, largely incorrect. That judgement of character had played some part in the social discourse of the earlier nineteenth century is of course undeniable; but such judgement did not have a major role in the mainstream of early Victorian social thought, which was rooted in utilitarianism and egoistic psychology.*
The 1834 Poor Law reformers had certainly viewed the bulk of paupers in a morally unfavourable light; but their immorality was viewed as a rational

* This may seem a surprising statement, in view of emphasis on character in the writings of J. S. Mill and Thomas Carlyle—particularly the claim made by Mill in *A System of Logic* (1843), that 'there exist universal laws of the Formation of Character'. But Mill was here anticipating the social science of the subsequent generation. The classic popular text on the subject, Samuel Smiles's *Character*, was published in 1871.

response to unwise public policies (comparable to the immorality of the aristocratic recipients of government sinecures) rather than as an expression of intrinsically bad 'character'. Similarly, much evangelical social thought, though often moralizing in tone, had little fundamental space for the role of personal character; on the contrary, all were deemed equally worthy of blame until redeemed by salvation and grace.

By contrast, 'character' in the later Victorian sense—as a powerful explanatory variable which discriminated clearly between good and bad moral behaviour—crept into social discourse in the mid-nineteenth century as part of a reaction against the more mechanistic vocabulary of the early Victorian age. As we have seen, it assumed a major role in the 1860s and 1870s in prescribing differential treatment for the deserving and undeserving poor, and in legitimizing the admission of some working men to the franchise and the exclusion of others. It played an important part also in the prolonged middle-class critique of aristocratic corruption, and in the attacks of feminists and purity reformers upon the sexual 'double standard'. It was increasingly invoked in the 1890s and 1900s—not just by puritanical middle-class moralists, but by working-class radicals and Kiplingesque conservatives—to denounce the rise of conspicuous consumption and the withdrawal of the rich from disinterested public service into anonymous private life. Its ascendancy in English social thought has been ascribed to the influence of Dr Arnold and the Broad Church/Christian Socialist school; but it may perhaps more properly be seen as the expression of a much wider movement for the revival of public spirit, patriotism, and civic virtue, of which Christian Socialism was merely a part. Moreover, though espoused by many Christians of different complexions, the notion of character that came to the fore in the 1860s and 1870s was not essentially a religious concept; on the contrary, it had roots in classical humanism, and markedly differed from evangelicalism in the belief that men and women *could* become virtuous by their own effort of will. It rejected the ethic of egoism in favour of altruism; and—in marked contrast to early Victorian notions of virtue—it suggested that virtue was an essentially public characteristic, which consisted not simply of private rationality or piety but of promoting the best interests of society as a whole.

Furthermore, far from being the antithesis of late Victorian social science, 'character' was one of its vital constituent parts. In the writings of Charles Booth character was viewed not as an archaism but as a scientific 'distress meter' for weeding out the 'fit' from the 'unfit'; likewise in Beveridge's work on unemployment, character was seen as a crucial variable in explaining, not the actual fact of unemployment, but why one worker rather than another became unemployed. Character in the guise of 'economic chivalry' underpinned the social philosophy of Marshallian economics. Both philosophical idealism and the mainstream of social evolutionary thought viewed 'character' as the life blood of the social organism, since without the catalysing role of altruism and conscience the whole conception of society as 'citizens unified by moral purpose' simply fell apart. In the discussions of the Sociological Society in the 1900s sociology was seen as a tool for the inculcation of moral character and civic virtue, in precisely the same light as the teaching of Latin and Greek a generation before.

Among the different social theorists of the period there was some disagreement about the precise role of character in the diagnosis of social problems. As we have seen, the Majority and Minority of the Poor Law Commission differed over the influence of character upon the actual gestation of poverty; and critics like J. A. Hobson and Samuel Barnett attacked the Charity Organisation Society for misusing 'character' as a stick with which to beat the poor. But the Webbs, Hobson, and Barnett, no less than T. H. Green, the Bosanquets, and C. S. Loch, all agreed upon the crucial role of character—or what Hobson preferred to call 'moral efficiency'—in the construction of schemes of practical social reform. Such perspectives were widely shared, not simply by intellectuals and the reformist middle classes but by large sections of the organized labour movement, who objected strongly to the patronizing moralism of charitable committees yet who themselves laid great emphasis on character, altruism and public spirit in the day-to-day management of their own collective affairs. In 1912 many leading members of the Labour party, headed by James Ramsay MacDonald and Philip Snowden, came together with prominent Liberals, Conservatives, Anglicans, and Nonconformists in the 'Prevention Movement', which was specifically designed to link the promotion of 'moral purity' with 'scientific social reform'. In marked contrast both to early nineteenth-century thought and to most schools of social theory a hundred years later, social theorists of late Victorian and Edwardian Britain believed almost without exception that a major purpose of social science was the promotion of public virtue. And they believed that moral character, active citizenship and 'public spirit' were the indispensable building-blocks of a well-ordered society and a virtuous state.

Conclusion

In any large and complex society it is wellnigh impossible to make generalizations about social processes and institutions to which exceptions cannot be found. The discussion in this book has aimed to move continuously between synoptic analysis of general trends and illustrative reference to concrete events and facts. Inevitably, large subjects have been left out, or treated in a superficial and oversimplified fashion; and doubtless numerous examples have been given to which readers will readily find counter-examples. Moreover, since I cannot share the belief of many of my actors that society is a finite 'organism' with a discrete and determinate 'body', the problem of boundaries—cultural, geographical, and institutional—has largely been left unsolved. If forced to find a metaphor for writing about Victorian and Edwardian social history I should prefer something like Penelope's web—a garment endlessly woven by day and unpicked again by night.

What conclusions, if any, may be drawn from the manifold cross-currents of this period of social history? The period ended with war on a scale that was almost wholly unforeseen by the vast majority of participants in the pre-war era. The impact of total war inevitably changed the detailed character and structure of British society and institutions in a myriad different ways. But the question remains that was posed in my introductory chapter, of how far the First World War transformed British society, or merely channelled and accelerated existing social change. The war clearly made a unique impact on life in Britain in terms of grief and sudden death, and it forced government to make demands on citizens of a wholly unprecedented and unexpected kind. It coincided and interacted with many important landmarks in social, economic and political history—not least among them the enfranchisement of women, the demise of the gold standard and the powerful emergence of Labour. Yet it is possible to exaggerate the degree of change uniquely wrought by the war, particularly in the social sphere. In fact many of the major configurations of British social life in the half-century after 1914 were already taking shape over the previous forty years. This is true not merely of the emergence of structures and attitudes that were to be dominant in Britain down to the 1960s, but of many of the subversive counter-currents that were to lead to the gradual dismantling of that later society and its ultimate dissolution. In so far as there have ever been great chasms rather than mere subterranean murmurings in the deep structures of British social history, it seems to me that they occurred in the 1870s and 1880s, and then again in the 1960s and 1970s, rather than in the apparently more dramatic and cataclysmic happenings of either of the two world wars. In so far as 'periods' have 'characters', late Victorian and Edwardian Britain resembled the Britain of the 1920s and 1930s, and even of the 1940s and 1950s, at least as much as, and in many ways far more than, the Britain of the early and mid-Victorian years.

Such periodizations are necessarily somewhat arbitrary and artificial; and throughout this book I have tried to emphasize the varying pace of time, the idiosyncrasy of local habits, and the frequent conjunction of quite dissimilar or contradictory social structures. Yet my overall point—that the true watershed came at the beginning rather than the end of the period, and that continuity was sustained until long after the First World War—can be supported on many levels. The shift to a 'modern' demographic structure began in the 1870s, and in the eyes of many contemporaries was already alarmingly far advanced by 1914. The structural and qualitative transformation of cities did not come with the Industrial Revolution but with the arrival of public utilities and municipal socialism after 1867—an epoch which determined the invisible infrastructure of city life until well into the late twentieth century. The global revolution in food production of the late 1870s and 1880s transformed the structure of wealth and the identity of the 'ruling class' in Britain far more profoundly than the agricultural and industrial revolutions of a hundred years before. It was not the early nineteenth-century factory system, but the onset of mass production and the retailing and financial revolutions of the 1880s that created the distinctive class, status, and consumer groups which were to characterize British society for much of the twentieth century. Mass education, mass culture, and mass leisure all date from the 1870s and 1880s, but from the 1870s down to the 1960s they were all to operate within a legal and cultural framework prescribed by a moral and intellectual élite. The serious-minded, public-spirited, sexually orthodox attributes of most early twentieth-century feminism had their roots in the women's education and purity campaigns of the 1860s and 1870s. The ethic of working-class voluntarism, independence, and self-help—celebrated in recent years as the lifeblood of 'Victorian values'—was far more widely disseminated in late Victorian and Edwardian society than had been the case earlier in Victoria's reign. The patterns of stable, monogamous, highly integrated family life that were established in the latter half of the nineteenth century were to be ubiquitous and morally mandatory down to the 1960s—in striking contrast to the more ramshackle, transient, and pluralist family arrangements that prevailed in many quarters in the early Victorian era, and that have re-emerged in more recent decades. The internal self-discipline and order of British society between 1870 and 1914 link it strongly with the society of the interwar years—and distinguish it sharply from the disorder and criminality of both the early nineteenth and the late twentieth centuries.

Nowhere was the watershed of the 1870s more powerful and decisive than in the ideological sphere: in religion, morality, civic consciousness, and social and political thought. The history of Victorian religion has often been portrayed by social historians in very crude terms, as a shift from evangelical conviction to agnostic doubt. It has been suggested in this book that the shift was a much more subtle and complex one, and that the predominant religion of the late nineteenth century was an undogmatic 'social' Christianity, which probably embraced more people and certainly was more publicly influential than the intense private conviction of the evangelical age. It was accompanied by a very widespread belief in moral self-regulation that extended far beyond the boundaries of organized religion. To large numbers of people in late Victorian England, including many who were not Christian believers, the virtues of self-restraint and 'repression' were just as commonplace and axiomatic as they were to be alien and incomprehensible to many of their descendants a hundred years later.

A parallel shift occurred in political thought. For perhaps the only time in the whole of British intellectual history most philosophers writing about politics after 1870 portrayed society as an organism rather than an aggregate—in Bertrand Russell's words, as more like a 'pot of treacle' than a 'heap of shot'—and continued to do so until the positivist counter-revolution of the 1930s and 1940s. Moreover, the belief that public as well as private life should be 'moral' was at least as strong—and certainly far more strongly embodied in legislation—than had been the case in the early Victorian era. Not simply Mr Gladstone, but post-Gladstonian philosophers and politicians of all complexions—Liberal, Conservative, and socialist—believed that it was possible and desirable for the state and public policy to pursue collective ethical goals. Both the Webbs and the Bosanquets, both the Fabians and the COS wholeheartedly dissented from the very widespead early Victorian view—famously epitomized in the conclusion of Dickens's *Little Dorrit*—that political power and the public sphere were intrinsically corrupt, and that virtue was attainable only within the confines of a purely private setting. The moralization of public life and the public enforcement of morality are often viewed as quintessentially 'Victorian' principles. If this be true, then this study must take issue with a long line of historians, from G. M. Young through to Patrick Atiyah, and conclude that it was not the period *before* but the period *after* 1870 which should be seen as constituting the 'age of principle' and the 'true Victorian age'.

From the very beginning of the period, however, there were rival undercurrents in British society that were working across or against the forces of moral unity and social integration. To some extent the very same conditions that made order, unity and self-regulation possible also precipitated trends that were in the long run to lead in the opposite direction. Once again this point can be demonstrated in many different spheres. The very openness to world markets that ushered in a modest degree of working-class affluence and stability was at the same time highly corrosive not merely of traditional popular culture but ultimately of the newer industrial culture that emerged during the late nineteenth century. The material fact of social class, though never so all-embracing a force as is often supposed, nevertheless constantly rivalled and subverted the moral aspiration towards a unified civic culture. The voluntaristic and communitarian ethic that many contemporaries viewed as the lifeblood of late Victorian social existence was eventually to be eclipsed by forms of business enterprise that appeared superficially to belong to that same ethic but were in fact its antithesis (such as large-scale commercial insurance and industrial life assurance). Throughout the period social life and thought were played out against the background of Empire, and it seems highly probable that a great deal of Britain's domestic peace and stability was related to that stupendous global fact. Yet the Empire was always a force for conflict and entropy as well as for world order. It injected ideas and assumptions into all layers of British society that were in many ways hostile to and in tension with domestic social growths; and Cabinet documents on Empire through-out the period often give the impression of a gigantic global juggernaut, spinning quite out of control.

Similar points may be made about democracy and morality. The fears of contemporaries about the 'swamping' of the constitution by the 'masses' were not entirely groundless: on the contrary, the ambitious vision of active and well-informed popular citizenship that seemed appropriate to the era of limited democracy *did* prove impossible to translate into a context of universal suffrage. Edwardian moral and political philosophy appeared on its face to provide an impregnable fortress of support for private virtue and public spirit; yet by the 1900s philosophers like Moore and Russell were already beginning to chisel away at that edifice, and to suggest that moral philosophy had nothing whatsoever to do with the prescription of right and wrong. The same was true of the sphere of private sexual behaviour. The vast majority of late Victorians and Edwardians appear to have endorsed the view that personal and sexual self-restraint was an indispensable element of freedom and progress; but biographies of the period suggest that the price was often intense psychological strain and suffering, amounting in some cases to varying degrees of inversion and mental disorder. Self-restraint was increasingly at war with the new notions of 'individuality' and 'self-expression' that were coming to the fore in the 1890s and 1900s; and by the end of the period an influential dissident minority was coming to regard the whole ethos of self-control and self-repression as intolerable cant.

All these points lend weight to the view, intuitively held by many contemporaries, that the late Victorian and Edwardian era was one of great contingency and contradiction. Fast-moving change was occurring on many fronts, but in a highly unpredictable, open-ended and often indecipherable way. A great deal of the vehemence and violence of Edwardian political and social debate stemmed from the fact that many outcomes seemed possible, and that participants were therefore especially anxious to bend the course of history in a particular way. The period is sometimes portrayed as one of great moral and political certainty: about the greatness of Britain, the possibilities of social and moral reform, the future of the Empire and the global destiny of the Anglo-Saxon race. Undoubtedly there were many who spoke in those terms, not least among them anxious foreign observers and competitors, who viewed British expansion and ascendancy from the outside. Throughout the period, however, even among imperialists, optimists and disciples of 'progress', there were those who viewed Britain's future in a far more ambivalent way, as inherently problematic and fragile. Even among the most avid promoters of Empire, the global federation of Anglo-Saxon peoples was never more than an ambitious imaginature vision—in Kipling's words, 'a semi-circle of buildings and temples projecting into a sea of dreams'. Gladstone in 1870 had struck chill into the hearts of the House of Commons by a speech which suggested that Britain's economic ascendancy would last just as long as her supplies of coal— provisionally estimated to be sufficient for another hundred years. Similar points were made forty years later by the radical economist Sir Leo Chiozza Money, who argued that, without massive investment in organization and technology, Britain with her slender natural resources was doomed to transience and decline. Fears of racial and national eclipse due to sheer failure of numbers have been discussed at several points in this study. Some at the turn of the century were already predicting a 'post-industrial' Britain. Beatrice Webb in 1890 noted with alarm the prophecy of her plutocrat brother-in-law, Daniel Meinertzhagen, about the future of the City of London as 'an island of capital in a sea of foreign investment—the land given over to sport'. And Sir Henry Maine in a famous passage conjured up a vision of the whole era of liberty, virtue, popular government, and economic progress as evanescent and arcane: 'The British political system, with the national greatness and material greatness attendant upon it, may yet be launched into space and find its last affinities in silence and cold.'

Bibliography

This book has been conceived and written at two different levels of analysis: it has attempted to piece together some of the vast body of specialist historical writing on different aspects of social history in Britain between 1870 and 1914. And, in areas where I judged received opinion to be inadequate, or where I happened to have particular knowledge, it has drawn upon 'primary sources' in the form of manuscripts, Blue Books, sermons, social and political tracts, reports of philanthropic and self-help organizations, memoirs, newspapers, journals, and numerous other contemporary printed works. The voluminous files of the John Johnson collection in the Bodleian Library supplied much illustrative detail, both structural and picaresque. In addition I have used the writings of nineteenth- and early twentieth-century social theorists, both British and Continental, at points where their theories seemed to offer some kind of insight or entrée into great masses of unwieldy social facts. Because of the synoptic character of the book it has been impossible to footnote all sources and references in the manner of a specialist monograph; but some indication of source material has been given at points where I thought my interpretation might appear particularly improbable or contentious.

The bibliography set out below makes no pretence at completeness (to do so would require a second volume larger than the first). It consists partly of works that I have found useful in writing this book (including some with which I have disagreed) and partly of indications for further and more detailed study. Many works that are listed as being of particular relevance to one topic or chapter were in fact of more diffuse importance throughout the whole book. Where a work is cited more than once full publication details are given only at first citation. Unless otherwise stated all works were published in London.

General

The period is covered by several major interpretative studies that have acquired quasi-classic status and become virtual sources in their own right. Of these the most important are:

Dangerfield, G., *The Strange Death of Liberal England* (1936)

Ensor, R. C. K., *England 1870–1914* (Oxford, 1936)

Halevy, E., *Imperialism and the Rise of Labour 1895–1905* (1926); and *The Rule of Democracy 1905–14* (1932)

Young, G. M., *Victorian England: Portrait of an Age* (Oxford, 1936)

Background perspectives were derived from many contemporary interpreters both British and foreign. These are far too numerous to list in detail, but mention may be made of:

Boutmy, Émile, *The English People; A Study of Their Political Psychology* (1904)

Escott, T. H., *England: Its People, Polity and Pursuits* (1879 and 1889); *Social Transformations of the Victorian Age* (1897); *Personal Forces of the Period* (1898); and *Society in the New Reign* (1904)

Gretton, R. H., *A Modern History of the English People, 1880–98 and 1899–1910*, 2 vols. (1913)

Jevons, W. S., *Methods of Social Reform and Other Papers* (1883)

Lazarus, Henry, *The English Revolution of the Twentieth Century: A Prospective History* (1894)

LePlay, F., *La Constitution de l'Angleterre* (Tours, 1875)

Masterman, C. F. G. (ed.), *The Heart of the Empire* (1902)

Taine, H., *Notes sur l'Angleterre* (Paris, 1860–70, trans. W. F. Rae, 1872)

Webb, Sidney, 'Social Movements', in *Cambridge Modern History, Volume 12: The Latest Age* (Cambridge, 1910)

White, Richard Grant, *England Without and Within* (Boston, 1881)

Excellent modern works offering general interpretations of British, English, Irish, Scots, and Welsh history during the period include:

Bedarida, F., *A Social History of England 1851–1975* (Paris, 1976, trans. A. S. Forster, 1979)

Harrison, Brian, *Peaceable Kingdom: Stability and Change in Modern Britain* (Oxford, 1982)

Lee, J., *The Modernization of Irish Society 1848–1918* (Dublin, 1973)

Morgan, Kenneth O., *Rebirth of a Nation: Wales 1880–1980* (Oxford, 1982)

Perkin, Harold, *The Rise of Professional Society: England since 1880* (1989)

Robbins, Keith, *Nineteenth Century Britain: England, Scotland, and Wales: The Making of a Nation* (Oxford, 1990)

Shannon, Richard, *The Crisis of Imperialism 1865–1915* (1974)

Smout, T. C., *A Century of the Scottish People 1830–1950* (1986)

Thompson, F. M. L., *The Rise of Respectable Society* (1989)

In addition the period is covered by some valuable collections of essays by different historians, of which I made most use of the following:

Benson, John (ed.), *The Working Class in England 1875–1914* (1985)

Bentley, Michael, and Stevenson, John (eds.), *High and Low Politics in Modern Britain* (Oxford, 1983)

Brown, Kenneth (ed.), *Essays in Anti-Labour History* (1974)

Burman, Sandra (ed.), *Fit Work for Women* (1979)

Crossick, Geoffrey (ed.), *The Lower-Middle Class in Britain 1870–1914* (1977)

Fraser, Derek (ed.), *The New Poor Law in the Nineteenth Century* (1976)

Gourvish, T., and O'Day, A. (eds.), *Later Victorian Britain 1867–1900* (1988)

Lewis, Jane (ed.) *Labour and Love: Women's Experience of Home and Family 1850–1940* (1986)

Mackenzie, John M. (ed.), *Imperialism and Popular Culture* (Manchester, 1986)

Thane, Pat (ed.), *The Origins of British Social Policy* (1978)

Thompson, F. M. L. (ed.), *The Cambridge Social History of Britain*, 3 vols. (Cambridge, 1990)

Wrigley, C. (ed.), *A History of British Industrial Relations 1875–1914* (Brighton, 1982)

The period coincides with the zenith of the 'realist' novel, many of which are of historical interest in both content and form. These are far too numerous to list in detail, but mention may be made of Ada Leverson, *The Little Ottleys* (1908, 1912, and 1916, reissued in one vol., 1962); W. H. Mallock, *The New Republic* (1877); George Meredith, *The Egoist* (1879); Arthur Morrison, *A Child of the Jago* (1896); Anthony Trollope, *The Way We Live Now* (1874–5); Mrs Humphry Ward, *Robert Elsmere* (1888); and H. G. Wells, *The New Machiavelli* (1911).

1. Themes and Interpretations: An Overview of British Society, 1870–1914

The scope of this chapter as a thematic survey of the whole period makes it peculiarly difficult to construct a bibliography that is other than selective and idiosyncratic. On the impact of Empire, J. A. Hobson, *Imperialism: A Study* (1902) remains controversial but indispensable. On the theme of class, my starting points were E. J. Hobsbawm, *Labouring Men* (1964) and *Worlds of Labour* (1984), supplemented by Peter Clarke, 'The Electoral Sociology of Modern Britain', *History* (1972) and Ross McKibbin, *The Ideologies of Class: Social Relations in Britain 1880–1914* (Oxford, 1990). On individualism, A. V. Dicey, *Lectures on the Relation between Law and Public Opinion in England in the Nineteenth Century* (preface to 2nd edn., 1914) is still a classic point of reference. My efforts to construct an alternative theory of socio-constitutional change owed much to Hansard debates on the 1867 and 1884 Reform Acts; to Walter Bagehot, *Physics and Politics* (1872); Sir Henry Maine, *Popular Government* (1886); and to John Davis, 'Slums and the Vote 1867–90', *Historical Research*, 64, 155 (1991). On the social history of language and cognate matters, invaluable guides were Lady Agnes Grove, 'Social Solecisms', *Cornhill Magazine*, 85 (1902); Lady Bell, *Landmarks: a Reprint of some essays and other pieces published between the years 1894 and 1922* (1929); and K. C. Phillipps, *Language and Class in Victorian England* (Oxford, 1984). On social mobility I made use of Helmut Kaelble, *Social Mobility in the 19th and 20th Centuries* (Heidelberg, 1983; trans., Leamington Spa, 1985) and Andrew Miles and David Vincent, *A Land of Boundless Opportunity: Mobility and Stability in Nineteenth Century England* (Sociological Review Monograph, 1990). Key works on women are Patricia Hollis, *Ladies Elect: Women in Local Government 1865–1914* (Oxford, 1987); Sandra Holton, *Feminism and Democracy 1900–1918* (Cambridge, 1986); Pat Jalland, *Women, Marriage and Politics 1860–1914* (Oxford, 1986); and Elizabeth Roberts, *A Woman's Place: an Oral History of Working Class Women 1890–1940* (Oxford, 1984). On the elusive subject of modernity it is difficult to cite an authoritative text, but my ideas were influenced by such diverse sources as George Bourne, *Change in the Village* (1912); Sir James Frazer, *The Golden Bough, Part I: The Magic Art and the Evolution of Kings,* 3rd edn. (1911); *The Letters of Evelyn Underhill*, ed. Charles Williams (1945); and H. G. Wells, *Anticipations* (1900). Relevant works of sociological theory were Émile Durkheim, *The Division of Labour in Society* (Paris, 1893), trans. G. Simpson (Glencoe, Illinois, 1960); Ferdinand Tönnies, *Gemeinschaft und Gesellschaft* (Berlin, 1887), trans. C. P. Loomis (1955); *From Max Weber: Essays in Sociology*, ed. H. H. Gerth and C. Wright Mills (1947).

The following are a few of the other principal items implicitly or explicitly cited in the text.

Contemporary works

Bodley, J. E. C., *The Coronation of Edward the Seventh: a Chapter of European and Imperial History* (1903)

Cobbe, Frances Power, *The Life of Frances Power Cobbe: as told by herself* (revised ed. 1904)

Dicey, A. V., *The Law of the Constitution* (1885)

English Dialect Society, *Reports* (1873–96)

Freeden, Michael (ed.), *Minutes of the Rainbow Circle 1894–1924*, vol. 38 (Camden Fourth Series, 1989)

Geddes, Patrick, and Thomson, J. Arthur, *The Evolution of Sex* (1889)

Grove, Lady Agnes, *The Social Fetich* (1907)

Hopkins, Ellice, *The Power of Womanhood; or Mothers and Sons* (1899)

International Congress of Women, Reports and Papers (1899)

Mill, J. S., *The Subjection of Women* (1869)

Pike, L. O., *The English and Their Origin: a Prologue to Authentic English History* (1866)

Royal Commission upon the Duties of the Metropolitan Police, Report (1908)

Stephen, Sir J. F., *Liberty, Equality, Fraternity* (1873)

Wallas, Graham, *Human Nature in Politics* (1908); and *The Great Society* (1914)

Webb, B., *My Apprenticeship* (1929); and (as Beatrice Potter) 'The Jewish

Community', in Charles Booth, *Life and Labour of the People in London*, First Series vol. 3 (1889)

Wedgwood, Frances Julia, 'Male and Female Created He Them', *Contemporary Review*, 56 (1889)

White, Richard Grant, *Words and Their Uses, Past and Present* (Boston, 1870 and 1881)

Historical works

Bradbury, Malcolm, and McFarlane, James (eds.), *Modernism 1890–1930* (1976)

Caine, Barbara, *Destined to be Wives: The Sisters of Beatrice Webb* (Oxford, 1986)

Cannadine, David, *Lords and Landlords: The Aristocracy and the Towns 1774–1967* (Leicester, 1980)

Colls, Robert, and Dodd, Philip (eds.), *Englishness: Politics and Culture 1880–1920* (1986)

Crossick, Geoffrey, *An Artisan Élite in Victorian Society: Kentish London 1840–1880* (1978)

Cunningham, Hugh, *The Volunteer Force: A Social and Political History 1859–1908* (1981)

Davidoff, Leonore, *The Best Circles: Society, Etiquette and the Season* (1973)

Davis, L. E., and Huttenback, R. A., *Mammon and the Pursuit of Empire: the Political Economy of British Imperialism 1860–1912* (Cambridge, 1988)

Dyos, H. J., *The Victorian City: Images and Realities*, 2 vols. (1973)

Harrison, Brian, *Separate Spheres: the Opposition to Women's Suffrage in England* (1978)

Harvie, C., *The Lights of Liberalism* (1976)

Hobsbawm, E. J., and Ranger, T. (eds.), *The Invention of Tradition* (Cambridge, 1988)

Jeffreys, Sheila, *The Spinster and Her Enemies* (1985)

Jones, Gareth Stedman, *Outcast London: a Study in the Relationship Between Classes in Victorian Society* (Oxford, 1971); *Languages of Class: Studies in English Working Class History 1832–1982* (Cambridge, 1984)

Joyce, Patrick, *Visions of the People: Industrial England and the Question of Class 1840–1914* (Cambridge, 1991); and *Work, Society and Politics: the Culture of the Factory in Later Victorian England* (Brighton, 1980)

Lyons, F. S. L., *Culture and Anarchy in Ireland 1890–1939* (Oxford, 1979)

O'Brien, P. K., 'The Costs and Benefits of British Imperialism 1846–1914', *Past and Present*, 120 (Aug. 1988), and subsequent debate in 125 (November 1989)

Pelling, Henry, *Popular Politics and Society in Late-Victorian Britain* (1868)

Perkin, H. V., 'Individualism versus Collectivism in Nineteenth Century Britain: a False Antithesis', in *The Structured Crowd: Essays in English Social History* (1981)

Sennett, Richard, *The Fall of Public Man* (1974)

Stearns, Peter, 'Modernization and Social History: Some Suggestions and a Muted Cheer', *Journal of Social History*, 14 (1980–81)

Stokes, Eric, 'Milnerism', *Historical Journal*, 5 (1962)

Vicinus, Martha (ed.), *Independent Women: Work and Community for Single Women*

1850–1920 (1985); and A *Widening Sphere: Changing Roles of Victorian Women* (1987)

Waller, P. J., 'Democracy, and Dialect, Speech and Class', in P. J. Waller (ed.), *Politics and Social Change in Modern Britain: Essays Presented to A. F. Thompson* (Brighton, 1987)

2. Demography, Death, and Disease

Major sources for this chapter were the decennial Census reports; annual reports of the Local Government Board; the *Journal of the Royal Statistical Society*; and numerous public inquiries into socio-medical issues. The most important of the latter were the reports and minutes of the *Interdepartmental Committee on Physical Deterioration* (1904) and the Royal Commissions on the *Care and Control of the Feeble-Minded* (1909), the *Poor Laws* (1909–10), and *Venereal Diseases* (1916). Other useful contemporary works were Sir John Simon, *English Sanitary Institutions* (1890); Dr H. A. Allbutt, *The Wife's Handbook*, 16th edn. (1891); Sir George Newman, *Infant Mortality* (1906) and *The Health of the State* (1907); *Public Health and Social Conditions: Memoranda and Charts* (Local Government Board, 1909); S. and B. Webb, *The State and the Doctor* (1910); Dr R. W. Johnstone, *Report on Venereal Diseases* (Local Government Board, 1913); and National Birth Rate Commission, *The Declining Birth Rate: Its Cause and Effects* (1916).

Modern sources of information included the journals *Population Studies*, *Medical History*, the *Bulletin of the Society for the History of Medicine*, *Ageing and Society* and *Continuity and Change*. Other helpful works were as follows:

Banks, Joseph, *Prosperity and Parenthood* (1954)

Barker, Theo, and Drake, Michael, *Population and Society in Britain 1850–1950* (1982)

Dyos, H., *Victorian Suburb: A Study of the Growth of Camberwell* (Leicester, 1977)

Gittins, Diana, *Fair Sex: Family Size and Structure 1900–39* (1982)

Hollingsworth, T. H., 'Illegitimate Births and Marriage Rates in Great Britain 1841–1911', in J. Dupâquier *et al.*, *Marriage and remarriage in the populations of the past* (1981)

Langton, John, and Morris, R. J. (eds.), *Atlas of Industrializing Britain 1780–1914* (1986)

Laslett, Peter, and Wall, Richard, *Household and Family in Past Time* (Cambridge, 1972)

MacLaren, Angus, *Birth Control in Nineteenth Century England* (1978)

Pinker, Robert, *English Hospital Statistics 1861–1938* (1966)

Porter, Dorothy, 'Enemies of the Race: Biologism, Environmentalism and Public Health in Edwardian Britain', *Victorian Studies*, 34 (1991)

Roberts, Elizabeth, *A Woman's Place: An Oral History of Working Class Women 1890–1940*

Seccombe, Wally, 'Starting to Stop: Working Class Fertility Decline in Britain', *Past and Present*, 126 (1990) and comment by Robert Woods, *Past and Present*, 134 (1992)

Smith, F. B., *The People's Health 1830–1910* (1979)

Soloway, R. A., *Birth Control and the Population Question in England 1877–1930* (Chapel Hill, 1982)

Szretzer, Simon, 'The importance of social intervention in Britain's mortality decline 1850–1914: A reinterpretation', *Social History of Medicine*, 1 (1988)

Thompson, F. M. L. (ed.), *The Rise of Suburbia* (Leicester, 1982)

Waller, P. J., *Town, City and Nation 1850–1914* (Oxford, 1983)

Webster, Charles (ed.), *Biology, Medicine and Society 1840–1940* (Cambridge, 1981)

Wrigley, E. A., and Schofield, R. S., *The Population History of England 1541–1871: A Reconstruction* (Cambridge, Mass., 1981)

3. Family and Household

This chapter relied largely on secondary works for questions of family size and structure, but drew upon a wide range of Victorian and Edwardian sources for discussion of norms, attitudes, role-sharing, parental and sexual relationships, and the structure of authority within the family. Use was made of the reports and minutes of the *Interdepartmental Committee on Physical Deterioration*, the *Royal Commission on the Poor Laws* and the *Royal Commission on Divorce and Matrimonial Causes* (1912). Useful material was gleaned from the journals *Feminist Studies*, *History of Childhood Quarterly*, *Journal of Family History* and *Oral History*. In addition the following were of particular importance:

Contemporary works

Bainton, George, *The Wife as Lover and Friend* (1895)

Barker, James, *A Secret Book for Men* (1888)

Barnard, A. B., *The Home Training of Children* (1910)

Bayly, Mary, *Home Rule: an Old Mother's Letter to Parents*, 3rd edn. (1886); and *Home Weal and Home Woe* (1892)

Bell, Lady Florence, *At the Works* (1906)

Booth, Charles, *Life and Labour of the People in London*, First Series (1902); and *The Aged Poor in England and Wales* (1894)

Bosanquet, Helen, *The Family* (1906)

Bowley, A., and Hurst, A. R. Burnett, *Livelihood and Poverty* (1915)

Caird, Mona, *The Morality of Marriage: and Other Essays on the Status and Destiny of Women* (1897)

Chadwick, H. C., *The Training of Children from Cradle to School* (1909)

Chapman, S. J., and Abbott, A., 'The Tendency of Children to enter their Father's Trades', *Journal of the Royal Statistical Society*, LXXVI (1913)

Drummond, W. B., *The Child: His Nature and Nurture* (1901)

Essays on Duty and Discipline (1911)

Gwynn, Stephen, 'The Modern Parent', *Cornhill Magazine*, new series, 8 (1890)

Hamilton, Cicely, *Marriage as a Trade* (1909)

Higgs, Mary, *The Evolution of the Child Mind* (1910)

Kelynack, T. N. (ed.), *Childhood* (1910)

Le Play, Frederic, *On Family, Work and Social Change*, ed. Catherine Bodard Silver (Chicago, 1982)

Loane, Margaret, *The Queen's Poor: Life as They Find It in Town and Country* (1905); *From Their Point of View* (1908)

Lyall, Edna, *The Burges Letters: A Record of Child Life in the Sixties* (1902)

Manson, Edward, 'Marital Authority', *Law Quarterly Review* 7 (1891)

de Montmorency, J. E. G., 'The Changing Status of a Married Woman', *Law Quarterly Review*, 13 (1897)

National Review, vol. 23, articles by 'A Family Man' and 'Felicitas' on family budgets (1894)

O'Hea, J. P., *The Rearing of Children* (1910)

Reeves, Maud Pember, *Round About a Pound a Week* (1913)

Riverside Visitor, *The Pinch of Poverty: Sufferings and Heroism of the London Poor* (1892)

Sully, James, *Studies of Childhood* (1895)

Waugh, Benjamin, 'Our New Protectorate for Children', *New Review* (1894)

Wells, H. G., *Socialism and the Family* (1906)

Whetham, W. C. D. and C. D., *The Family and the Nation* (1909)

Women's Co-operative Guild, *Maternity: Letters from Working-Women* (1915)

Historical works

Anderson, Michael, *Family Structure in Nineteenth Century Lancashire* (Cambridge, 1971)

Cominos, Peter, 'Late Victorian Sexual Respectability and the Social System', *International Review of Social History*, VIII (1963)

Gillis, John, *For Better, For Worse: British Marriages, 1600 to the Present* (Oxford, 1985)

Holcombe, Lee, 'Victorian Wives and Property: Reform of the Married Women's Property Law 1857–1882', in Vicinus, Martha J. (ed.), *A Widening Sphere: Changing Roles of Victorian Women* (1980)

Kern, Stephen, 'Explosive Intimacy: Psychodynamics of the Victorian Family', *History of Childhood Quarterly*, 1, 3 (1974)

Laslett, P., and Wall, R. (eds.), *Household and Family in Past Time*

Lochhead, Marion, *The Victorian Household* (1964)

Lowe, Nigel, 'The Legal Status of Fathers', in Lorna McKee and Margaret O'Brien (eds.), *The Father Figure* (1982)

Lummis, Trevor, 'The Historical Dimension of Fatherhood: a Case Study', in Lorna McKee and Margaret O'Brien (eds.), *The Father Figure* (1982)

May, M., 'Violence in the Family: an Historical Perspective', in J. P. Martin, *Violence and the Family* (1978)

Roberts, Richard, *The Classic Slum* (1971)

Robertson, Priscilla, 'Home as a Nest: Middle-Class Childhood in Nineteenth Century Europe', in Lloyd DeMause (ed.), *The History of Childhood* (New York, 1974)

Ross, Ellen, 'Fierce Questions and Taunts: Married Life in Working-Class London 1870–1914', *Feminist Studies*, 8, 3 (1982)

Smith, Richard, 'The Structured Dependence of the Elderly as a Recent Development: Some Sceptical Historical Thoughts', *Ageing and Society*, 4 (1984)

Smout, T. C., 'Scottish Marriage, Regular and Irregular 1500–1914', in R. B. Outhwaite (ed.), *Marriage and Society: Studies in the Social History of Marriage* (1981)

Thompson, Thea, *Edwardian Childhoods* (1981)

Thomson, David, 'The Welfare of the Elderly in the Past: A Family or Community Responsibility', in Margaret Pelling and Richard M. Smith, *Life, Death and the Elderly: Historical Perspectives* (1991)

Tomes, N., 'A Torrent of Abuse: Crimes of Violence between Working-Class Men and Women in London 1840–1875', *Journal of Social History*, XI (1978)

Wohl, A., *The Victorian Family* (1978)

4. Property

Major sources for this chapter were John Bateman, *The Great Landowners of Great Britain and Ireland* (1876); Leo Chiozza Money, *Riches and Poverty* (1905 and 1912); *The Land: Reports of the Land Enquiry Committee* (1912 and 1913); Josiah Stamp, *British Incomes and Property* (1915); and report of the *Select Committee on Land Values* (1920). Important modern studies are Y. Cassis, 'Bankers in English Society in the Late Nineteenth Century', *Economic History Review*, 2nd series, 38 (1985); Paul Johnson, *Saving and Spending: The Working-Class Economy in Britain 1870–1939* (Oxford, 1985); Avner Offer, *Property and Politics 1870–1914* (Cambridge, 1981); Harold Perkin, *Élites in British Society since 1880* (SSRC report, 1975); and W. D. Rubinstein, 'The Victorian Middle Classes: Wealth, Occupation and Geography', *Economic History Review*, 2nd series, 30 (1977); 'Wealth, Élites and the Class Structure of Modern Britain', *Past and Present*, 76 (1977); and *Men of Property: the Very Wealthy in Britain since the Industrial Revolution* (1981).

Other works found useful were as follows:

Contemporary works

Brodrick, G. C., *English Land and English Landlords* (1881)

Dicey, A. V., 'The Paradox of the Land Law', *Law Quarterly Review*, 21 (1905)

Gore, C., *Property: Its Duties and Rights* (1913)

Higgs, Henry, 'Workmen's Budgets', *Journal of the Royal Statistical Society*, LVI (1893)

Loane, Margaret, *From Their Point of View* (1908)

Money, L. G. Chiozza, *The Nation's Wealth: Will It Endure?* (1914)

Porter, G. R., *The Progress of the Nation* (revised ed. 1912)

Quail, Jesse, 'The Wealth of the Workers', *Contemporary Review*, 92 (1907)

de Rousiers, Paul, *The Labour Question in Britain* (1896)

Stamp, Josiah, 'The Wealth and Income of the Chief Powers (1914)', in *Studies in Current Problems in Finance and Government* (1924)

Historical works

Campion, H. H., *Public and Private Property in Great Britain* (1939)

Cannadine, David, *Lords and Landlords: The Aristocracy and the Towns 1774–1967*

Cassis, Youssef, *La Cité de Londres 1870–1914* (Paris, 1987)

Daunton, Martin, *House and Home in the Victorian City: Working-Class Housing 1850–1914* (1983); and 'Financial élites and British society, 1880–1950', in Youssef Cassis (ed.), *Finance and Financiers in European History 1880–1960* (Cambridge and Paris, 1992)

Langley, Kathleen M., 'An Analysis of the Asset Structure of Estates, 1900–1949', *Bulletin of the Institute of Statistics*, 13 (1951)

Lisle-Williams, M., 'Merchant banking dynasties in the English class structure: ownership, solidarity and kinship in the City of London 1850–1960', *British Journal of Sociology*, 35 (1984)

Matthews, R. C. O., Feinstein, C. H., and Smee, J. C. Odling, *British Economic Growth 1856–1973* (Oxford, 1982)

Perkin, Harold, *Professionalism, Property and English Society since 1880*, Stenton lecture (Reading, 1981)

Revell, J. S., 'Changes in the Social Distribution of Property in Britain during the Twentieth Century', *Third International Conference of Economic History* (Munich, 1965)

Richards, E., 'An Anatomy of the Sutherland Fortune: Income, Consumption, Investments and Returns 1780–1900', *Business History*, 21 (1979)

Rose, Mary B., 'Diversification of Investment by the Greg Family', *Business History*, 21 (1979)

Rubin, G. R., and Sugarman, D., *Law, Economy and Society: Essays in the History of English Law 1750–1914* (Abingdon, 1984)

Rubinstein, W. D. (ed.), *Wealth and the Wealthy in the Modern World* (1980)

Solow, Barbara, *The Land Question and the Irish Economy 1870–1903* (Cambridge, Mass., 1971)

Tebbutt, Melanie, *Making Ends Meet: Pawnbroking and Working-Class Credit* (Leicester, 1985)

Thompson, F. M. L., *English Landed Society in the Nineteenth Century* (1963)

5. Work

Important sources of information for this chapter were the reports and minutes of the *Royal Commission on Master and Servant* (1874–5), *Royal Commission on Labour*

(1892–4), and *Royal Commission on Trade Disputes and Trade Combinations* (1906). Use was also made of factory inspectors' reports, trade union reports and rule books, and reports of the *Tariff Commission* (1906–9) and the *Census of Production* (1907–12). Classic contemporary works were Charles Booth, *Life and Labour of the People in London*, Second Series (1902); B. L. Hutchins, *Women in Modern Industry* (1915); David Schloss, *Methods of Industrial Remuneration*, 3rd edn. (1898); G. von Schulze-Gaevernitz, *Social Peace: A Study of the Trade Union Movement in England* (1893); S. and B. Webb, *The History of Trade Unionism* (1894) and *Industrial Democracy* (1897). Major modern studies are E. J. Hobsbawm, *Labouring Men* and *Worlds of Labour*; Patrick Joyce, *Work, Society and Politics: Culture of the Factory in Later Victorian England* (1982); Ross McKibbin, 'Why was there no Marxism in Great Britain?', *English Historical Review*, XCIX (1984); and Harold Perkin, *The Rise of Professional Society: England since 1880.*

Other useful works were as follows:

Contemporary works

Anon. ('A Working Man'), *Working Men and Women* (1879)

Anon. ('One of the Crowd'), *A Working Man's Philosophy* (1886)

Barnes, George, *et al.*, *Life and Labour in Germany: Report of the Labour Party and Trade Union Commission on Wages, Hours of Employment, Working Conditions and the Standard of Living* (1910)

Bell, Lady Florence, *At the Works* (1906)

Best, R. H., Davis, W. J., and Perks, C., *The Brassworkers of Berlin and of Birmingham: a Comparison* (1905)

Black, Clementina, 'Women and Work', *New Review* (1891); and *Married Women's Work* (1915)

Bourne, George, *Change in the Village* (1912)

Brassey, Thomas, *Work and Wages*, 3rd edn. (1872)

Brentano, Lujo, *Hours and Wages in Relation to Production* (1894)

Butler, C. V., *Domestic Service* (1912)

Chapman, S. J., and Marquis, F. J., 'The Recruiting of the Employing Classes from the Ranks of the Wage-Earners in the Cotton Industries', *Journal of the Royal Statistical Society*, LXXV (1912)

Dilke, Lady, 'Trades Unionism for Women', *New Review*, 8 (1890)

Dueckershoff, Ernst, *How the English Workman Lives* (trans., 1899)

Fawcett, Henry, *The Economic Position of the British Labourer* (Cambridge, 1865)

Flux, A. W., 'Gleanings from the Census of Production Report', *Journal of the Royal Statistical Society*, LXXVI (1913)

Freeman, Arnold, *Boy Life and Labour* (1914)

Galton, Frank W. (ed.), *Workers on Their Industries* (1895)

Jeans, J. S., 'On the Comparative Efficiency and Earnings of Labour at Home and Abroad', *Journal of the Royal Statistical Society*, XLVII (1884); and 'On the Recent

Movement of Labour in Different Countries in Reference to Wages, Hours of Work and Efficiency', *JRSS*, LV (1892)

Lavollée, René, *Les Classes ouvrières en Europe: Études sur leur situation matérielle et morale, III: Angleterre* (Paris, 1882–90)

Malvery, Olive, *The Soul Market* (1906)

Owen, Thomas (ed.), *Dangerous Trades* (1902)

Potter, Beatrice, *The Co-operative Movement in Great Britain* (1891)

Rogers, Frederick, *Life, Labour and Literature* (1913)

Rousiers, Paul de, *The Labour Question in Britain* (Paris, trans., 1896)

Smith, H. L., and Nash, Vaughan, *The Story of the Dockers' Strike* (1889)

Steele, Henry, *The Working Classes in France* (1904)

Thornton, William T., *On Labour: Its Wrongful Claims and Rightful Duties; Its Actual Present and Possible Future* (1869)

Tozer, Basil, 'The Unemployed Gentleman', *National Review*, 49 (June 1907)

Williams, Alfred, *Life in a Railway Factory* (1915)

Working Gentlewomen's Journal (1906–8)

Working Ladies' Guild, *Reports* (1878–86)

Wright, Thomas, *Some Habits and Customs of the Working Classes* (1867); *The Great Unwashed* (1868); *Our New Masters* (1873)

Historical works

Benson, John, *British Coalminers in the Nineteenth Century: a Social History* (1980)

Burnett, John, *Useful Toil* (1974)

Business History, 31, 2 (1989), special issue on 'Labour and Business in Modern Britain'

Daunton, M. J., 'Down the Pit: Work in the Great Northern and South Wales Coalfields 1870–1914', *Economic History Review* (1981)

Davidoff, Leonora, and Westover, Belinda (eds.), *Our Work, Our Lives, Our Words: Women's History and Women's Work* (New Jersey, 1986)

Floud, Roderick, *The British Machine Tool Industry 1850–1914* (Cambridge, 1976)

Harrison, Royden, and Zeitlyn, Jonathan (eds.), *Divisions of Labour: Skilled Workers and Technological Change in Nineteenth Century England* (Sussex and Chicago, 1985)

Horn, Pamela, *The Rise and Fall of the Victorian Servant* (1975)

Jones, Gareth Stedman, 'Working-Class Culture and Working-Class Politics in London, 1870–1900: Notes on the Remaking of a Working Class', in *Languages of Class: Studies in English Working-Class History 1832–1982*

Keating, Peter, *Into Unknown England 1866–1913* (Manchester, 1976)

Lenin, V. I., *British Labour and British Imperialism: a compilation of writings by Lenin on Britain* (1969)

Melling, Joseph, 'Employers, Industrial Welfare, and the Struggle for Work-Place Control in British Industry, 1880–1920', in Howard F. Gospel and Craig R. Littler, *Managerial Strategies and Industrial Relations* (Aldershot, 1986)

Penn, Roger, 'Trade Union Organization and Skill in the Cotton and Engineering Industries in Britain 1850–1960', *Social History*, 8, 1 (1983)

Price, Richard, *Masters, Unions and Men: Work control in building and the rise of labour 1830–1914* (1980)

Roberts, Elizabeth, *Women's Work 1840–1940* (1988)

Routh, Guy, *Occupation and Pay in Great Britain 1906–60* (1965)

Samuel, Raphael, 'Workshop of the World: Steam Power and Hand Technology in Mid-Victorian Britain', *History Workshop*, 3 (Spring 1977)

Vicinus, Martha J., *Independent Women: Work and Community for Single Women 1850–1920*

6. Religion

Contemporary sources for this chapter were the 1851 religious census, recorded in *Religious Worship: England and Wales* (1853); the *Religious Census of London, reprinted from the British Weekly 1886* (1888); and R. Mudie Smith, *The Religious Life of London* (1904). Use was also made of the report and minutes of the *Select Committee on Public Worship* (1875), the *Royal Commission on Ecclesiatical Discipline* (1906), and the *Archbishops' Committee on Church and State* (1916). Other important contemporary works were Charles Booth, *Life and Labour of the People in London*, Third Series (1902); the annual *Church Congress Reports*; and the *Review of Churches*, published from 1891 as a supplement to the *Review of Reviews*. Invaluable modern studies were Robert Currie, Alan Gilbert, and Lee Horsley, *Churches and Church-Goers: Patterns of Church Growth in the British Isles since 1700* (Oxford, 1977); and Gerald Parsons and James R. Moore (eds.), *Religion in Victorian Britain*, 4 vols. (Manchester, 1988). Much useful detail was gleaned from the *Journal of Ecclesiastical History*, *Studies in Church History* and the *Sociological Yearbook of Religion*.

Other helpful works were as follows:

Contemporary works

Adderley, James, 'Has the Anglican Crisis Come?', *Fortnightly Review*, 101 (1914)

Baverstock, A. H., *The Failure of the Church in the Villages* (1913)

Booth, William, *In Darkest England and the Way Out* (1890)

Campbell, R. J., *The New Theology* (1907)

Clark, W. G., *The Present Dangers of the Church of England* (1870)

Clarke, W. K. Lowther (ed.), *Facing the Facts, or An Englishman's Religion* (1912)

Davies, C. Maurice, *Orthodox London* (1874–5); *Unorthodox London* (1873); *Heterodox London* (1874); *Mystic London* (1875)

Dearmer, Pearcy, *et al.*, *The English Hymnal* (1906)

Denison, H. P., *The Catholic Revival: a Retrospect and a Warning* (1911)

Dolling, Robert R., *Ten Years in a Portsmouth Slum* (1896)

Figgis, J. N., *Religion and English Society* (1910); *Civilization at the Cross Roads*

(1912); *Churches in the Modern State* (1913); and *Some Defects in English Religion and Other Sermons* (1917)

Gore, Charles (ed.), *Lux Mundi: a Series of Studies in the Religion of the Incarnation* (1889); and *Essays in Aid of the Reform of the Church* (1898)

Gray, J. Forbes (ed.), *Non-Church-Going: Its Reasons and Remedies* (1911)

Greg, W. R., 'Is a Christian Life Feasible in These Days?', *Contemporary Review*, 21 (1871–2)

Henson, Hensley (ed.), *Church Problems: a View of Modern Anglicanism* (1900)

Hymns of the Liberal Faith (1906)

Moore, Mrs Stuart (Evelyn Underhill), 'The Magic and Mysticism of Today', *Hibbert Journal*, VI (1908)

Newman, John Henry, 'On the Inspiration of Scripture', *Nineteenth Century*, 15 (1884)

Oxford House Papers, 3 vols. (1904–7)

Palmer, William Scott, *The Diary of a Modernist* (1910)

Smith, R. Bosworth, 'Sunday', *National Review*, 49 (July 1907)

Sturt, Henry, 'Do We Need a Substitute for Christianity', *Hibbert Journal*, V (1906)

Underhill, Evelyn, *The Letters of Evelyn Underhill*, ed. Charles Williams (1943)

Valentin, J. P., *The Latest Phase of the Oxford Movement* (1912)

Historical works

Bebbington, D. W., *The Nonconformist Conscience: Chapel and Politics 1870–1914* (1982); 'Nonconformity and Electoral Sociology 1867–1918', *Historical Journal*, 27, 3 (1984); and *Evangelicalism in Modern Britain* (1989)

Binfield, Clyde, *So Down to Prayers: Studies in English Nonconformity 1780–1920* (1977)

Chadwick, Owen, *The Victorian Church*, Part II (1970)

Cox, Jeffrey, *The English Churches in a Secular Society: Lambeth 1870–1930* (Oxford, 1982)

Gay, John, *The Geography of Religion in England* (1971)

Haig, Alan, *The Victorian Clergy* (1984); and 'The Churches, the Universities and Learning in Late-Victorian England', *Historical Journal*, 29, 1 (1986)

Heeney, Brian, *The Women's Movement in the Church of England* (Oxford, 1988)

Inglis, K. S., *Churches and the Working Classes in Victorian England* (1963)

Koss, Stephen, *Nonconformity in Modern British Politics* (1975)

Lipman, V. D., *Social History of the Jews in England 1850–1950* (1954); and *A Century of Social Service: The Jewish Board of Guardians* (1959)

Machin, G. I. T., *Politics and the Churches in Great Britain 1869–1921* (Oxford, 1987)

MacLeod, Hugh, *Class and Religion in the Late Victorian City* (1974); 'White Collar Values and the Role of Religion', in Crossick, Geoffrey (ed.), *Lower Middle Class in Britain 1870–1914* (1977)

Malmgreen, Gail, *Religion in the Lives of English Women 1760–1930* (1986)

Martin, David, *A General Theory of Secularization* (Oxford, 1978)

Moore, Robert, *Pitmen, Preachers and Politics: the Effects of Methodism in a Durham Mining Community* (1974)

Nicholls, David, *Church and State in Britain since 1820* (1967)

Norman, Edward, *Church and Society in England 1770–1970* (1976)

Obelkevich, J., Roper, L., and Samuel, R. (eds.), *Disciplines of Faith: Studies in Religion, Politics and Patriarchy* (1987)

Orens, John R., *The Mass, the Masses and the Music Hall: Stewart Headlam's Radical Anglicanism* (1979)

Rowell, Geoffrey, *Hell and the Victorians* (Oxford, 1974)

Waller, Philip, *Democracy and Sectarianism* (Liverpool, 1981)

Yeo, Stephen, *Religion and Voluntary Organizations in Crisis* (1976)

7. Society and the State

In this chapter I attempted to extract the 'social' history of the state from sources that were primarily political, legal and constitutional. Use was made of the Royal Commission and Select Committee materials cited in earlier chapters, together with the reports of the *Committee of Enquiry into the Featherstone Riot* (1893), the *Royal Commission on Local Taxation* (1900), and the *Royal Commission upon the Duties of the Metropolitan Police* (1908). Reference was made to reports of the Trades Union Congress, the Labour Representation Committee and the Tariff Reform Commission. Important contemporary works were G. C. Brodrick *et al.*, *Essays on Reform* (1867); Walter Bagehot, *The English Constitution* (1872); T. H. Escott, *England: Its People, Polity and Pursuits* (1879 and 1905); and A. V. Dicey, *The Law of the Constitution* (1885) and *England's Case against Home Rule* (1892). Valuable modern works were Patrick Atiyah, *The Rise and Fall of Freedom of Contract* (Oxford, 1979); Peter Clarke, *Lancashire and the New Liberalism* (Cambridge, 1971); E. P. Hennock, *Fit and Proper Persons: Ideal and Reality in Nineteenth Century Urban Government* (1973); H. C. G. Matthew, *Gladstone 1809–1874* (Oxford, 1986); Geoffrey Searle, *The Quest for National Efficiency* (Oxford, 1971); and Gillian Sutherland (ed.), *Studies in the Growth of Nineteenth Century Government* (1972).

Other relevant studies were as follows:

Contemporary works

Ambrose, W. J. L., 'The New Judiciary', *Law Quarterly Review*, 26 (1910)

Braithwaite, William J., *Lloyd George's Ambulance Wagon*, ed. Sir Henry Bunbury (1957)

Branford, Victor, 'Science and Citizenship', in J. E. Hand (ed.), *Science and Public Affairs* (1906)

Flexner, Abraham, *Prostitution in Europe* (1914)

Harrison, Frederick, *Order and Progress* (1875)

Jones, Sir Henry, *The Working Faith of a Social Reformer* (1911)

Lindsay, A. D., 'The State in Recent Political Theory', *Political Quarterly*, 1 (1914)

Malmesbury, Lord (ed.), *The New Order: Studies in Unionist Policy* (1908)

Parry, Edward, *The Law and the Poor* (1914)

Spencer, Herbert, *The Man versus the State* (1884)

Tönnies, Ferdinand, *Der englische Staat und der deutsche Staat* (Berlin, 1917)

Historical works

Abel-Smith, Brian, and Pinker, Robert, *Changes in the Use of Institutions in England and Wales between 1911 and 1951* (Manchester Statistical Society, 1961)

Abrams, Philip, *The Origins of British Sociology* (Chicago, 1968)

Adonis, Andrew, 'Aristocracy, Agriculture and Liberalism: the Politics, Finances and Estates of the Third Lord Carrington', *Historical Journal*, 31, 4 (1988)

Behlmer, G., *Child Abuse and Moral Reform in England 1870–1908* (Stanford, 1982)

Blewett, Neil, 'The Franchise in the United Kingdom 1885–1918', *Past and Present*, 32 (1965)

Brown, Kenneth D. (ed.), *The First Labour Party* (1985)

Cannadine, David (ed.), *Patricians, Power and Politics in Nineteenth-Century Towns* (Leicester, 1982)

Clarke, Peter, *Lancashire and the New Liberalism* (Cambridge, 1971)

Davis, John, *Reforming London: The London Government Problem 1855–1900* (Oxford, 1988); and 'Radical Clubs and London Politics', in David Feldman and Gareth Stedman Jones (eds.), *Metropolis: London. Histories and Representations since 1880* (1989)

Emsley, Clive, *Crime and Society in England 1750–1900* (1987)

Fraser, Derek, *Urban Politics in Victorian Britain* (1976)

Gattrell, V. A. C., 'The Decline of Theft and Violence in Victorian and Edwardian England', in V. A. C. Gattrell, B. Lenman and G. Parker, *Crime and the Law: the Social History of Crime in Western Europe since 1500* (1980)

Gattrell, V. A. C., and Hadden, T. B., 'Nineteenth Century Criminal Statistics and Their Interpretation', in E. A. Wrigley (ed.), *Nineteenth Century Society: Essays in the Use of Quantitative Methods for the Study of Social Data* (1972)

Gillis, J., The Evolution of Juvenile Delinquency in England 1890–1914', *Past and Present*, 67 (1975)

Goldman, Lawrence, 'The Social Science Association 1857–1886: a context for mid-Victorian Liberalism', *English Historical Review*, CI (1986)

Hennock, P., *Fit and Proper Persons: Ideal and Reality in Nineteenth Century Urban Government* (1973); and *British Social Reform and German Precedents* (Oxford, 1986)

Hollis, Patricia, *Ladies Elect: Women in English Local Government 1865–1914*

Jackson, Alvin, 'Unionist Politics and Protestant Society in Edwardian Ireland', *Historical Journal*, 33, 4 (1990)

Jalland, Patricia, *Women, Marriage and Politics 1860–1914*

Jones, David, *Crime, Protest, Community and Police in Nineteenth-century Britain* (1982)

Lambert, Roysten, 'A Victorian National Health Service: state vaccination, 1855–71', *Historical Journal*, v (1962)

Langan, Mary, and Schwarz, Bill, *Crises in the British State 1880–1930* (1985)

Laybourn, Keith, and Reynolds, Jack, *Liberalism and the Rise of Labour 1890–1918* (1984)

Lester, V. M., 'Insolvency and Reform of English Bankruptcy Law 1831–1914' (Oxford D.Phil. thesis, 1990)

MacBriar, A. M., *An Edwardian Mixed Doubles: the Bosanquets versus the Webbs, a Study in British Social Policy 1890–1929* (Oxford, 1987)

McCord, Norman, 'Ratepayers and Social Policy', in Pat Thane (ed.), *Origins of British Social Policy* (1978)

Manchester, A. H., *Sources of English Legal History 1750–1950* (1984)

Matthew, H. C. G., 'Disraeli, Gladstone and the Politics of Mid-Victorian Budgets', *Historical Journal*, 22 (1979)

Meller, H. E., *Leisure and the Changing City 1870–1914* (1975)

Nicholls, David, 'Positive Liberty 1880–1914', *American Political Science Review*, LVI (1962)

Pellew, Jill, *The Home Office 1848–1914: from Clerks to Bureaucrats* (1982)

Pelling, Henry, *Social Geography of British Elections 1885–1910* (1967)

Pugh, Martin, *The Tories and the People 1880–1935* (Oxford, 1985)

Radzinowicz, Sir Leon, and Hood, Roger, *History of the English Criminal Law and Its Administration*, vol. 5 (1986)

Rodgers, Brian, 'The Medical Relief (Disqualification Removal) Act 1885', *Parliamentary Affairs*, 9 (1955–6)

Russell, Bertrand, *Portraits from Memory and Other Essays* (1956)

Searle, Geoffrey, *The Quest for National Efficiency* (Oxford, 1971)

Shannon, Richard, *Gladstone and the Bulgarian Agitation 1876* (1975)

Smith, Paul (ed.), *Lord Salisbury on Politics* (Cambridge, 1972)

Tanner, Duncan, *Political Change and the Labour Party 1900–1918* (Cambridge, 1990)

Thane, Pat, 'The Working Class, and State Welfare', *Historical Journal*, 27, 4 (1984)

Thomas, J. A., *The House of Commons 1832–1901* (1939); and *The House of Commons 1906–11* (1958)

Walkowitz, Judith R., *Prostitution and Victorian Society: Women, Class, and the State* (Cambridge, 1980)

Waller, P. J. (ed.), *Politics and Social Change: Essays Presented to A. F. Thompson*

Wiener, Martin J., *Reconstructing the Criminal: Culture, Law and Policy in England 1830–1914* (Cambridge, 1990)

8. Society and Social Theory

Sources for this chapter included many of the Royal Commissions and public enquiries already cited in previous sections. Extensive use was made of contemporary periodical publications, particularly the *Charity Organisation Review*, the *International Journal of Ethics*, *Sociological Papers* (1904–8) and the *Sociological Review*. Major contemporary authorities were Herbert Spencer, *The Study of Sociology* (1873); T. H. Green, *The Collected Works*, ed. R. Nettleship, 3 vols. (1899); T. H. Huxley, *Evolution and Ethics, and Other Essays* (1894); Bernard Bosanquet, *The Philosophical Theory of the State* (1899); and A. C. Seward (ed.), *Darwin and Modern Science: Essays in Commemoration of the Birth of Charles Darwin and the Fiftieth Anniversary of The Origin of Species* (Cambridge, 1909). Important modern interpretations may be found in John Burrow, *Evolution and Society* (1966); Stefan Collini, *Public Moralists: Political Thought and Intellectual Life in Britain 1850–1950* (Oxford, 1991); Michael Freeden, *The New Liberalism* (Oxford, 1978); Gertrude Himmelfarb, *The Idea of Poverty* (New York, 1984); Greta Jones, *Social Darwinism and English Thought* (Brighton, 1980); and P. J. Nicholson, *The Political Philosophy of the British Idealists* (Cambridge, 1990).

Other key works are as follows:

Contemporary works

Anon., 'Communism and Co-operation' (a review of *Das Kapital*), *Church Quarterly Review*, VIII (Apr. 1879)

Argyll, Duke of, *The Unseen Foundations of Society* (1893)

Arnold, Matthew, *Culture and Anarchy* (1869)

Beveridge, W. H., 'The Problem of the Unemployed', *Sociological Papers*, 3 (1906); and *Unemployment: a Problem of Industry* (1909)

Booth Charles, *Life and Labour of the People in London*, First, Second and Third Series, 17 vols. (1902)

Bosanquet, Bernard, *The Introduction to Hegel's Philosophy of Fine Art* (1905)

Bosanquet, Helen, *The Strength of the People* (1902)

Branford, Victor, *On the Origin and Use of the Word Sociology* (1903)

Essays on Duty and Discipline (1910)

Fawcett, Henry, *The Economic Position of the British Labourer* (1865)

Haldane, R. B., 'The Teaching of Civic Duty', *Contemporary Review*, 64 (1893)

Hand, J. E. (ed.), *Ideals of Science and Faith: Essays by Various Authors* (1904)

Hobhouse, L. T., *Mind in Evolution* (1904)

Hobson, J. A., *The Evolution of Modern Capitalism* (1894); *The Problem of the Unemployed* (1896); *The Social Problem* (1901)

Kidd, Benjamin, *Social Evolution* (1894)

MacIver, R. M., *Community: A Sociological Study* (1917)

McLennan, J. F., *The Patriarchal Theory* (1885)

Maine, Sir Henry, 'The Patriarchal Theory' (review of McLennan), *Quarterly Review*, 162 (1886)

Maitland, Frederick William, *The Collected Papers of Frederick William Maitland*, ed. H. A. L. Fisher, vol. I (1911)

Marshall, Alfred, *Official Papers by Alfred Marshall*, ed. J. M. Keynes (Cambridge, 1926)

Nadaud, M., *Histoire des Classes Ouvrières en Angleterre* (Paris, 1872)

Prevention: A Quarterly Journal Devoted to Public Morals (1910–14)

Rae, John, 'The Socialism of Karl Marx and the Young Hegelians', *Contemporary Review*, XL (1881)

Rowntree, B. S., *Poverty: A Study of Town Life* (1899)

Smith, Goldwin, 'The Greatness of England', *Contemporary Review*, 34 (1878–9)

Synthetic Society, *Papers read before the Synthetic Society 1896–1908* (1909)

Washington, Booker T. (with Robert Lynd), *The Man Farthest Down: a Record of Observation and Study in Europe* (Chicago, 1912)

Webb, Sidney, *The Decline of the Birth Rate* (1907)

Historical works

Annan, Noel, *The Curious Strength of Positivism in English Political Thought* (Hobhouse Memorial Lecture, 1959)

Bevir, W. Mark, 'British Socialist Thought 1880–1900' (Oxford D Phil. thesis, 1989)

Biddiss, Michael D. (ed.), *Images of Race* (Leicester, 1979)

Brown, A. W., *The Metaphysical Society: Victorian Minds in Crisis 1869–1880* (New York, 1947)

Burrow, John, 'The Village Community and the Uses of History in Late Nineteenth Century England', in N. McKendrick (ed.), *Historical Perspectives: Studies in English Thought and Society in Honour of J. H. Plumb* (1974)

Coats, A. W., 'Sociological Aspects of British Economic Thought (ca. 1880–1930)', *Journal of Political Economy*, 75 (1967)

Collini, Stefan, 'Sociology and Idealism in Britain 1880–1920', *European Journal of Sociology*, 19 (1978)

Freeden, Michael, 'Eugenics and Progressive Thought: a Study in Ideological Affinity', *Historical Journal*, XXII (1979)

Goldman, Lawrence, 'Social Science Association', *English Historical Review*, CI (1986) and 'A Peculiarity of the English: the Social Science Association and the Absence of Sociology in Nineteenth Century Britain', *Past and Present*, 114 (1987)

Hearnshaw, L. S., *The Shaping of Modern Psychology* (1987)

Jenkyns, Richard, *The Victorians and Ancient Greece* (Oxford, 1980)

Kadish, Alon, *The Oxford Economists in the Late Nineteenth Century* (Oxford, 1982)

MacBriar, A. M., *Edwardian Mixed Doubles: Bosanquets versus the Webbs—a Study in British Social Policy 1890–1929*

McKibbin, Ross, *The Ideologies of Class: Social Relations in Britain 1880–1950* (Oxford, 1991)

McKillop, I. D., *The British Ethical Societies* (Cambridge, 1986)

Otter, Sandra den, 'The Search for a "Social Philosophy": the Idealists of Late Victorian and Edwardian Britain' (Oxford D.Phil. thesis, 1990)

Parsons, Talcott, 'Society', in *Encyclopaedia of the Social Sciences*, vol. 14 (1934)

Pick, Daniel, *Faces of Degeneration: Aspects of a European Disorder, c. 1848–1918* (Cambridge, 1989)

Richter, M., *The Politics of Conscience: T. H. Green and His Age* (1964)

Searle, Geoffrey, *The Quest for National Efficiency*; and *Eugenics and Politics in Britain 1900–14* (Leyden, 1976)

Soffer, Reba N., *Ethics and Society in England: the Revolution in the Social Sciences 1870–1914* (Berkeley, 1978)

Soloway, Richard, *Demography and Degeneration: Eugenics and the Declining Birthrate in Twentieth-Century Britain* (Chapel Hill, 1990)

Turner, Frank, *The Greek Heritage in Victorian Britain* (New Haven, 1981)

Turner, Frank, 'British Politics and the Demise of the Roman Republic: 1700–1939', *Historical Journal*, 29, 3 (1986)

Wiener, Martin, *Reconstructing the Criminal: Culture, Law and Policy in England 1830–1914*

Willis, Kirk, 'The Introduction and Critical Reception of Marxist Thought in Britain 1850–1900', *Historical Journal*, 20, 2 (1977)

Wright, T. W., *The Religion of Humanity: the Impact of Comtean Positivism on Victorian Britain* (Cambridge, 1986)

Index

READ MORE IN PENGUIN

In every corner of the world, on every subject under the sun, Penguin represents quality and variety – the very best in publishing today.

For complete information about books available from Penguin – including Puffins, Penguin Classics and Arkana – and how to order them, write to us at the appropriate address below. Please note that for copyright reasons the selection of books varies from country to country.

In the United Kingdom: Please write to *Dept. EP, Penguin Books Ltd, Bath Road, Harmondsworth, West Drayton, Middlesex UB7 ODA*

In the United States: Please write to *Consumer Sales, Penguin USA, P.O. Box 999, Dept. 17109, Bergenfield, New Jersey 07621-0120*. VISA and MasterCard holders call 1-800-253-6476 to order Penguin titles

In Canada: Please write to *Penguin Books Canada Ltd, 10 Alcorn Avenue, Suite 300, Toronto, Ontario M4V 3B2*

In Australia: Please write to *Penguin Books Australia Ltd, P.O. Box 257, Ringwood, Victoria 3134*

In New Zealand: Please write to *Penguin Books (NZ) Ltd, Private Bag 102902, North Shore Mail Centre, Auckland 10*

In India: Please write to *Penguin Books India Pvt Ltd, 706 Eros Apartments, 56 Nehru Place, New Delhi 110 019*

In the Netherlands: Please write to *Penguin Books Netherlands bv, Postbus 3507, NL-1001 AH Amsterdam*

In Germany: Please write to *Penguin Books Deutschland GmbH, Metzlerstrasse 26, 60594 Frankfurt am Main*

In Spain: Please write to *Penguin Books S. A., Bravo Murillo 19, 1° B, 28015 Madrid*

In Italy: Please write to *Penguin Italia s.r.l., Via Felice Casati 20, I–20124 Milano*

In France: Please write to *Penguin France S. A., 17 rue Lejeune, F–31000 Toulouse*

In Japan: Please write to *Penguin Books Japan, Ishikiribashi Building, 2–5–4, Suido, Bunkyo-ku, Tokyo 112*

In South Africa: Please write to *Longman Penguin Southern Africa (Pty) Ltd, Private Bag X08, Bertsham 2013*

READ MORE IN PENGUIN

HISTORY

Frauen Alison Owings

Nearly ten years in the making and based on interviews and original research, Alison Owings' remarkable book records the wartime experiences and thoughts of 'ordinary' German women from varying classes and backgrounds.

Byzantium: The Decline and Fall John Julius Norwich

The final volume in the magnificent history of Byzantium. 'As we pass among the spectacularly varied scenes of war, intrigue, theological debate, martial kerfuffle, sacrifice, revenge, blazing ambition and lordly pride, our guide calms our passions with an infinity of curious asides and grace-notes ... Norwich's great trilogy has dispersed none of this magic' – *Independent*

The Anglo-Saxons Edited by James Campbell

'For anyone who wishes to understand the broad sweep of English history, Anglo-Saxon society is an important and fascinating subject. And Campbell's is an important and fascinating book. It is also a finely produced and, at times, a very beautiful book' – *London Review of Books*

Conditions of Liberty Ernest Gellner

'A lucid and brilliant analysis ... he gives excellent reasons for preferring civil society to democracy as the institutional key to modernization ... For Gellner, civil society is a remarkable concept. It is both an inspiring slogan and the reality at the heart of the modern world' – *The Times*

The Habsburgs Andrew Wheatcroft

'Wheatcroft has ... a real feel for the heterogeneous geography of the Habsburg domains – I especially admired his feel for the Spanish Habsburgs. Time and again, he neatly links the monarchs with the specific monuments they constructed for themselves' – *Sunday Telegraph*

READ MORE IN PENGUIN

HISTORY

The Making of Europe Robert Bartlett

'Bartlett does more than anyone before him to bring out the way in which medieval Europe was shaped by [a] great wave of internal conquest, colonization and evangelization. He also stresses its consequences for the future history of the world' – *Guardian*

The Somme Battlefields Martin and Mary Middlebrook

This evocative, original book provides a definitive guide to the cemeteries, memorials and battlefields from the age of Crécy and Agincourt to the great Allied sweep which drove the Germans back in 1944, concentrating above all on the scenes of ferocious fighting in 1916 and 1918.

Ancient Slavery and Modern Ideology M. I. Finley

Few topics in the study of classical civilization could be more central – and more controversial – than slavery. In this magnificent book, M. I. Finley cuts through the thickets of modern ideology to get at the essential facts. 'A major creative achievement in historical interpretation' – *The Times Higher Education Supplement*

The Penguin History of Greece A. R. Burn

Readable, erudite, enthusiastic and balanced, this one-volume history of Hellas sweeps the reader along from the days of Mycenae and the splendours of Athens to the conquests of Alexander and the final dark decades.

The Laurel and the Ivy Robert Kee

'Parnell continues to haunt the Irish historical imagination a century after his death ... Robert Kee's patient and delicate probing enables him to reconstruct the workings of that elusive mind as persuasively, or at least as plausibly, as seems possible ... This splendid biography, which is as readable as it is rigorous, greatly enhances our understanding of both Parnell, and of the Ireland of his time' – *The Times Literary Supplement*

READ MORE IN PENGUIN

HISTORY

Citizens Simon Schama

The award-winning chronicle of the French Revolution. 'The most marvellous book I have read about the French Revolution in the last fifty years' – Richard Cobb in *The Times*

To the Finland Station Edmund Wilson

In this authoritative work Edmund Wilson, considered by many to be America's greatest twentieth-century critic, turns his attention to Europe's revolutionary traditions, tracing the roots of nationalism, socialism and Marxism as these movements spread across the Continent creating unrest, revolt and widespread social change.

The Tyranny of History W. J. F. Jenner

A fifth of the world's population lives within the boundaries of China, a vast empire barely under the control of the repressive ruling Communist regime. Beneath the economic boom China is in a state of crisis that goes far deeper than the problems of its current leaders to a value system that is rooted in the autocratic traditions of China's past.

The English Bible and the Seventeenth-Century Revolution
Christopher Hill

'What caused the English civil war? What brought Charles I to the scaffold?' Answer to both questions: the Bible. To sustain this provocative thesis, Christopher Hill's new book maps English intellectual history from the Reformation to 1660, showing how scripture dominated every department of thought from sexual relations to political theory ... 'His erudition is staggering' – *Sunday Times*

READ MORE IN PENGUIN

POLITICS AND SOCIAL SCIENCES

National Identity Anthony D. Smith

In this stimulating new book, Anthony D. Smith asks why the first modern nation states developed in the West. He considers how ethnic origins, religion, language and shared symbols can provide a sense of nation and illuminates his argument with a wealth of detailed examples.

The Feminine Mystique Betty Friedan

'A brilliantly researched, passionately argued book – a time-bomb flung into the Mom-and-Apple-Pie image ... Out of the debris of that shattered ideal, the Women's Liberation Movement was born' – Ann Leslie

Faith and Credit Susan George and Fabrizio Sabelli

In its fifty years of existence, the World Bank has influenced more lives in the Third World than any other institution yet remains largely unknown, even enigmatic. This richly illuminating and lively overview examines the policies of the Bank, its internal culture and the interests it serves.

Political Ideas Edited by David Thomson

From Machiavelli to Marx – a stimulating and informative introduction to the last 500 years of European political thinkers and political thought.

Structural Anthropology Volumes 1–2 Claude Lévi-Strauss

'That the complex ensemble of Lévi-Strauss's achievement ... is one of the most original and intellectually exciting of the present age seems undeniable. No one seriously interested in language or literature, in sociology or psychology, can afford to ignore it' – George Steiner

Invitation to Sociology Peter L. Berger

Sociology is defined as 'the science of the development and nature and laws of human society'. But what is its purpose? Without belittling its scientific procedures Professor Berger stresses the humanistic affinity of sociology with history and philosophy. It is a discipline which encourages a fuller awareness of the human world ... with the purpose of bettering it.

READ MORE IN PENGUIN

POLITICS AND SOCIAL SCIENCES

Conservatism   Ted Honderich

'It offers a powerful critique of the major beliefs of modern conservatism, and shows how much a rigorous philosopher can contribute to understanding the fashionable but deeply ruinous absurdities of his times' – *New Statesman & Society*

The Battle for Scotland   Andrew Marr

A nation without a parliament of its own, Scotland has been wrestling with its identity and status for a century. In this excellent and up-to-date account of the distinctive history of Scottish politics, Andrew Marr uses party and individual records, pamphlets, learned works, interviews and literature to tell a colourful and often surprising account.

Bricks of Shame: Britain's Prisons   Vivien Stern

'Her well-researched book presents a chillingly realistic picture of the British sytstem and lucid argument for changes which could and should be made before a degrading and explosive situation deteriorates still further' – *Sunday Times*

Inside the Third World   Paul Harrison

This comprehensive book brings home a wealth of facts and analysis on the often tragic realities of life for the poor people and communities of Asia, Africa and Latin America.

'Just like a Girl'   Sue Sharpe
How Girls Learn to be Women

Sue Sharpe's unprecedented research and analysis of the attitudes and hopes of teenage girls from four London schools has become a classic of its kind. This new edition focuses on girls in the nineties – some of whom could even be the daughters of the teenagers she interviewed in the seventies – and represents their views and ideas on education, work, marriage, gender roles, feminism and women's rights.

READ MORE IN PENGUIN

THE PENGUIN SOCIAL HISTORY OF BRITAIN

General Editor: J. H. Plumb

English Society in the Later Middle Ages Maurice Keen

In 1350, the traditional idea of the 'three estates' – priests, knights and labourers – offered an idealized but essentially accurate picture of society. By 1500, a far more complex structure based on landowning wealth, the city commercial élite and 'bastard feudal' relations was in place. Maurice Keen traces this great transformation to give us a subtle and three-dimensional portrait of England during a major watershed in our history.

Sixteenth-Century England Joyce Youings

The Tudor period is generally considered to have been a time of great enterprise, a 'golden age' in the history of civilization. Here Joyce Youings exposes a darker side and reveals how inflation, poverty and the population explosion, changes in domestic affairs and the collapse of the traditional church affected the ordinary people. Her richly detailed account provides an illuminating backcloth to the times.

English Society in the Eighteenth Century Roy Porter
Second Edition

'A brilliant work of synthesis . . . Porter has triumphantly accomplished what many regard as the impossible task of writing a book that is valuable both to the historian and to the general reader' – *London Review of Books*

British Society 1914–45 John Stevenson

With two world wars sandwiching the Depression years, the essential flavour of British society from 1914 to 1945 was one of moderation and consensus. John Stevenson creates a vivid picture of the trends and changes, from broadcasting and the cinema to mass unemployment, votes for women and improved welfare services.

British Society since 1945 Arthur Marwick
Second Edition

'A *tour de force* . . . Without serious distortion or omission . . . he moves dexterously through a wide variety of sources, ranging from poetry through film and novels to opinion polls . . . it is astonishing how much he gets in' – *The Times Educational Supplement*